MY SEVERAL WORLDS

By Pearl S. Buck

Excerpt from a letter to Sir Horace Mann
from Horace Walpole, *September 26, 1781*

"All sublunary objects are but great and little by comparison.
. . . Is anything more lean than the knowledge we attain by
computing the size of a planet? If we could know more of a
world than its size, would not size be the least part of our contemplation? . . .

"What is one's country but one's family on a large scale?
What was the glory of immortal Rome but the family pride of
some thousand families?"

MY
SEVERAL
WORLDS

A Personal Record
by
PEARL S. BUCK

The John Day Company
New York

I

Green Hills Farm,
Pennsylvania,
June, 1953

THIS morning I rose early, as is my habit, and as usual I went to the open window and looked out over the land that is to me the fairest I know. I see these hills and fields at dawn and dark, in sunshine and in moonlight, in summer green and winter snow, and yet there is always a new view before my eyes. Today, by the happy coincidence which seems the law of life, I looked at sunrise upon a scene so Chinese that did I not know I live on the other side of the globe, I might have believed it was from my childhood. A mist lay over the big pond under the weeping willows, a frail cloud, through which the water shone a silvered grey, and against this background stood a great white heron, profiled upon one stalk of leg. Centuries of Chinese artists have painted that scene, and here it was before my eyes, upon my land, as American a piece of earth as can be imagined, being now mine, but owned by generations of Americans, and first of all by Richard Penn, the brother of William Penn, who founded our state of Pennsylvania. Had I prayed Heaven, I could not have asked for a picture more suited to the mood for this day's work, which is to begin my book.

The reader is warned, however, that the story is incomplete, and, worse still, that it is told upon different levels and about different places and peoples, the whole held together merely by time, for this is the way my life has been lived and must be lived until I die. Geographically, my worlds are on opposite sides of the globe and for me, too, only the years of my life tie them together. There is yet another diversity and it is within myself. I am a creature instinctively domestic, but the age in which I am born, combined with whatever talents have made me a writer, have compelled me to live deeply, not only in home and family, but also in the lives of many peoples. But of my several worlds, let me begin with the personal since that, in truth, is where we all begin.

This book is not a complete autobiography. My private life has been

3

uneventfully happy, except for a few incidents whose disaster I was able to accept, and a human being could not, I believe, have less than I to complain of against fate. A happy childhood, marriage in its time, love and home and children, friends, and more than enough success for a creature singularly without ambition and born with no competitive sense whatever—this is the story of my secret years.

The fortunate chance I have had, above all else, has been the age into which I am born. Never, or so it seems to me as I read history, has there been a more stirring and germinal period than the one I have seen passing before my conscious eyes. I might have grown up secure and secluded in the comfortable and pleasant small town of my ancestors, taking for granted the advantages of families accustomed to more than their share, perhaps, of comfort and pleasure. Instead I had as my parents two enterprising and idealistic young people who, at an early age and for reasons which still seem to me entirely unreasonable, felt impelled to leave their protesting and astonished relatives and travel halfway around the globe in order to take up life in China and there proclaim the advantages of their religion. To them the task seemed inevitable and satisfying and they were devoted to it for more than half a century, and this in spite of coming from no missionary stock. There was nothing in either family to produce two such Christian adventurers as my parents, and none of their children has continued the zealous mission. I can only believe that my parents reflected the spirit of their generation, which was of an America bright with the glory of a new nation, rising united from the ashes of war, and confident of power enough to "save" the world. Meantime they had no conception of the fact that they were in reality helping to light a revolutionary fire, the height of which we still have not seen, nor can foresee.

As a result of this early voyage of my young parents-to-be, I grew up on the Asian side of the globe instead of on the American side, although I was born, quite accidentally, in my own country. My young mother, who was only twenty-three years old when she went as a bride to China, had four children rather rapidly, and as rapidly lost three of them from tropical diseases which at that time no one understood how to prevent or to cure. She was distracted enough so that the doctors ordered her to be taken to her home in West Virginia for two years. It was in the last few months of this long rest that I was born, and thereby became an American citizen by birth as well as by two centuries of ancestry.

Had I been given the choice of place for my birth, I would have chosen exactly where I was born, my grandfather's large white house with its pillared double portico, set in a beautiful landscape of rich green plains and with the Allegheny mountains as a background. I was a

4

welcome child, a circumstance conducive, I believe, to natural good nature and a tendency to optimism. At any rate, I had a happy beginning in a pleasant place, and at the age of three months, my mother's health being restored, I was transported across the seas to live and grow up in China. Thereafter Asia was the real, the actual world, and my own country became the dreamworld, fantastically beautiful, inhabited by a people I supposed entirely good, a land indeed from which all blessings flowed.

My parents, who were my sole source of information concerning this dreamworld as I came to the age of questions, certainly did not mean to tell me lies. Their own memories had not indeed been entirely pleasant. The war between North and South had shadowed their early years, four of my father's older brothers had fought on the Southern side, and had shared in the stinging defeat. The hardest blow of all was that an arbitrary line had divided their beloved Virginia and had left their ancestral homesteads in the new state, albeit only by a few miles. But they were spared the worst hardships of the reconstruction period, and by the time they had finished their education, my father at Washington and Lee University and my mother at the then fashionable Bellewood Seminary in Kentucky, the discomforts of war were gone, if not forgotten. Moreover, both families were glad to see the end of slavery, a burden far too heavy to be carried by a people committed to the Constitution and the Bill of Rights, not to speak of the Christian religion.

In China, however, my parents conveniently forgot all the less admirable aspects of their country, and while I was a child they regaled me with memories of quiet village streets, large houses set far back in trees and lawns, decent folk walking to church on Sundays to worship God in beautiful old churches, law-abiding men and women, children who obeyed their parents and learned their lessons in school. Doctors cured the few sick folk, or sent them to wonderfully clean hospitals, and certainly no one had cholera or dysentry or typhus or died of bubonic plague. Neither were there lepers to be seen lounging along the streets, intimidating the pedestrians and shopkeepers, and beggars there were none. I am not to be blamed therefore for having grown up with illusions about my own country.

If America was for dreaming about, the world in which I lived was Asian. The actual earth was Chinese, but around China clustered a host of other nations and peoples, whose citizens I frequently saw and some of whom I knew well. Thus I learned about India very early indeed, and that was because our family physician was an Indian and so was his stout and kindly wife, although they spoke English and were members of an English mission and there was certainly some admixture of white blood in their veins, for India's blood does not run pure after hundreds of years of domination by white men. When in my insatiable thirst for stories I pressed these friends to tell me about their own childhoods, for I was a tiresome child for questions, the tales they told were of India, and listening, I shared their lives in a torrid land, where whole populations sat and waited, almost fainting, for the rains. I became acquainted with fabulous snakes and with apes swinging in distant trees. I learned of other gods, I heard a language different from the two I spoke as my own, and early I knew the woes of India and what her people dreamed.

And high on the hillside across the valley above which we lived in our low brick house, a Japanese lady lived with her English husband, and from her I learned of Japan, until I went there myself time and again, first with my parents and then later alone, and thereafter so often that Japan became my third country. Among our friends were Asians, too, from the Philippines and Siam, from Indonesia and Burma and Korea, and thus early I conceived a world wherein China was the center, and around us were these other peoples, all friendly, all interesting and ready to be visited.

To the dreamworld of the West, however, belonged the English friends we had, who lived behind the barred gates of the British Concession in the port city of Chinkiang on the great Yangtse River, and among them were also a few French and Italian families. But the French and Italians I really knew well were the Catholic priests who came to visit us sometimes, and three or four nuns who had an orphanage for children abandoned on the streets or the hillsides but still alive. I could imagine India, or Java, but Italy I could not, nor France, and scarcely England.

For in the secret thoughts of the Chinese, thoughts often confided to me by my Chinese playmates who caught them from the talk of their elders, these westerners were "foreigners," as my playmates called them and as I thought of them, too, and they were potential enemies. "Foreigners" had done evil things in Asia—not the Americans, my small and even then tactful friends declared, for Americans, they said, were "good." They had taken no land from Asian countries, and they sent food in famine time. I accepted the distinction and felt no part with other Western peoples of Europe, whom at that time I considered also my enemies. Our version of the universal game of cops and robbers in those days was the endless war of Chinese and all good Asian allies against the imperial powers of the West, and as the sole American in the game, it was my duty to come forward at the height of battle and provide food and succor for the ever-victorious Chinese. Thus half a

6

century ago did the children of Asia play at the game of later reality, and it was quite by chance that a small yellow-haired American represented her country among them.

Halfway between the two worlds, however, were the children of my Chinese adopted sister. Years before I was born, when my parents had lived in an interior Chinese town on the Grand Canal, my mother was called one night to the house of a Chinese lady who was dying. My mother would never tell me her name, but I knew that she was the first wife of the head of an old and wealthy Chinese family. My father had become acquainted with the head of this family through their mutual scholarly interests and had tried to influence him to be a Christian. In the course of this endeavor, he had asked my mother to call upon his friend's wife, which she did, and the lady was attracted to my mother, and my mother to her, so that when a sudden illness became obviously mortal for the lady, she called my mother to her bedside and asked her to take her small daughter, who she feared would suffer if left alone with the concubines. With the father's consent the child was given to my mother for her own and my parents adopted her. Her name was Ts'ai Yün, or Beautiful Cloud, and I remember her as a lovely gentle young woman with a soft pretty face. She was already married by the time I was born, and had begun to bear the large family of girls who became such an embarrassment for her. My mother had followed the Chinese tradition for Beautiful Cloud, and when she had finished her education in the mission school for girls, my mother betrothed her to a handsome and also good young man who was the son of my father's assistant pastor. It was a happy marriage and a suitable one, the young man followed in his father's footsteps and became a pillar of the Church in a mild and agreeable way, and the only embarrassment was the regularity with which the girl babies appeared in their home. A first girl they accepted with welcome, a second one a year later with equanimity, a third with gravity, a fourth with consternation. By the time the sixth one came the situation was critical. People were asking, how is it that Christians have nothing but girls? Inasmuch as the matter had become a subject of prayer for the church members after the third girl, the next question was, how is it that our prayers are not heard? Actual doubt of the foreign god began to arise and my father, who had tried to take no notice, exclaimed "Oh, pshaw" several times a day, as was his habit when perplexed. We were too humorous a family not to see the absurdity in the situation and yet we were quite aware of its seriousness. No one suffered more than my pretty adopted sister, who felt that all was her fault, and never was her husband's goodness more manifest than

7

when he refused to allow her to take the blame. He was at least an example of Christian fortitude, as my father remarked.

As for me, I loved the children and enjoyed them as much as sisters. The eldest two were nearly my age and we had wonderful playtimes when they came to visit us or we went to visit them in their home some miles away. I have told this story for my American children in a little book, *The Chinese Children Next Door,* and those who have read that book will remember that there was a happy ending, for after six girls, my distracted Chinese sister did give birth to a fine boy. This ended the family. Neither she nor her husband dared to risk an eighth child who might be a girl again. It gives me pleasure to remember that I was told by an Indian friend that Jawaharlal Nehru once read my little book aloud to Mahatma Gandhi, who was lying ill at the time, and it made him laugh very much, because it was the sort of thing that might have happened in India, too.

It was a happy world for a child, even for a white child, and in spite of lepers and beggars and occasional famines, and our ruler, if you please, was a proud old woman in Peking, the Empress Dowager, or as her own people called her, The Venerable Ancestor, and I supposed that she was my Venerable Ancestor, too. When I think of that world of my early childhood, I remember the Empress Dowager as the central figure, and one as familiar to me as though I had seen her myself. Everybody knew how she looked, and any little Chinese girl, in our games, was proud to represent her and for a throne to sit upon the tussock of one of the tall pointed earthen graves that dotted our hillside.

I did not realize, then, that the Empress was not Chinese, but Manchu. She had black hair and eyes and the lovely cream-pale skin of the northern people. She was not tall, but she wore embroidered satin shoes set high on padded soles in the Manchu fashion, and her shining black hair was worn high on her head so that actually she looked tall. When she sat on the Peacock Throne, its dais raised several steps above the tiled floor of the Throne Room of the yellow-roofed Imperial Palace in The Forbidden City in Peking, everybody said she looked as tall as a man. But the height was more than physical. She was proud and wilful and her eyes could make anyone tremble. She was dangerous, we all knew that. The meekest little brother among us had to play the part of the young Emperor in our games, so that the Empress could terrify him and lock him up in prison.

I cannot remember when I first learned that the Empress Dowager was not Chinese, and that many Chinese thought of the dynasty as alien. I knew the Manchus, for every important city had a special reservation for them and we had one in Chinkiang, too. It was on the

8

edge of the city and a high wall surrounded all the Manchu houses. At the front gate stood Chinese guards, and no one was allowed to come in without their permission. It was not imprisonment, supposedly, but simply that all Manchus needed special protection because they were related to the royal house and so were part of officialdom. Actually it was a luxurious imprisonment, for this was the Chinese way of conquering enemies. When the Manchu invasion of 1644 was successful in a military sense—and almost any people could invade China successfully, it seemed, in a military sense—China did not resist. The people were apparently passive, mildly curious, and even courteous to their conquerors. The real struggle came afterwards, but so subtly that the conquerors never knew they were being conquered. The technique of victory was that as soon as the invaders laid down their arms the philosophical but intensely practical Chinese persuaded them to move into palaces and begin to enjoy themselves. The more the new rulers ate and drank, the better pleased the Chinese were, and if they also learned to enjoy gambling and opium and many wives, so much the better. One would have thought that the Chinese were delighted to be invaded and conquered. On the pretext of increased comfort, the Manchus were persuaded to live in a specially pleasant part of any city, and to be protected by special guards against rebellious citizens. This meant they were segregated and since they were encouraged to do no work, the actual and tedious details of government were soon performed by Chinese, ostensibly for them. The result of this life of idleness and luxury was that the Manchus gradually became effete while the Chinese administered the government. The Manchus were like pet cats and the Chinese kept them so, knowing that when the degeneration was complete, a Chinese revolutionary would overthrow the rotten structure. Revolution was in the Chinese tradition and every dynasty was overthrown, if not by foreign invasion, then by native revolution.

As a child, of course I did not know how nearly the end had come for the Manchus. Until I was eight I did not know. Those early years were carefree ones for me and for my little Chinese playmates. Looking back, it seems an idyl of happiness. I had many people to love me. My parents, though busy, were always kind and ready to heed me, the Chinese servants were tenderly indulgent and spoiled me dangerously, always taking my side against discipline. Did my mother set me a task as a much-needed punishment, I had only to look sorrowful and my Chinese amah would secretly perform the task, or if it had to do with outdoors, then the gardener or the second boy would do it, and the cook himself was not above helping me in a pinch. My mother discovered them eventually, and tried to show them that they were not

9

really helping me, and indeed were preventing me from learning the proper lessons of self-discipline, to which their reply was bewilderment and murmurings that I was only a child and must not be expected to know everything at once. Discipline, in their estimation, was the expression of adult anger and the child must as a matter of course be protected, since anger was merely a sort of dangerous seizure. My mother gave up persuasion and learned to set me tasks that the loving Chinese could not perform for me, such as looking up words in the English dictionary and writing down their meanings. And then how the agitated Chinese tried to help anyway, and comforted me in the cruel labor by smuggling in sweetmeats, or rewarding me with a toy that one of them rushed out to buy on the market place, a pottery doll dressed in bright robes of paper, or a bamboo whistle or a sugar tiger stuck on the end of a stick!

Once, before I was eight, my father whipped me for telling a lie, and horror spread through the servants' quarters and even among the neighbors. I had broken the gardener's hoe and then said that I had not, and in his grief, in order to stave off the whipping, the gardener swore that it was he who had done it. My father had seen the event, however, and the whipping was swift and hard and the gardener stood weeping in the doorway with peanut candy bulging in his pocket. Such foods were forbidden, for the germs of tropical diseases were hidden in them, but they were fed to me secretly and I ate them without qualms because the Chinese did, and built up a like immunity, I suppose, for I was the healthiest child imaginable, and suffered from none of the ills which seemed to beset the average white child. Nor did I consciously deceive my parents, I think, for I believed what they said about white people, who seemed to die or at least to fall ill with amazing ease. But I did not consider myself a white person in those days. Even though I knew I was not altogether Chinese, still I was Chinese enough to eat sweets from the market place with impunity.

Thus I grew up in a double world, the small white clean Presbyterian American world of my parents and the big loving merry not-too-clean Chinese world, and there was no communication between them. When I was in the Chinese world I was Chinese, I spoke Chinese and behaved as a Chinese and ate as the Chinese did, and I shared their thoughts and feelings. When I was in the American world, I shut the door between.

In the Chinese world, it is true, we often discussed the Americans. My parents fortunately were well beloved by the Chinese, and except for a few unfortunate facts, such as my father's absurdly large feet and immense height, and my mother's quick temper, I had nothing to be ashamed of. My father was revered as a man of kindness. But other white people did not always fare so well, and their characters were sometimes dissected with mirth and thoroughness. I knew what no other Americans knew about the white people and their secret lives. I knew that a certain man kept a secret whiskey bottle in his closet, and that a certain woman would not sleep with her husband. I knew that an old gentleman, actually fastidious, suffered monstrously from indigestion, and that another, a lonely young man, tried to make love to any woman who would allow it, even to the gateman's wife. Nothing was private in the Chinese world, nothing could be kept secret, the very word for secret also meant unlawful. It was a richly human world, steeped in humor and pathos, for more often than not when the laughter was over, some kindly old Chinese would say tolerantly, "But these Christians are good, nevertheless. They do their best and we must not blame them for what they do not know. After all, they were not born Chinese. Heaven did not ordain."

I had no direct contact with the Empress Dowager, of course, however real she seemed. She lived far away in Peking and I was an American child living outside a vast old city some two hundred miles from the mouth of the Yangtse River. Shanghai was the only exit to my Western world. Through that motley place foreigners came and went, and brigands grown rich, and retired war lords lived there under British or French protection. But the whole of China behind that gate to the Pacific Ocean was remote indeed from Western ways, and it was this world that the Empress governed. She was the more fascinating to me because she had not been born a queen, but a commoner. Her father had been a small military official and the family was almost poor. She had worked hard as a child, the eldest daughter compelled to take care of younger children. Yet she had one advantage as a Manchu, and one that I had, too, as an American. Her feet were never bound as the Chinese then bound the feet of their girls, and she grew up with a free and imperious air. When she was sixteen she was a beauty but even had she not been she would have been compelled, as Manchu girls usually were, to go to the Emperor's palace and stay for the inspection period. If she were chosen as a possible royal concubine, then she would leave her home and family and live the rest of her days in The Forbidden City, a concubine who could be claimed by her lord, or who might never be so claimed. It was a tragic immolation if she were not noticed, but this girl was noticed, and she became the Emperor's concubine and bore him a son. And then because she was born to power she moved toward it by the very strength of her own nature until she ruled the greatest kingdom in the world, The Middle Kingdom, which the West called China. It was a romantic success story and the Chinese admired the woman for it and forgave her many sins that she later committed even against them, and which in the end brought the walls of empire crashing down.

We did not dream of such disaster. When I think of that first world I ever knew, it was all peace. I see a circle of green hills and purple mountains beyond. Between the green hills were the greener valleys, tilled to the last inch by farmers of four thousand years. Ponds full of fish lay outside the gates of farmhouses, and every family had a pig and some hens and a cock and a water buffalo. Beggars were on the city streets, but unless there were refugees from a famine in the north, those beggars were as professional as the city thieves. They were organized under a beggar king and from all shopkeepers they exacted a certain alms, if not daily then regularly, and did any shopkeeper fail to pay the usual sum, the most hideous of the lepers and the deformed were stationed outside his doors to scare away his customers. But to be a beggar was to accept a lowly life, unless one went still lower and became a professional soldier, lower because soldiers destroy and consume and do not produce. We had no beggars in the hills and the villages, but we did have soldiers. There was an earth-walled fort on top of one of the hills near our house, and the terror of my life was that I might meet a soldier on the road to the Chinese girls' school where I went every day. If I saw one of those lazy fellows lounging along the road in his yellow uniform I ran more fleetly than any deer into the big clanging gate of our compound.

"What is the matter?" my mother inquired one afternoon.

"A soldier!" I gasped.

"So what of that?" she asked too innocently.

I could not explain. She belonged to the little white world and she could not understand. But in my other world I had been taught that a soldier is not a man, in the civilized sense of the noble word. He is separated from the laws of life and home, and it is well for a girl child to run fast if he comes near.

"True," old Madame Shen said one day when she was instructing me with her granddaughters, "not every soldier is a devil, but it is hard for him not to be. He has a devilish trade."

Madame Shen was a neighbor, a matriarch in her own domain as much as the Empress Dowager was in the palaces of Peking. Her granddaughters were my schoolmates, for the Shen family was enlightened and there was already talk of not binding the feet of their youngest girls. The older girls had bound feet, and while I did not envy the pains and aches of that dire process whereby the toes of each foot were turned under into the sole and the heel and the ball of the foot brought together under the arch, still there were times in those early days when I wondered if I were jeopardizing my chances for a good husband by having what would be called big feet, that is, unbound feet. The older girls of the Shen family would not think of unbinding their feet, although my mother did some practical missionary work on the subject. When one of them was later sent to board in a missionary school, she was compelled to loose the foot bandages, but she confided to me that every night she bound them tight again. In that world it was important to be a woman and if possible a beautiful woman, and small feet were a beauty that any woman could have, whatever her face.

The Empress in Peking was careful never to interfere with the customs of the Chinese she ruled and when once a Manchu Princess returned from abroad in Western dress, she asked her to show her what she wore to make her stout figure so narrow at the waist. The Princess turned to her own daughter, a slender girl in a Parisian gown, and said,

"Daughter, take off your garments and show Her Majesty your corset."

The young Princess obeyed and the old Empress surveyed the grim garment of steel and heavy cloth.

"Of the two tortures," she observed, "it is easier to bear the Chinese one."

It was perhaps because the Manchu rulers were always careful not to disturb the customs of the Chinese that their dynasty lived longer than it might have otherwise. Certainly we were scarcely conscious of being ruled at all. There was a magistrate in each county seat who was understood to be a representative of the Viceroy and at the head of each province was the Viceroy, the representative of the Throne in Peking, the capital of the nation, but the main duty of these officials was to see that every family continued free to live its life, interfering only when some injustice was done. I never saw a policeman in that early world of China, and indeed, saw none until I went to Shanghai and in the British Concession stared at the dark Sikhs, imported from India, their heads wrapped in intricate and brilliant turbans, or in the French Concession at the trimly uniformed Annamese policemen. I used to wonder why they stood there in the streets obstructing the traffic and waving clubs at people.

In the world of our hills and valleys and even in the city we needed no police. Each family maintained firm discipline over every member of the group, and if a crime was committed the family elders sat in conference and decided the punishment, which sometimes was even death. For the honor of the family the young were taught how to behave, and though they were treated with the utmost leniency until they were seven or eight years old, after that they learned to respect the code of human relationships so clearly set forth by Confucius.

Yes, Chinese children were alarmingly spoiled when they were small, my Western parents thought. No one stopped tantrums or wilfulness and a baby was picked up whenever he cried, and indeed he was carried by somebody or other most of the time. Babies ate what they pleased and when they pleased, and little children led a heavenly life. The Chinese believed that it was important to allow a child to cry his fill and vent all his tempers and humors while he was small, for if these were restrained and suppressed by force or fright, then anger entered into the blood and poisoned the heart, and would surely come forth later to make adult trouble. It was a knowledge as ancient as a thousand years, and yet something of the same philosophy is now considered the most modern in the Western world in which I live today.

Right or wrong, these spoiled children emerged like butterflies from cocoons at about the age of seven or eight, amazingly adult and sweet-tempered and self-disciplined. They were able by then to hear reason and to guide themselves in the accepted ways. Since they had not been disciplined too soon, when they reached the age of learning they progressed with great rapidity. The old Chinese, like the most modern of the Western schools of child psychology, believed that there is an age for learning each law of life, and to teach a child too young was simply to wear out the teacher and frustrate the child. As an example, for the greater convenience of both child and parents, little children went naked in summer and in winter had their trousers bisected, so that when nature compelled all a tiny creature needed to do was to squat. Thus was he spared the nagging of a mother who wanted to be relieved of diaper washing. As for the babies, they were simply held outside the door at regular intervals and encouraged by a soft musical whistling to do their duty if possible. It was a delightful and lenient world in which a child could live his own life, with many people to love him tolerantly and demand nothing. Instead of the hard pressed father and mother of the Western child, the children of my early world had grandparents, innumerable aunts, uncles and cousins and servants to love them and indulge them.

If the child were a boy, when he reached the age of seven still another person became important in his life. This was his schoolteacher. In that Chinese world the teacher held the place next to parents for the years of childhood and adolescence. His was the responsibility, not only for the mental education of the child, but for his moral welfare, too. Education was not merely for reading and writing and arithmetic, not only for history and literature and music, but also for learning self-discipline and proper conduct, and proper conduct meant the perfecting and the practice of how to behave to all other persons in their various stations and relationships. The fruit of such education was inner security. A child learned in the home how to conduct himself toward the different generations of grandparents and parents, elder and younger uncles and aunts, elder and younger cousins and brothers and sisters and servants, and in school he learned how to conduct himself toward teacher and friends and officials and neighbors and acquaintances. Being so taught, the youth was never ill at ease, never uncertain of how to behave or of how to speak to anyone. The essential rules were simple and clarified by the usage of centuries, and so the growing personality was poised and calm.

The very houses were ordered in the same fashion. We young persons knew where to sit when we came into a room. We did not take the seats of our elders until we ourselves became the elders. With each year we knew that we would be given certain privileges, and if we claimed these too soon we were the losers, in the respect and estimation of other people. We were patient, therefore, knowing that time would bring us all things. How much easier it was for me to live in that world where I knew exactly what to do without being told or scolded than it is now for my children to live in my present world! How confusing for my American children not to know, for example, whether an adult wants to be called by his first name, or by his last! I know a family where the children call their parents by their first names, and I feel the confusion in those children's hearts. The relationships are not clear and therefore they do not know where they belong in the generations. They know they are not adults, they know that the adults are not children, yet the lines are not defined as they should be, and children lose security thereby.

In my early world we were all taught not to sit until our elders sat, not to eat until they had eaten, not to drink tea until their bowls were lifted. If there were not enough chairs we stood, and when an elder spoke to us, however playfully, we answered with the proper title. Did we feel oppressed? I am sure we did not, nor did that word occur to us. We knew where we were, and we knew, too, that someday we would be elders.

And school! We all loved school and knew it was a privilege, especially for girls, to go to school. Most boys and certainly most girls could never go to school. The Old Empress favored girls' schools in her latter years, but she said that she feared to increase the taxes to an amount necessary for public schools. Nevertheless, after she heard of Western schools, she sent out an edict commending the idea of education for girls as well as boys, and many private schools were opened as a consequence. I wonder sometimes nowadays, when I see reluctant children forced to school, whether compulsory education really educates. In my early world it was a priceless opportunity to go to school, and to say that one did go was to declare himself a member of the aristocracy of the educated.

For our class consciousness in that Chinese world was entirely based upon education, and the object of education was not only mental accomplishment but moral character. Our teachers made us understand and indeed believe that a well-educated person was well-bred and had moral integrity as a matter of course. Much was forgiven the ignorant and the illiterate, but nothing evil or foolish was forgiven the educated man or woman, who was supposed to be a superior person in the old Confucian sense of the princely being. Plato once taught the same lesson.

Since education insisted upon moral as well as intellectual attainments, the governors of the country were chosen from among the educated, and the old Imperial Examinations were the narrow gate through which all educated persons must pass if they wished to get the good jobs of the government. The material of the examinations was excellent test material, involving memory as well as thought, and a knowledge of history, literature and poetry was necessary. Those who passed with the highest marks were chosen for government administration, and since the best minds were naturally the most successful, it was inevitable that superior men became the actual rulers of the people. The hit-or-miss methods of modern times would never have been accepted in that old ordered world. It was from the Chinese Imperial Examinations that the English adopted their own Civil Service Examinations, and later the United States based our own Civil Service upon the English system.

I am glad that my first years were in an ordered world, for though it passed, still the memory holds of what it means to a child to live in such a world, where adults were calm and confident and where children knew the boundaries beyond which they could not go and yet within which they lived secure. My parents had their work of teaching and preaching their religion, and this kept them busy and happy and out of their child's way. I had lessons to do, the lessons of my own country which could not be taught in a Chinese school, American history and literature, the history and literature of England and Europe and of ancient Greece and Rome, and I confess those countries seemed to have little to do with the world in which I lived. But a solitary child learns lessons quickly and most of my day was free for play and dreaming.

How sorry I feel nowadays for the overcrowded lives of my own children, whose every hour is filled with school and sport and social events of various kinds! They have no chance to know the delight of long days empty except for what one puts into them, where there is nothing to do except what one wants to do. Then the imagination grows like the tree of life, enchanting the air. No wonder I was a happy child, and that my parents were happy, too. We met briefly, we smiled and made communication about necessary matters of food and clothing and the small tasks of my day. My mother bade me hold my shoulders straight, and my father reminded me at table to hold my knife and fork as he did. Upon this subject of the knife and fork my mind was kept divided, for my mother ate her food as Americans do, cutting her meat and then putting down the knife to take up her fork, but my father ate as English people do, holding the fork in his left hand and the knife in his right, and piling the chopped food against his fork. Each gave me directions and sometimes I obeyed one and sometimes the other, wondering at first, and then accepting, as children do, the peculiarities of parents and letting chance decide each meal. Meanwhile my private choice was chopsticks.

My early memories are not of parents, however, but of places. Thus our big whitewashed brick bungalow, encircled by deep arched verandas for coolness, was honeycombed with places that I loved. Under the verandas the beaten earth was cool and dry, and I had my haunts there. The gardener made a stove for me from a large Standard Oil tin with one side cut away. He lined the three sides with mud mixed with lime and then set into it a coarse iron grating. When I lit a fire beneath this and put in charcoal I could really cook, and of course I cooked the easy Chinese dishes I liked best and that my amah taught me. I had a few dolls but my "children" were the small folk of the servants' quarters or the neighbors', and we had wonderful hours of play, unsupervised by adults, all of whom were fortunately too busy to pay us heed. I remember going to bed at night replete with solid satisfaction because the day had been so packed with pleasurable play.

Under those verandas, too, I kept my pet pheasants and there I watched the tiny thimbles of tawny down pick their way out from the pale brown eggs, and there I smoked my first corn silk cigarette, an unknown sin in my world, but introduced to me by the red-haired small son of a visiting missionary who had lately returned from America.

"All the kids smoke in America," the rascal said and so we smoked in the latticed cellars while our elders talked theology upstairs. It was not exciting enough for me, however, for in my other world any child could take a puff from a Chinese grandparent's water pipe and adults only laughed when children choked on the raw Chinese tobacco smoke. Opium I knew I must never taste, even though sometimes the parents of my best friend might administer it for an ache in a small stomach, for opium was an evil. My parents spent weary hours trying to help some addict break the chain that bound him and I feared the sweet and sickish stuff, imagining, as children do, that if once I tasted it I would grow thin and yellow, like the father of my next door playmate, and never be myself again.

There was more than that to opium. Our city, which lay beyond the fields and ponds and down by the river's edge, had once been captured in July, 1842, by the British during the Opium Wars, when China had tried to stop the entrance of opium from India under the English flag and had failed. The Manchu general, Hai Ling, was in charge of the defense of our city in those years, and feeling himself disgraced by defeat he retired into his house and set it on fire and so perished. The English, incensed at the loss of revenue, had insisted on their right to trade, maintaining that it was not they who had introduced the opium habit to the Chinese, that opium was grown on Chinese soil and greedy Chinese traders merely wanted all the income for themselves. Probably this was partly true, for nothing in this life, it seems, is simon-pure, and the hearts of men are always mixed. Yet there were many Chinese who were not traders and who honestly enough were frightened at the tremendous increase of opium-smoking among their people, and it was also true that most of the opium, especially the cheaper kind, did come from India, and not only under the English flag, but also under the Dutch and the American flags. My vigorous parents sided entirely with the Chinese and did their doughty best to help many a man and woman to break the opium habit.

The use of opium, it may here be remarked, was not native to China. It was first brought in by Arab traders during the Middle Ages, and was then introduced as a drug beneficial in diarrhea and intestinal diseases. The Chinese did not begin smoking opium until the Portuguese traders taught them to do so in the seventeenth century when it became a fashionable pastime for officials and rich people. Most Chinese, even in my childhood, considered it a foreign custom, and indeed their name for opium was *yang yien,* or "foreign smoke." The feelings of the average Chinese can therefore be understood the better when a substantial part of the English trade was in opium, grown in India for markets developed in China.

The Chinese lost the Opium Wars, and after each loss the price was heavy. Treaty ports were yielded, the rights of trade and commerce were demanded and given, and high indemnities had to be paid. The story can be read in any good history of China, and I will not retell it here, except as it influenced my world. Chinkiang, my home city, had been deeply affected by the wars, although it was still an important city, for it stood at the junction of the Yangtse River and the Grand Canal, and so was in a key position for the transmitting of tax money and produce to Peking. An early writer, J. Banow, in his book, *Travels in China,* says of my Chinese home town in 1797: "The multitude of ships of war, of burden and of pleasure, some gliding down the stream, others sailing against it; some moving by oars, and others lying at anchor; the banks on either side covered with towns and houses as far as the eye could reach; as presenting a prospect more varied and cheerful than any that had hitherto occurred. Nor was the canal on the other side less lively. For two whole days we were continually passing among fleets of vessels of different construction and dimensions."

In my time, however, Chinkiang was a treaty port and the stretch of land along the river's edge was a British Concession. High walls surrounded it, broken by two great iron gates that were always locked at night. Within the boundaries lived the British Consul, his vast house set high on a wooded hill, and all the English and Americans and other foreigners, except for a few missionary families who preferred to live among the Chinese. My parents were among these. They were constitutionally unable to preach what they did not practice, and the discrepancy between a gospel of love and brotherhood and the results of the Opium Wars was too much for them. They could not live happily behind the high walls and the iron gates, although the streets there were clean and shaded by trees and beggars were not allowed. Happy for me that I had such parents, for instead of the narrow and conventional life of the white man in Asia, I lived with the Chinese people and spoke their tongue before I spoke my own, and their children were my first friends.

Did I not see sights which children should not see and hear talk not fit for children's ears? If I did, I cannot remember. I saw poor and starving people in a famine year, but my parents bade me help them in relief, and I learned early that trouble and suffering can always be relieved if there is the will to do it, and in that knowledge I have found escape from despair throughout my life. Often I saw lepers, their flesh eaten away from their bones, and I saw dead children lying on the hillsides, and wild dogs gnawing at their flesh, and I saw rascals enough and heard rich cursing when men and women quarreled. I cannot remember anything evil from these sights and sounds. The dead taught me not to fear them, and my heart was only made more tender while I chased the dogs away as best I could. It is better to learn early of the inevitable depths, for then sorrow and death take their proper place in life, and one is not afraid.

19

And how much joy I saw and shared in! Our Chinese friends took me into their homes and lives, and that wonderful simplicity which is the result of long living mellowed all their relationships with me. The kindliness of servants was warmth at home, and so was the friendliness of our Chinese neighbors. Their laughing curiosity, their unabashed ignorance of our Western ways, their pleasure in seeing our house and what we ate and how we dressed were all part of the day's amusement. If my kind was different from theirs, I never felt it so, and I did not discern in them the slightest dislike of what we were.

For much of this I must thank my parents who in their quiet way made no difference between peoples. We were the only missionary family I knew in those days who welcomed Chinese guests to spend the night in our guest room and eat at the table with us. I am sure this was partly because my parents were themselves cultivated persons and drew to them Chinese of like nature and background. They disliked a crude and ignorant Chinese as much as they disliked such a person were he white, or even American, and thus early we learned by their example to judge a man or woman by character and intelligence rather than by race or sect. Such values held, and they were natural to the Chinese, too.

How shall I conjure again those childhood days? I rose early in the morning because my father demanded it. He got up at five o'clock and when he had bathed and dressed he prayed for an hour in his study. He expected then to find the family waiting for him at the breakfast table. If any one were not there he would not seat himself at the end of our oval teakwood dining table, that piece of furniture imperishable in my memory. There he stood, tall and immovable, his blue eyes gazing across the room at the landscape beyond the high windows. When a small girl hurried through the door and slipped panting into her chair he sat down, and with him all of us. He then asked grace, not carelessly gabbling, but with a moment's preceding silence. In a solemn voice peculiar to his prayers, he asked divine blessing and always that this food might strengthen us to do God's will.

The food itself was simple but it seems to me it was always good. In the morning except in the summer we had oranges, the beautiful sweet oranges that were brought by ship and bearer from Fukien, where such oranges grow as I have never seen elsewhere, although I have seen even the orange groves of California. For we had a great variety of oranges. There were tight-skinned Canton oranges for the winter, and there were a dozen varieties of mandarin oranges or tangerines and there were large loose-skinned oranges, but the best of all were the honey oranges, the *mi chü*, which came in the season of the Chinese New Year in late January or February, and were often sent to us as

New Year's gifts. The skin peeled from them easily, and inside the sections parted at a touch, each so full of sweet juice and fine fragrant pulp that to eat this fruit was one of my great pleasures. There was always a plate of oranges on the sideboard, I remember, during their long season, and we ate them when we liked, sucking them if the skins were tight.

When the oranges were gone we had loquats, those bright yellow balls of delicate flesh deep about the brown stones within, and then came apricots, not just one variety but several, and perhaps fresh lichees, imported from the South, and sometimes tree strawberries in their brief season. When the peaches ripened we were well into summer. The earliest peaches were the blood-red ones, enormous and slightly tart, and then came yellow ones and the sweet flat ones, and finally the huge white peaches that were best of all. My mother canned them in the American fashion, buying her jars from Montgomery Ward and Sears Roebuck. Of course we had bananas and pineapples and melons of many kinds, watermelons, red, white and yellow, and little sweet golden muskmelons. Melons were summer fruits and we ate them freely but never if they had been cut in the streets, for we knew that flies were deadly enemies, carrying dysentery and cholera and typhoid in their tiny claws. Years later it took me a while to endure the sight of flies in my own country, for somehow I had not expected to see them here, too. And let me not forget the many varieties of persimmons that were ready to eat in the late autumn. The best of them, the big golden seedless ones, came from the North where they were ripened in the warm ash of charcoal ovens, but I liked very well, too, our small scarlet seeded ones, filled with sweet juice. From Peking came also the dried persimmons, dusty with powdered sugar, and as big and flat as pancakes.

After the fruit at breakfast we always had a special sort of porridge invented by my father. It was made of whole wheat and the servants ground it at home on a Chinese stone quern. I hear a good deal nowadays from dietitians about the superiority of slowly ground grains, but I learned about it long ago from the Chinese. All the grain there was ground by hand on stone querns, and the breads were delicious. Our porridge was delicious, too. My mother roasted the cleanly washed wheat slightly, before it was ground, and when the porridge was cooked by a long slow process it had a toasted flavor. We ate it with sugar and white buffalo cream, richer than cows' cream. It made a nourishing dish, and it was followed by eggs, and hot rolls or hot biscuits, for my family came from the American South and seldom ate their bread cold. Coffee for grownups was inevitable, but my mother got her coffee beans whole from Java and ground them in a little square wooden mill with an iron handle. I drank water, boiled and cool.

Breakfasts were always solid and American, for my parents worked hard and expected their children to do so, but the other two meals were less hearty. To these meals I was indifferent and usually ate first within the servants' quarters, to the consternation of my mother, who was astonished at my frequent lack of appetite without apparently ever guessing its cause. The servants' food was plain but delicious. Indeed the diet of the poor in China was remarkable for its flavor, if not for the variety which richer people had. Even their breakfast I liked much better than my own. In our region it was rice gruel served very hot, with a few small dishes of salt fish, salted dried turnips and pickled mustard greens, and an egg, now and then, hard-boiled and cut into eighths. The servants' midday meal was the best, and that one I ate heartily enough and as often as I dared. It was rice, cooked dry and light, a bowl of soup of some sort, another bowl with Chinese cabbage and fresh white bean curd, and still another with a bit of meat or fowl. We needed no dessert, for fruits and sweets were considered between-meal dainties. At night I supped alone with my amah, and in secret, well before our own family night meal. We ate the leftovers from noon or we drank a soup made from the browned rice at the bottom of the big rice pot.

Years later when I went to North China to live, but that was in another world, I did not eat rice but wheaten breads with vegetables and infrequent bits of meat. Feather-like twisted crullers, salt and not sweet, and tea made breakfast, with dates and persimmons for fruits, or roasted bread, paper-thin and a foot in diameter, wrapped around chopped garlic. For the second meal of the day, since in North China people eat only two meals a day except in the harvest season, we ate noodles or bread roasted against coal embers and dotted with sesame seeds, or steamed bread-rolls filled with chopped meat and garlic, or boiled dumplings, very small and dainty and filled with bits of meat and fresh ginger, or with chopped spinach and bean vermicelli. I am never in the least homesick for past worlds, for I live in the present, yet I come nearest to nostalgia when I think of the variety of Chinese food. Each province had its own fruits and vegetables and dishes, and every city was famous for some dish or other, and every restaurant had its specialty and every family its private recipes, and no one thought of food and cooking with anything except lyric pleasure.

The other evening, sitting with Chinese friends here upon my own terrace in Pennsylvania, we remembered together a few of the most famous dishes of our childhood world—the Yellow River fish soup so deliciously cooked in Ching-chow, the steamed shad of West Lake, the cured fish and beef of Chang-sha, the plum flower fragrant salted fish of Chao-chow, the steamed crabs of Soochow, the sweet and sour fish of Peking, and the dried shrimps of Tung-ting Lake.

And of wines, the best, we agreed, was the Shao-hsing wine of Chekiang, and then the Mao-tai wine of Kweichow and the distilled Fen-chow liquor of Shansi. And of teas the green Lung-ching tea of Chekiang was our favorite, but also the Pu-êrh tea of Yünnan, plucked from the mountain named P'u-êrh, and the Chi-men red tea, and the Lin-an green tea of Anking or the jasmine and the Iron Lo-han tea of Foochow and the Hangchow chrysanthemum tea.

As for fruits and vegetables, there are so many that only a very few could be mentioned. We spoke of the oranges of Hsin-hui, in Kwangtung, the pumelos of Sha-tien, in Kiangsi, the taro of Li-pu, the red and white dates of Tê-chow in Shangtung, the Chefoo apples and T'angshan pears, the watermelons and grapes of Sinkiang, the Shanghai muskmelons and the Peking persimmons, the kumquat oranges of Foochow, and the olives of Kwangtung province, the bamboo shoots and mushrooms of South Hunan, and the Kalgan mushrooms, Ho-p'u lichee nuts and Nanking lotus root.

But other foods cannot be altogether forgotten, as for example, Tê-chow smoked chicken, Canton steamed young pigeon, Nanking salted duck, Peking roast duck, Canton's one-chicken-three-tastes, Fuchow hash, King-hua ham, Szechuan's pickled salted greens, arrowroot from West Lake, a Peking summer drink made from sour prunes, mushroom oil from South Hunan, rice flour from Kwei-lin, bean curd and sauce from Anking in Anhwei province.

And we stopped there only because one must not go on forever.

The gala days were the days when we were invited to wedding and birthday feasts, and then the menu included a score and more of different dishes, each perfected by centuries of gourmets. For Chinese are always gourmets. The appearance of a dish, its texture and its flavor, are subjects for endless talk and comparison. A rich man will pay his cook a prince's salary, and yet he will humbly heed the criticisms of his friends concerning a dish set before them, for in China cooking is pure art in its most fundamental and satisfying form, and when a dish is criticized by those who know all that it should be, none can take offense, since there is nothing personal in criticizing an art.

One item of significance—the best dishes were always seasonal as well as local. I am a great believer in the seasons. Even here in my own world, I have no relish for sweet corn in January or strawberries in November. Such seasonal monstrosities are repulsive to me. I want my corn in August, young and green, and I do not want it for a longer time than it should continue, because other vegetables must in justice have their turn. Freezing is inevitable in this day and age and I have the implements, but I am lackadaisical about the whole affair, and had I my will, I would never eat a dish out of season. Turkey should appear at Thanksgiving and at Christmas, and for me the bird does not exist at other times.

So in my earliest world I ate rice flour cakes at New Year's but never thought of them at other times, and in the spring I ate glutinous rice wrapped in green leaves from the river reeds and steamed, and with it hard-boiled duck eggs, salted and sliced, or if I longed for sweet, then with red sugar, which I know now is full of vitamins, but which I ate then merely because it was delicious. And in the summer we ate crabs with hot wine, but not in the autumn when they were dangerous, and the only delicacy we children ate at any time of the year was the barley taffy, covered with sesame seed, which the travelling taffy vendor sold as he wandered along the narrow earthen roads of our hills and valleys. Whatever I was doing, intent at my books or playing games in the long grass outside the gate, when I heard the tinkle of his small bronze gong, struck with a minute wooden hammer, which he did while holding the gong and hammer in one hand, I gathered a few copper cash from my store and ran to beckon to him. The taffy, dusted with flour to keep it from being sticky, lay in a big round slab on the lid of one of the baskets he carried suspended on a bamboo pole across his shoulder. When we had argued over the size of the piece I could buy with my coins, each of which was worth the tenth of a penny, he took his sharp chisel and chipped off a portion. It was a delicious sweet, congealing the jaws, long lasting and very healthy, since it contained no white cane sugar.

One of the benefits of sharing the food of the poor, and how generous they always were, was that I ate brown rice and brown flour and brown sugar. Yet the strange human passion for whiteness possessed the Chinese, too, and when a poor man became rich, which he did as often as among other men, immediately he took to eating white polished rice and flour and white imported cane sugar and wondered why he did not feel as well as he used to feel in his days of poverty. And though I was pitied for my blue eyes and yellow hair, my white skin was always praised, and it was counted a misfortune if a daughter in a Chinese family was born with brown skin instead of with a skin of light cream color. The northern Chinese are tall and fair in comparison to the dark short brown people of the South, and so the women of the North are much admired, although Soochow has its share of beautiful girls and must always have had, since old Chinese books are full of their praises. I find this same desire for whiteness here in my present world, where a darker Negro will try to marry a fairer one, and where I am told that

24

gentlemen naturally prefer blondes. A friend explained it the other day by saying that the desire of all people is toward the brightness of the sun and their fear is toward the night and darkness. I doubt it is a matter of such profound anthropological meaning, but it may be.

Throughout those long and glorious days of my early childhood there was always something to see and to do. Behind our compound walls, whose gates were never locked except at night, a warm and changeful life went on. My father was often travelling, but my mother did not leave her children and when she had to go we went with her. This meant, too, that many visitors came to see her, Chinese ladies who were curious to meet a foreigner and see a foreign house, and these my mother led gravely through our simple home where there was actually nothing more wonderful than a sewing machine but where everything seemed strange and therefore wonderful to eyes that had seen only the age-long furnishings of the usual Chinese house. My own friends came and went, and our favorite playing place was the hillside in front of the gate, where the pampas grass grew tall above our heads. Here in the green shadows we pretended jungles one day and housekeeping the next. Or we played in the wheat straw in the little stable where my father kept his white horse. In a sunny corner of the south veranda I spent many winter afternoons reading alone, and in that spot I read and re-read our set of Charles Dickens, refreshing myself meanwhile with oranges or peanuts. Here let me say that to my taste we Americans ruin our peanuts with over-roasting. Peanuts are not meant to be brown but creamy white, roasted barely enough to take away the raw edge of their earthy flavor, and not until they look like coffee beans.

For change and excitement we went on rare occasions to the hills for picnics or to see Golden Island, where a giant lived, who froze my heart when I looked into his fat bland face. He was in an inner room of the vast and famous Buddhist monastery, an immense figure in the grey robes of a priest, eight and a half feet tall, and broad in proportion. He sat with huge hands placed on his knees, and he would not get up unless he were paid to do so. Even then he would not always get up to show us how tall he was, for he was often in a surly mood and kept the money anyhow. If I had nightmares, it was about that hideous gigantic priest.

Golden Island is one of the famous spots of Chinese history and it was visited by Marco Polo. Long ago it ceased to be an island for the river moved its bed and left it standing in dry land, and the historic temples and monasteries, once the possession of emperors, in my time had only remnants left of the imperial green and yellow porcelain tiles of the Ming dynasty. The pagoda still stood, however, elegant and grace-ful against the sky.

In the river was the bigger but less famous Silver Island, and a picnic there was an expedition requiring the hiring of a boat to carry us to and fro, and we had to spend a day for the trip. It was a fascinating one, however, for the narrow pathway clung to the steep rocky cliffs and when I had climbed to the top and looked down upon the yellow whirl-pools of the river, here as wide as a sea, I was pleasantly terrified.

The Chinese moon year was rich with treasures, too, of feast days, each with its particular dainty to be made and eaten, and each with its special toys and delightful occupations. Thus at the Feast of Lanterns our faith-ful servants bought us paper rabbits pulled upon little wheels and lit within by candles, or lotus flowers and butterflies or even horses, split in two, one half of which I carried on my front and the other strapped upon my back, so that I looked like a horse walking in the dark, to my great joy. And in the spring there were kites made in every imaginable shape, and sometimes we made them ourselves of split reeds and rice paste and thin red paper, and we spent our days upon the hills, watch-ing the huge and intricate kites that even grown men flew, a mighty dragon or a thirty foot centipede or a pagoda that needed a dozen men to get it aloft. We played with birds in cages and birds that could talk if we taught them carefully enough, black macaws and white-vested magpies, or we had nightingales for music. We listened to the wander-ing storytellers who beat their little gongs upon the country roads or stopped at villages at night and gathered their crowds upon a threshing floor. We went to see the troupes of travelling actors who performed their plays in front of the temples far or near, and thus I early learned my Chinese history and became familiar with the heroes of the ages. The Chinese New Year was of course the crown of all the year's joys, and on that day my two childhood worlds came near to meeting, for we exchanged gifts with our Chinese friends and received calls and went calling, dressed in our best and bowing and wishing "Happy New Year and Riches" everywhere we went. Such occupations and pleasures be-longed to my Chinese world into which my parents seldom entered with me, for they remained foreign, whereas I was not really a for-eigner, either in my own opinion or in the feelings of my Chinese friends.

Yet there was always the other world on the fringe of my Chinese world, the white world, and the white world had its own holidays and pleasures. Halloween, for instance, I faithfully observed with a jack-o'-lantern made from a yellow Chinese gourd and the kindly Chinese neighbors pretended to be terrified when a fiery grinning face shone through their windows on the October night. Christmas, too, was a foreign festival, a family joy, and so were the Fourth of July and Thanksgiving. My parents were careful to observe all such days and to teach us what they meant. And these were not all. When Queen Victoria's birthday came around, every American as well as every other white family received an invitation to the British Club, a forlorn little house up in the hills surrounded by a small racecourse for ponies. On the Queen's Birthday the Club took on dignity. The hall was decorated with the British colors draped around the black and white portrait of Queen Victoria, a plump and severe-looking little woman, and we all sat on benches and stared at her and listened to a discourse by the British Consul and diplomatic replies by the other Consuls, usually only the American and the French.

Then we stood and sang "God Save the Queen" as heartily as we could, although I could never understand why the tune was the same as "My Country, 'Tis of Thee," and after it tea was served, a very English repast of buttered buns and jam and hot Indian tea and sweet biscuits, and the children, half a dozen or so of them, ran races and received prizes. My memory of those white children is that they were always wan and pale and ran so listlessly that it was easy to win, and win I did, being brown and strong, until my parents were ashamed because I took so many prizes.

"On the Queen's Birthday, too!" my mother whispered to me reproachfully. "You should let an English child win." But I was not able to do less than my best, even for the Queen.

That early world seemed as stable as the sun and moon and all its ways were peace. And yet, before I was eight years old, even I could discern that it might come to an end. In Peking the Empress Dowager was having trouble with her heir, her adopted son, the young Emperor Kwang-hsü. Parents of only sons sympathized with her, especially if such sons were wilful, handsome, intelligent, rebellious youths. I heard the young Emperor discussed in my own family and thought of my brother, eleven years older than I, whom I scarcely knew because he had been sent away to college when I was but three. He was sometimes a trouble, too, and I knew that my mother was often sleepless when he did not write and she could not know what was happening to him in faraway America.

We all knew about the young Emperor, for his life had been dramatic from the first. When the Empress Dowager had entered the Imperial Palace, she soon became the favorite concubine of the Emperor Hsien-feng. Yet so tactful and graceful was she in his house that even his consort, the First Empress, had not been jealous of the beautiful courteous

27

girl. When she bore a son she was raised to the rank of Western Empress, the First Empress being given the title Eastern. The two Empresses continued as friends, twenty-five years in all, and it was a legend in our countryside that these two ladies, the wives of one man, had never quarreled throughout that long time. They were very different, for the Eastern Empress was quiet and retiring, a fine scholar and a real connoisseur of art and music and literature, while the Western Empress, who became the regent after the Emperor's death, was a good executive, active in many ways, and interested in political life.

The Emperor had died in a very strange and tragic way during the Arrow War, but long before I was born, so that I knew about it almost as a legend from my Confucian tutor, Mr. Kung, who was supposed only to teach me to read and write Chinese. Since he loved to talk and I loved to listen to the melodious flow of his beautiful Peking language, I knew all about the Arrow War. It was a little war and I doubt that many westerners have even heard of it, yet it was one of those incidents, seemingly slight, upon which turn mighty events. Some time between the years 1850 and 1860 a few enterprising Chinese merchants bought a small ship, named it *The Arrow* and had it registered under the English flag in Hong Kong. They then plied a trade in the southern waters which was called honest trade but certainly smelled of piracy, and since the Viceroy of one of the southern provinces wanted to rid the coast of the pest of pirates, he seized *The Arrow* among other ships and pulled down the English flag and put the Chinese crew in jail.

The British heard of the insult to their flag and were immediately angry, whereupon the Viceroy, terrified because of the previous Opium Wars with Great Britain, sent the prisoners in their chains to the British Consulate, but neglected to apologize for the flag, which doubtless he considered merely a bit of cloth. The Chinese had no sacred associations with flags, and looked upon them as no more than decorative banners. The British Consul flew into a rage, however, and sent the men back, whereupon the harassed Viceroy had them all beheaded for making so much trouble.

At this Britain declared war again and seized the Chinese Viceroy and sent him to India where he died in exile. France, Russia and America were invited to join with Great Britain in the new war, but only France accepted, using as her excuse the fact that a French missionary had recently been killed in the province of Kwangsi. The foreign troops marched upon Peking, and the Emperor and the Empress and their baby son fled to Jehol, a hundred miles away. There the Emperor suddenly died, and the young Western Empress was left alone with the heir.

She had no time to mourn. At such a moment it was always possible that discontented men might snatch away the throne. While the dead Emperor's brother, Prince Kung, still in Peking, persuaded the invaders to a treaty, although not until the beautiful Summer Palace outside the city had been burned down, the resolute Western Empress returned quickly to see that her little son, T'ung-chih, was set in his father's place. From then on she never ceased to keep her firm hand upon the throne.

She had need of firmness and she knew it. No one realized better than she that the times were dangerous. The Western powers were pressing hard upon China as still another colonial possession, and the Manchu dynasty was dying. Hsien-feng had been a weak Emperor, and the heir was a baby. She needed to be strong and to find strong men to help her. Prince Kung and the two Empresses were appointed regents, yet Prince Kung was too able a man, and the strong young Western Empress soon felt that it was he who was the real ruler. She deposed him and thereafter she and the gentle Eastern Empress were the regents until T'ung-chih was seventeen. Then she married him to a lovely Manchu girl named Alute.

In these days, in this Western world in which I now live, the marriage of Elizabeth of England and Philip reproduces in modern terms that old and beautiful love story of T'ung-chih and Alute. A whole nation rejoiced then as now, and the Western Empress, who had become the Empress Dowager, planned to yield her regency to her son. She was eager for a grandson that the throne might be secure. Three years passed, however, without a child, and then suddenly the young Emperor was smitten with smallpox and died. The throne was empty again.

Again there was no time for sorrow. Within the palace, the capital and the nation, there was a strong party that wished to displace the two Manchu Empresses and set a Chinese upon the throne. Once more the Empress Dowager had to act quickly. She sent for her great general, Li Hung-chang, then in the city of Tientsin eighty miles away, and ordered him to bring to The Forbidden City four thousand of his best men on horseback, with artillery. In thirty-six hours, exactly at the planned moment, they arrived without any one outside knowing yet that the Emperor was dead. The men had wooden bits in their mouths to prevent their talking and the metal strappings of the horses were wrapped in cloth for silence.

As soon as she knew she had this military support, the Empress Dowager stole out of the palace to the house of her sister and lifted from his bed her eldest nephew, a little boy of three, and took him, asleep, back to the palace with her. When dawn came she proclaimed him her heir, the throne had an Emperor again, and the little boy became the Emperor Kwang-hsü.

All this was only story to me, for it had happened before I was born. What I knew actually was the trouble that Kwang-hsü made now when he had become the Emperor. I suppose the Empress Dowager was already dreaming of something like retirement and enjoying herself, for she had many interests and amusements. She liked to paint, and had she been free to devote herself to art she could have become notable. She was a fine calligrapher, she loved flowers, she had a magnetic and enchanting way with birds and animals, so that she could coax wild birds to come to her at call, and cicadas to sit upon her wrist while she stroked them with her forefinger. She had a profound love of nature and was fond of certain vistas about the palaces, especially about the rebuilt Summer Palace, and she would have been glad, I think, to leave the affairs of state to her adopted son. But she did not deceive herself. He, too, was impetuous and weak, and though she had provided the finest of teachers for him, he was unable to think and plan as a statesman. Moreover, and this really terrified her, he seemed bewitched by the ways of the West. It had begun in his early childhood, in a manner which had seemed innocent enough. The eunuchs who were his servants had been hard put to it to amuse the lonely little boy, torn from his home and family, and they had searched the city for toys. But he grew tired of kites and clay dolls and paper lanterns and whistles, and at last one of the eunuchs remembered that there was a foreign toyshop in the capital, kept by a Dane, who stocked a few Western toys for the children of the foreign legation families. Thither the Imperial eunuchs went and they bought a toy train for the little Emperor, a magical toy which could be wound up to run. He was delighted with it, and they, poor souls, pleased and relieved to find something that could amuse their tiny sovereign, hurried to the shop again and again until the astonished Dane found himself on the way to riches. Every imaginable trinket and toy was bought and at last he searched the European countries to find something new for the baby Emperor.

Thus from early years Kwang-hsü believed that from the West came strange and wonderful objects which his own country did not know how to make. As he grew older he read of machines and railroads and he wanted to study science and he began to dream of reforming his nation and making China as modern as were the Western nations. Nor was he the only one. There were men who had the same dreams, and two of them were the Emperor's own tutors. Unknown to the Empress, they encouraged their young ruler to imagine himself as the head of a vast modern people, a new China, and they tried to persuade him to the first dreadful step toward his complete power. It was to murder the Empress Dowager, his adoptive mother.

Here was the stuff of Shakespearean drama. The young Emperor was torn between loyalty to the great woman who had brought him in her own arms to the Imperial Palace and his sincere belief that China must be changed. He loved and admired the Empress with the force of all the tradition which had trained him to obedience to her not only as his sovereign but also as his adopted mother, and filial piety made his conscience tender. Yet he saw clearly enough what she would not, that China was in peril if she did not modernize to defend herself. Hungry Western powers were nibbling at her coasts and inland rivers, and she had no ships of war, no armies with which to beat them off. It was the age of empire, and any country not strong enough to defend itself was considered fair prey for Western empire builders. But China had never built an army or a navy, for she had not needed such defenses. The strength of her superior civilization until now had conquered every invader.

"We are being carved into pieces like a melon," the old Empress groaned, and indeed they were, and yet she could not trust the impetuous young Emperor. She was partly justified for in a burst of reforming energy as soon as he became Emperor, within a hundred days, he had sent tens of edicts flying over the country, announcing new schools to be set up in temples, new railways, new laws and customs. Everything was to be changed and at once.

The people were confused and inside the palace immediately there was deep division. The old princes told the Empress Dowager that order must be restored. The modern advisors of the Emperor and his reformers must be routed and killed. The Emperor, they said, must be restrained.

When the Empress Dowager had to act, she acted quickly. Though I was a child and far away in another province, I can remember the consternation of my parents and our liberal Chinese friends and the satisfaction of our conservative Chinese friends, including my tutor, Mr. Kung, when we heard the news one early morning that by a *coup d'état* the young Emperor had been taken prisoner and locked up on an island, that Yuan Shih-k'ai, the Commander of the new Western-trained Chinese army, had deserted the Emperor to take his side with the Empress Dowager, that six of the reformers had been killed and only two of the leaders, K'ang Yu-wei and Liang Ch'i-ch'ao, had escaped. A strange silence pervaded our region that day and doubtless it spread over the whole country. What now was to happen? The foreign governments, it became evident during the next few weeks, would do nothing. Opin-

31

ion was divided but on the whole it sided with the Empress Dowager and with the conservative party. The foreign governments did not welcome reforms which might rouse the people of China to knowledge of what had been going on.

The first edict we next received was signed by the Emperor, but every one knew that the Empress had written it and sent it out over his name and the imperial seal. It was moderate enough, mildly saying that the reforms were going too fast and the people were becoming confused.

"Our real desire," the edict announced reasonably, "was to make away with superfluous posts for the sake of economy; whereas, on the contrary, we find rumors flying abroad that we intend to change wholesale the customs of the Empire, and, in consequence, innumerable suggestions of reform have come to be presented to us. If we allowed this to go on, none of us would know to what pass matters would come. Hence, unless we hasten to express our present wishes clearly before all, we greatly fear that petty officials and their underlings will place their own construction on what commands have gone before, and create a ferment in the midst of the usual calm of the people. This will indeed be contrary to our desire, and put our reforms for strengthening and enriching our empire to naught."

Then followed the retraction of all the young Emperor's edicts during the past hundred days, and we knew that The Venerable Ancestor was back on the throne again and in full power.

It was in the year of 1900, when I was eight years old, that the two worlds of my childhood finally split apart. I had held them tied together by my very existence, I could see them clearly and combined from our vantage point on the hill above the Yangtse River. Sometimes in the morning when I looked abroad from our veranda, my mind flowed on beyond the green hillsides and the greener valleys, their ponds like diamonds in the sunshine, beyond the dark-roofed city and the bright breadths of the river, beyond to the sea. Across the sea was America, my own land, about which I knew nothing, and so upon which my imagination played with fantastic freedom. It all belonged to me, the near hills and the valleys, the city and the river, the sea and the land of my fathers.

In an academic fashion I knew, of course, even in those early years, that I was not Chinese, and I felt a rough justice in street urchins calling me "little foreign devil," or in their pretending when they saw me that it would soon rain, since devils, they said, come out only when it is going to rain. I knew that I was no devil, and to be called one did not trouble me because I was still secure in my Chinese world. Did these naughty children know me, they would not call me a devil, and I merely made reply that they were the children of turtles—that is to say, they were bastards, a remark which sent them into shocked silence. My parents did not know for years the significance of the retort, and by that time I was old enough to be ashamed of it myself.

In the year of 1900, however, throughout the spring, the beautiful springtime of the Yangtse River Valley, I felt my world splitting unexpectedly into its parts. The stream of visitors thinned and sometimes days passed without a single Chinese friend appearing before our gates. My playmates were often silent, they did not play with the usual joy, and at last they too ceased to climb the hill from the valley. Even my schoolmates did not clamor to share my desk seat. I was a child spoiled by love and gifts and at first I was bewildered and then sorely wounded, and when my mother saw this, she explained to me as best she could what was happening. It had nothing to do with Americans, she said, for surely we had never been cruel to the Chinese nor had we taken their land or their river ports. Other white people had done the evil, and our friends, she promised me, understood this and did not hate us. Indeed, they felt as warmly to us as before, only they did not dare to show their feelings, since they would be blamed. At last I comprehended that all of us who were foreigners were being lumped together in the cruel fashion that people can adopt sometimes, for particular and temporary reasons, which are no real reasons but merely vents for old hatreds. But I had never known what hatred was. I had neither been hated nor had I ever hated anyone. I could not understand why we, who were still ourselves and unchanged, should be lumped with unknown white men from unknown countries who had been what we were not, robbers and plunderers. It was now that I felt the first and primary injustice of life. I was innocent, but because I had the fair skin, the blue eyes, the blond hair of my race I was hated, and because of fear of me and my kind I walked in danger.

Danger! It had been an unknown word to me. Noxious insects and reptiles were dangerous, but now we were in danger from people, I and my family and all white men, women and children like us. For there came creeping down from Peking in the North to our mid-country province the most sickening rumors about the Empress Dowager, she whom I, too, had learned to think of as The Venerable Ancestor, not only of the Chinese but of all of us who lived under her rule. She had turned against us. Because greedy Europeans and Englishmen were gnawing at the shores along the Chinese seas and the rivers, she, we heard, wanted to rid herself of all white people and lock the gates of China forever against us. She was scarcely to be blamed, my grave father said, for being angry or for wanting to free China of invaders and the plunderers, and how would we like it if our own country, the United States, were fastened upon by strangers and stolen away from us bit by bit, by nagging petty wars and huge indemnities in money and land and railroad rights? He sympathized with the Empress Dowager, but his sympathy could not save us. We had to take our place with our own kind, guiltless though we were, and we had to suffer for their guilt.

I remember the faultless summer day when we heard of the first massacre of missionaries in Shantung, and that the little children had been murdered with their parents. It was the death of the children that made my mother's face turn pale and made my father decide that we must all be sent away. He had not believed until then that the Empress Dowager could be so foolish as to trust herself to the Boxers, that clan of monstrous imposters who pretended to her that they could by their secret magic withstand the foreign guns. For it was the foreign guns she feared. She knew that she had no armies or weapons which could match the armies and weapons of the Western peoples, and wanting desperately to find a means of protection and retaliation, she let herself believe in the magic pretensions of the Boxers. But by this time hysteria was raging over the whole nation. The foreign powers had demanded one concession after another from the weak young Emperor, and the people had, it was true, been only the more terrified by his Hundred Days of Reform, when he had sent the edicts which, if obeyed, would have destroyed the very structure of their ancient society. Meanwhile France had taken Annam, England insisted upon Weihaiwei, France upon Kwangchow, Germany upon Tsingtao and Russia upon Dairen. These were called "leased territories," but actually they were colonies. And where were the armies and the navies for which the Chinese people had been paying so heavily through taxes? It was clear that the money had been absorbed, spent, squandered, not only by the old Empress Dowager herself upon such follies as the marble boat on the lake by the Summer Palace, but through the private hoardings of her officials. When her full guilt began to be suspected she was glad to turn the attention of the angry people to the plundering foreigners, and so she listened to the Boxers, against the advice of her best ministers. By now the young Emperor had no power at all, for he was locked up and his helpers were decapitated or gone.

Into this storm and fury our quiet bungalow was swept one day like a leaf upon a whirlpool. The air that summer's day was hot and still and from the verandas the landscape was beautiful, the valleys green as jade with their earthen farmhouses shaded beneath the willow trees. White geese walked the paths between the fields and children played on the threshing floors while their parents in blue cotton peasant garb tilled the fields. Beyond the dark city the shining river flowed toward the sea. There was not a sign to show that the world was changed. I remember, though I was only eight years old, that long moment I stood on the veranda, gazing upon the scene that was home to me because I knew no other. It was the same and yet I knew, child though I was, that it could never be the same again.

Half a century and more has passed over my head since then, two world wars and the cruel snarl in Korea, and yet I see myself upon the veranda of the bungalow that was long ago torn down, a child, facing the changing world. The feelings then in my childish heart, the forebodings and the sadness, were right enough, for all has come to pass as I felt it might.

We left our home on that perfect summer's day and took ship on one of the sturdy steamboats that plied the Yangtse down to Shanghai. There had been plenty of argument in the mission bungalow before we left. My mother and father did not leave their post easily, and it was only the murdered children that gave the better argument now for escape, and even at that there was no thought of my father accompanying us. He was to take us to Shanghai and stay only long enough to see us established in some modest flat, and then return alone. We left the house as it was, for him, but my mother took some of the family silver she had brought from her West Virginia home and buried it in a corner of the yard to save it. Long ago she had learned such lessons in her childhood, when in the War between the States her family had hidden their treasures, too, but against the Yankees. I realize now that the calm with which my parents faced our danger was the result of their childhoods in a wartime.

The actual leave-taking was entirely unreal. I went about the house from room to room, saying to myself that perhaps I might never see it all again. My books I could not take, except a few of the best loved, for we were leaving in haste. The signal for instant flight had been long planned. When the flag on the American Consulate was changed to one of solid red, we must go, and it had changed at noon. But there was more than the house to leave. I said farewell to my favorite haunts inside our compound, the big Chinese elm, three feet in diameter, which I had climbed so often, and wherein was my favorite seat, a nook in the branches where unseen I could look down upon the road. There was, too, the garden bench under the bamboos where I went to read, and there was the little play kitchen under the verandas. And there were the animals, my pheasants, a rabbit, and an old grey dog, Nebuchadnezzar, whom we called Neb, a humble, mangy, pleading, too affectionate creature that no one could love except me. I could not be sure

35

that anyone would feed him when I was gone, for our amah was going with us, and she alone had the heart to keep old Neb alive for my sake.

And yet I could not believe that I was never to return. My father would be here, I could not imagine him not living, and there was the buried silver to be dug up, and the trees must remain, and the permanent hills and the valleys. Sometime we would come back, when the Chinese dared to like us again. And with irrepressible hope, I followed my family to the Bund and crossed the wooden bridge to the hulk and after due hours of waiting we went aboard the steamer and so were on our way to Shanghai.

It was a journey I enjoyed, for we took it seldom, and I could not keep from enjoying it even now. There was something delightful about the neatness of the ship, the pleasant little dining saloon, the compact cabins and the white-robed Chinese servants. The Captain was a Scotchman, for my father thought it wise to take an English vessel rather than one of the China Merchants' ships, and only when I saw the Captain did I feel shy. English captains, I had learned, did not approve of missionaries, especially proud and stubborn ones like my father, who made no effort to seem other than he was, a severe man of God. Most of all I enjoyed the actual movement of the ship along the river, the green banks sliding by and the ports at which we stopped by day or in the night. Once in the night when I lay in my berth I listened to a two-stringed Chinese violin weave a melody which I cannot repeat but which I remember to this day as the most bewitching that I have ever heard. Sometimes it still catches in my mind and I try to spin it again out of that long past midnight, out of the magic darkness. But I cannot lay hold upon it, although I hear it echoing through the manifold cells of my brain.

We reached Shanghai, I know that, but thereafter for the next months I think it was almost a year, my memory falters. I see scenes clear and separate, but no stream carries them on together. Whatever happened seems accidental and disjointed, unrelated to my real life. We were merely refugees. Shanghai was hot, breathlessly hot after our hilltop, but I was used to semitropical heat and the memory was not of suffering but of pleasure. At home our daily baths were in a tin tub, filled by buckets of water which the water-bearer brought in. Here in Shanghai I saw for the first time water coming out of the wall from faucets. It was pure magic, the self-coming water that I heard about from Americans and from Chinese who had been to America. The tub was still of painted tin, but it was a big one, and it was set in a wide shallow wooden platform fenced about with board and lined with tin, at one end of which was a drain. My mother stopped the drain with a big cork and then let cool water run into the walled platform and there on hot afternoons my baby sister and I played. It is a childish memory, slight enough, except that it diverted my mind from larger woe. Our small three-room flat was somewhere off Bubbling Well Road, on a quiet dead end, and there I learned to skip rope from two well-bred little English girls next door. But my favorite neighbor was a Portuguese lady, the soul of kindness, who lived two doors down the street and she invited me often to tea. Thither I went always with joy, dressed in a fresh white dress and my hair curled, and I remember that once I ran so fast to her gate that I fell and scraped my elbow badly and arrived bleeding, though not in tears, and the Portuguese lady bound me up with enormous bandages and plied me with viands. The scar is on my elbow yet as a souvenir of her kindness, although I have long ago forgotten her name.

For a treat our mother or our amah took us to a little park along the Whangpoo River, where an artificial rockery seemed to me a castle of delight, and when the steps were climbed, there at the top in a grotto was a tiny stone boy holding a stone umbrella perpetually over his head, whence dripped eternal rain. For something very special we visited the big park where horse racing went on, and there Chinese and white men mingled together in equal zeal to gamble. We, of course, had nothing to do with that. We walked along the gorgeous flower beds and looked at some monkeys in cages and came home again.

Such are my slight memories of a year when elsewhere in China there was beginning the most dreadful upheaval of our age, whose end is not yet nor can it be foreseen.

A final incident of that refugee period is rooted in my mind. One day we were walking along a crowded street, my mother and I, and I do not know what street. It was crowded and ahead of me, stifling me, I thought, was a wide Chinese gentleman in a blue satin robe and a black sleeveless jacket. Straight in front of my face was the swinging end of his queue, a black silk woven cord ending in a large tassel. The heat became unbearable, the gentleman seemed immovable, and at last in a sort of wilful impatience I did what I had never done before. I pulled the tassel gently, as a hint that he walk a little faster. Instantly he turned around and bent upon me a black look of wrath. He did not frighten me, but my mother did. For I saw her face go quite white, and quickly she begged the Chinese to forgive me.

"She is only a child," I remember her very words. "But she is a naughty child, and I will punish her. Please overlook her fault."

The gentleman did not reply but he did not look mollified, and my mother drew me away and we went down another street.

"Never," she said more sternly than I had ever heard her speak, "never do such a thing again! It might be very dangerous."

What frightened me was the look on her face. I had never seen it before. She was afraid, afraid of a Chinese! I had never seen her afraid before in my life. It was indeed the end of an era.

II

TODAY we have been travelling over Pennsylvania mountain country and then as afternoon came on, our direction being westward, we reached Ohio and by nightfall came to this quiet small city, which was the home of William McKinley. The American President and his wife lie in an enormous tomb in a park. A long flight of steps leads to the tomb and at the head of the steps there is a statue of the dead statesman.

By a curious coincidence McKinley had something to do with my life in that second world which followed after the troubled Boxer years in China. My father was not killed, nor were any of the white men in our province of Kiangsu killed, and that this could be was the result of the wisdom and courage of one man, our Viceroy, who when he received the edict of the Empress Dowager, refused to obey it. It was more than mercy, it was also foresight, for our Viceroy understood what our old Empress did not or could not, and it was that no one, not even she, could stay the progress of time. The Viceroy knew that it was not white men alone who had bred revolution in China. Their presence and deeds, more evil than good, had only hastened the awakening of the Chinese people. Why, the people asked themselves, had they no weapons to resist the arrogance and robbery of the invaders from the West, who were different from any others of the past? The white men had seized lands and rivers instead of the throne, and they had built railroads to the coast so that they could carry away their loot in ships. Nor did they yield as the others had to the superior civilization of China. On the contrary, the westerners considered their own civilizations superior and they tried to prove them so by guns and cannon. Such weapons were as terrifying to the unarmed Chinese people as a hydrogen bomb might be to an undefended city here in Ohio, to this very city in which we sleep tonight.

Even this city has its direct relation to those years of early revolution in China, since a reason for this journey of ours is something more than

41

pleasure alone. Our family has three sons, the elder two nearing draft age and the third one not far behind. The hideous possibility has become a reality. I who have been reared in one world, a Christian one, and taught that love and brotherhood must be the law of life, and reared too, in another world yet kindlier, with the Chinese belief that life is sacred and that it is evil to kill even a beast, and how much more a human being, I now face the tragic probability that my sons must deny both Christian and Asian teaching. They must join our armed forces and fight perhaps an Asian people, a people whom I love and admire and to whom I am deeply indebted. To prevent this I am helpless, although it could have been prevented long ago in Asia, and prevented many times since, but now perhaps it is too late, since it is not we who have won in Asia, although we might have done so easily had we but understood the nature of the peoples there.

And McKinley, whose bronze statue towers over this small Ohio city? What has he to do with the child I once was? Little enough and yet very much. For when the strange year of 1900 was over, the year in which I saw in my American mother's eyes the fear of a Chinese, so that from that day on I too had that fear, all mingled with love and friendship at it was, we came to the United States, my own country. My first shock here was the assassination of President McKinley. I scarcely knew the difference then between Emperor and President. In China our young Emperor had died suddenly, murdered, it was rumored, by the command of the Empress Dowager, who was by then herself within hours of her own death from old age and illness. But she would not, could not die until the dangerous heir was first gone. And now suddenly here in my own country the President was murdered, too!

I cannot remember everything, for much had happened and worlds were tumbling about me. But I do remember that I was in my grandfather's house in West Virginia, where I had been born, a place of peace and beauty, and there on a particular day I was gathering white and purple grapes with my cousins. It was September, hot, still and fragrant, and I was happy and quiet, enjoying to the full my country, my own, where there was no war any more, no hatred, no revolution. Then someone called to us to come quickly and we ran into the house. We went to the parlor, uncles, aunts, my parents, my brother, my cousins and I. There my grandfather stood very straight in his black suit, his stiff white wing collar, his black tie, his snowy hair brushed up from his forehead. His dark eyes were somber and his face was grave, and when we were all assembled he said in a solemn voice:

"Children, the President of the United States has been assassinated. Our President is dead."

Of all of them only I broke into loud weeping, to their astonishment and dismay, and my mother put her arm about my shoulder.

"Oh," I cried, "must we have the revolution here, too?"

"What is the child talking about?" my grandfather demanded.

Nobody answered for nobody knew except my mother, and she understood so well that she said nothing at all while she let me sob. And what I was afraid of I did not know until years later.

Indiana

Indiana, I read in books, is of all our states the most valid sample of our whole country. Agriculture and industry, fourth generation immigrants and first generation, plains and hills, rivers and lakes, Indiana has them all. There is even a picturesque corner where rounded tumbling hills have attracted the most American of our artists, and surely some of the best American writers have come from this state, that is, the ones least affected and to a degree the least experimental. I smile at the word experimental! Nothing is new, and everything has been done before. I read this week a reviewer's comment on a book, a criticism that the author had not used "the modern technique of cutback." New? Five hundred years ago Chinese novelists were using the cutback with consummate skill, and in Europe, whose history is comparatively recent, French writers were using the cutback when America was new. Joseph Conrad was a master of the cutback, and when I have used it, it has not occurred to me that I was doing anything modern, for I was not. The cutback is an admirable technique for portraiture, but not for edifice.

I feel Indiana is plain American. Sometime or other it went a little mad and people built a few astonishing huge and turreted houses. One such I saw today, painted snow-white and looking like an enormous iced cake. Somebody evidently was proud of it as an antique and quite rightly so, for it was imposing and bizarre.

But the houses of our country are a revelation of our variety. No man knows what an American will construct when he is able to afford his own house. He pays no heed to history or landscape. On the contrary, he behaves as though he were Adam in some Eden of his own. I confess I do not know what to make of our newest building developments, accompaniments of industry, but I assume that they are merely merchandise and that no one will live in them beyond a temporary necessity.

The houses here in Indiana are decently ugly except for the notable few, and they are as various as are the houses in other states. How long did it take, I wonder, for the Chinese people to become so unified, so molded by history and geography combined through centuries, that their architecture became stylized, a distillation of centuries of family living? It was nothing in my Chinese world to find a family that had lived a thousand years in the same place. Homes grew slowly from the landscape. The wide plains of the North created wide gently sloping roofs, and the abrupt upward lines of volcanic southern mountains tilted the roofs sharply. Under the roofs, north and south, however, the rooms were arranged in the same patterned order with the same tolerant allowance for independence and privacy in the midst of a complete family life. Each generation lived separately in one-story rooms, but were united by courtyards to the other generations. Thus the Chinese realized the need of the human individual to be alone and yet close to others, especially of his own kind. Thus children grew in free security, surrounded by loving adults of various generations, and thus adults shared the burdens of family responsibility. There was no terror of losing one's job, for in such a circumstance one simply lived on with the family and without reproach, until a new job was found. There was no need for orphanages for there were no orphans, since the family kept its own. And the old were loved and revered and never put away into institutions as sometimes they are put away here, and must be put away, I am told, because of small flimsy houses where there is only room for two people and their two children.

I am glad I once had the grateful joy of living, even for that year of McKinley's assassination, with my grandfather and my uncles and aunts and cousins in a big porticoed house. I did not know my own good fortune, for then I took it for granted that everywhere in my country everybody so lived. I was only nine, and I may be forgiven for my ignorance, and yet I still believe that the generations need each other and should live together.

Yung, my Chinese friend, spent last month at our farm and out of long quiet talk I remember two scenes she put before me. The first one had nothing to do with families but with fish. She began in her usual gentle fashion, and very seriously.

"I have something to say to you."

"What is it?" I asked.

She had spoken in English and now she changed to Chinese, the mid-Chinese Mandarin that was our childhood language. She said:

"Dear Elder Sister, I went to the Museum of Natural History in New York that I might learn something useful and scientific."

"And did you learn something useful and scientific?" I inquired.

She looked sad. "Scientific, perhaps, but not useful—only trouble-some."

"Tell me," I suggested.

She hesitated and then went on. "A man there told me such a strange thing. He said that we human beings are come from fish. Must I believe this? It makes me so sad. Only a fish!"

She shook her head and sighed. "So disappointing, isn't it? A fish! Elder Sister, is it necessary to believe this?"

"No," I said. "Don't believe it. The man was guessing. There are many stories of our beginning. Believe what is nearest to your heart as well as your mind."

She brightened. "You really think so?"

"I do," I said firmly.

It was also Yung who put into clear and pitiful words the picture of an old lady, an American old lady, or old man for that matter. She said, in the way she has, seeming sudden, but not sudden because she has been thinking long before she speaks, and this time she spoke in English, "I feel sorry for American old lady and old man."

"Why?" I asked.

For answer she gave me an example out of her life in the New York apartment house in which she lives with her excellent husband. She said, in her ever-gentle voice, still in English, "In our apartment house lives a nice old lady alone. We did not know her. But our neighbor came in one day so happy saying, 'Do come downstairs with me to see my friend's granddaughter. My friend is very joyful. Why? Because to-day for the first time the little girl, five years old, is allowed to come to visit grandmother and to spend the night.'

"I cannot believe such a thing—five years old and never spending the night with grandmother! We went downstairs and it was true. There were the little girl and the grandmother, both happy, and the grand-mother told me the story. She said such a long time she had hoped the child could come to visit her but she dared not to ask it. But on this day happily the child herself suggested it, when the old lady went to visit her son's family. 'Grandmother,' the child asked, 'may I spend the night in your house?' The old lady dared not to cry out, 'Oh, come!' Instead, very quiet, she said, 'Whatever your mother wishes, my dear.' So the child asked the mother, who said, 'Wait until your father comes home.' So the old lady waited long until her son came home and again she waited for the child to ask, not daring to seem eager for fear it would not be allowed, and she was so happy when the father, her own son, said, 'Why not?' And then the child's mother said, 'Just this once.' All this the old lady

45

told and I really did weep, because in China the grandmother could not be so afraid of the younger ones. It is not right."

I agreed with my Chinese friend and then remembered, contrariwise, what a young American man had said to me only a few weeks before. He said, "I wish my mother would stay with us always the way you say Chinese grandparents do, but she doesn't want to be bothered by young children, even her grandchildren. She wants to travel, to hear music, to go abroad, to live her own life, as she calls it, and so my children have no opportunity to know their own grandmother."

Two sides of the same story, and the only sense I can make out of it is that our American pattern is to be patternless, unless individualism is the pattern.

In my own case, my grandfather was remote but comforting. He had his place in the house where I was born, an upright, somewhat rigid figure, but always kind, and though the few months of that year in which McKinley was killed passed quickly and I stayed with my grandfather no more, yet I had seen him, I had lived in the house with him, I had felt him the source of my being, because he was my mother's father, and his other children were my uncles and aunts and their children were my cousins, and so I was one of a clan and not solitary. When my parents took me back to China with them, I went back knowing where they had come from, and so where I had come from, and we were not a solitary little group lost in a vast and alien China, alien now because the Chinese did not love white people and had killed many of our kind. No, we were Americans, and I had a country of my own, and a big white house where my kinfolk lived, and there were generations of us there, all belonging together. So a child ought to feel, and if he so feels, he can wander to and fro upon the earth and never walk alone.

Sioux Falls, South Dakota

We have been driving over the beautiful uplands of Illinois and Iowa, and cutting deeply into Minnesota. We arrived here in Sioux Falls to spend our first night in South Dakota.

I wonder what dream or experience, or both, led to the naming of American towns and villages? We passed in Iowa a little hamlet named Polo, in honor of Marco Polo. But why Marco Polo in Iowa, U.S.A.? His is a familiar name to me, for Yangchow is across the river from Chinkiang, my Chinese home town, and in Yangchow Marco Polo was governor for some years. It is a city famous for beautiful women, one of whom was my Chinese nurse, although I remember her old and missing some

46

teeth, but still beautiful. What American in Iowa, then, dreaming of those travels on the other side of the world, called his town Polo?

And we passed a town called Woosung, but why Woosung in the heart of Iowa? What musing, wandering mind, compelled to stay at home, named his inland town for that port on the flats of the Yangtse Delta, that gateway to Shanghai and so to China? And while I was pondering on this, our car passed into Minnesota and there was Ceylon on a signpost but the only Ceylon I know is the jewelled island that clings to India's foot.

Earlier in the journey we passed, too, through a bare little town in Illinois, all open to the sun. It was Galena, ancestor or relative, I suppose, to our little New Galena in Pennsylvania. Galena, Illinois, is the town where Ulysses S. Grant, not yet President, went with his family before the Civil War, to set up his tanning trade. He built a solid square red brick house, graceless, comfortable and commonplace, and from there he was called to lead the Union Army. He took with him some of his cronies to support him, a number unsurpassed before or since, I am told, by any administrator, but I confess I see no wrong in choosing friends for one's supporters.

What interests me is that Ulysses S. Grant could have reached so high a position. Perhaps the chief weakness of a democracy is that seldom can a truly great person rise high, for people elect those whom they can understand and therefore admire, and these are usually men like themselves. And even as I write these cynical words the noble ghost of Abraham Lincoln stands before me. He, too, was a man of Illinois, the middle country, and I first heard of him from Mr. Kung, who revered him because he had freed the colored slaves. When I asked my parents, however, they were Southern enough to say proudly that the slaves were being freed anyway, and not by Abraham Lincoln.

Be this as it may, I see myself, a child of ten, returned again to China with my parents. It is the year 1902 and I am in the small old dining room in the mission bungalow on the hills above the Yangtse River, and I am listening to the grave voice of the old Chinese gentleman who is my Chinese tutor. He is a Confucian, which seems not to have troubled at all my Christian parents, although he instilled into me Confucian ethics while he taught me Chinese reading and writing, and I listened and learned and called him Teacher Kung. He prided himself on the surname Kung, which was also the surname of Confucius, this name again being a corruption of the Chinese Kung-futse or Father Kung. But I, as a Christian child, supposed that Confucius was the same as Our Father in Heaven, that is, God the Father, and I accepted all gods, having been accustomed to seeing temples full of many gods. Among

47

them was my special goddess, she of mercy, the Kwanyin, always so beautiful and graceful, such a lady in her looks as well as in her kindness, and tenderhearted toward all female creatures. To be sure, there was her younger sister, The Virgin Mary, but a vague cloud I did not then understand surrounded The Virgin, an immaculate cloud, but producing also The Son. And the patient Joseph, standing always to one side in the Sunday-school pictures, how I pitied him, for somehow it seemed as though he had been cheated. I heard talk of this among the Chinese Christians who had no enthusiasm for Mary and felt sorry for Joseph. And this talk must have reached my own American Christian father, for he ceased trying to explain how Jesus was born of The Virgin. It was one of the mysteries and the less said about it the better. But the Goddess of Mercy was really immaculate and there was never any talk there about a god-father or a god-son. She was pure goodness. Besides, Chinese history or mythology, and often they merge, is rich in stories of beautiful virgins impregnated by gods to conceive divine sons, and this Mr. Kung taught me, too.

But the important lesson which he taught me was that if one would be happy he must not raise his head above his neighbor's.

"He who raises his head above the heads of others," Mr. Kung said, "will sooner or later be decapitated."

It was true in China as in other democratic nations that when a man became too famous, too successful, too powerful, mysterious forces went to work and the earth began to crumble under his pinnacle. The Chinese are a proud and envious people, as a nation and as individuals, and they do not love their superiors and never did, and the truth is they have never believed that their superiors could exist. This fact partly explains the present anti-Americanism, this and the attitudes of missionaries and traders and diplomats, all white men indeed, who considered themselves whether consciously or unconsciously superior to the Chinese, so that a smouldering fury has lived on in Chinese hearts for more than a century and this fury, which white men could not or would not recognize, is the chief reason why Chiang Kai-shek lost his country and why the Communists won it. Had he been wise enough he would have expressed boldly his own anti-Western feelings and had he done so he might have held the leadership. But he thought he could win by American force and this his people could not forgive him, and, sadly for us, Mao Tse-tung seized the opportunity that Chiang threw away, and the power of history today is turned against us. It is hard for Americans to believe that American charm, so warmly expressed in the ready smile and the outstretched hand, does not win the Chinese. What then can the American do? He must read history afresh. He must prove to the Asian that he is not to be confused with the past, of which he is relatively innocent, and therefore he must not be compelled to bear its burdens. American boys must not die because England once ruled India and in China won the Three Opium Wars and fastened a ruinous tax upon the people, or because an Englishman allowed Japan to stay in Manchuria, and so established a foothold for an imperial war. Nor should American people be asked to share the intolerable and ancient burdens of France in Indo-China. We shall have enough to do to prove to Asia that we are not as other white men have been.

Yet we are only relatively innocent, for in those days after 1900 when white armies punished the Old Empress so bitterly, when her palaces were looted and incalculable treasures stolen from Peking by soldiers and officers with equal greed, Americans were among the white men. And we did not heed the history being made, and so we could not understand and do not yet understand its dreadful fruit. After the storm was over—so strangely called in Western history The Boxer Rebellion, but rebellion against what ruler except the white man?—after the storm and after the defeat, the white men went back again to China without a lesson learned. They went back in complacency, thinking that by force they had taught the Chinese a lesson, so that never again would they rebel against the white man's rule. We were to be allowed to come and go as we liked over the Chinese earth, our ships of merchandise and our men of war were to be permitted to sail the waters and dock at any port. Our missionaries were given the freedom to live where they wished, to open schools foreign in all they taught, to establish hospitals which practiced foreign medicine and surgery, and strangest of all, these missionaries were free to preach a religion entirely alien to the Chinese, nay, to insist upon this religion as the only true one and to declare that those who refused to believe would and must descend into hell. The affrontery of all this still makes my soul shrink.

It made me unhappy enough even in the days when Mr. Kung was my teacher. He explained it to me gently and being an intuitive and feeling child I remember one afternoon that I wept. We had only just come back from America and the year in my kindly grandfather's house, and I wept because I knew that if Mr. Kung and my grandfather could meet and talk things over they would understand each other and agree together. But how could they meet when one lived in China and the other in America, and even if they could have met, what common language could they have spoken? And yet I knew and know to this day that could such men as they have met and could they have found a common language, and it did not matter whether this was English or Chinese, all that has happened need not have happened. Pearl

49

Harbor would never have been, and the atomic bomb would not have fallen and American prisoners of war would not have come back wounded and dying from a Communist China, for Chinese would not have yielded to Communism had they known there was hope in the white men of the West. It was when the last hope died that the Chinese turned away from us in final despair. And we cut the last golden cord ourselves, in innocent ignorance, if ignorance can be innocent any more in this day and age.

All this in some dim foreseeing way I think I vaguely understood that day when I leaned my forehead down upon the oval dining table in the mission house and sobbed because of what Mr. Kung had just told me. For what he said in his beautiful polished Peking Mandarin was something like this:

"It will be peaceful for you here again, Little Sister, but not for long. The storm is still rising and when it breaks, you must be far away from here. You must go to America and stay there and not come back, lest next time you be killed with all your kind."

"There must be a next time?" I asked, terrified.

"Until justice is done," he said gravely and with infinite pity.

And I could say nothing, for I knew that his ancestral home in Peking had been destroyed by German soldiers, men to whom the German Kaiser had given the imperial command in some such words as these: "Germans, so behave that forever when a Chinese hears the name of Germany he will quake with fear and run to save himself." And the Germans had obeyed their Kaiser.

Yet as the days passed, I forgot my fears as a child forgets, and I still took comfort because we were Americans. Surely, I argued, my Chinese friends would see how different we were from other white people. For a long time it seemed they did perceive our difference. I can see now, looking back, how changed I myself was after the Boxer defeat. My worlds no longer interwove. They were sharply clear, one from the other. I was American, not Chinese, and although China was as dear to me as my native land, I knew it was not my land. Mine was the country across the sea, the land of my forefathers, alien to China and indifferent to the Chinese people.

I used often to ponder that indifference, child that I was, and I was not deceived in the eleven years I was to live between the outburst of the Boxer leaders and the one led by Sun Yat-sen, a young fiery Chinese who grew up in a southern village. Could it be indifference when clearly my parents had made real sacrifice in leaving their comfortable American homes and all the delights of a clean and fruitful country-side to live here and preach and teach their religion? They were deeply devoted to the Chinese we knew and indeed to all Chinese, and in greater or lesser degree so were all the missionaries. Few of them were selfish or lazy, and most of them in those days came from homes well above the average. And yet I knew intuitively that they were not in China primarily because they loved the people, even though during years they did learn to love a people naturally lovable. No, they were there, these missionaries, to fulfill some spiritual need of their own. It was a noble need, its purposes unselfish, partaking doubtless of that divine need through which God so loved the world that He sent His only begotten Son for its salvation. But somewhere I had learned from Thoreau, who doubtless learned it from Confucius, that if a man comes to do his own good for you, then must you flee that man and save yourself. And I was troubled when my father preached his doctrines and I wished he would be silent, content only to live what he preached, and so, lifted up, to draw men to him without words. And this I wished, knowing that my father would never have preached had he not felt it his duty, for he was the gentlest preacher any heathen could ever hear, avoiding all mention of hell fire and dwelling only upon the wonderful love of God, surpassing the love of man. But I could not bear preaching from any white man, knowing what white men had done in Asia, even as today in my own country I cannot go into a church and hear a white man preach when I know that were a black man to enter that church it is likely that no place could be found for him to sit and listen to the story of God's love for all mankind, and so there is no seat for me, either, in such churches. And this is because I grew up in China, in one world and not of it, and belonging to another world and yet not of it.

Notwithstanding, they were good years in many ways for a child, and it was not every day that I pondered upon such large grave matters. And of course there was much that I did not know. I knew that the Old Empress was dead and so was the Young Emperor, but she had, before she died, once again declared a little child her successor, the small Pu Yi. We saw pictures of him sometimes in the papers, a plump baby with an astonished wooden little face above his stiff satin robe and sleeveless jacket. There was a Regent, but nobody seemed to care and life went on as usual apparently, and had it not been for the inescapable past, I might have been the same child. But I was not. For one thing, I was old enough now to read history for myself and I perceived that Chinese historians and English ones gave entirely different versions not only of the same events but of each other, and that each despised the other as a lesser breed, although neither knew what the other was.

Those were strange conflicting days when in the morning I sat over American schoolbooks and learned the lessons assigned to me by my mother, who faithfully followed the Calvert system in my education, while in the afternoon I studied under the wholly different tutelage of Mr. Kung. I became mentally bifocal, and so I learned early to understand that there is no such condition in human affairs as absolute truth. There is only truth as people see it, and truth, even in fact, may be kaleidoscopic in its variety. The damage such perception did to me I have felt ever since, although damage may be too dark a word, for it merely meant that I could never belong entirely to one side of any question. To be a Communist would be absurd to me, as absurd as to be entirely anything and equally impossible. I straddled the globe too young.

All this learning went on quite pleasantly and painlessly and I was aware of no particular insecurity and certainly of no frustrations and boredoms. Indeed I had a happy life, though my days would perhaps have seemed intolerably slow and boring to my children now, who do not love books as I have ever done, perhaps because their imaginations were not caught young, as mine was, by the visions of minds between covers. Perhaps Mr. Kung had something to do with that. I see him still as he arrived upon all fine afternoons, except on Sundays, and he could not come upon rainy days because his mother forbade it, lest he wet his feet and fall ill, and being a filial son he did not wish to cause her anxiety, and there was nothing strange to me in that, although Mr. Kung was nearly fifty and his mother seventy-two. She was his mother, was she not, and would be until she died, and the web that held the Chinese together as a people, solid and eternal, was the love and respect between the generations. "Honor thy father and thy mother that thy days may be long upon the land" is an Asian precept as well as a commandment.

And so Mr. Kung arrived punctually on fine afternoons at two o'clock, carrying his treasure of books wrapped in a soft old piece of black silk. This he unfolded but only when he had given greeting to me and received from me a suitable bow and salutation, after which I, too, could seat myself. Then only, I say, did he open the silk with tender care and bring forth the book which we might then be studying. For two hours we read and he expounded, not alone the past contained within the book, but also the relation of that past, however dim and distant, to the present and even to the future yet to come.

Thus it was from him in those days of my early youth that I learned the first axiom of human life, and it is that every event has had its cause, and nothing, not the least wind that blows, is accident or causeless. To understand what happens now one must find the cause, which may be very long ago in its beginning, but is surely there, and therefore

52

a knowledge of history as detailed as possible is essential if we are to comprehend the present and be prepared for the future. Fate, Mr. Kung taught me, is not the blind superstition or helplessness that waits stupidly for what may happen. Fate is unalterable only in the sense that given a cause, a certain result must follow, but no cause is inevitable in itself, and man can shape his world if he does not resign himself to ignorance. Mr. Kung liked to quote also from the Christian Bible, partly, I imagine, to prove to me his liberal Confucian mind, and his favorite text was the one about reaping the whirlwind if one sowed the wind, and he reminded me often, in his gently lofty manner, that one could not expect figs from thistles.

When four o'clock came the lesson was over. He covered his tea bowl and wrapped the book again in the square of soft black silk and we rose and I bowed and he inclined his head, reminding me of tomorrow's preparation and of a few mistakes I might have made. So we parted, I following him to the gate as a pupil should follow a teacher, and there standing until his swaying robes and black silk queue had disappeared.

It would still be years before the demands of revolution, smouldering under the surface of our everyday life, would cut the queue away as the last sign of servitude to the dying Manchu Empire. But Mr. Kung was dead by then, taking his queue with him to the grave, and what I made of those later days I had to make without him.

Meanwhile our life went on in strange and silent peace. I was too old by now to play in the pampas grass outside the gate, and my free time in the afternoons after Mr. Kung was gone was divided between our home and my friends in the small white community or among the Chinese we knew. I did not run down the hill any more to visit the women and girls in the valley farms. I was getting to be what was called "a big girl" and if my mother was not with me then my Chinese nurse accompanied me when I went outside the gate. She was far more strict than any mother and she pursed her wrinkled lips if I stopped to buy a sweet from a vendor or some bit of jewelry that took my fancy at a silversmith's. The Chinese silver was beautiful, soft and pure, and the smiths carved it in delicate patterns in a bracelet or a heavy chain, or they twisted hair-fine wires into exquisite filigree as delicate as cobweb, and studded it with plum blossoms and butterflies inlaid with blue kingfisher's feathers.

For the first time, during these post-Boxer years, I tried to find a few friends among people of my own race. I remember a sweet-faced, brown-eyed English girl whose father worked for the English Bible Society, a gentle creature with whom I could find no profound companionship, for she had lived the secluded, almost empty life of most white families, entirely unaware of the rich culture of the Chinese people. Her home was built upon a high and narrow hill which had once been an island in the restless Yangtse until the river receded from the city to gnaw away the opposite bank. I remember less of this English Agnes than I do of her English home and the entirely English garden which surrounded it. That bit of England created above the turmoil of a particularly poor and crowded Chinese slum taught me love for England, nevertheless. The father, dark-eyed and brown-bearded, always in rough tweeds, was as English as if he had never left his native land, and the mother, an impetuous Scotch woman, was untouched by any idea that she was surrounded by other human beings who were Chinese. In spite of my knowing that this was entirely wrong of them, I enjoyed the family, the two older sons, home only for the holidays from the English school in Chefoo, and the two girls, my friends, and a Wee Willie, as they called him, who died somewhere in those years and who always, in his fragile gentleness, reminded me of Tiny Tim and then, very late, a loud and robust English baby, a postscript of a child embarrassing the whole family by his birth. Each of them enchanted me in his own way and nothing was more delightful than to sit down at tea with them and to enjoy real English cheer on a chill winter's afternoon, when the houses of my Chinese friends were damp and cold. For however reprehensible they were, I loved my English friends and never more than when we gathered in a little dining room stuffed with ugly English furniture, secondhand from Shanghai shops, and had an English tea. There was no dainty nonsense about that meal. It might have taken place in any honest middle-class family in London or in Glasgow. There were no silly sandwiches, no hint of lettuce or olives. The big rectangular table was covered with a solid white linen cloth, and upon this were set the silver-covered plates of hot scones and dishes of Australian butter and Crosse and Blackwell English strawberry jam. There was no puttering with pale Chinese tea. We had strong black Indian tea, stout Empire stuff, enriched with white sugar and proper English condensed milk. And when we had helped ourselves to scones, the plate was set on the hearth beside the black polished grate, wherein coals burned cheerfully, beneath a mantelpiece and an overmantel, a hideous structure of carved shelves reaching to the ceiling, whereon every shelf was crowded with bits of porcelain or painted glassware, not from China, but from various spots within the blessed British Isles—"Greetings from Brighton" (in gold upon pink), or "Hearty Good Wishes from Dundee." Never mind, it was hideous but it was warm and cozy and friendly and in its hideous funny way I loved it. And after the scones, but not until the last bit of scone and jam was eaten, and one did not take butter and jam for the same scone, we had fresh pound-cake or English raisincake and more and more cups of tea, poured for us by the comfortable Scotch mother who sat at the foot of the table and talked unendingly while she poured, cheerful chatter as guiltless of wit and wisdom as any charwoman's, but amusing and kind, for all of that. And this good English tea was prepared in a dark little English kitchen by a thin Chinese man of years, who survived the harrying scolding of his foreign mistress and consoled himself by cheating her richly when he shopped, and learning meanwhile to cook so well that when the white folk departed, forever so far as he was concerned, he found a job as head cook for a famous war lord who had a fancy for foreign food. And we were served at table by a table boy who afterwards burned down the house in which we sat. But how were we to know such effects, when we did not know the causes that we made?

Rapid City, South Dakota

If this state were anywhere else in the world, it would be such a wonder that people would be streaming here to see it by land and air and sea. As it is only where it is, today when we drove through it slowly—trying to assimilate its miracles—we saw few cars and those all American. It was a fearfully hot day, so hot that the air conditioning in our car promptly broke down in the devilish way that machinery does when it is most needed. This peculiarity is nothing new to me. We had no machinery in our Chinese bungalow, only the reliability of human hands and feet. Therefore the oil lamps always shone every night and no thunderstorm or even typhoon could put us into darkness, as any slight storm can do with electricity in our Pennsylvania house.

I had an exaggerated idea of machinery before I knew anything about it, and finding reliable human hands and feet very rare, after I left China, and frighteningly expensive when and if found, impulsively I set up a way of life upon our American farm entirely entrusted to electricity and machines. The years have taught me that nothing is less reliable than these can be at times, singly or in combination. Electric current can stop and render useless an otherwise perfect machine. Or the electric current may flow full and free and be repulsed by the indifference of a machine made idle by some cog or contact which will not work. Such accidents, if they are accidents, almost invariably take place on weekends when we have guests or when the entire family is home for holidays and a large turkey is roasting in the electric oven. I have never known the electric dishwasher to stop except when it was full of silver, china and glass, and another lot waiting, necessitating the removal of everything and washing and drying all by hand. This, too, happens only on Sundays or important holidays when essential experts cannot be found, because they have prudently learned to spend their own holidays far from home. The machine must therefore stand idle, perhaps for days, a hideous monument to its own power and the helplessness of men.

For the first few years I was innocent enough to think this perfect timing was pure accident, but I know better now. It is some devilish coincidence of which no scientist has dared to tell us. If, as one reads, the human being is merely a handful of minerals and a gallon or two of water, the only magic in us to make us think and dream must be the combination of these simple elements. And I read, moreover, that the secret of the atomic bomb itself is not in its materials, which are fairly common knowledge, but in the combination of those materials. It is the formula, so to speak, which compels being. This being so, it is not difficult to wonder whether that combination of elements which produces a machine for labor does not create also a soul of sorts, a dull resentful metallic will, which can rebel at times.

It must be so, it may be so, for why should our otherwise obedient car decide to cease its cooling upon a summer afternoon in South Dakota, when the temperature under nonexistent shade was said to be ninety-eight degrees and in the Badlands, so burning and so beautiful, was at least ten degrees more hot? We had rolled along all morning in a landscape as fabulous as the moon, shining silver under the wicked sun, and yet we had been as cool as a November day behind our closed windows. Suddenly, because we wanted to move slowly through the ancient wind-carved hills, our car made up its dim mind to rebel. The air conditioning stopped. We put down the windows, gasping, and were struck by such a blast of dried heat that we were parched and scorched, although we did not yield. We would travel on, we decided. At this the car stopped entirely, and we were towed shamefully to a garage, a big, new, handsome hulk, while merrily there passed us a hundred small decrepit cars fit for nothing but the junk pile. I cannot believe that the expensive and complex machine did not enjoy our confusion, meanwhile caring nothing for its own disgrace.

I confess that sometimes I find myself nostalgic for a house where the servants are humans and not machines, the while I know and hate the poverty that makes human labor cheap. And yet the servants in our Chinese home enjoyed their life, and they respected themselves and their work and us. They would not work for masters they did not like, and they expected and received respect from us. The relationship was irreproachable, and a decent servant would give up his livelihood immediately if he felt a lack of due regard from the master and his family. If he did stay on, he took some secret reward which compensated him for what he suffered.

Thus I knew a certain missionary, an American of a lesser breed, who being unaccustomed to the role of master, was arrogant and often bad-tempered, so that he could keep no servants in his house. One old woman remained with the family for years, however, and in apparent peace of mind. The Chinese never marvelled, although the white folk did, and only because I belonged as much to the one as to the other did I learn the secret, and it was told me by the old woman herself, a gay old soul with a devilish sense of humor. I did not ask, but this is what I heard. Her room was in the attic of the white man's house, and her little window opened upon the tin roof. The wells in that region of North China are shallow and their waters bitter, and the white folk were accustomed to have cisterns dug to catch the rain water from their roofs. So it was with this house, too. The rain water ran down the roof into tin gutters and through tin pipes into the cistern. And what sweet revenge did this old woman find for the white man's tempers? Each morning when she rose she emptied out upon the roof the contents of her chamberpot, and then went blithely about her day, while she with all the other servants drank the clean and bitter waters of the well.

But such old women are rare, doubtless. In our house our parents taught us to be as mannerly to the servants as we were to guests and elders, and each side maintained its pride. We kept our servants for years and belonged to them and they to us, and how many happy childhood hours I spent with them and how lonely might I have been at evening when the gates were locked for the night had I not been free to sit in the servants' court, to play with their babies and listen to the music of a country flute or a two-stringed violin! Sometimes our cook, a small thin artist of a man who looked, by the way, like Fred Astaire, except that his skin was yellow and his eyes and hair were black, sometimes, I say, he would tell us a story from the past, because he could read. And he read *The Three Kingdoms, All Men Are Brothers, Dream of the Red Chamber,* and other books he kept in his room.

Certainly machines are not so companionable. At home in Pennsylvania I went not long ago to call upon a neighbor, a young farmer's wife. It was the early afternoon, and I had perhaps half an hour to spare. I entered at the kitchen door, for she would have been astonished otherwise, and encircling her big kitchen I saw monumental machines, washing machine, drier, mangle, two freezers, refrigerator, electric stove, sink. With such help her daily work was soon done, and we went into the neat living room where there was no book, but where a television was carrying on. She paid no heed to it, and inviting me to sit down, she took her fat baby on her knee, immaculate and well fed, and we talked small stuff while minutes passed, and then I had to leave. Said she, real disappointment in her voice and look, "Oh, can't you stay? I thought you'd spend the afternoon. I get so bored after dinner—I haven't a thing to do."

I thought of Chinese farm wives who take their laundry to the pond and chatter and laugh together while they beat their garments with a wooden paddle upon a flat rock, a long tedious process, it might be said, except what would they have done of an afternoon without it? And by their talk and merriment they were more amused, I do believe, than was that young neighbor of mine by the television rattling all day long, with its unknown voices and its pictured faces.

Two worlds, two worlds, and one cannot be the other, and each has its ways and blessings, I suppose.

At any rate, here in South Dakota the night has fallen, and I prepare for sleep in a comfortable roadside motel. The South Dakota sky is brilliant with bright stars, the wilful car has been hauled into a garage and tomorrow will have its inner organs cleansed and healed, we hope, and so its soul restored. And I am glad enough to turn the chromium faucet in the porcelain bathroom and fill the tub with water, hot and comforting, although without a human hand to bring it to me.

Dayton, Wyoming

A pretty sight passes the window at this moment near high noon on a summer's day. I hear the clatter of hoofs, and looking out I see a string of horses cantering up the dusty road from the canyon. These are the riders who set out this morning after breakfast, with a wrangler in command, to spend the morning in the Big Horn Mountains. The horses are eager to get home and the riders sit them well. The riders are young, boys and girls still in their early teens, but late enough so that some are beginning to be sober folk, thoughtful because the armed services lie just ahead. The girls, I think, have it harder than the boys for they will stay at home, most of them. I notice that in spite of enticing posters, seducing propaganda and noble appeals, most women stay at home. There is something in their natures that cannot accept the necessity of warfare, even after centuries.

The horses pass and the dust settles again, the riders dismount and go their way. The scene is mountains, rock and sage and pine, and sands

58

golden under the hot Wyoming sun, and I sit here writing in my book.

I have, as I well know, been avoiding those years between 1901 and 1911 after the Boxer Rebellion when I was growing up in China. As I look back upon them they seem now to be strangely hesitant years, their transience concealed beneath a sort of everyday happiness so brittle that I think we all felt that it could at any moment be shattered. Peace covered China like a sheet of thin ice beneath which a river boiled. Outwardly our life was better than ever. My mother dug up the buried family silver, our faithful servants gathered around us again, and my father came and went in such freedom, with so little cursing on the streets against foreigners, that I think even he was troubled, knowing what a price had been paid for such peace.

For after the Boxers had been dispelled and disgraced, after it was plain to the simplest villager that his country had been defeated, the new treaties guaranteed the safety of the white man wherever he might choose to travel, to live, to preach, to trade. In addition, China was compelled to pay vast indemnities for the desperate folly of the old dead Empress, and though my own country later chose to spend its share in scholarships for young Chinese in American universities, that time was not yet.

The Chinese are a practical people and very wise. They knew their own defeat and could not then risk another. The time for the next struggle lay far ahead. For ten years at least they must recuperate, reflect and plan. In those ten years I passed from childhood into adolescence. I am grateful for one aspect of that decade—the years contained a freedom which perhaps no white child had ever known in China and certainly could not know after the revolution broke again in 1911. Had it not been for that freedom, that perfect safety, insured by treaties, indemnities and punishments with which I had nothing to do and yet in whose benefits I unwittingly shared because I was a white man's daughter, I could not have come and gone so easily upon the city streets and country roads. Only the dogs dared bark at me, for those savage, starving village dogs alone still dared to show the hatred they had been taught to feel against the foreigners. No, there were the children. Sometimes a child having heard his family talk at night behind closed doors, would still shout "Yang kwei-tse"—foreign devil!—as I passed, but if he did his mother clapped her hand across his mouth, frightened because she had heard how cruel was the revenge that white folk took.

This fear always broke my heart, I think, and wherever I found it, I stopped and spoke gently to the mothers and asked them not to be afraid, and if I could I lingered long enough to talk and play with the child and I left only when I saw fear gone and friendly looks taking its place. This gave me comfort and it pleased me when they wondered that I spoke their language so easily, for then I had the chance to tell them about my country and how my people were not hateful and did not hate them and how much I wished that we could be friends, because indeed our hearts were all the same.

Here I must confess a secret, for which I hope my dear parents in their graves will forgive me, for I never let them know. Often I would have liked to have invited these friends I made to come to our house and visit us and see how harmless our family was, how kindly were my parents, how tenderhearted my little sister, but I could not invite them because I did not want them preached at. I understood the deep burden of my father's soul, the duty that he felt to preach the love of God and his own yearning to save, as he said, their precious souls. I did not blame him, but I could not cast my friends into that white fire of his own spirit. And would they not distrust me if I put them in his power? They were naturally courteous, they would not have refused to hear him, but would they not say that I had used friendship to win them to a foreign god? I could not risk it, and so for years I had many Chinese friends whom I took care to keep away from my good parents, and this not only because I thought it right, but also because, quite selfishly, I could not risk their doubt.

I was richly repaid for their trust, for to this day I value what they shared with me, their homes, their work, their laughter and good talk. Once the trust was established, we talked, questioning each other in close human ways. There was plenty of time in those years. We still lived in the country, and my mother taught me in the mornings but there were the long lonely afternoons and I had few companions of my own race. It was natural therefore that my paths led me to the red gate between the stone lions of the Lu family a half mile or so away and that I spent hours in the courtyards there, playing with the babies, listening to the young wives gossip, and sharing the thoughts of a schoolmate, a pretty girl of my own age. And how she happened to be a schoolmate was that Mr. Kung died in 1905, and since I was so tall my parents felt I had better not be taught by a strange man but go instead two or three times a week to a mission school for girls. But I never again learned as much as I had learned from Mr. Kung. I wept at his funeral and wore a white band of mourning on my sleeve and I bowed before his coffin with the lesser members of his family. He died of cholera, in September. He rose as usual in the morning but he was dead by night and my mother did not want me to go to his funeral because of the danger of contagion and when I insisted she let me go with my father only on the promise that we would not touch our lips even to so much as a bowl of tea and certainly not to any funeral meats. She had good reason to demand such promises for she had nearly died of cholera once, before I was born, and had on the same day lost my sister whom I never saw, a child of four. And my father, having found a doctor, for that dreadful day took place in Shanghai where there were white doctors, was forced to decide which life was to be saved, his daughter's or his wife's.

"I cannot save them both," the doctor had said.

He chose his wife, but sometimes I wonder if my mother forgave him for it. It would have been like her to have insisted on saving both and somehow getting it done, but she was unconscious and had no say. She always felt, I think, that my father accepted too easily the will of God.

Well, there were six or seven families not too far away where I was welcome and where I learned the other side of the victory the white men had won and I knew then what my life has taught me since, that in any war a victory means another war, and yet another, until some day inevitably the tides turn, and the victor is the vanquished, and the circle reverses itself, but remains nevertheless a circle.

From those long and happy hours of visiting I came home more torn in heart than any child should be, for I saw that each side was right as well as wrong, and I yearned over both in a helpless fashion, unable to see how, history being what it was, anything now could be done. I used to look at my parents, wondering how to tell them what I felt and feared, not wanting to betray my Chinese friends, either, for who knew what use my parents might make of what I told, reporting it in duty to the Consul, perhaps, or forbidding me to go again to my friends' courtyards.

And yet I knew my parents were so wholly good, so utterly innocent, that surely I ought to tell them that Mr. Lu said there were wars ahead and more wars.

I never told them, and I comforted myself that if I had they would have said merely that what would be was in the hands of God. This I did not wholly believe, knowing very well that much can be done by men's hands if they have the wit and will.

Looking back, I see my life in parts, each part fitting into the age in which I lived. If my childhood was different from that of other children of my time, and it was very different, then the deepest difference was that I always knew that I was a mere leaf in the gathering storm to come. Yet day by day I had plenty of love and kindness and I knew no personal unhappiness. There were no pressures on me, I had hours for myself and blessed freedom, for my parents were lenient and undemanding. And I had the fortune to be born with a nature easily diverted and amused, with a gift, if I had any gift, for enjoying what was around me, both landscape and people. I was healthy and full of good spirits and never idle or bored, a curious child plaguing everyone with questions sometimes too intimate and personal, and yet I will forgive myself to this extent: I had no interest in gossip, but only in story. I was entangled in every human story going on about me, and could and did spend hours listening to anyone who would talk to me, and there were always those ready or needing to talk. Of course I absorbed much useless information, and yet I wonder if any of it was really useless. I took deep interest, for example, in the farming problems of our neighbors, the difficulties of raising crops on five acres or so of land, and yet learned the miracle of how it was done, by hand actually, so that every rice plant was thrust into the paddy field by hand, and not by hired hand at that, but by farmers and their wives and daughters and sons and sons' wives and their children. I watched the turn of seasons and was anxious with the farmers when there was no rain and yearned with them in their prayer processions and was grateful when sometimes the rain did fall. All knowledge was useful to me later when I began to write.

My own growth, perhaps, was from outside in, or to put it otherwise, I lived outside myself and lived richly. There was another life, however, and it was still imagined and dreamed much more than real. I never quite forgot the months I had spent in America, though my memories dimmed as time went on. I remembered certain hours, such and such an event, rather than consecutive time, and in an effort to hold what I had, I read incessantly. I had always read but now I read to search for and find my own world, the Western world, to which some day I would return, and must return, when the gates of Asia closed against me and my kind.

And yet I found few American books. Literature, it seemed, was English rather than American. Mark Twain my mother considered slightly coarse and though we had *Tom Sawyer* and *Huckleberry Finn,* and I read them, they were unreal to me. I had not seen such persons for myself. Now, decades later, I can see well enough that Mark Twain caught something American and true that none other has, or so I think. Indeed, I have a son whose ways are so foreign to my ways that I would never have known what to make of him, I think, did I not have Mark Twain on my shelves. I read *Tom Sawyer* once a year or so, to help me understand this American boy who is my own.

The truth is that very few American books reached our part of the world in my youthful days, but Kelly and Walsh, the excellent English bookshop in Shanghai, carried a good stock of the new English novels and secondhand editions of the old ones and their lists reached us up-country and I spent every penny given me, or earned, on books. My parents had already as part of the furnishing of our home the sets of

Dickens and Thackeray and George Eliot and Walter Scott and their company, and we had the English poets and a fine edition of Shakespeare, and all these were a solid part of my childhood. My mother took *The Delineator* as her choice in American magazines and my father took *The Century* magazine and we had *St. Nicholas* and *The Youth's Companion* to keep us in touch with the young of our own country. I doubt the validity of the touch, however, for I somehow got the notion of incredible perfection in America, and I grew up misinformed and ripe for some disillusionment later, though not severe, at that, for common sense came to the rescue.

One interlude broke those tranquil years before I was sent "home," as we were always taught to call our country, for college. There was always something tragic, though I did not know it then, in the word "home," used by white men far from home. Wherever these lived, in whatever country of Asia, with or without their wives and children, they spoke of their native lands as "home." In India one would meet Englishmen who at eighteen had been sent there by their parents to seek a fortune, and had never once gone back, and though they were grey-headed and surely had established homes of some sort for themselves, yet they spoke of England as "home." And saddest of all, if they had Indian wives or merely lived with Indian women, was to hear the little half-Indian children call England "home," although they could never be at home there, or in India, either. There were such children in Chinkiang, too, and while my mother insisted that we never speak of them as anything but English or American, as their fathers were, yet I knew they knew that for them "home" was nowhere. I felt this plight so heartily sorrowful that I almost thought it wicked for me to be so lucky as to be wholly an American, my parents insuring all my blood.

So before I went "home" to college there was the interlude. The circumstances were that I was really too young for college, a natural result of being taught only by my mother in Western subjects. The year must be spent somehow, for my father's furlough was not until 1910 and it was still only 1909.

I think, too, my mother felt that I was not ready to be left alone at college, even in my own country, composed as I was of innocence and an Asian sophistication, a combination resulting from daily living with a people as naturalistic as the Chinese were. I had had little chance to mingle with my own kind. Two months each summer, it is true, we went up into the high Lu mountains to escape the heat of the river levels and there I met the sons and daughters of missionaries and of businessmen. But I was so charmed by the landscape of those mountains that I spent more time in walking and climbing than I did in parties and playing tennis. Besides these yearly holidays, I had met only one American family who had girls of my own age. For a few months or perhaps for a year or two, I cannot remember, for huge events that have since befallen continue to destroy my sense of time, I made friends with the three daughters of a missionary family, healthy, gay and newly come from America. They did not stay long because the malarial climate of our river province made the mother ill. Yet I had a glimpse, at least, of American girls and their delightful ways. I was quiet, not so much from shyness as from the need to discover them entire. I watched them not as individuals but as the whole of America must be, full of such girls, laughing, noisy, wilful, teasing. They went away again and suddenly I was alone as I had never been before.

That was when my mother, always sensitive and observant, decided that I must spend a year away in a boarding school. I had one other such experience, when for a few months I had stayed on at a small new American boarding school in Kuling. It made no impression on me, apparently, certainly I learned nothing, for after three months I was not sent back, and the lessons with my mother were resumed. This time, however, I was to go to Shanghai, to Miss Jewell's School, the most fashionable and indeed the only good school, supposedly, in our part of the China coast for Western boys and girls. A year or two later the American School was started and to it went the generations of white children after me, mainly American, and they were prepared for American life quite differently and certainly far more adequately than Miss Jewell's School could do, at least in its latter days when I was there.

When I look back on the months spent in that strange place, the memory is unreal, fantastic, separate from any other part of the times in which I have lived. There was, in the first place, Shanghai, a city altogether unlike any Chinese city. It was a city created by foreigners and for foreigners. Decades earlier Manchu emperors had assigned a living space to the intruding westerners, and in contempt had allowed them nothing better than mud flats on the Whangpoo River, where the Yangtse flows into the sea. Out of this malarial waste the foreigners had made a city. Great buildings lifted their bulk along the handsome Bund. Parks were opened, the famous parks which later provided a slogan for the simmering revolution, "No Chinese, No Dogs." Fine English department stores did a thriving business, extending themselves from the modern cities of India and from Singapore and Hong Kong, and specialty stores for the arts, for books and for music, completed a metropolis. There were excellent hotels for tourists and local businessmen as well as apartment houses, and expensive clubs for sports and amusements as well as great private homes belonging to the wealthy of all nationalities.

My own knowledge at that time of a city already fabulous around the world was meager enough. Shanghai had been for me merely the gateway to the Pacific Ocean, through which we had to come and go when we left China. No, there was the memory, too, of the few months we had spent there as refugees from the Boxers. Now as an oversensitive and too observant young girl I was to see Shanghai from the windows of a gloomy boarding school, and it was quite a different city. I learned then that, like most great cities, Shanghai was many cities wrapped in one and my knowledge of it depended entirely upon my experiences in it.

Miss Jewell's School was established in buildings of somber and indestructible grey brick. Never have I seen, except in London, such buildings, shaped, it seemed, for eternal life. Upon the ground floor by the front door was the parlor and there on the day upon which I was to be received my mother and I sat waiting for Miss Jewell. Shades of *Nicholas Nickleby* enveloped me as I looked around that dreary parlor. The windows were partly sunken beneath the pavement of the street outside and they were heavily barred against thieves, a reasonable condition but one which added something dreadful to my impression of the room. Texts from the Bible, framed in dark oak, hung upon the pallid walls, and the furniture was nondescript and mixed. In a small English grate beneath a black wooden mantel an economical fire smoked up the chimney, a handful of coals carefully arranged to smoulder and not to burn.

There we sat, not knowing what to think, and I felt my own misgivings growing deeper as I saw my mother's usually cheerful face gradually losing its cheer. She was not one to give up easily, however, and so we waited and presently into the room came a short, heavy-set, white-haired, black-eyed woman. It was Miss Jewell herself. She wore a dark full dress whose skirt came to the floor, and she entered silently because, as I was to discover, she always wore soft-soled shoes, partly so that no one might know when she was coming and partly because she suffered grievously from corns. I looked at this handsome sad-faced woman and did not know what she was. I felt most persons immediately, but this was someone new. She greeted us in a low voice and I noticed that although her hands were beautiful they were cold and she had a limp handshake. No warmth came from her. In fairness I must admit that she was already an aging woman and one always tired. She had been the headmistress of her own school for many years and dependent solely upon herself, and in spite of her seeming coldness, she did many good works. During the months I was to stay under her care not a few strange lost women came to her for shelter and somehow she always gave it and arranged work for them or a passage home. It took time for me to discover the hidden goodness, however, and on that first day I felt only a sort of fright.

Perhaps I never understood Miss Jewell fully, nor some of the women she gathered about her, until years later when in a New York theater I saw Eugene O'Neill's plays about people dying of dry rot. Out of a proud but desiccated New England background Miss Jewell had brought to China a severe goodness, a passionate resignation, a will of steel. She was not like anyone I had ever seen, neither my cheerful parents nor my warmhearted Chinese friends. I kissed my mother goodbye and reminded her in a whisper that she had promised that I need not stay if I did not like it, and then when she had gone I followed Miss Jewell up a wide dark stair behind a Chinese houseboy who carried my bags.

The effect upon me of this school is not important except as it opened to me a strange subterranean world of mixed humanity. I had an attic room which I shared with two other girls, both daughters of missionaries whom I had not known before. Their lives had been wholly different from mine, and although we were soon acquainted, we remained strangers. This was because my parents were so unorthodox as to believe that the Chinese were our equals in every way, and that the Chinese civilization, including its philosophy and religions, was worthy of study and respect. My roommates came of orthodox folk, they had spent their lives in mission compounds, and as a consequence spoke only "servant" Chinese and had no Chinese friends, at least in my sense of the word. They despised me somewhat, I think, because I had been taught by Mr. Kung, and wrote letters regularly to dear Chinese friends. The nearest that we ever came to quarreling, however, was on the subject of Buddhism about which they knew nothing. I, on the other hand, knew a good deal about it in spite of my youth, because my father, always a scholar, had studied Buddhism for many years, among other religions of Asia, and he had written an interesting monograph on the similarities between Christianity and Buddhism. My parents never talked down to their children. On the contrary, they conversed upon matters of their own interest, and we listened, perforce, and joined in as we were able. Thus I knew rather clearly the general ideas my father had about Buddhism, one of these being that the likeness between that religion and Christianity was not accidental but historical since it is quite possible that Jesus may have visited the Himalayan Kingdom of Nepal when he was a young man, and during the twelve unrecorded years of his life. Such tradition is widespread in northern India and is even mentioned in *Vishnu Purana,* the ancient Hindu Scripture. Two thousand years ago all religions were a brotherhood and religious leaders and disciples communicated. My father believed that Jesus knew the teachings of Confucius as well as of Buddhism, for the almost identical expression by Confucius and by Jesus of the Golden Rule, for one example among many, could scarcely be accidental similarity of thought. In short, although my father was a conservative Christian, he had come to the conclusion that in Asia, where human civilization had long ago reached an unparalleled height of philosophical thought and religious doctrine, all religions had contributed their share to the profound and steady movement of mankind toward God.

These were shocking ideas to my two roommates, and though I presented them in innocence and in the course of bedtime talk, they reported me to Miss Jewell as being a heretic. I, on the other hand, was shocked that they could call the Chinese people heathen, a term my parents never allowed to be spoken in our house, so that even certain hymns were forbidden to us because they contained this ugly word. Miss Jewell, informed of my monstrous views, removed me from the attic room lest I contaminate the others, and put me in a little room alone. This pleased me for I could read after lights went out elsewhere, and from the veranda outside my room I could look across the street and observe a large and friendly Portuguese family. I never knew their surname, for I never met them, but I knew all their personal names, since they had loud lively voices and they called to one another from floor to floor and lived on their upstairs veranda with careless intimacy. Mama and Papa, Rosa, Marie and Sophie and little Dee-Dee were the ones still at home. On Sundays after Mass a married son and daughter and their children came home to spend the day, and on that day I too had leisure after compulsory church, and so I could watch them and share in their merry life. I grew fond of them in my way, for perhaps it is my weakness to be fond of people easily, although intimacy is difficult for me, and they gave cheer to what might otherwise have been a shadowed existence in those great dark buildings.

For once in my life I took no interest in my lesson books. I did not, I found, enjoy studying in classes, for I was accustomed to my mother's quick mind and imaginative teaching and other teachers bored me, with the exception of my English teacher, a frail blue-eyed little woman whose oversensitive spirit I discerned and dreaded somewhat, I think, because I felt in it depths for which I was not ready.

We had good teachers, Miss Jewell saw to that, but I was a restless pupil, informed in some subjects far beyond my age, thanks to my parents, but impatient when confronted with the more technical aspects of Latin grammar and mathematics. What I really learned had nothing to do with formal subjects. Miss Jewell, feeling that I needed a stricter Christian theology, endeavored to instill it in me by taking me to prayer meetings and then to places of good works. Both terrified me. The prayer meetings were unlike any I had ever seen. I do not know to what sect Miss Jewell belonged, but for her prayers she went to one private house or another where her fellow Christians met to pray. She was a busy woman and we usually arrived late, after the meeting had begun. We entered a dark hall, admitted by the usual blasé Chinese houseboy who led us to the room of prayer. It was always dark and we stumbled over legs and reclining figures until we found a space wherein to kneel. There we stayed as long as Miss Jewell could spare the time, and stiff with repulsion, I listened to voices in the darkness pleading for the presence of the Holy Spirit, or fervent beseeching for forgiveness of unmentioned sins, accompanied by moans and groans and sighs. The experience became so frightening, so intolerable to me, that I asked my mother to let me come home. Religion I was used to, but not this dark form of it, this grovelling emotion, the physical confusion, a loathsome self-indulgence of some sort that I could not understand but at which my healthy instincts revolted. In my father's house religion was a normal exercise, a combination of creed and practice, accompanied by music. My mother had a fine strong clear soprano voice, well trained, and at any hour of the day she sang, not only the better hymns but solos from great oratorios and noble church music. My father's sermons, inclined, it is true, to scholarly dryness, did not, however, contain any talk of hell. Infant damnation, a horrid idea from which I am happy to say all Christians have now recovered, was nevertheless in those days still part of the normal creed, but my father, heretic that he was, would have none of it, and my mother, having lost four beautiful little children, was raised to fury at the very mention of any child descending into hell. I had heard her comfort more than one young missionary mother beside the body of a dead child. "Your baby is in heaven," she declared. "There are no babies in hell—no, not one. They are all gathered round the Throne of God the Father, and Jesus takes them in his bosom when they first come in, when they still feel strange to heaven." Upon the common tombstone of three of her children, who died before I was born, she had their names inscribed and then the text, "He gathered them like lambs in His bosom." And as long as she lived there hung on the wall of her bedroom opposite her bed, where she could see it night and morning, the picture of a shepherd with his sheep, and in his arms were baby lambs.

68

My parents were alarmed, then, when I told them of the dark rooms and the strange prayers, and they wrote my headmistress and requested that I be taken to no church services except on Sunday mornings in the Community Church, where Mr. Darwent, a short stout little Englishman with a bald rolling head and no neck, could be trusted to preach harmless sermons, sincere and brief. Thus one burden was removed from me.

Miss Jewell, however, did not give me up. She felt that I was old enough to have some share in her good works, and so I took her turn, when she was busy, at the Door of Hope, a rescue home for Chinese slave girls who had cruel mistresses. It was really an excellent work, and the municipal authorities gave it every support, even to the extent of legal help in freeing slaves from their owners. I was supposed to teach the girls to sew and knit and embroider, all of which tasks I disliked, but which my own beautifully educated mother had taught me to do well. She believed that it was still part of a woman's education to know the household arts. "Even if you always have servants," she was fond of telling me, "you ought to know how to teach them to do their work properly. And home is the place to learn home-making."

She was right in this as in so much else, and I have never regretted knowing all she taught me, even though I complained enough then when I had to learn fine crocheting and lacework as well as cooking meals and baking delicate hot breads and cakes. I have not been able to impart these feminine arts to my own daughters. My mother had one advantage over me—we had to make American foods if we wanted to eat them. Nowadays, here in the United States, young women can buy such miracles of ready frozen stuff, wanting only to be thrust in an oven to be finished, that it is hard to make them believe that they have lost an art. And this ignorance extends even to the daughters of farmers. I had once a little Pennsylvania maid who could not cook or sew, and did not feel her ignorance unfitted her in the slightest to be a wife and mother. She would buy both food and clothes ready-made, she said, and laughed when I said I felt sorry for her because she had missed so much.

The Chinese slave girls at the Door of Hope, however, were eager to learn. They were wretched children, bought young in some time of famine and reared to serve in a rich household. We had only the ones from evil households, of course, for a bondmaid in a kindly family received good treatment as someone less than a daughter but more than a hired servant, and at the age of eighteen she was freed and given in marriage to some lowly good man. But these who ran away were the ones beaten with whips and burned by cruel and bad-tempered mistresses with live coals from pipes and cigarettes and ravished by growing adolescent sons in the family or by lecherous masters and their menservants. Such slavery was an old system and perhaps no one was entirely to blame for it. In famine times the desperate starving families sold their daughters not only to buy a little food for themselves but often, too, to save the daughter's life. It seemed better to allow the child to go into a rich and hopefully friendly family rather than certainly to die of starvation. The girl was sold instead of the boy because the family still hoped to survive somehow and the son must be kept, if possible, to carry on the family name. Sooner or later, it was reasoned, the girl would have to leave the family, anyway, when she married. There are many romantic and beautiful love stories in Chinese literature centering about the lovely bondmaid who is the savior and the darling of the family, and these perhaps added to the hopefulness of the starving family when they sold their girl child. Nor was it always a girl who was sold. Sometimes if there were no girls, or if all the girls had been sold and there was more than one boy, a younger boy would be sold to a rich family, also. But a girl was more salable. A boy was less useful as a servant.

It was an old system, I say, and like all systems in human life, everything depended upon the good or evil of the persons concerned. The best government in the world, the best religion, the best traditions of any people, depend upon the good or evil of the men and women who administer them.

At the Door of Hope I saw the dreadful fruit of evil and still another aspect of human and certainly Asian life. Since I spoke Chinese as if it were my native tongue, the slave girls, unless they knew only Shanghai dialect, could talk to me freely and they did. Most of them could speak Mandarin for they had come from northern families who had travelled southward as refugees, although in famine times there were also men or women who deliberately went northward to hunt for children to sell again at profit in the large cities.

Many a night I woke up in my little room at Miss Jewell's School to ponder over the stories these young girls told me and I wept to think there could be such evil in the world. This grieving either makes a heart grow more hard, in self-protection, or it makes a too tender heart. In my own case, perhaps there was something of both. I had early to acccpt the fact that there are persons, both men and women, who are incurably and wilfully cruel and wicked. But forced to this recognition, I retaliated spiritually by making the fierce resolution that wherever I saw evil and cruelty at work I would devote all I had to delivering its victims. This resolution has stayed with me throughout my life and has provided a conscience for conduct. It has not always been easy to follow, for I am not an aggressive person by nature. Once in India I was travelling by train from Calcutta to Bombay. In the compartment next to me was an English captain who disliked the Indians, it seemed, with an unusual virulence. When the train stopped, crying beggars and shouting vendors crowded as usual around the windows, and while it was not pleasant to be thus surrounded on a hot day, nevertheless these people were trying to earn a few anna to buy food. The Captain, however, did not use his reason. He carried a rawhide whip and he ran out upon the platform and beat off the half-naked Indians with vicious blows.

It was a horrid sight, yet if I had not made my resolution years before at the Door of Hope, I doubt I would have had the courage to speak to him. Much as I hated it, I did speak.

"How can you be so cruel?" I demanded. "They have not hurt you, and they are only trying to get a little money. There is no law against that."

He was astonished for a moment, then he shrugged his shoulders. "Filthy beasts!"

Anger came to my aid. "Someday," I said, "other white men and women and children, quite innocent, will suffer for what you are doing now."

He shrugged again and walked away. I am not so foolish as to think he changed, for people seldom change once the mold is set, and he was past his youth. But I have never forgotten the dark Indian faces wearing the grave and bitter look I used to see on Chinese faces, too, when some white man was unjust. And the tragedy is that we are now reaping that very fruit. I read this morning in the newspaper of the cruel treatment given to the American prisoners of war in Asian camps. Part of it, I suppose, is not conscious cruelty but merely the difference in standards of living. The average Chinese workingman's daily fare would seem near starvation to a hearty American boy, used to the best, and walking endless miles over hard roads under a heavy burden is only what many an Asian does every day for his living. If he is ill, it does not occur to him to go to a doctor or a hospital because a thousand chances to one there are none. Part of the cruelty, therefore, is the inevitable difference between poverty and riches. But the worst of it is undoubtedly really cruelty, instinctive and conscious at the same time, and the Asian is punishing the American because he is a white man now in his power and white men have been very cruel to the Asians in the past. The few good deeds done by a handful of missionaries do not change the history of centuries gone—not enough. The nightmare of my life has always been, since I understood anything at all, that someday a son of mine would have to stand in hand-to-hand battle with a Chinese, and that

71

the Chinese, who knew his people's history, would take revenge upon the innocent American. It has already happened to the sons of other Americans and may yet happen to my own.

Billings, Montana

This up-to-date Western town is built along the railroad, as so many Western towns are, like beads on a string, and I have just been wakened from a sound sleep in a very comfortable roadside inn by the noise of an engine and a few cars racketing past not fifty feet from the head of my bed. When the bed stopped shaking and the dust had settled, I fell to thinking of the difference between night noises here and the ones to which I was accustomed in that other world of mine. At home on our farm in Pennsylvania there are the house noises, the crack of old beams on a cold night, or the first peepers of spring and then the summer croaking of the bullfrogs in the pool, and later the autumn crickets. The dogs bark on a moonlight night and across the road sometimes a cow bawls in heat and must wait until dawn for the farmer to come and lead her to the bull. Or in the deep silence, and this sound I dislike for it always makes me afraid, a plane rushes through the night, too low, it seems to me, always too low, and I fall to wondering what the pilot's mission is and why it must be done by night and what it is like to be speeding through the black sky, borne upon the beams of his own lights, with nothing between heaven and earth except himself, and what awful loneliness that must be.

Here in the West the train rushes past, making its mournful cry, and I do not know why these western trains have such a sad long echoing whistle as they fly past, a cry nearly human, so wild, so lost. It makes me think of human voices I have heard in the night elsewhere, the mournful monotony of voices singing in an Indian village, and I do not know what that song is, either, or why it is sung so often in the night, a few notes repeated over and over, thin and high until at last one's very heart is caught and twisted into it. But the voice I remember most clearly is the cry of a Chinese woman, a mother, any mother whose child was dying, his soul wandering away from home, she thought, and so she seized the child's little coat and lit a lantern and ran out into the street, calling the wailing pitiful cry, *"Sha-lai, sha-lai!"* and this meant, "Child, come back, come back!" How often have I heard that cry, and always with a pang of the heart! Lying in my comfortable bed and safe under our own roof, I could see too vividly the stricken family and the little child lying dead or dying and all the calling in the world could never bring his soul home again.

The Shanghai streets had their own noises, and often wakeful at Miss Jewell's School, I heard the creak of a late riksha rolling along and the swift patter of people's feet, and I heard the call of voices, girls' laughter sometimes, or a hearty English voice, a man saying good-bye to someone. And deep in the night I woke to hear the endless slip-slip of Chinese feet in their cloth shoes, walking along the pavements, and I wondered where they went and why they never seemed to go home but always on and on.

In the spring of that strange year I spent at Miss Jewell's School, she took me with her to still another of her good works. At a house whose name I cannot remember and where it was I have forgotten, too, there was a shelter for destitute white women, many of them prostitutes too old or ill to work any more, but some of them still young and even with babies. This place struck me with a profound horror, and actual terror. Here, for the first time in my life, I saw people of my own race, and women at that, so low in poverty and disease and loneliness that they were worse off than the Chinese slave girls at the Door of Hope. I could pity the slave girls because they had not chosen to be slaves, but I could not comprehend these white women of every Western nation. French, English, German, Belgian, American—how had they let themselves come to such a pass and where had the first step been taken and how could they be made innocent again? I suppose my horror must have been plain, for the women fell silent when I came near, and though I did my best, playing games and reading aloud and teaching them to sew, there was never any communion between us. It was impossible, I had no background for it, nor did they understand me.

When I went home for the spring holidays my mother said I was too pale and thin and when I told her of Miss Jewell's good works and my part in them, she pressed her lips together and her dark eyes sparkled with anger and I knew that I would not be sent to boarding school again. I had learned enough. Into the short year I had crowded human knowledge not only of a Shanghai underworld but of New England women, my headmistress and the teachers, the little Scotch music mistress who was engaged that year to a good young man and whose innocent romance was comforting, the dark and passionate woman who taught us geometry and whom I never understood until years after she was dead, and the other teacher, and I forget even what she taught me but I think it was Latin, who later married and became the mother of a delightful American writer, John Espey. And among those I remember there was also our matron, a tall elderly English woman, whose false

73

teeth slipped back and forth whenever she spoke, but whom we all loved because she had no judgment, and left in charge she could be as silly as any schoolgirl with us, and she was always to be counted on for extra bread and butter at teatime.

Of my schoolmates I remember even less, and those I do remember are for no reasons except foolish ones, such as the missionary boy who would eat the eyes of the baked carp we always had at Friday luncheons. I was and am convinced that he hated fisheyes as much as any of us, but he could not forego the pleasure of seeing us all shudder and hearing us cry out and so he ate them. Yet he grew up into a very good American man, an artist, I believe, who has done well enough at commercial art in his own country.

Perhaps the one I remember best was the half-Chinese daughter of a distinguished American who, when his English love refused him for another man, devoted himself to the education of young Chinese men in a great university, and to help him in his work, he married a Chinese lady, plain-faced but of noble character. Of their children all were boys except one and the boys were handsome like their father but the girl was plain like her Chinese mother and she used to talk to me about herself, and wonder what would become of her because she was plain and because she was afraid no white man would marry her and she did not want to marry a Chinese. I think she never married, but I do not know whether she lived or died.

I was glad to be home, although it was lonely for a while, but not too lonely, for when summer came my parents were to take me to America to college. Would I come back again or not? I did not know, and the few months passed in a sort of sweet melancholy while I wondered if each day were a sort of last farewell to China.

And I have not mentioned the sound I liked best there at night but perhaps the memory belongs here. It is the voice of the great bronze bell that stood on a pedestal in the Buddhist temple halfway down our hill. As long as I could remember I had heard it sound in the night, not often, but at certain hours the round rich note of music reverberated through the darkness. When I was small I used to be afraid, the sound was melancholy and made me feel alone. But in the years of my childhood when I had been so free, more free than any white child before or since, I had often visited the temple in the daytime and had seen for myself how the bell was struck by a small kind old priest who grasped with both hands a piece of wood, the end of which was wrapped into a club with cloth. He swung out his arms and let this club fall against the bell hanging within its frame, and out rolled the great pure sound.

I remember the last night at home and all the bags packed and ready to close. I was sleepless and when I heard the bell strike its last note at dawn as we left the house, I had a strange premonition that I would never hear it again, and I never did.

Sauk Centre, Minnesota

This town was once the home of Sinclair Lewis and it is because of him that we have turned aside from the straight road home. I saw him only once, and it was at a dinner given in New York by the P.E.N. Club upon the occasion of the award of the Nobel Prize in Literature in 1938. I went as the guest of honor, but never was there a guest so faint of heart, and even dispirited, as I was that night. This mood went back to my childhood and perhaps partly to good Mr. Kung, who could not possibly know that even then I had intended to be a teller of tales, a writer of novels, though how that end was to be achieved I did not know. One longs to make what one loves, and above all I loved to hear stories about people. I was a nuisance of a child, I fear, always curious to know about people and why they were as I found them. Moreover, I began to read Charles Dickens at the age of seven and he had his usual influence, and this is always to stir alive the young imagination and create wonder about human beings. My first Dickens book was *Oliver Twist,* which I read twice through without delay. After that I read any of the dark blue clothbound set that filled a shelf in our parlor. My mother became alarmed at my absorption, especially as she herself resisted an instinctive love of Dickens—resisted, because in her young days he was considered coarse and a novelist of "the lower classes." No such instincts troubled me. I spent my afternoons reading one volume after another, in summertime in the crook of the huge elm, and in winter sitting in the sunny corner of our back veranda. For ten years, I daresay, I read Dickens complete each year from cover to cover, laughing aloud, though alone, over *Pickwick Papers* and weeping quietly over the death of Little Nell and the cruelty of *Hard Times.* Sissy Jukes has remained with me always as a part of myself because she replied sensibly, though faltering with shyness when Thomas Gradgrind asked her if a mortality of seven to a thousand people was high, that it *was* high because it was just as hard on the seven who died as it would have been if more had died. Thomas Gradgrind shouted that she was a fool, but I have always known that she was right, and the more I see of life and humanity the more sure I am that she was eternally right and that it is the Thomas Gradgrinds of this world who are the fools and not the Sissy Jukeses.

75

The result of having few childish books and therefore of being compelled at an early age to read adult novels was that I decided well before I was ten to be a novelist, and only Mr. Kung confused my mind. He, as a Confucian scholar, had been trained in the early Chinese classical tradition that no reputable writer condescends to produce novels. Novels, he taught me, cannot be considered literature. They are designed to amuse the idle and the illiterate, that is, those persons who cannot appreciate a true literary style and moral and philosophical content. This discouragement was maintained during my most formative years, and was even increased by the religious feelings of my parents who considered novel-reading a mere pastime. Indeed, my mother and I played a sort of hide-and-seek all through my childhood, although neither of us ever referred to it. She hid the novels I read and I hunted for them until I found them. I cannot remember that I bore her any ill will for this. She was far too lovable and good, nor did she, apparently, feel any anger toward me for almost invariably finding her hiding places. The whole performance was carried on in silence by both of us. When I grew up I forgot about it and have since wished that I had remembered to ask her why she hid the books in such easy places. But she died too young. There were many questions I meant to ask her and did not until it was too late and she was forever gone.

The result of all this was that somehow I grew up feeling that the writing of novels was a lesser work than it is. Certainly I never felt that novels were literature and I was secretly ashamed of my continued interest in reading them. When *The Good Earth* took on a life of its own, no one was more astonished than I, and I was even apologetic that my first appearance, so to speak, in the world of literature, should be with a novel. I remember when the publisher of that book gave me a very handsome dinner in New York, at which various notables were present whose names I had only heard from afar, and I was required to make some sort of speech, I could only do so in the words of the ancient Chinese novelist, Shih Nai-an, whose masterpiece of compilation and original writing I had just finished translating under the title of *All Men Are Brothers*. This Chinese novelist, too, felt humble before his fellow scholars, for his vast work was still only a sort of collective novel, and sharing his feelings, I gave as my own speech the preface to his book, which illustrates the attitude of the Chinese scholars toward novels and the writing of novels. It closes with these sentences: "How can I know what those who come after me and read my book will think of it? I cannot even know what I, myself, born into another incarnation, will think of it. I do not know if I, myself, afterwards can even read this book. Why therefore should I care?"

All this may explain my own small estimate of my powers, so that one day in the autumn of the year 1938, when I heard that I had just been awarded the Nobel Prize in Literature for that year, I did not believe it, nor could I believe it until a telephone call to Stockholm confirmed it. My feelings then were still very confused. I could not understand why it should be given to me and I remember that I exclaimed, "Oh, I wish that it could have been given to Theodore Dreiser instead!"

I did indeed so wish, for I admired Dreiser greatly as a writer. He was, to my mind, far more than a mere novelist. He had in his deep, ponderous, gigantic fashion got hold of something profoundly American, and if before twenty I read Charles Dickens, after twenty I read Dreiser and after Dreiser, Sinclair Lewis, and of the two of them I felt Lewis the more brilliant but I knew Dreiser would be the more nearly permanent. And he was getting old, whereas I was still young, young enough to wait for future rewards.

If I had doubts about myself, they were doubled and tripled by my fellow writers who were men. The gist of such criticisms, and there were more than a few, was that no woman, except possibly the veteran writer, Willa Cather, deserved the Nobel Prize, and that of all women I deserved it the least because I was too young, had written too few books of note, and was scarcely even to be considered an American, since I wrote about the Chinese and had lived only in their remote and outlandish part of the world. With my background and literary education, I was only too ready to agree with all this, and yet I did not know how to refuse the award without seeming even more presumptuous. In real distress, for it made me very unhappy to feel that my fellow writers were against the choice, I could only continue making melancholy preparations to go to Stockholm and accept the award which had been given me so unexpectedly and without any knowledge on my part that I was even considered a candidate.

It is only honest to say that I am sure the blast from my fellow writers fell upon me with a severity they had scarcely intended. I had for years worked so entirely alone in my writing, in such remote places in Asia, among people who could not understand my yearning to associate with others, especially Americans, who were writers and with whom I could communicate as kindred minds, that I was oversensitive to this American criticism which did indeed fall upon me too soon. And it must be confessed that I have never quite recovered, though years have passed, so that I have been too diffident, ever since, to mingle much with American writers or, perhaps, to undertake my proper responsibilities with them. To go among them even now revives painful memories of that autumn in 1938, when I was still new in my own country, still eager and hopeful and, as I can see now, absurdly worshipful toward my elders in the golden field of American letters.

And all this leads me to the kindly memory of Sinclair Lewis, himself a winner of the Nobel Prize in Literature. As I said, I met him at a P.E.N. dinner, the only one, I think, which I have ever attended, and he sat next to me. I said very little because I felt reticent before so great a writer, and I listened with appreciation to what he said. He was already sad and disillusioned, and I felt a sort of reckless honesty in his words, his fine homely face turned away from me most of the time so that I had to listen carefully while he talked quickly on. Suddenly my turn came to make a little speech, and I got up, intensely mindful of the criticism from some of the very persons who sat that night before me, and looking back to what I had been taught in my Chinese childhood, I told them somehow, and I cannot remember exactly the words and I did not think them important enough to write down, that I had long ago learned that a mere teller of tales is not to be considered a literary figure, and that my novels were only stories to amuse people and make a heavy hour pass a little more easily, and a few more sentences of the sort. Mr. Kung would have approved all I said.

Sinclair Lewis, however, did not approve. When I sat down again, he turned to me with an animation sparkling with anger.

"You must not minimize yourself," he declared, and I remember every word because they fell like balm upon my wounded spirit. "Neither must you minimize your profession," he went on. "A novelist has a noble function." And then, as though he understood all I had been feeling, he went on to speak of that function, and how a writer must not heed what others say. I would weary, he said, of the very name of *The Good Earth,* for people would act as though it were the only book I had ever written, but never mind people, he said, never mind! He had often wished, he said, that he had never written *Main Street,* so sick did he get of hearing people speak of it as "your book."

"You must write many novels," he cried with an energy intense and inspiring. "And let people say their little say! They have nothing else to say, damn them!"

What comfort that was from him, and how warmly I felt toward him ever after! Years later, when I heard that he had died in Italy so alone that he was reduced to playing his beloved chess games with his maidservant—though he said sadly she was so stupid that she could never remember how the knight moves—I wished that I could have known of his loneliness and could have made some return for his kindness to me. But I had supposed that a man so famous and so successful would have been surrounded by old and faithful friends, and I cannot understand how it was that he was not. I had heard of his faults and difficulties, but his genius was a burden heavy enough for him to bear, and because of it all his sins should have been forgiven, certainly by his friends.

I made this pilgrimage, therefore, to Sauk Centre and today I went about the town, trying to see it as perhaps it had seemed to him. I went into a little grocery store and asked the proprietor, a youngish man, if he knew of Sinclair Lewis. Oh, yes, he said, everybody knew about him here. They hadn't liked him much after his *Main Street,* but people got over that and nobody cared now.

"Is there a monument to him anywhere?" I asked.

"Oh, no," the man said cheerfully, weighing hamburger meat for a young woman with a fat baby, "there wouldn't likely be any monument put up to him—not here."

"Can you tell me which was his house?" I asked.

He told me in an offhand way while he wrapped the meat and the young woman stared at me.

"It's not open to the public," he warned me. "It belongs to other people now."

I thanked him and went away and found the house, a sober, comfortable middle-class house with gables and a porch and a neat lawn. And why, I wondered, should that fiery, honest, impatient spirit have come out of such a house? What accidental combination of elements produced him? I could only see him bursting out of those walls, and out of the town and what it stood for, loving it so much that he hated it for not being all he wanted it to be and knew it could be.

That was the way he loved his whole country, and that, too, I can understand.

Forest Haunt, Vermont

Our journey ends here in the Green Mountains of Vermont and across my memory stretch the broad reaches of our country. I am heartened, as always, by its size and its variety. There are many alarming possibilities in the fluid trends of our culture, and when I am oppressed by one shadow or another, as at times every thinking creature must be oppressed in the light of human history, I take to the car and, with as many of the family as possible, make a cross-country tour, sweeping widely and yet slowly enough to talk with people as I find them. Without fail I come home with confidence revived. The mere size of our land is an obstacle to any man who might imagine himself a Hitler or a Stalin. Yet size alone would not be a safeguard without the variety of our people, the many minds, each thinking with extraordinary vitality and independence within his individual limits. This variety is due, I suppose, to the variety of our ancestors and the customs they brought with them when they came here as immigrants to make a new country for themselves. We have not lived long enough together to become unified as the Chinese are, their racial differences all intermingled and melted into a common color, and their habits smoothed into uniformity by centuries of living together.

The Germans were well educated, far better than we are on the average, nevertheless they succumbed to Hitler, mainly perhaps because Germany is so small as to be physically manageable by one man and his adherents. And yet Russia succumbed to what is now called Communism, although she is so vast. But her people were ignorant and miserable and her intellectuals were persecuted and imprisoned, and when peasants and intellectuals revolt together, revolution is inevitable, although out of revolution invariably there comes chaos or dictatorship, and history is the proof.

And well I remember that old Russia, although I was very young when I crossed her wilderness of land. We left our home on the Chinese hill, after the night when I heard the temple bell strike for the last time, and we set out for America. Ordinarily, or had we been an ordinary family, we would have gone to Shanghai and taken a ship across the Pacific Ocean. But my mother suffered from a peculiarly virulent and incurable form of seasickness, and since she had during the years developed a tendency to a heart weakness, the doctor decided that she could not face the month of constant sickness which such a journey involved. Moreover, she wanted me to see Europe. She loved Switzerland and France and Italy and England, and she wanted to visit Holland again, whence her own ancestors had come. I think that she had some idea, too, of inducting me into my country for the four years of college by taking me first through the continent of Europe which had produced the new nation. At any rate, she bought a trunkful of books on Europe and we began reading them together the very day we left our Chinese home and settled ourselves in our tiny cabins on a Jardine-Matheson steamer going up the Yangtse River to Hankow, where we would then take the train for Peking, and Harbin in Manchuria. With European art and music we were already fairly familiar, for from the time we were young children our mother had supplied us with reproductions of famous paintings, and with biographies, suited to our ages, of great artists and composers. We had learned to play Bach and

Mendelssohn, Handel and Beethoven on our little English-made Moutrie piano, sent from Shanghai, and upon which we practiced faithfully, if not always willingly, under her supervision.

Our preparation now for Europe was far more serious. My mother was an inspired if uneven teacher. She illuminated by her own enthusiasm any subject in which she was interested, and if she were not interested, she skipped shamelessly and openly. For Europe we could scarcely have had a better teacher. Her own appreciation, not only of art and music but also of history, communicated itself to me, and long before we reached Europe I had quite clearly in mind the differences among the peoples, their characteristics and their achievements. In addition, my mother described to me many of the beautiful places she remembered from her former visits, and I could scarcely wait to see them with my own eyes. Germany she scorned for some reason unknown to me, but my father supplied something for this lack, since he spoke German perfectly, among his other languages, and his religious studies had given him a perspective quite different from my mother's. Then, too, his own ancestral origins were in southern Germany. In the year 1760, three brothers, his ancestors, the sons of a well-known German scholar, decided to leave their home and the company of men like themselves in order that they could have religious and academic freedom in America. Their father was willing, but required each of them first to have a trade, wisely declaring that a university education would be worth nothing to them in a wilderness. Within a few years after their arrival in the new country the War of Independence began and at least one of them achieved some fame as an aide to George Washington, although he was taken prisoner at Fort Washington, in Pennsylvania. The family traditions were strong in their later home in Virginia, and when my father was growing up there, German was still spoken as a second language in the family.

Looking back, I find that my memories of China grow suddenly dim on that day when we left our compound on the hill and this must have been because my mind was already turned toward Europe and my own country. At any rate, I remember amazingly little of the long train journey northward, and even of our stay in Peking, a city I learned later to know well and to love very much. I did find a deep interest in The Forbidden City, for my impressions of the Old Empress, that dominating figure of my childhood, had remained vivid. The Imperial Family, now weak and inconsequential, were still in residence, and of the famous Summer Palace we could see only the outside, the pagoda beautifully set against the hills. But it is all vague, very vague, and my true memories of Peking came decades later, in another world, and then

The Forbidden City was open to any tourist, the doors swinging and the beautiful rooms empty, and the Summer Palace was a picnic place for pleasure seekers.

Harbin, our first stop in Manchuria after we left Peking, was not interesting, being but the familiar medley of a crossroads town, a mixture of peoples and buildings, and I remember only odd and outlandish bits, such as a Mongol camel driver walking briskly at the head of his caravan of dingy camels, and he was remarkable to me because as he walked he was knitting with two long bamboo needles, and his yarn was strands of raw wool which he pulled out from the loose mat of the grey and hairy coat which the camel behind him was shedding. The garment looked like a long wide scarf, although how it could be worn I do not know, except by a man who slept and ate with his camels, for the reek of the camel is eternal, and not to be removed by the best of washings. In the First World War a group of patriotic American ladies in Kuling knitted vests for soldiers in Europe and the only plentiful and cheap wool was that spun from camel hair, and although it was carded and spun and done up nicely in skeins, the smell of camel was still in it and so strong that my mother held her nose and dropped all the yarn into a pail of strong carbolic solution to soak for a day or two. When it was taken out and dried, the camel reek was still there, triumphant over the carbolic, and I remembered it from the knitting Mongol.

Once in Russia itself, my memories grow suddenly strong and clear. The background is vast, endless days of train travel across a flat wooded country, the trees of birch and pine, a weary dreary monotone, with very little change except the intervals, once or twice a day, when we stopped at a station for food and water. Then descending from the train I stared at the strange, wild-looking people, as different from the Chinese as they were from the Europeans I was to meet later. I had seen poverty in China and starvation in famine times and I was later to see poverty in my own country in city slums and in southern towns but never had I, nor have I since, seen poverty to equal that of pre-revolutionary Russia. I saw the poverty, although I was also to see the vast wealth of the nobles and the priests, but at first I thought all Russians were like the savage hungry people in the country, peasants and villagers clad in skins with the fur turned inside and filthy with crusts of aged dirt. Besotted ignorance was on the faces of these poor people, and a terrible despair, as though it was beyond their memory or their imagination that anyone had ever cared for them or ever could care for them, so that all they could think of was a little coarse food to stuff into their empty mouths. Yet they had their feelings, these wretched ones. They embraced one another, a man seizing his friend warmly in his arms and smacking kisses on his cheeks, and they talked with rough voices and laughed loudly in a childlike eager fashion.

I remember my father looking very sober indeed and saying to my mother, "Carie, this can't last. There'll be a revolution here within the next ten years—mark my words! People can't live like this and look like this without an explosion ahead."

When we reached Moscow we saw a different Russia. Here were plenty of poor people, too, but there were also rich and well-fed ones, wearing handsome furs and satins and English woolens. They rode in carriages or hired droshkies and they talked in French as easily as in Russian, and many of them lived in France or Italy, but especially in France, for most of every year. Moscow was a handsome city, far more interesting to me than Saint Petersburg, but what impressed me, and perhaps depressed me, were the vast cathedrals, those palaces wherein the priests were the ruling princes. The lights, the gold and the silver, the immense and cavernous groined ceilings and in the naves the gilded images and jewelled icons, the smouldering incense and the thousands of candles, were in terrifying contrast to the ceaseless stream of poor people who came in to pray, their sad faces brooding and yearning. And what really broke the heart was the worship of the relics, the bits of dead saints, the fingerbone, the wisp of hair, the fragment of dried skin, which the ignorant pressed to their lips. It made me weep because it was so hopeless, the prayers lost and all the suffering still there. No wonder that a day was to come when the people turned in frightful anger even against the priests. "The hungry sheep look up and are not fed."

And I wandered with my parents and a guide through the dark small rooms of the ancient parts of the Kremlin and I can still feel upon me the speechless weight of human history as the guide described the tortures of prisoners and the tribunal chambers under the Czars who had been despots, although the present family, he told us, was far more gentle than most of the Imperial Families had been, both the Czar and Czarina much absorbed with their children and especially with their son, the Crown Prince, who suffered from haemophilia. Yet it was this gentle family who a decade or so later was murdered by the angry people, who forgot their gentleness and remembered only that their rulers had done too little to make the lives of the people more bearable.

Even then, young as I was, I felt a fearful premonition of a world to come, when many innocent would suffer because of the anger of an outraged people. I remember hoping again and as usual, with a sort of awful fear, that my own would escape the punishment we did not deserve and that when the peoples of Asia rose up against the white

83

men who had ruled them, Americans could be recognized as different. It was possible that the day would come, and now it has come, and, alas, even American boys lie dead in the earth of Korea.

Years later, after the revolution had broken in Russia and Communism had taken it over, I was curious to know how the people fared. Time was then in the middle of the Second World War and Russia was a friend and an ally and not yet a potential enemy to the United States, and we still had the will to understand each other. I did not want to go to Russia again, however. I cannot speak the language, and unless I can speak the language of a country I find myself constricted and consequently impatient. Moreover, I had already a deep distrust and fear of Communism, for by then I had seen its effects in China. Yet I knew that the average people of any country judge their government by what it does for them and not by its theory, and remembering the misery I had seen in Russia thirty years before, it seemed to me at that time quite possible that the new Russian government might have improved the lot of the common man. At least it could not be worsened. I sought and found, therefore, a Russian woman in New York, one young enough to have grown up under the new regime and yet old enough to have been born under the old, and we became friends. Our long discussions were so interesting to me that I put them verbatim, though arranged and edited, into a short book, entitled *Talk About Russia*. There Masha, the daughter of Russian peasants, told me the story of her life as a child and a young girl in a new Russia entirely strange to me. I could never have endured its restrictions, and yet I could see, nevertheless, that Masha had lived a better—that is, an easier —life than had her parents, and if I felt that the tyrannies of the new regime were intolerable, I had to agree that at least there were compensations in food and opportunities for education. Thus Masha's parents were illiterate but she and her brothers and sisters all went to college at the expense of the State. It was easy to understand her enthusiasm for her own country as we wrote our book together.

Even so, we differed often. For example, when we came to the matter of the right of free speech, so dear to an American, Masha could not understand why I felt it was an essential for happiness as well as for democracy.

"You Americans are always wanting so much to talk!" she exclaimed. "Why do you need always to talk?"

And we differed, too, on the absolutes of right and wrong as well as on the right to one's own beliefs. For example, two books on Russia had just been that year published, both by American writers. One was favorable, the other unfavorable to the Soviet system. This Masha could not understand.

"One of the two is right and therefore the other is wrong," she declared with indignation. "The one that is right should be kept, the other should be abolished."

"But Masha," I reasoned, "every American has the right to decide for himself which book is true."

"And if some decide one is true and some decide the other is true?" she inquired.

"They have the right to differ," I said.

"You call it the right, I call it the confusion," she retorted.

To such discussion there can be no end. We were in this way as far apart as our two countries, and yet we became dear friends, and have so remained, accepting our difference.

Not long ago, however, I asked Masha how she felt now about Russia. She has lived a long time in the United States as a citizen and the wife of a well-known American, and years have passed since our book was published. And she is very changed, in many ways, from the girl who had come, so young and so Russian, to live in New York. She had longed for her own country and had been homesick until her husband let her go to visit her Russian family, "not knowing," he told me, "when I put her on the train, whether I would ever see her again."

And on the train, Masha told me, she was set back, and not to say shocked, because some Russian officers who were her compartment mates treated her as an American instead of a fellow countrywoman.

"Did you visit your parents, Masha?" I asked.

Her mother and father had been central figures in our book together. They had reminded me of other peasant couples I had known in China, and though I had never seen them, I had grown fond of them. Mother had been the typical humble Russian peasant wife until the revolution came and then she had caught at the one straw which she could use, which was that women and men were to be equal. The next time Father raised his hand to emphasize a command by a blow she had stood her ground. "I have the same equality you have and I am not afraid," she had told Father. "Father was better to Mother after the revolution," Masha had said, "so he stopped beating her. When he was mad he still threatened her, but he was afraid to touch her."

"I did visit my parents," Masha now replied. "And they were well and happy and glad to see me. They are old and retired but they live comfortably."

She laughed, her grey eyes crinkling. "Do you know what Father said to me the first thing? He had seen our book. Someone had read it aloud to him, and so he said, reproachfully, 'Masha, your book was su nice, but only one thing was not nice. Why did you tell all those Americans how I beat Mother? I didn't beat her so very hard!'"

We both laughed and then Masha was serious. "As for other things, I found them not altogether the same. Someone's husband, whom I knew, someone near to me, was sent away to Siberia for making criticism of the government. Nine years he must stay and still he did not come back when the years were over. So my friend went to look for her husband in Siberia and she found him in the labor camp, very thin and sick, and still working, and when she complained, the commissar laughed and said, 'Oh, yes, it is time for him to go home—I forgot it—' and they let him go and she thought they could now go home where the children waited. But when they reached the border they were stopped and told that never could they leave Siberia. This happens now and I could not believe it would have happened before when I was in Russia. And I know another friend who hides because he too had said something about Stalin and it was known."

She sighed. "Perhaps revolutions are only good at first—I don't know. But now I just live here quietly in America, not thinking at all about politics or such things, but only to be a good wife to John and a good mother to the children and to make the garden and so on. I have some roses, too, in my small greenhouse John made for me. Certainly my life is good now."

And so Masha, too, could not tell me about Russia today. I have only the memory of that old country as I saw it decades ago, and all that happens has been and is the fulfillment of the inevitable, the premonition that lay so darkly upon me even when I was only a young girl.

And then we were in Poland, in the great beautiful city of Warsaw, where so much history and destruction have since taken place, and then in Berlin, and I could feel no quivering of its foundations. Yet only a few years later it became the storm center for the First World War. Paris lay dreaming in beauty that summer and if any Frenchman guessed what lay ahead in fewer years than could be counted upon the fingers of one hand he did not show it. I felt no more premonitions after we had left the dark Russian land. Europe was only a pleasure ground, and England when we went there was a bulwark. Uneasy though I had often been through my childhood when I watched the doings of individual Englishmen in Asia, I felt nothing in London and in the little English towns and villages except a life as solid as the globe itself. I used to watch, as a very small child, the bearers from the wharfs of river steamers on the Yangtse as they carried bags of sugar from the English ships that had come in from Java and bales of cotton from

India and boxes of tinned butter from Australia. Those were heavy loads and the thin wiry figures of the Chinese men, naked to the waists, trembled under their weight. Every man had a tally stick when he left the hulk to which the ship was tied, and this tally stick had to be checked by an Englishman, sitting in a comfortable chair at a table under an umbrella on the street that ran along the Bund of the British Concession. Too thoughtful a child I doubtless was, for I was troubled by the sad humility of the brown men and the cold impartial calm of the white man. I was troubled because the load was too heavy and the white man did not care that it was, and because I knew each bearer was poor and I could imagine his family, working and perhaps living on one of the little river sampans, and I knew where the white man lived. He lived, he and his wife and his son, Tony, in a fine brick house plastered white, and surrounded with cool verandas and standing in a compound full of flowers and shade trees. The contrast was very troubling indeed, and that trouble has followed me all the days of my life. I thought of it in England, so compact and so beautiful and safe as it was, and I wondered if the English people knew, and of course they did not know or dream that the very safety of the loveliest country in the world depended upon the feelings between that brown burden bearer far away and that white man who checked his tally stick. And this trouble I carried with me to my own country, not full-blown but folded like a tight bud in the core of my heart.

Before we left Europe, however, we went to Switzerland, a country for which my mother had a great love, partly because of its natural beauty but most of all, I think, because there three different peoples had agreed to live together in peace with themselves and the world. There, too, she had found comfort in earlier years after the loss of her two daughters and her son, all so small, who had not survived swift and deadly tropical diseases, one after the other dying so quickly that she had not been able to recover. Now we spent months in a pleasant little pension near Neuchâtel, and my mother sent me to a French school to improve my French accent.

I do not remember such things, I fear, as school. What I see is the pension family of decayed gentility, Madame La Rue, a thin little widow in perpetual black, seated at the head of her scanty table and with much dignity serving the watery soup as though it were vichyssoise, while Monsieur, her eldest son, sat at her right hand to measure each ladleful with his sharp dark eyes. I came to grief with them both in the garden one day when I picked a blackberry and ate it. Monsieur saw me through the parlor window and reported the crime to Madame his mother, and she came out and with the utmost courtesy informed me that the guests were not supposed to pick the fruits. I apologized, burning red, for I had not meant to rob anyone, but only to give myself the joy of eating a berry fresh from the vine.

And I remember that a Russian countess and her two daughters had rooms at the pension also, and that they complained bitterly of the meager menu, and that neither Madame nor Monsieur paid the slightest attention to them, Madame, indeed, turning her fine worn profile away and conversing with her son on the right as though Russians did not exist. I had then long thick blond hair, and one day my mother sent me to the hairdresser with the Russian lady, who wished also to have "the hairs of my daughters washed," as she put it. At the hairdresser's she sat waiting and watching and talking without stay, while her daughters were tended, and when my hair was loosed from its braids and brushed and combed with a fine toothcomb, as the "hairs" of her daughters had been, she exclaimed because my hair was "clean," as she put it.

"Never," she said in her fervent fashion, "have I seen the hair long and thick, so, but without the insects!"

She beamed admiration and incredulity, and I was too shy to declare that we never had insects, lest her feelings be hurt. Looking back upon her robust and cheerful personality, I doubt she could have been hurt by anything.

And I remember, still instead of improvement in my French, that there were huge black cherries for sale in the countryside about Neuchâtel and one day we bought a bagful, my little sister and I, and we ate the half of them before we discovered minute white worms in them. We could not refrain from examining each of the remaining cherries and we found worms in every one, and so we had to believe the worst, gloomy as it was.

Such small scenes took place against an immense background of scenery, the blue lake at Geneva, the waters of Lucerne, and above all the high white Alps.

On the ship crossing to America I spent more thoughtful hours, perhaps, than I had ever before. My mind was full of all I had seen in Russia and Europe and of the talk that I had with many people wherever I went. I was a shy young girl, not used to young people of my own age and race, but I was drawn easily into human lives partly by my own curiosity but more, I think, by imagination which led me to understand feelings and thoughts and compelled me to conversation. I learned early that people are always ready to tell their opinions and troubles and problems and these drew my deepest and unfailing interest, wherever I was. I left the continent of Europe with a fairly clear idea of the peoples there, and especially, perhaps, of England and the English people, whom I could not keep from loving, now that I knew them, although when I saw them in China I had always taken sides against them with the Chinese.

What I realized was that these pleasant peoples, and especially the wonderful English, had no knowledge and therefore no conception of what their representatives in Asia were doing to destroy them. These peoples were living, each in their own beautiful country, entrenched each in their own civilization, without the slightest foreboding of what I knew then was inevitable, the uprising of Asia against them. When I talked with my father about this one evening while we were still on the ship, he said something which I never forgot. "The uprising," he said, "will begin in Russia, for there the people are oppressed not by foreigners but by their own rulers. The Russians are the most miserable and wretched people on earth today, and there the world upheaval will first show itself. It is clearly foretold in the Scriptures and it will come to pass. When it breaks in Russia it will spread to other countries of Asia, and because men of the white race have been the oppressors, all the white race must suffer."

I remember the fear that fell upon me and then the passionate pity for those pleasant and endearing people in England and Europe, and I said to my father,

"Can't we tell them? Can't we warn them?"

He shook his head. "They have their prophets," he said.

I knew he was thinking of the Biblical story, a sort of parable, of the man who, in hell for his sins, wanted to send a warning to those he loved, who were still upon the earth, that they might escape his fate, and God's stern reply was that they had their prophets and would not heed them.

My father and I did not often talk together. He was in some ways an unbending man. One had to enter his world of intellect and religion, for he never left it. But that evening we understood each other. And then because I was on my way to my own country, so unknown and yet so eagerly longed for, now that I knew the old days in China were gone forever, I could not keep from asking him the old question I dreaded to hear him answer.

"But Americans won't have to suffer, will they? We have no colonies —no real ones, like India—and we have no concessions in China, and we are using the indemnity money from the Boxer Rebellion for Chinese students in American colleges, and we have done so much good for the Chinese people—hospitals, schools, food in famines—"

He listened to this with a quiet patience and then he said, "We must never forget that missionaries went to China without invitation and solely from our own sense of duty. The Chinese therefore owe us nothing. We have done the best we could, but that, too, was our duty and so they still owe us nothing. And if our country has taken no concessions, we have kept silent when others did, and we too have profited from the unequal treaties. I don't think we shall escape when the day of reckoning comes."

A chill came over me when he said this and I feared that he was right. Today, worlds later, though we are innocent, we Americans, of the guilt of the weight of history of the white man in Asia, we are not innocent of the guilt of silence. The burden of Asia has fallen upon us, and for what other white men have done, we too must suffer.

Green Hills Farm,
Pennsylvania

I entered America in September, 1910, with a sober heart and a mind too old for my years. We had used up all our days in England and there was none to spare and so we travelled directly to the town where my college was. I had originally hoped to go to Wellesley and had taken the examinations for entrance there, but my Southern relatives, still haunted by the War between the States, had objected sufficiently by letter to my parents so that a compromise had to be made between a Yankee college and the Southern finishing schools against which I rebelled. A Southern college for women, Randolph-Macon, was chosen for me. My mother approved it because the education there was planned to be exactly what a man would get. After being married to my father for thirty years she had developed into an ardent feminist, and I must say with cause. My father, who based all his acts upon Biblical precedent, followed strictly some careless remarks made centuries before by Saint Paul, in which that saint stated flatly that as Christ was head of the Church, so man was head of the woman. My mother had an intrepid and passionate nature, but my father was a monument of calm, and as usual the monument won. In our home my father was the head, and although my mother battered at him, he held his position. To her eloquent and sometimes angry assaults on the subject of being a woman, as for example when she felt that the family bank account, always slim, should be a joint account so that she could draw checks as well as he, he never answered anything more violent than a quiet protest, "Oh, now, Carie, don't talk that way!"

The result of years of defeat, although she never acknowledged subjection, was that my mother determined to give her daughters every possible advantage over their future husbands, and so she was charmed by the idea of educating me exactly as though I were a boy.

Arrived at Lynchburg, Virginia, I found my college to be a collection of red brick buildings, still new enough to look raw, at least to my eyes accustomed to years of the finest and most cultivated scenery in the world, which certainly the best Chinese landscapes are. Within those buildings there was no beauty to be found, and the minimum even of comfort. I can measure how long ago that was when I return now occasionally to visit my college and find it mellowed with beauty everywhere and a place already enriched by tradition. In my day, however, it was stark, and it was hard to have no beauty to look at as I came and went along the wide halls down which the only carpeting was a strip of dull brown linoleum, thick as leather. But other promises were fulfilled. We were soundly taught and the curriculum carried no hint that we were young women and not young men. We were not corrupted by home economics or dressmaking or cookery or any such soft substitute for hard thinking. We were compelled to take sciences whether we liked them or not, and mathematics and Latin were emphasized and excellently administered. Each year the student body petitioned for a course in home economics, for in that day no girl thought it possible that she might not marry, and each year the faculty sternly refused to yield to the request. The theory was, and I think it entirely correct, that any educated woman can read a cookbook or follow a dress pattern. It is the brain that needs education and it can teach the hands. I was proud of my college when I discovered recently that while the students still petition each year for a course in home economics, the faculty still refuses to yield.

Of my college days I remember shamefully little and this is no one's fault except my own, for my life was limited by my personal situation. My parents returned to China immediately after depositing me and I had no home for the next four years. My life was confined, therefore, to the college buildings. True, my elder brother was married and was living in the same town, but unhappily there was a shadow over his house, and I did not enter it willingly. The greatest sacrifice of my college life was in my senior year, when he wished to take a new job in a distant city, and not wishing to leave his children he asked me to live in his house instead of in the college buildings. I loved him and we were understanding friends, and I loved his two attractive children, and I did what he asked, but it was a hard year, and for me tragic, because it was my first insight into the danger which besets any marriage when the man and woman are too unlike in their background of birth and education. Yet I did not learn enough to save myself, some years later, from the same mistake.

But it is too soon to speak here of marriage. When I look back from this distance upon those four college years, I see them as an experience, divided again by my different worlds. I had grown up in Asia, a region of the globe in which my college mates had not the slightest interest and certainly of which they had no knowledge and this fact lent me an aura of strangeness, more unkindly called queerness, which after a short time I perceived well enough in their attitude toward me. With some fortitude I saw that unless I did something about it, I would spend four lonely and unhappy years, for no one is more cruel than the young American female unless it be the young American male, and that it was carelessness rather than conscious cruelty only made the cruelty seem the more severe, especially as I had been reared in a culture where human relationships were the first concern. It took some weeks of thinking to orient myself in this new culture of complete individualism. Meanwhile I could not complain of lack of notice—rather, the opposite, for I had too much attention. Girls came in groups to stare at me, and I soon began to understand the detachment of the only Chinese girl in the student body, a senior, who came and went with friendly indifference to her fellow students. In their way they were even fond of her, but while she accepted their good intentions she never yielded herself. I was not satisfied with her position. I wanted to belong to my own kind and to belong, as I soon saw, meant that I must separate my two worlds again. I must learn to talk about the things that American girls talked about, boys and dances and sororities and so on, and I must look like them, and above all I must conceal the fact that inside me was a difference that I could not escape, even if I would.

After reflection I decided to live as fully as possible in my college world, to achieve as far as I could its modest awards, and above all to enjoy everything. The first necessity was to buy myself some American-made clothes, and so I put away the fine Chinese linen and silk dresses with which my mother had outfitted me. They had been made with affectionate care by our Chinese tailor and he thought he had copied them faithfully from models my mother showed him in *The Delineator*. But I soon saw that there was an infinite difference between his dresses and those my college mates wore, and not the quality of the linen and the silk nor the exquisite perfection of his embroidery and drawn work could compensate for the questionable fit of his sleeves and the wrong length of the skirts. I bought a few American dresses and I put up my hair, which I still wore in a thick braid doubled up and tied with a ribbon, and instead of the handmade leather shoes made by our Chinese cobbler I bought American ones. Externally I became an American. I learned the proper slang and exclamations, and by the end of my freshman year, I was indistinguishable from any other girl of my age and class. And so I joined my world.

I was happy enough at college, although often I was desperately lonely without my family and my home. Vacations were a misery, for I felt obligated to go to my brother's house, and there was the inescapable shadow, mitigated only by the sweetness of the little children. The long summer vacation was a blank to be filled somehow, and I filled it the first year by going to see my uncles and aunts and cousins. They were kind, but remote indeed from any life I had ever known, and while I loved the countryside and the magnificent Allegheny Mountains rising behind my grandfather's house like a stage backdrop, yet I did not know how to communicate with my American family. They were immersed in their own life, very naturally, and while I tried to share it, yet it was strange to me, and many of the things we had to do, the visiting, the afternoon calls, the small daily household tasks, seemed trivial and uninteresting, and the talk, lively as it was, incurably local. I had been accustomed to world thinking and world living and it was hard to center in the little town. Yet I learned to enjoy it, as I might enjoy for the moment the reading of a closely knit family novel or watching a play, and I began to see the drama of personalities in close range. My grandfather, so completely the head of the family, was dead by then, and his place was taken by my elder uncle, a gentle and kindly man, black-haired and black-eyed as my mother's people were. There was a haunting physical resemblance to my mother in all my aunts and uncles proper, and this drew me to them. Yet they were all different from my mother, and sometimes I fancied in them an unexpressed disapproval of her because she had left the family and gone so far away—and to be a missionary! We were not missionary folk by ancestry, and perhaps they did not quite forgive my mother for being different from the rest of them, and I do not know why she was. She was talented enough to have been anything she chose, but some emotional discontent must have made her impetuously willing at a certain moment in her life to give up her pleasantly comfortable home and follow my father across the world, for her soul's sake, whatever else the reason. With the family I went on Sundays to the white-spired Presbyterian church where my father's eldest brother was the minister and I did all that I could to seem like everyone else, while I knew I never could be, however I tried. Meanwhile I lost my heart to my country itself. The cleanliness which made it safe to drink water unboiled, the freedom from the possibility of dysentery and cholera which made it pleasant to pluck an apple from a tree and eat it skin and all, the abundance of water to bathe in, the spaces wherein no one lived, the miles of fields and lawns and country-side, the coloring of autumn forests, all these won my heart.

One thing I could not understand and do not yet and this was the apparent lack of interest or curiosity in Americans about other countries and peoples. I remember my wonder that my college mates never asked me about China, or what the people there ate and how they lived and whether China was like our country. So far as I can remember, no one ever asked me a question about the vast humanity on the other side of the globe. Certainly no member of my family asked me anything, and years later I remember my father, too, returning after half a century in China for a last visit to his family, coming back again sorely hurt be-cause none of his family had asked him any questions about the people to whom he had given his life. More decades later when I came to America to live, I found the same incuriosity or disinterest, and today, after I have made my home for twenty years here in as pleasant a com-munity as can be found anywhere, I have to report that still I have never found an everyday American in the least interested in any of the ways of life of Asia. No farmer has ever asked me about the Chinese farming, or the crops that are harvested there, no doctor has ever in-quired of the interesting and indeed invaluable medical knowledge of Chinese physicians, no housewife has ever asked me how Chinese women do their work, and no American boy or girl has ever asked me how the Chinese young people live. True, sometimes when I am asked to talk to school children, their teachers prompt them and they ask proper little questions and forget what I answer. Once in New York, in a lecture in the Town Hall series at eleven o'clock in the morning, an hour when ladies of leisure and cultivation attend, I gave what I hoped was a penetrating analysis of Chinese thought upon modern problems, and at the end of the time allotted me I waited for questions. There was one question. It came from a portly old lady in the front row. She wanted to know whether the chop suey she ate in Chinese restaurants in New York was really a Chinese dish. I told her it was not. I must admit that questions do follow a lecture, but they are more likely to be political than human.

This lack of interest in other peoples would be of no importance, per-haps, except that it limits the field of mental enjoyment, were it not for the fact that the United States is at a crucial point in her history. It has already been disastrous that we have not known and therefore have not understood other peoples, and especially the peoples of Asia, so that again and again we have lost opportunities for influence. It is almost too late, I fear, to expect other opportunities, but I hope that it is not quite too late. Yet I doubt that the habitual indifference of our people can be changed in a decade or even in a generation. People do not change easily anywhere.

Long ago when I was in college I pondered upon this aspect of my college mates and it was reflected even in their parents when I went home with them occasionally for visits. But I was young and I shut out of my mind the danger and the possible results, and I went on to enjoy myself as an American girl. By my sophomore year I had my techniques established and was able to feel a genuine interest in the activities of the group, except that I could never be deeply concerned over sports. The competitive instinct was either not born in me or my childhood in China had not developed it. Thus it did not seem to me of the slightest importance who won a game, and in sports therefore I did not shine. I was inclined, too, to waste little time on studies I did not enjoy, such as Latin, mathematics and physics, and stole hours from them to spend in the library reading books I had always wanted to read and had not found before at my hand. I read prodigiously, extravagantly and greedily, in season and out, and certainly lowered my general level of grades thereby. But here, too, my noncompetitive nature prevented me from trying to get higher grades than others. When I did so, it was accidental. Years later I went back to visit my college, and I found a legend among the freshmen that I had once failed an English course. It was not true, but when I observed what a comfort it was to them to believe it, I had not the heart to spoil it. What did it matter whether I had failed it or not?

By my junior year I was sufficiently American to be elected president of my class, and then I had really to identify myself with my college mates in fairness to them. That was the best year of my college life and I enjoyed it. Other honors came my way, I do not remember them all now, but they had their part in my happiness and I was too innocent or young or unconcerned to realize that many honors do not make one better loved. Such revelation and premonition of the future came in my senior year, when, needing some extra money, I competed for prizes for the best short story and the best poem of the year and won them both. I was glad for the cash and not, I think, unduly impressed by the honor, since I had written stories and poems equally badly, I am sure, as long as I could remember. But what astonished and wounded me was that in the congratulations of my fellows I discerned a slight hostility, a hint of complaint that one person had been given the two best prizes. Upon reflection, I felt the justice of this, and yet what could I say?

Of my senior year I can remember very little that is pleasant or that added to my growth. I lived off campus at my brother's house and I was burdened with a secret my brother now shared with me, that he had decided upon a divorce. He asked me to write to my parents and I did so, and they wrote back in such horror and shock that he postponed the whole matter for several more years. Our families on both sides were extremely conservative in every way, and there had never been a divorce in our history. To my parents it seemed unthinkable that their son, particularly, should commit such a sin. My mother wrote to me, weeping, as I could see from the tear splotches on the paper, and blaming herself that she had sent my brother to America at fifteen.

We met in secret, my brother and I, and talked long hours, and after much thought the decision for postponement was made, for the sake of our parents. True to his decision, he did not seek divorce until after their death, years later, although he lived separately and alone in the intervening years, except for visits from his growing children. This crisis of personal life so near me was an isolating experience, for it meant that the normal life I might have had in my bother's home during the years I was in America was denied, although I gained in the knowledge of human nature and the difficult and delicate relationships of marriage.

So I came to the end of college and took my place in the long procession of graduates. I received my diploma, lonely to know that my parents were not in the chapel crowded with other parents, although by then I was used to loneliness of that sort, at least. Summing it up, I am amazed at how little I learned in college. No one except myself was to blame for this, I am sure. College was an incident in my life and out of its main stream, an experience which remains incidental. My attempt, successful enough in its own way, to be like other American girls, was not permanent, I fear, and after my graduation I was faced with my two worlds again. Which should I choose? Should I stay to become permanently American or should I go home again to China?

All during the days of packing and farewells, I pondered this choice. I wanted to stay, that I knew. Between the two countries my heart chose my own, for I was beginning now to understand that beyond the college walls was a whole country I still did not know, although it was mine and I was born to it. I had my living to earn but that was no problem and I felt secure enough in myself. I could choose among several teaching jobs, including one to remain on in the college as an assistant in psychology with the professor under whom I had majored. Already during my senior year I had been a minor assistant to the extent of helping him correct freshman papers and examinations. Yet my conscience moved me to return to my parents. I did not want to be a missionary, for I knew I could never preach or persuade people to change their religion. I had seen enough of that dangerous business in years gone by. Moreover, I had not the spiritual attitudes which could make it possible for me to proclaim my religion superior to all others. I had seen too many good people who were not Christian, and, as my father used to remark, it took the arrogance out of anybody to have to acknowledge that the best Christian converts were always good people anyway, the best Buddhists or Mohammedans or Taoists or what not, even before their conversion to Christianity.

One day a letter came from my father that my dearly loved mother had been taken with sprue, a tropical disease which at that time no physician knew how to cure and scarcely to treat. Yet it was a slowly fatal disease, robbing the blood of its red corpuscles until in the end the victim died of a deadly anemia. My mind was made up on the instant. I wrote to the Presbyterian Board of Foreign Missions under whom my parents worked and asked to be sent to China as a teacher, and I packed my bags and prepared to sail as soon as I could get passage. I did not think of my return as permanent, but only until my mother was well again, or if she did not get well, then until—but that end I could not face.

No sooner was my passage assured than there came a letter from the Board saying that war threatened in Europe and all passages abroad would be postponed until it was clear to what extent our country would be involved. It is an example of the remoteness of our college life that this news came to us all like a thrust of lightning. We had been studying European history, and yet our study had not prepared us for the uprising of the Germanic peoples in an effort to control the European continent. Our history professor had, it is true, spoken of such a possibility, years hence, but none of us thought of it as part of our lifetime. To me it came with special foreboding, for I saw it as the beginning of the inevitable struggle between East and West, the inflaming incident for a long period of war. Yet I persuaded myself, or tried to, that the murder of an uninteresting archduke in a little European town could not ignite the world. But I did not understand how charged and supercharged were the feelings beneath that small incident, meaningless in itself. It was the touching off of the tinder of human hostilities and fire lit fire around the globe.

Meanwhile I could only cable my parents, unpack my bags and settle down. I accepted the assistantship at college as the easiest job, making it clear that I could only take it with the understanding that at any moment I must be allowed to resign and go home to my sick mother. Thus I began the task of teaching freshman psychology to the incoming class of girls from all over the country. There was no necessity now to be one of them. I was their teacher, and being so young it was all the better if I carried my head high and kept my distance.

In November my mother was worse, and by dint of anxiety and pressure, although the war loomed darker than ever, I persuaded the Presbyterian Board to let me go home anyway. A classmate and close friend generously came to take over my job, and I set forth alone across the wide spaces of land and ocean to return to the country I had known better than any other, and yet which had changed very much in the four years that I had been away. I began again to think in Chinese. During the four years I had not spoken a single word of Chinese, for our one Chinese student came from Shanghai and did not speak Mandarin, and I did not know her dialect. Chinese was my first language, but for the college years I had spoken only my second language, English, and I had unconsciously absorbed the soft drawl of Virginia speech. I remember that a young American on the ship corrected my pronunciation even of the word China, which he insisted I called "Chahna."

He was a meticulous young man, on his way to the Philippines to work for the Standard Oil Company, and during the idle weeks on the ship, he was part of my American education. I had known a few American men merely as casual companions, but he was another sort. Somewhere along the way we decided firmly, at first individually and then together, that while we would be friends on the ship we would not continue our friendship after parting at Shanghai, and we did not. I do not remember why we came to this stern decision, for nothing was serious between us, but I imagine that it had to do with his contract and certainly with my own determination not to get myself involved with anybody until the question of my mother's life was settled. But ship friendships are brittle stuff, and certainly the magic of the wide Pacific ended abruptly when the yellow waters of the Yangtse rushed out to muddy the blue.

At any rate, reality began for me when the tall thin figure of my father and the little figure of my younger sister appeared upon the pier to meet me. The very fact of my mother's absence struck me to the heart. Neither of them had the slightest ability to tell less than the truth. She had not been well enough to come to Shanghai, but she hoped to meet me at the train in Chinkiang.

I read many warnings nowadays against too deep an attachment between parents and children, and I am sure that such dangers are overrated. There should be a deep attachment, heart should be tied to heart between parent and child, for unless the child learns how to love a parent profoundly, I believe that he will never learn how to love anyone else profoundly, and not knowing how to love means the loss of the meaning of life and its fulfillment. I loved both my parents but at different times and in different ways. During my childhood all my love went to my mother, and I felt very little for my father, even going to the extent of remarking one day at the age of eleven that I hated him. My mother rebuked me but there was no other fuss made about it and my father, although he had overheard me, said nothing. I was not made to feel wicked or ungrateful and so I continued to hate my father mildly until I was old enough to appreciate him, which was not until I was grown. During the years when he was seventy to eighty years old, I adored him and found him delightful and charming, affectionate and amusing, and he knew it and expanded in the friendly atmosphere between us. Yet it was not my fault nor his that we had both to wait until such an age for mutual understanding. He did not know earlier how to accept my world and I did not know how to enter his. We had to grow together in time and maturity, and I am glad he lived long enough for that.

My love for my mother was a thing apart. It was rooted in my blood and my bones. I felt her every pain, I knew when she was wounded, and she was wounded always too easily, so that toward the end of her life she suspected people unfairly of wanting to hurt her, and while I knew this was wrong and I argued against her judgments, yet I could not forgive the ones who wounded her even when they did not know what they did. I wanted her to have the happiest life possible for a human being, and this desire was perhaps made the more passionate because I discerned, although she never acknowledged it, that as she grew older she was desperately homesick for the land she had left too young. It was impossible for her to return, she could not leave my father, and she could not cross the ocean again with her weak heart and enfeebled frame.

How weakened she was I had not been able to imagine until I saw her at the railway station in Chinkiang. There she stood, and instead of the strong upright figure I had remembered, wearing her thick white hair like a crown, her dark eyes bright, her lips firm, I saw a small little lady, very dainty in dress as always she was, but shrunken and tiny, so tiny that I lifted her up in my arms when I ran to her.

"Mother, how little you are!" I cried.

"Daughter, how big you are!" she retorted, laughing.

My heart trembled at her fragility and I tried not to weep and she saw it and made me turn to greet the crowd who had come to welcome me, my old Chinese friends, my English Agnes and her family, a few American missionaries, our servants and neighbors. What a heart-warming home-coming it was, with all of them trying to hug me at once and clinging to my hands and making speeches and giving me flowers and little gifts and packages of Chinese spongecakes and sesame cookies! It was a mild and glorious afternoon although the season was late November and we lingered so that I could speak to everyone and the station gang gathered around to stare and remark upon our goings on. I was home again, even though during the years I had been away the compound in which I had grown up had been given over to a boys' school and the old bungalow torn down to make place for a new two-story modern dormitory. My parents had moved to another hill and another modest mission house had been built for them. But the hills and the valleys were the same, and as we walked along the familiar roads of beaten earth, the farmers looked up from the fields and saw me and put down their hoes and came to speak to me and their wives and children ran out of the earthen houses to call to me.

"And have you come back?" they shouted. "It is good—it is good."

And when we came to the new house, unfamiliar though it was to me, I found that my mother had set aside for me the pleasantest upstairs room, facing the distant river and overlooking the green valley. It was a bare room, I suppose, with the minimum of plain furniture and there were no rugs on the floor, but bowls of late roses stood on the desk and the dressing table, and my mother had made white curtains for the windows and my old bed was there and my childhood books were in a little bookcase built in the wall, and it was home again.

That night my mother and I sat long in talk and I made her tell me about herself and how it was that sprue had begun and then fastened itself on her, and unwillingly she showed me her poor mouth, sore and red, and told me that the vicious disease, a sort of fungus growth it was thought to be, was destroying the mucous membranes of her mouth and throat and intestines, so that it was painful for her to speak very much or to eat anything but the mildest of bland foods, and this she had hidden from me! I put my arms about her and wept, and she comforted me, saying that she intended to fight the disease with all her strength and get well again now that I was home, and I dried my eyes and swore myself to the task with her. I was glad I had chosen to come home and I was sure that I had decided rightly to leave America. It was not so much China that I chose. It was my mother's life.

My own life now was divided again. My daily duty, besides teaching in the new boys' school, and supervising seventeen to twenty young Chinese women who were being trained for various types of work in other schools, was to care for my mother. I took over the management of the house in order to relieve her, and in her place I carried on the work among women for which she was responsible. I could not and would not lead religious meetings, but my mother did not do much of this sort of thing herself. She was too sensitive to impress upon others directly the advantages even of the religion in which she still fervently believed. Her meetings were usually friendly gatherings where the women told of their difficulties and problems and opportunities and needs, and my mother endeavored as best she could to fulfill each demand. I was too young to take her place, but I could listen and promise to get her advice for the next meeting. It was an invaluable experience thus to hear Chinese women open their hearts because of their faith in my mother and I was always touched and moved at their acceptance of me in her place.

Beyond this I made a fierce and determined attack upon the disease which threatened my mother, working with the doctors to learn all I could about it. Nothing but diet was then tried as a cure, and we experimented with all the known foods to find the one most suitable to her. Some victims professed to recover upon bananas and my long-suffering mother fed for months upon bananas, never a favorite food at any time with her. Then we heard that fresh strawberries were helpful and we set about the cultivation of strawberries. Milk, however, fresh raw milk, seemed to be the most approved food and how to get fresh raw cow's milk became my problem. I do not know whether it is only Chinese milkmen who are the most wily of their kind or whether milkmen everywhere are below the average of human beings in integrity. But certainly in those days it seemed impossible to find an honest milkman. The Chinese had never been used to drinking cow's milk, indeed the very idea of it was repulsive to them, partly because Buddhists considered that to drink milk was to rob the calf of its life, and partly because of the cow smell of those who drank milk, or so they declared. Yet cow's milk was beginning to be thought of as a Western source of health, and the more modern among the Chinese eagerly bought canned milk from American stores in Shanghai for their children. Human milk the Chinese had always considered beneficial for young children and old people but it was expensive and not suitable for the average person. A few enterprising Chinese therefore bought a cow or two and sold raw milk to foreigners. Sometimes the cows were only water buffaloes, and although their milk was good, it was scanty and very high in butter fat, too high for my mother's delicate digestion. All milk, of course, had to be boiled, and this destroyed much of its value. Also, boiled milk is very binding to the bowels and to exist upon a boiled milk diet is to complicate the system. How to get clean unwatered raw milk was my task, and knowing nothing about cows at that time, I conceived the idea of having the milkman lead his cow up the hill to our back yard and there milk her product into a pan before my eyes, after I had seen his hands scrubbed with hot water and soap and dipped into disinfectant. We did this for a few days, and still the milk seemed disconcertingly blue and thin. It was our faithful cook who asked me to observe closely one day that the milkman's dirty cotton sleeves hung down over his wrists. I did so, and discovered a thin rubber tube under his right wrist, and from that wrist ran a small stream of water into the milk pail. I stooped and twitched back the wide sleeve and disclosed a rubber hot-water bag which he had bought from some servant of a foreigner. It was filled with water. I was speechless and for a moment I could only look my reproach.

He was ashamed enough, though only for the moment, too, I fear, and then he said, "But I boiled the water, Little Sister—truly I boiled it, knowing that foreigners always drink only boiled water. Besides, the milk is so rich I feared it would make your honored mother ill."

We gave up on raw milk after that, and experimenting further we worked out a diet of rice gruel and fresh fruit juice and soft-boiled eggs and liver which served at least to prolong my mother's life, though she was never really well again during her few remaining years. Now, of course, doctors of tropical diseases know that sprue is a deficiency disease, and while the bananas and fresh strawberries and raw milk and liver were useful in providing some vitamins, far more were needed. But the knowledge came too late for my mother.

Outside this home battle I lived another life. I was intensely interested in my teaching, for my students were not children. They were senior high school students, and far more mature than Western boys of the same age. Many of them were already married men and some had children. I could treat them as adults, although I was not much older than they were. My task was to teach them English and in this tongue we attempted to carry on conversations upon the profound subjects which interested them. They taught me far more than I taught them. For, as I said before, while I had been away at college great things were happening in China. I had left in a period of confusion. The weak little Emperor Pu Yi sat upon the throne but with the passing of the doughty old Empress Dowager there had been no real ruler and the Manchu dynasty was near its end. As usual in such times, the Chinese people were waiting philosophically for a new head to appear and various local leaders were developing into war lords. It was a process thoroughly Chinese and essentially democratic, and tradition compelled the new ruler to do the best he could to comfort the people in order that his seat might be secure. The throne was seldom secure in the first generation, however, for the Chinese were accustomed to criticizing their rulers and they did not revere easily, any more than Americans do. By the second generation national affairs settled down, and the dynasty began to rise towards its full power.

This historical process I now found was disturbed. The war lords were swarming as usual when the dynasty came to an end, but there was no throne for a prize. While I had been peacefully at college a real revolution had been going on, fed by a dozen fires, but chiefly by the intrepid Sun Yat-sen. His name, of course, I had long known, but it was always surrounded by doubt, for no one knew what to think of him. He was the son of a village farmer in South China, but he had been sent to a mission school and when he was only a boy he had been taken to Honolulu by his elder brother, who was a merchant there. There, too, he had attended a Christian school and had seen American government at work. He was no mean missionary himself, for he soon conceived the vast notion of modernizing his country, not by education or by writing essays and translating books as the two famous scholars, Liang Ch'ih-ch'ao and K'ang Yu-wei, were doing in exile, but by inciting other Chinese to help him overthrow the throne and set up a republic based on the constitutional form of the Government of the United States. With this idea as big as a melon in his head, he had given up his profession as a doctor of medicine and set out as a sort of patriotic pilgrim to find Chinese in every part of the world and collect funds from them for his revolution. Meanwhile he hoped to persuade foreign governments to help him with the new China.

It was one of those mad dreams which can succeed only when the mood of many people is at the point of readiness to accept any hope of improving their state. The foreign governments, as was to be expected, only shrugged Sun Yat-sen off, but the Chinese overseas gave him all they had and put their faith in him. Exiled as they were by the demands of business, they were patriotic Chinese still and they longed to see their country strong and great and safe from colonization. They agreed with Sun Yat-sen that only modernization could save them.

The story of this remarkable man has been told so often that I am not inclined to repeat it here. In my sophomore year in college he did actually succeed in his dream. While he was travelling in the United States collecting his funds, the revolutionaries he had left behind him in his own country became impatient and rose up and overthrew the dynasty representatives in the province of Kiangsi and declared Sun Yat-sen the first President of the Republic of China. He saw the news in an American newspaper while he was on a train in one of the Western states. No one recognized him, of course, and it is fascinating to imagine his thoughts as he read that paper and saw his own name in great headlines while he sat in the dingy day coach, lonely and unknown. The anger of the Chinese people, meanwhile, had risen to its height and everywhere they killed the Manchus whom hitherto they had protected in contempt. In a letter my mother had written to me in 1911 she had said, "I look from the window this morning and see poor Manchu women and children hiding for their lives behind the graves on the hillside. I shall have to go out and see what I can do."

It was characteristic of my parents that while the American Consul had warned all Americans to leave for Shanghai until the trouble was over, lest the revolution take its usual anti-foreign turn, my parents did not go, and it is characteristic, too, that the Chinese said nothing when my parents helped the Manchus to escape death. It was a good deed, according to Chinese ethics as well as Christian, and they did not reproach my parents for saving the very people whom they themselves were killing. The paradox is part of Chinese human nature, but the explanation is that they believed that religion and religious acts were entirely individual responsibilities and privileges.

All these doings had seemed vague enough to me while I was at college, and I had not mentioned them to my college mates because it would have taken too much explaining. I should have had to go far back in world history and begin with the Portuguese sailing vessels pushing their way across the oceans in search of treasure in the East, and laying lasting hold on Goa in India and Macao in China and I should have had to tell of Spanish ships snatching the Philippines, and how, long after Americans drove the Spanish out, the Filipinos supposing meanwhile that we intended to give them independence, we had stayed for half a century bringing both good and evil to those islands. And I should have had to remind them that Columbus himself did not want to discover America, that it was only an accident in his search for the jewelled treasures of India, and I should have had to tell them that we Americans would not so easily have freed ourselves from the English in 1776 had not the East India Company at that very hour been discovering the extravagant wealth of India, so that England concentrated her effort there instead of upon thirteen little stretches of wilderness in an uncivilized continent. "You Americans owe us a great deal," my Indian friends are fond of saying to me today. "If the English had not discovered how much richer we were than you were in 1776, you would still be part of the British Empire." It may be true for all I know, for certain facts of history point in that direction. And I would have had to explain to my college mates the whole disgraceful story of the Western Powers and how they were still robbing the great peaceful countries of Asia, which on principle had never developed the use of gunpowder and modern weapons, and I should have had to explain about the Opium Wars and the Boxer Rebellion and the Unequal Treaties, the extra-territoriality whereby any white man walked the earth of China free from arrest by a Chinese authority. He could commit murder and rape and sometimes did and yet he could not be arrested because all white people had what amounted to diplomatic immunity. I should have had to explain the arrogance of the white man in Asia, unmatched, I believe, since the days of the cruel Roman Empire.

And how could I have explained the evolution of this history, clear though it was from the very first days of rapacious tradesmen and bigoted priests? My college mates had nothing in their experience wherewith to understand. All that they knew about China was that they had heard a missionary beg for money in a church so that he could teach the Chinese or feed them or buy Bibles for them and they thought of the great and beautiful country as a land of beggars and savages instead of the most ancient existing civilization in the world, with a culture older than any in Europe. So I did not explain. I read my mother's letters alone and pondered the changes which she described so vividly and then I put them aside to face when I returned.

Now, however, the struggle of Sun Yat-sen was a matter of daily study in the newspaper and daily talk with my Chinese friends. Could he organize a republic or not? If not, what would then happen? Would we have a throne again and a new Emperor and if so, who would he be?

Meanwhile as usual in the midst of political confusion the life of the Chinese people went on in its accustomed ways, with no ferment and no uproar. The greatest change that I could see outwardly was that the men and boys had their queues cut off, and their hair cut in Western fashion, since the queue had been a sign of subjection to the Manchu dynasty and that dynasty was ended. Even so, many a Chinese peasant clung to his queue and did not want to cut it off. He did not know why he had it, but his father and forefathers for generations had worn the queue and therefore it must be good. But peasants were overcome by the strong forces of revolution and young men, some of them my own students, stationed themselves at the city gates through which the farmers had to pass to carry their vegetable baskets and bundles of fuel to the markets, and when one wore a queue they sat him down on a stool and lectured him and cut off his appendage, even though he wept while they did so. In a matter of some years all the queues seemed to be gone, although when I was living in North China after my marriage a few years later, I still occasionally saw dusty-haired farmers from the back country with modest little queues curled under their felt caps, and now and then I found an old woman who did not know that the Empress Dowager was dead although she had been in her jewelled tomb for twenty years. I considered this ignorance remarkable at the time but have discovered since that it was not. The *New York Times* recently published the results of an American history test given to thousands of college freshmen throughout the United States. Among other amazing discoveries were these: that thirty percent of them did not know Woodrow Wilson was President during the First World War; that only six percent were able to name the first thirteen colonies—many even listed such states as Texas and Oregon; and a third of them did not know who was President during the Civil War. People everywhere do not concern themselves much beyond the common round of everyday, and this is the chief problem for a democratic government, whose success depends upon an informed and responsible citizenry.

There were many conservative and well-educated old Chinese, however, who heartily disapproved of Sun Yat-sen and the revolution and all the doings of the young people, and who wished the Throne back again. Some of them were friends of my parents, and while I heard the arguments of the young during the day in my classes, I had the other side from these older Chinese. I was hard put to it sometimes to answer the questions which the students asked in class. One of their favorites was to demand of me in halting English, which nevertheless improved daily, "Why does not your country give freedom to the Filipinos?"

I did not know why, but later the rising ambitions of Japan helped me and I could then reply, "If Americans leave the Philippines, the Japanese will come in. Would you rather have the Japanese?"

They had to acknowledge that they would not. At that time the United States was the most popular of the Western nations. In spite of resentment against our demand that we share the benefits of extraterritoriality and trade agreements, the Chinese did not fear us as an imperial power, for that was before the days of Communism, but they did very much fear the new strong Japan.

Yet even that Japan had, I knew, its roots in the old evil of empire and colonization. I had Japanese friends who insisted to me that the only way to insure Japan's continuing freedom was to make her too strong for any Western power to colonize.

"You must remember, my dear young lady," Mr. Yamamoto said to me one day. He was a rich merchant who had a home in our town as well as in Japan and he was responsible, as were others like him, for filling the Chinese shops gradually over the years with a plethora of cheap but remarkably good merchandise and driving out to the same extent the more expensive products of Britain and the United States. "You must remember," he repeated, wagging a long pale forefinger at me, "every Asian country has either been seized by a Western power, as India has been, or it has been despoiled and weakened by excessive demands and the Unequal Treaties and frightful indemnities as China has been. Only Japan remains free, and we are in great danger. We could never tolerate colonization. It is necessary, therefore, for us to make ourselves an empire as Britain has done, and China is the logical place for us to begin. We will develop China, we will not despoil her— it would not be to our interest."

What could I say? It seems to me now, looking back, that I spent those first years of my return in almost complete silence. I listened and could not reply. Sometimes even my father, impatient because of the lack of central government and the confusion of rising war lords and revolutionists in China, would exclaim that "it might be a good thing if Japan came in and cleaned China up."

To this I could and did make retort that I was sure it would not be a good thing. The Japanese and the Chinese are as nearly opposite in their national characteristics as it is possible for human beings to be. There is more difference between them than there is between any two peoples in the white race. Their geography has shaped their history, and their history could not be less alike. The Chinese are actually much more like the Americans, also a continental people, than they are like the Japanese who are an island people, and I knew that the Japanese, much as I liked and admired them and do still, would be tyrants if they were able to rule in China. They could never understand the Chinese, and not understanding, they would, out of fear and insecurity, try to rule by force and that, of course, the Chinese could not tolerate.

Many years later, on a bright Sunday afternoon in December in Pennsylvania I heard that Japanese bombs had fallen upon Pearl Harbor. I remembered instantly the words of Mr. Yamamoto, spoken so long ago, and again I saw the path of history clear from the very first Portuguese vessel that sailed the seas to maraud on the coasts of Asia to the Japanese ships of the air flying to destroy as much as they could of the strongest Western power in the world. Step by step, cause always preceding result, history marches on.

Young as I was in those early years, and filled with conflicting and youthful interests and impulses, I tried very hard to understand what was taking place in my worlds. I was lonely in many ways. My years in college had separated me from the Chinese girls with whom I had once been such close friends. They were all married and busy with household affairs, and they felt strange with me, perhaps because I had been away to college. They asked me a thousand questions for, unlike the Americans, the Chinese are full of curiosity about other peoples and will stop at nothing in the way of intimate detail, and I answered as best I could. Invariably our sessions together ended with the one important question they put to me anxiously, a very personal question—"When are you going to be married?"

"I don't know," I always replied.

The next question was also invariable and concerned. "Are your parents doing nothing about finding a husband for you?"

Without exception their parents had found husbands for them in the approved old Chinese fashion. It was still too soon for the later wave of impetuous rebellion of youth against traditional marriages, and a Chinese girl or young man would have been astonished and embarrassed to be told that she or he must find a mate. Marriage was a family affair, and the parents pondered with much care upon the nature of their child and the sort of person that should be found to complete his or her life. It was also essential that this person fit into the family group, for where the generations lived together in the old Chinese custom, it could only bring unhappiness if the new person did not fit into the circle, both in birth and breeding. The results of these arranged marriages were usually good. Most of them were happy, an even higher percentage, I think, than in the individualized and romantic marriages of the West. This is only to be expected, for marriage, after all, is basically a practical matter and romantic aspects pass into solid love and companionship. Usually love did develop after marriage, sometimes romantic and passionate love, but it was not an essential. Such marriages had perhaps the greater chance for survival because the expectations of romantic love were not as high as they are in the West.

At any rate, my Chinese friends were happily married and busy with babies, and although I was young enough they were troubled about my solitary state. As far as my own race went, I had no possible friends except my English Agnes, and she, alas, I had outgrown. The nearest American woman to me in age was thirty-five years old, a missionary's wife and the mother of three children. It was another generation. Nor was I allowed to accept the attentions of any of the few young white men in the British Concession in our city. Among them were even two or three Americans with the Standard Oil Company or one of the tobacco companies. I did accept their invitations at first without thinking, until one of the older missionary women in the narrow circle lectured me one day severely. "You cannot continue in both ways of life," she said solemnly. "If you go with the business people you must leave the missionary circle."

"I am not a missionary," I insisted. "I am a teacher."

"You are a teacher in a missionary school," she reminded me, "and your parents are missionaries."

"My parents don't mind," I persisted.

"The rest of us do," she retorted.

For the sake of my parents I refused all invitations from then on and scheduled my days severely between work and home. I began to study Chinese books and as my mother's health grew a little better I travelled about the country within walking and riding distance. My Chinese friends, however, were still concerned, and I know they talked with my parents about arranging a marriage for me. This resulted in a curious argument between my father, who had become far more Chinese in his mentality and feelings than he was American, and my mother, who remained American to the core. My father, it seemed, would have been pleased to have me marry a young Chinese gentleman of his own choice but my mother was wholeheartedly against it. I listened and reflected and did not take sides, for I saw no danger from the handsome and brilliant Chinese whom my father had in mind, since his family would not have tolerated his marriage to an American, even though she were my father's daughter. I decided, instead, since my mother's health was better, that I would like to go to some other part of China, and carve out my career alone.

I knew in my heart as I had always known, that someday I would be a writer, but I was not yet ready. I still felt empty. I know now, of course, that emptiness is the normal state of youth. No writer, I believe, should attempt a novel before he is thirty, and not then unless he has been hopelessly and helplessly involved in life. For the writer who goes out to find material for a novel, as a fisherman goes out to sea to fish, will certainly not write a good novel. Life has to be lived thoughtlessly, unconsciously, at full tilt and for no purpose except its own sake before it becomes, eventually, good material for a novel.

I did not want to travel to other parts of China to find material for writing but I did want to find more life. I was caught in too small a circle and I wanted to break away, as all young people do and should, from the childhood environment. I wanted to move out from being the child of my parents and make my own place among strangers. Yet it did not occur to me to go back to America, partly because I did not want to leave my mother at such a distance, for her malady was only better and not cured and it would never, I feared, be cured. Therefore I must be within distance of possible return. Beyond this, however, I was genuinely part of my Chinese world again, a new world changing from day to day, and China was destined, as even then I could see, to be a pivotal country in the future. She had always been a source country in culture, and India alone, although completely different, could be her rival. Now I wanted only to be free to live in China as I liked, in some place where I could escape the confines of dogmatic religion. Casting about I thought of a woman who had stirred my imagination ever since I had first heard of her. She lived alone in a distant and ancient city of the province of Yünnan, itself, I had always heard, a supremely beautiful part of a beautiful country. I sat down one day at the little Chinese desk in my room and wrote to Cornelia Morgan and asked her if she would let me come and work with her. Somehow or other, weeks later, her friendly reply fell into my mother's hands and then I saw a new aspect of my mother. She broke down and wept and said that if I went away she did not want to live and why was I dissatisfied here, where everyone loved me so much? And what would the Chinese say if I deserted my parents when they believed in filial piety?

I said, "But you left your home when your father did not want you to do it. Grandfather even forbade your marriage."

Her dark eyes were tragic. "I know it," she said, "and I did wrong. I wish I had obeyed him."

This was a terrifying revelation, and I was struck speechless. I neither promised to stay nor insisted upon going. I was simply silent, and a few days later she fell seriously ill again and the doctor said that someone must take her up the mountains of Lu, to Kuling. There was no one to do that except me, for my father would not have thought of leaving his work. I asked for leave of absence from my school and my mother and I boarded one of the clean little English river steamers and set sail for Kiukiang, where we would take sedan chairs for the climb up the mountains. My fate, at least for the time being, was settled.

The importance of Kuling in the lives of the white people in the central provinces of China must now be explained. There were other summer resorts, but none of them, we felt, compared with Kuling. It was much more than a summer resort, it was a lifesaving station, especially in the early years of my childhood before it was known how some of the worst of the tropical diseases, against which white people seemed to have no immunity whatever, were carried. I can remember the devastation of malaria, for example, from which the Chinese suffered and grew thin and yellow but from which they recovered far more often than the white people did. At the first rumor that mosquitoes were the carriers my father had promptly nailed cheesecloth over all the windows of our house, and people thought he had gone insane. As soon as he could buy wire screening from Montgomery Ward ours was the first house to have it. Cholera, the autumn menace, we knew was somehow carried by flies, and certainly conveyed by mouth, and I can remember how terrified my mother was lest we eat any raw fruit or anything indeed which had come from the Chinese markets until it was cooked, and how when an epidemic was raging, which was every autumn during my childhood, we never used even eating utensils until they had first been placed in briskly boiling water, and this at the table where my mother could supervise the process, and dishes and silverware were wiped with boiled dish towels kept by my mother. Yet none of us was easy from the middle of August until the first of October, and we children learned, on pain of death, not to put anything in our mouths, not even fingers, until boiling water or soap and water and disinfectant had been applied.

The death of children had really compelled white parents to find some place where families could go for the worst months of our tropically hot summers, and my father had been one of the little group of white men who explored the famous Lu mountains, where old temples had existed for centuries in a climate so salubrious that it was said the priests lived forever. I can still remember the day when I was a small child that my father came home from the expedition and reported that high in those mountains, six thousand feet above sea level, he had found the air as cold as early winter, though the season was midsummer. There was a rough stone road up the mountainside, carved no one knew how long ago by priests and pilgrims, and bamboo mountain chairs were available and the bearers were the neighboring farmers.

"The air up there is like the Alleghenies," my father said, "and the brooks run clear."

This was enough for my mother. Her joy in the thought of escaping the torrid months of summer and particularly the hot rainy season, when the rice fields were flooded and the mosquitoes swarmed, was something I can still see. We were among the first, then, to buy a plot of ground after negotiations had been made with the Chinese for us to do so—a long lease it was, actually, for foreigners could not own the soil of China. I remember our first little house, made of stone, for stone was the building material on those mountaintops where only low trees grew. The temples, too, were of stone and the pagoda on a neighboring peak was of stone.

As a child I took Kuling for granted, and every summer I gave up my birthday party in order that we might go there. My mother disliked leaving my father alone to cope with housekeeping in addition to his work, but her struggle always ended in favor of the children. I knew, each June, when the rice seedlings were transplanted from the dry beds to the flooded fields, that the time had come for Kuling. It was a time

I loved at home, too, for the valleys were beautiful, green lakes in the sunshine and mysterious by night under the moon. It was heaven for the frogs and the chorus of their croakings and pipings could be heard clearly even at our house.

The whole process of the growing of rice is a cycle of beauty, from the seedbeds, greener than any green on earth, to the last harvested golden sheaf. I was charmed always by every change, and especially by the transplanting, when the dry fields were filled with water and the farm family rolled up the legs of their blue cotton trousers and waded into the water and planted the seedlings neatly and exactly spaced over the fields. The rice grew swiftly while we were gone during the summer and when we came back in late September the fields were dry again and the grain stood high and yellow. Then came the harvesting when once more the farm family sallied forth and with hand sickles cut the sheaves, and tied them and stacked them and carried them to the threshing floors in front of the farmhouses. There the sheaves were spread and men and women lifted the swinging bamboo flails and beat out the grain. Women swept up the grain and spread it in winnowing baskets and men tossed it up for the wind to clean. When at last the rice was harvested it was piled into vats made of clean rice straw woven into matting and shaped and tied into containers. There was poetry in every movement of the blue-clad peasants, and I see it all clear in my mind today, a series of exquisite and symbolic pictures, memorized through half my lifetime.

Only in Java, years later, did I see the process whole and simultaneous, for there upon the richest soil and with the finest rice climate in the world, planting and harvesting went on in adjacent fields, the earth in continual production so that while some farmers transplanted seedlings into the water others bore home the sheaves. When I think of Java, I see handsome brown men carrying on their shoulders sheaves of rice, heavy-headed and cut as exactly even as strands of yellow silk.

Between planting and harvesting we stayed in our little stone house in the mountains. Other white people, missionaries and tradesmen and their families, joined those of us who had pioneered and gradually, as years went on, a beautiful little town developed there in the top of the mountains. A church was built and at one end of the property shrewd Chinese merchants opened shops. Farmers from the plains below carried up the mountains baskets of eggs and fruits, fowls and vegetables, and we had an abundance of food. Near our house was a clear spring bubbling up from under the top of the mountain and this water we drank without boiling and considered it pure luxury.

As time went on many white people seized the chance to escape from

China for a few weeks and mingle with their own kind. Missionaries held meetings and conferences and businessmen and their wives had bridge parties and dances, and everybody went on picnics and walks. Each summer there was a tennis tournament and a sacred concert, where my mother sang in *The Messiah* or in some other oratorio. Each week, too, there was a meeting only for amusements, where amateurs did their best with whatever talent they had. Besides such arranged entertainment there were tea parties, dinners and much visiting, while people who had no chance to see one another during the year could meet here and compare adventures and children and share their news. Kuling did indeed mean many different things to different people, but to my mother it meant first of all a place where her children were safe and the air was clean and where she could renew her own soul. For me, as I look back, I realize that it meant a kind of beauty I knew nowhere else, the beauty of clear brooks and wild ferns and lilies, a place where I could wander safely and explore to my own content. Each morning during the years when I was small it was my task to climb the mountain behind our house and come back with fresh ferns and flowers, and never have I seen so many flowers growing wild as I found there. The little fireplace in our living room my mother filled with bracken, and she wanted the delicate ferns for her pots, and the tall white Madonna lilies, the red, black-spotted tiger lilies or the white ones with red spots were always welcome. Yellow and orange day lilies grew everywhere, and since they lasted but a day, I did not pick them except for our amah who cooked the buds into a delectable dish for her midday meal. Grass-of-Parnassus and club moss were special finds, and my mother loved, too, the long leafy strands of wild clematis, set with hundreds of little white stars of flowers, and this she twined along our mantelpiece. The simple house became a fresh bower, and not for anything would I have missed that morning climb and the return laden with treasures for my mother's joy. There was only one danger, and it was the short slender grass-green snake that climbed the trees and hung down like a swaying branch. Its bite was fatal, and I kept my eyes sharp as I walked along the trails or climbed the grey rocks.

One fearful aspect of those beautiful mountains of Lu was the flash floods. Springs at the top of the mountains had through the centuries cut deep gorges into the soil, and since the forests had long ago been destroyed, a cloudburst on the top of a mountain could pour water into a gorge so suddenly that within minutes a great wall of water was built up, although below the sun might be shining. Every summer some lives were lost in these flash floods. Picnickers enjoying their meal by the side of a small and peaceful brook looked up to see descending upon them a mass of water twenty feet high. Before they could escape they were swept away, sometimes over high falls. I remember the tragedy of a neighbor, an American woman whose husband was dead and who had only one child. Upon the child's sixth birthday she had put their supper in a basket and the two of them had gone to a nearby brook to make a little celebration. In the midst of their meal she heard a roar and looking up she saw the flood rushing toward her. In her fright she seized what she thought was the child's frock and clambered up the side of the gorge only to discover that what she had grasped was her own skirt and that the child was gone. The possibility of death always at hand lent an undertone of terror to the pleasantest summer day in Kuling.

All that was in my childhood, and now when I went to Kuling with my mother, one early June, before even the rice fields were flooded, I went back as a young woman. Kuling was changed, too. I had caught rumors of it in my parents' talk. Wealthy Chinese wanted to buy land there and it had become a point of hot disagreement between the white people as to whether Chinese could or should be kept out any longer. In the early years no Chinese had thought of coming but now they wanted to buy in the white concession and not in the Chinese section outside the Gap where tradespeople lived. Kuling had developed very much, I discovered when I reached the top of the mountain and I did not like it so well, although the journey up the mountain had been even more beautiful than I remembered. We had left the ship at the river port the day before and had gone by riksha to the resthouse in the city to spend the night on our own bedding rolls spread upon Chinese bed bottoms resting upon two wooden benches. Early the next morning we were waked as usual by the chair bearers, clamoring to get off, and we rose and ate a hearty breakfast of rice and eggs prepared by the rest-house cook, and then we climbed into our chairs, much improved now, and made of wood and rattan instead of bamboo. Thus we set off across the plains and up into the foothills to the second resthouse, where other chairs waited with mountain bearers, for the plainsmen could not climb. Now came, as always, the magical part of the journey. One caught the first hint of it when a clear mountain brook tumbled past the resthouse and the village houses were made of stone instead of the gray brick of the plains. We seated ourselves in our chairs and four bearers carried each chair, suspended by ropes from poles across their shoulders, and thus they mounted the first flight of stone steps with light rhythmic stride. Up the mountain we climbed and soon the frothing bamboos changed to pines and dwarf chestnuts and oaks and we were on our way. The road wound around the rocky folds of the cliffs, and beneath us were gorges and rushing mountain rivers and falls. Higher and higher the road crawled, twisting so abruptly that sometimes our chairs swung clear over the precipices as the front bearers went on beyond the rear ones, still behind the bend. One misstep and the chair would have been dashed a thousand feet into the rocks and swirling waters, but there was never a misstep. In all the years I never heard of an accident, even though the bearers went at an astonishing speed, every step in rhythmic movement.

Somewhere near the top of the mountain we turned a certain corner and were met, as I had remembered, by a strong cold current of mountain air. Until then the air had gradually cooled, but at this spot it changed suddenly and the bearers welcomed it with loud hallooing calls and a spurt of running, the chair swaying between them. It was still exciting. As a child I could never keep from laughing, and this time, although I was grown up, I still felt exhilaration. The air of the plains had been hot and heavy, breathed in and out by millions of human lungs, but here on top of the mountain it was charged with fresh cold purity, and one breathed it in like lifesaving oxygen.

So we reached the same little old house, my mother and I, and very small it looked to my grown-up eyes, but the trees were big and the ferns had grown thick on the terrace walls. The two servants we had brought with us cleaned the house swiftly and we settled in, my mother to rest in bed for a while and I to care for her and read to her. I studied my Chinese books while she slept and every day I went for a long and solitary walk. There were few people to be seen and most of the houses were still closed, for the season had not begun, but it was interesting to walk about the settlement and see the changes. A sanatorium had been built for tuberculosis patients, all white, and Russian traders had developed a separate piece of land beyond the mountain and named it Russian Valley and outside the settlement limits rich Chinese had built immense stone houses for themselves. The streets were named and the trees had grown tall and arched above them and the atmosphere of the place had become worldly and cosmopolitan.

My mother and I talked together about it, and she admitted the change and said, symbolically, that she no longer dared to drink the spring water unboiled because houses were built above it now. Then she said, "We must let the Chinese come in—I can see it. Perhaps we white people ought never to have built a separate place for ourselves but we did it so that we could keep our children. We lost so many little children."

She could never mention the lost children without thinking, I knew, of our four, buried in little walled cemeteries, three in Shanghai and one in Chinkiang, who died when I was six. The eldest, my sister Edith, my mother considered her most beautiful and brilliant child, and she was the one who had died of cholera when she was four. There was a portrait of her in my mother's bedroom in the mission house, a handsome sturdy blue-eyed child, her dark hair in bangs across her fine forehead and hanging in thick curls on her shoulders.

"Someday," my mother was saying, "the Chinese will take everything back again."

And so they did, though not until she was dead.

During the two years of her convalescence in Kuling she rebuilt the house, tearing down the old one and putting up one larger, though still modest, because she wanted it big enough, she said, for my sister and me when we married and had children. But when she was dead, and my father dead, and China was changing indeed and all that belonged to the white people was being taken from them or they were giving it back for the sake of their own consciences, then my sister and I sold the house to a good Chinese family and so for us Kuling was returned. By that time it had become a stronghold for Generalissimo Chiang Kai-shek and Madame Chiang and their many relatives, and the new officials were more rigorous than the white people had been about keeping out the poor Chinese. But it was no more our business.

I felt, that year when I was alone there with my mother, that the end was inescapable, as she had said it was, but I did not fear it. I wanted more than ever to be rid of the burden which had weighed upon me all my life, the burden of knowing that my race had been unjust to another. It is easier to receive injustice than to inflict it, for conscience is a fox gnawing at the vitals. Then, too, I had forgotten by that time the hatreds of the old Empress Dowager and her followers against foreigners, and feeling again the warm friendliness of the Chinese people, the easy courtesy and unfailing consideration, I longed to see every inequality between us removed, and all people living with equal opportunities for self-development. Rich and poor there would always be, of course, and some people would be clean and some dirty, some educated and some ignorant, but these inequalities were fluid and natural, and depended to a large extent upon individuals themselves. What I wanted to be rid of, merely as a burden, was the declared discrimination between the dominant white and the rebellious Chinese. They were right and we were wrong in that particular matter. After all, we were still only guests upon the Chinese soil, not rulers and not even citizens.

But I was removed again from life, for the time being, by our return to Kuling. The First World War was raging, but I knew nothing of it except through the newspaper which reached us weekly from Shanghai, an English paper which gave very little report of American forces. I had no idea, indeed, until years later when I was visiting Europe again, how many Americans had fought in the First World War and had died on foreign soil. I learned it then as I wandered through the vast memorial halls which had been built as monuments to the American soldiers who had died and had never been found. There on walls high and wide were carved in small print the myriad names of the missing. And I wandered through the cemeteries in France and elsewhere and saw little white crosses set as closely as human bodies could lie, and the magnitude of what my country had done overwhelmed me and I wept belated tears for the young men whose flesh was already dust.

We stayed the summer through in Kuling, our old friends and many new ones returned to their summer homes, and my sister came from boarding school in Shanghai and we took up much of the old childhood life, except that I was no longer a child. An English doctor had my mother in charge, and he changed her diet again, so that she fed now upon an obnoxious mixture of boiled liver and spinach, consuming it with a fortitude that was amazing. She was slow to get well, and after my father had come for his brief vacation and gone, and my sister had returned to school, my mother and I stayed on while the frost turned the leaves scarlet and the chinquapin burrs burst and dropped their small sweet nuts. Then, because so few white people remained, we were asked to move lower into the valley where it would be easier for the doctor to visit my mother and easier to reach supplies of food and coal. We moved into the house of a Swedish friend, a pink and white cottage, and I began what was to be the loneliest winter of my life, so far as human beings were concerned. The nearest person to my age was a young man in the sanatorium recovering from tuberculosis, but he was only a boy to my newly adult eyes, and our friendship was brief, ended indeed by the alarm of his missionary parents at his growing interest in a young woman. My own mind was concerned with far different matters. I was struggling with the decision of what I was to do with myself. My problem was the variety of my interests, all leading someday of course to writing, but not yet. I enjoyed too many employments.

Meanwhile, as winter passed my mother was better. My school was clamoring for my return, and so with the doctor's permission and on her own insistence, I left her surrounded by a few good friends and cared for by our servants, and one cold February day I walked down the mountain.

It was strange to get back to the mission house and take charge of it alone, my father its only other occupant, strange and a little exciting to be my own mistress, to go to classes and teach and to come home and study Chinese literature with my own teacher, order the household affairs and plan our simple meals, and even invite a few guests now and then. I enjoyed my independence, in spite of my great love for my mother, and yet I knew all the time that this was not permanent, neither this place nor this time. Something else lay ahead but I did not know what. While I waited I busied myself.

There was plenty with which to be concerned. The year 1914, in which I was graduated from college, had been a year of importance in much larger matters. Many young Chinese were being graduated from other American colleges and universities at about the same time, young men who were destined to clarify the new age by their writings. Sun Yat-sen and his followers were still struggling with political problems, for Yuan Shih-kai, the military leader, had finally assumed the Presidency of the new Republic of China as a compromise between the old guard who rejected Sun Yat-sen, and the impetuous radicals who would not acknowledge Pu Yi as Emperor. Sun Yat-sen had been set back, but he had accepted the situation with Chinese grace. Now, however, it became apparent that the ambitions of Yuan Shih-kai were leading him to try to establish the Throne again with himself as the First Emperor. It was still doubtful whether the people would allow this, for if I could judge from my own students and young Chinese friends, the revolutionary stimulus constantly applied, not only by Sun Yat-sen, but also by Liang Ch'ih-ch'ao and K'ang Yu-wei and others, had permeated the people more than one might guess was possible when eighty percent of the people could not read and write. The Chinese are a very articulate people, however, always curious and mentally awake, and hearsay and rumors ran fast over the nation, and it was evident that they would not tolerate the setting up of a monarchy, especially under old Yuan, who carried with him quite a stink from the dead regime, for it was he who had betrayed the Young Emperor to the Old Empress and was therefore morally responsible in the end for his death. The people did not forget.

It was a wonderful time in which to live in China, and I was at the right age for it. Young, interested in all that went on around me, able to read Chinese as well as English, surrounded by friends far beyond the Christian circle of missions, I found myself stirred and stimulated by many events. True, the center of new movements was far from our quiet rather old-fashioned city and countryside, but we knew what was going on. Even the Church was growing, and my father was surprised at the number of businessmen and farmers who were interested in becoming Christians. None were scholars of the old-fashioned sort, and few were young students in schools and colleges and this grieved him, for if he had a snobbish tinge it was in the direction of the literate rather than the illiterate person. There was no hiding the fact that when he baptized an educated man, whether old or young, he felt such a one was worth at least a baker's dozen of the ordinary uneducated sort. Yet a solid group of Chinese was becoming interested to some extent in the Christian religion, and it was, I am sure, although my father refused to agree with me, because this religion did give promise of creating a new society where all men could be equally valuable as human beings.

The mission schools, too, had a very strong part in the revolution. I do not know how missionaries liked the idea that they helped to bring about chaos in China, but they did, nevertheless. It was more than that they insisted upon unbinding the feet of girl students, that they taught Western subjects including science and mathematics rather than the old classical and literary subjects of Chinese schools. More even than these was the fact that they taught the revolutionary and world-shaking principles of Christ. The wonder is that none of them, at least in that day, realized how revolutionary those principles were. They had been reared in the Western atmosphere where church members do not take literally the teachings of Jesus, and practice them only as far as is convenient in the total framework of their society. The Chinese, however, tended to be practical even about religion, and the result was often very upsetting indeed.

But perhaps the most powerful force came, after all, from the graduates of mission schools, who had not been allowed to compete in the old Imperial Examinations and even after these were abolished in 1905 were still not considered sufficiently educated in Chinese ways to apply for high political positions. There was a deep jealousy between the two groups of scholars, the old traditional ones who had earned their Chinese degrees by dint of knowing the classics, and the new ones who had Western degrees but were deficient in the classical and traditional requirements. Each group held the other in contempt, and the young new scholars were determined to build a society where they and not the men they considered old fogies would be in power. Sun Yat-sen had many of these young men among his followers.

What troubled me, however, as I looked upon my Chinese world with my own young and too idealistic eyes, was that really first-rate minds were not turning to Christianity. I was troubled, not for my own sake, but for my parents', for I feared that the good which they and others had undoubtedly brought to China with their living expression of Christianity would be outweighed by the evils that had accompanied it, and eventually the whole structure would fall. I did not foresee how soon it would fall, but I knew enough to understand that in China coming changes would be shaped by the best minds. The Chinese people had for centuries revered learning and there was little danger that they would live under the leadership of ignorant men for any length of time. Confucianism had built itself too strongly into the mental and spiritual texture of the people, and Confucius had dinned into them the qualifications of the superior man. The failure of missions and of Christianity, insofar as they have failed in China, was that no first-rate Chinese minds joined the Christian movement. I make this statement without qualification. Liang Ch'ih-ch'ao, who was the spiritual and mental leader of the young in that period, declared openly that religion, and especially Christianity with its record of meddling in the political life of many Western nations, would always be the weapon of the State.

No fundamental change in any people is sudden, however, and change in China was not sudden, either. Chinese educated in the West had been returning since 1880, bringing with them ideas of other ways of life. Laborers and merchants had gone to Hawaii and the United States in large numbers and had also brought their versions of Western ways. Most tragic and amusing of all, some of the so-called "coolie" labor corps, which was China's contribution to the First World War, were bringing back French wives or concubines, whose stay was long or short depending upon the conditions they discovered in a man's home when they arrived. Of course the "coolie" lovers had assured the French women that life in China was comfortable and modern. Railways? Certainly China had railways. The French women wanted to be sure they could get away easily if they did not like what they found. As a matter of fact, there were a few excellent railroads. One of them, connecting Shanghai with Peking, ran through our city. It had been opened when I was twelve years old, and I remember the excitement it had caused, because a tunnel had to be built under the hill upon which the fort stood, and our whole community was in a state of distraction, lest the spirits of the dead people buried in the graves on that hill would be disturbed by the roar and rattle of the trains shaking their bones. Those were the days when the Old Empress was feeling her defeat, however, and trying to prove how modern she intended to be, she favored railways at last, or said she did, and so the tunnel was made and the trains ran.

Nevertheless, prudent French women, and most of them were prudent, did not give up their French citizenship by marriage, and they kept tucked away enough money to get home again, and these, with the cooperation of French consulates, were no trouble, except for the one problem they left behind them. This was that a Chinese uneducated laborer could and did boast of having been married to or at least connected with a white woman and his stories destroyed even more of the prestige of the white race.

The two men whose names were magic at this time, to me as well as to my young Chinese friends and my pupils, were still K'ang Yu-wei and Liang Ch'ih-ch'ao, who had been tutors of the Young Emperor. Both had been exiled after 1898, and of the two, Liang Ch'ih-ch'ao during the years had gradually assumed the stronger position. This was not, I think, because he had the better mind, for it would have been difficult to find in any country a mind so versatile and yet so profound and original as that of K'ang Yu-wei. K'ang had a breadth of understanding and vision which made partisanship impossible, and he early saw that East and West, if they would cooperate in friendship and mutual benefit, could help each other in complementary ways. He was stimulated by Western history and science and was not abashed by any false sense of Chinese inferiority. But after he went into exile in Japan he never again had the same influence, mainly, I believe, because he did not approve the radical trend of the revolution. He was convinced that China ought not to be a republic, and that her people were not ready for this form of government. He was right, of course, but he was unpopular, as those who are right at the wrong time always are, and so Liang Ch'ih-ch'ao became the idol of the literate young.

As early as 1902 Liang Ch'ih-ch'ao had begun his remarkable writing. Hu Shih in his autobiography describes the profound influence which he and others like him felt when they read Liang's essays, published then in Japan in the *Ming Pao,* or *People's Newspaper.* There Liang set forth a doctrine which was different indeed from the old Chinese belief that civilized man is never aggressive or even active except in passive ways. Instead he told the young Chinese, who were longing for activity and change, that Darwin had proved the theory of the survival of the fittest, that this in itself declared aggression to be the law of nature, and it was because Western peoples were aggressive that they had conquered. Therefore Chinese must make themselves into a new and aggressive people.

Everywhere this phrase, *the new people,* became fire set to tinder. Sun Yat-sen had thought that when the Manchu dynasty was overthrown, the people would then inevitably become "new." Like the Nationalists in recent years, however, the Manchus were overthrown too easily and quickly, before anyone had had time to think out exactly how to make the people new. Rueful indeed did I feel when I heard from a Chinese friend in Hong Kong a few years ago that the Communists were actually alarmed when Chiang Kai-shek's soldiers surrendered so readily. "We had counted on five years of struggle," the

Communist general is reported to have said, "and we needed those five years in which to learn how to govern the people. Now victory has come so quickly that we are not ready for it. We shall make many mistakes."

The same thing had happened after the revolution of 1911, when the rotten defenses of the Manchu rulers, even with their three million Bannermen clustered in villages about Peking to protect them, and in every province capital as well, gave way to the revolutionists. What does one do with a vast country and hundreds of millions of people without rulers? No one had a plan, and it was doubtless due to this planlessness that Sun Yat-sen was able to put forth his ideas of a republican form of government. At least, people said, such a government could be organized without the usual era of civil wars and the trouble and expense of setting up a new dynasty. The common man, peasant or merchant, was glad to think that he would not be taxed any more to keep up expensive palaces and pleasure gardens for officials. There was a great deal of democracy in China, deep and inherent in the people. They had accepted their Emperors, follies and all, as necessary government, but when it appeared that there were countries which had none, a change seemed sensible to them. When Yuan Shih-kai dreamed of setting up the imperial system again, they decided against it. So decided were they that it permeated even his bemused brain that the people not only did not want him, they did not want any emperor at all. They wanted some form of modern self-government.

As a matter of fact, the Chinese had always governed themselves. They distrusted and even held in contempt governments. They were cynical to the last degree about official honesty and considered it inevitable that every official was corrupt. Their ancient adage is that the best government is the one that governs least. A country folk song runs thus:

> *When the sun rises I work;*
> *When the sun sets I rest.*
> *I dig the well to drink;*
> *I plow the field to eat.*
> *What has the Emperor to do with me?*

And the Chinese people were quite capable of self-government. Their traditional family system, wherein every individual man, woman and child belonged to a clan and each clan was responsible for all individuals in it, was a sound basis for a new kind of modern democracy. It is hard for Americans to realize the soundness of the family clan as the unit for democratic government, but indeed it is so. In China before Communism began its destructive work on the family system, there was no need, for example, for the expense of institutionalism which lies so heavily upon our own democracy. There were no orphanages, for no child was orphaned, since the family as a whole continued responsible for the care of the child who had lost his immediate parents. There were no insane asylums, for the family cared for its insane. As a matter of fact, there were very few insane, for the family system provided individual security without disgrace and thus removed one of the main causes for modern insanity, the lost individual. There needed to be no relief rolls, for again the family as a whole cared for its members who were jobless. Only in times of widespread famine and catastrophe did there have to be outside help, and even then the family stayed together. Business was stable in a large middle class, for the generations carried it on in the same family. Nepotism, it is true, tended to be a problem, since it was natural that a man would try to get jobs for his relatives. Yet I do not see the difference between family nepotism in China and political nepotism in the United States, and of the two, family nepotism in China seems the less dangerous to society because the family still remained morally responsible for each of its members, and the disgrace of any member was a family disgrace.

Could Sun Yat-sen and his followers, and this includes the later Nationalist government under Chiang Kai-shek, have understood the value of the family system and have built upon its responsible democracy, there is little doubt that Communism would not be ruling in China today. One proof of this is that the Communists, wishing to establish their political theory, have made their main attack upon the family system, and the measure of the length of their stay will be to the degree to which they are able to separate the members of the family from each other and thus to destroy the fabric which has kept China alive, functioning and vital for centuries after her contemporaries in history were dead.

The failure of the early revolution was not evident at first, of course. Sun Yat-sen continued to struggle for political unity although the country was drifting toward the old trend of war lords, helped this time by the rising tide of militarism in the West. I suppose few Americans, then as now, thought about China at all and fewer still could have realized that events in the West were working with an old historical process to produce the Chinese war lords, called "generals," who began to be the real rulers in their own regions. I lived under war lords for many years in that period, and peacefully enough, although we had always to watch the mood and the temper of our local war lord. He was usually uneducated and he was given as much to pleasure as to war. After a combat, whether he were victor or vanquished, he tended to settle down for a while, take a few new concubines and perhaps yield to opium or some such diversion and so we would have peace again until the next time. War lords seldom disturbed white people, because they did not want trouble with Western governments, but they had another vice, maddening to the young radicals, which was that they needed endless amounts of money to support their ever-increasing armies of ne'er-do-wells and malcontents, and needing money they sold off bits of their country to Japan, who was during the First World War making great hay. She had joined the war on the side of the Allies, and thus had been in a position to take over the German holdings in China, gaining a foothold for later aggressions. She leased or bought mines and ports and concessions from greedy war lords, and became indeed our ogre and portent.

Educated Chinese despised the war lords, but ordinary folk were, more often than not, amused by them so long as they kept off bandits and let other people alone, and the war lords were usually strong, wilful, humorous, rough-and-ready individuals, afraid of no one, and often very funny. One of our neighboring war lords was famous because of the three things he did not know—how many soldiers he had, how much money he had and how many wives he had. I remember the war lord in the province next to ours who was twice defeated by another war lord. At last he declared in loud and public tones that he intended to fight once more and if he were defeated he would come home in his coffin. We all waited the outcome of this much-touted battle, and when it ended as the others had, in defeat, an elaborate funeral was prepared for the return of the body. The funeral went off in high humor with every detail complete, except that instead of a corpse in the enormous coffin, the old war lord, very much alive though vanquished, was seated therein, dressed in his best robes and grinning at the astonished crowds while he smoked a large foreign cigar. The people burst into roaring laughter and instantly forgave the old ruler all his sins because he had made such a good joke, and this is characteristic of the Chinese, then and now, for they love laughter. My own father saved his life more than once by a quick-witted joke.

Meanwhile young Chinese, many of them the husbands of my friends, or even my own students, were trying their best to create the new China. Unfortunately, instead of beginning with reality, and this was to know and understand what they had in their own people upon which to build, they tried to apply Western ideas cold. For example, they began to believe in the necessity of militarism, since, they argued, the strength of the West lay in its armed forces and weapons, and certain young reformers attached themselves to the war lords and tried to modernize their large and irregular armies. Others felt that the strength of the West lay in its standards of law and that China was weak because her government did not depend upon law but upon individuals and their human relationships, and such young men studied law abroad and then came home and tried to build up a legalistic government, modeled after the American and the French. Their attempt failed because Sun Yat-sen insisted that the parliament thus set up must be the ruling body of the country whereas the old-fashioned Yuan Shih-Kai, while he was President, determined to keep power in his own hands. Provincial assemblies were actually set up but the war lords soon put an end to them as they continued to rise to power.

It was a fantastic era. I felt sometimes as I read the newspapers that I was a juggler trying to keep a dozen balls in the air at the same time. Here were the Western-educated young, quarreling over parliaments and legalities and mechanistic theories as opposed to the old idealistic philosophies, and here were the crude, hearty, entirely selfish war lords building up their little separate empires, and here was imperial Japan gnawing diligently at the land and resources and preparing for her future empire, and here was the desperate Sun Yat-sen, fighting bravely without money or army for his own ideals, and here was old Yuan Shih-kai, determined to restore the monarchy. The air became clear to some extent when Yuan understood that the people would not have him, and so plain was this made that he had to back down, or resign and acknowledge his mistake, a disgrace which he did not long survive. When he died in 1916 we were all relieved.

The aspect of the revolution which interested me most, however, was still the literary one. While the country was struggling to find a political form suitable to the modern age, a profound change was going on in the writing and reading of books. Before I begin to describe this part of the revolution I must make clear, or as clear as I can, the place which books have had in China ever since the era of Confucius, five hundred years before Christ. If there was an aristocracy in China it was one not of birth or even of wealth, it was of scholarship. The Imperial Examinations had been open to all candidates and those who passed them most successfully could even be the sons of peasants. They often were, for if a village recognized a boy genius among its inhabitants, it was quite usual for all the villagers to join together and provide for his education, in the hope that if he passed the Imperial Examinations he would bring honor to the home village and would also give the villagers a return for their investment in him. Automatically the young scholar joined the elite of the intellectuals and thereafter never put his hands to any menial labor. He was a scholar and lived a scholar's life, rich or poor. Even if he never achieved fame he never lost his position, and he could at least support himself by opening a village school. Whether he became an advisor to the Emperor or only a village schoolteacher, he received respect as a scholar. This national attitude of reverence for learning made the task of teaching young Chinese a pure pleasure, for instead of lackadaisical lounging in the classroom or childish absorption in sports, my pupils were alert and eager to learn all they possibly could, since academic achievement was the key to success in Chinese society. There were practical rewards for the intellectual.

As long as the Manchu government stood and especially as long as Imperial Examinations continued, strength remained with the old classical scholars, who would not recognize Western university degrees. When the Examinations ended, however, and the Throne fell, the old scholars were at a loss. Their protection was gone as well as their jobs, and so the young Western-trained scholars became powerful through the political revolution they had created. It was characteristic of these young intellectuals that instead of tackling the practical problems of the country, which were political and economic, they plunged with fervor into a literary revolution. Fully eighty-five percent of the Chinese people could not read and it is doubtful if more than five percent read with ease, and among the five percent were all the scholars, both old and new. Yet here the young intellectuals spent their energies. They attacked first the written language itself, the language of the old scholars, the classical wen-li, which was the only language used for literature. Fiction, or "wild writing" as it was called, was not considered literature. It was pastime reading, and a true scholar of the old school was ashamed to be seen reading novels, although all read them in private. This classical language, however, did prevent the ordinary Chinese from getting information, much as Americans might be prevented if Latin were used instead of English. Years of study were necessary in order to learn proficiency in wen-li, and the young intellectuals, who had spent those years in studying science and other Western subjects and therefore were poor in classical Chinese, declared themselves against wen-li. The language of the people, the spoken language, they said, should also be the written language. It was more than language—the old literary tricks of allusiveness and allegory and parable were also to be sternly rejected. From now on, young intellectuals said, they would write with simple clarity in the vernacular. Ts'ai Yuan-p'ei, the renowned president of the National University in Peking, headed the revolutionary movement, and he enriched his teaching staff with first-rate minds from among the new group. Among them I think before all others of Ch'en Tu-hsiu, brilliant, bold, and radical, who was later lost to Communism. His magazine,

Ch'ing Nien, or *Youth,* was an inspiration to thousands of restless young Chinese, and when in 1916 the magazine took up the cause of the literary reform, the flame of new intellectual life spread everywhere through China.

Old scholars, of course, and even average conservative minds, literate or not, were horrified at what they considered the destruction of the literary past while discussion went on in scores of new little magazines, in newspapers and in teashops. When Hu Shih, in an article in *Youth* magazine, startled us all by the brilliance and persuasiveness of his argument for the use of the pai-hua, or vernacular, as against wen-li, we recognized a fresh force in modern China.

Both Ch'en Tu-hsiu and Hu Shih based their arguments not merely on Western literature, which had obviously influenced them strongly, but also upon the revolutionary spirit of the West. Older Chinese minds were revolted by what seemed to them the foreign and unpatriotic attitudes of the two young men and those who flocked to follow them, but the fact is that Ch'en Tu-hsiu and Hu Shih did search the history of their own people and did find there the periodic appearance of the same revolutionary spirit which had changed their country, too, again and again, as well as the culture of Europe, and this revolutionary spirit, they felt, was simply the renewed determination in progressive generations of human beings, wherever they lived, to do away with old clutter and meaningless phrases and to try instead to approach freshly and directly the problems of life.

The greatest interest for me in all this was the fact that these modern intellectuals were considering for the first time the Chinese novel as literature instead of the despised possession of the common people, through wandering storytellers and theatrical groups, and which, if it was produced by a scholar, was always done under the cover of anonymity or a pseudonym because it was always written in the vulgar spoken tongue. Now Hu Shih came forward with a stimulating essay on the Chinese novel, a theme never before taken up by a scholar, and I myself, who had never quite dared, under the tutelage of Mr. Kung, to acknowledge how much I enjoyed reading stories and novels, found that Mr. Kung was dead indeed, for not only did all the young people of my age begin to read fiction and feel it quite smart to do so, but they began to write fiction, not in the old classical allusive fashion, but straightforwardly, with unashamed self-revelation and emotion.

This was an enormous release to educated men and women. To be able to say what one felt and thought without having to think whether it was written in a rigid and antiquated style was to free an energy suppressed for centuries. The new intellectual life began to flow with a strength and an influence far out of proportion to the numbers who were actually engaged in it or were able to understand and profit from it. It was still the five percent of the population who were concerned, and yet they were the leading young minds, and from them even the illiterate and the ignorant caught something of the new China. It was a wonderful hour, young enough to be still pure. The young Chinese lost their animosities and prejudices for the time being and they searched the world in their hunger for new ideas, new forms, new intellectual companionship. So alive were they that I felt myself filled with their enthusiasms, and my faith in China was born again. At this rate, I thought, she would run ahead of all other countries, and compared to the vivid articulate world—questioning minds of my young Chinese friends, both men and women, my American college mates seemed puerile indeed.

One of my own particular absorptions was a most unusual man named Lin Shu. He knew not a word of English, but he happened one day by chance upon a Western novel, and moved by curiosity, he engaged a friend to read it to him, translating it as he read. Lin Shu was charmed by the story. I wish I knew what novel it was that he first heard. I think, although my memory is not sure, that it was one of the novels of Sir Walter Scott. Whichever it was, he demanded that it be read to him again, and while he listened to the rough translation of the reader, he rewrote it in his own beautiful Chinese style. In this fashion he translated the novels of Scott and Dickens, of Conan Doyle and Victor Hugo and Robert Louis Stevenson, Tolstoi, Cervantes, and others, until he had translated ninety-three English books, nineteen American ones, twenty-five French, and six Russian. Rider Haggard was perhaps his favorite Western writer. He translated for his own pleasure at first but he soon found that Chinese readers enjoyed the foreign novels as much as he did and in the end he became wealthy by this innocent piracy. Of course other Chinese writers, always poor, and particularly the young, were quick to copy his example, and, I must say, not always acknowledging foreign authorship. By this means Western literature was made known even to the average Chinese reader, since it was no longer a disgrace to read fiction, at least foreign fiction.

Years later when I began to write, I found myself subject to the same honor, or annoyance, depending upon how one wishes to think of it, and my books, too, were cheerfully pirated over and over again. I remember that I saw seven different translations, some in full and some in shortened versions, of *The Good Earth,* and on two of them my name did not appear at all and the translator's name was given as that of the author. Young writers lifted certain incidents and characters out of the book and wove amplified stories about them and sold them as original works. The same fate befell others among my books, but nothing could be done about it. There were no copyright laws to which to appeal. I doubt whether the situation has changed under the Communists, since in Russia herself, although I know that my books have been translated there freely, no permissions have been asked and no royalties given me. International altruism may move one to accept a certain amount of the inevitable, but not, I think, the assumption of authorship by a translator.

From all this fascinating new life I was suddenly removed, or perhaps it would be more accurate to say that I suddenly removed myself, by my marriage to a young American, not strictly speaking a missionary since he was not at all religious, so far as I could see, but who was employed as an agriculturist by the Presbyterian Mission Board. The time had come for marriage, as it comes in the life of every man and woman, and we chose each other without knowing how limited the choice was, and particularly for me who had grown up far from my own country and my own people. I have no interest now in the personal aspects of that marriage, which continued for seventeen years in its dogged fashion, but I do remember as freshly as though it were yesterday the world into which it transported me, a world as distant from the one I was living in as though it had been centuries ago. It was the world of the Chinese peasant.

III

THE landscape outside my big window this morning is a forest clearing, and beyond the pines and the maples at its edge green mountains rise in rounded peaks. Our simple house is the result of a plan and the plan is the result of a mild revolt on my part. These American children of mine were growing up without knowing how to use their hands. On the farm the boys rode tractors and fastened the milking machine to the cows. They sat on a combine and harvested the grain and called it farming. It is farming, of course, the American way, but I was dissatisfied with it. They had no touch with the earth direct, and I feel that there must be the direct touch, hands upon stones and earth and wood, in order that life may have stability. My own life has been spent in many places, but it has not lacked continuity or stability because everywhere I have made gardens and lived on farms and planted and harvested in the unchangeable turn of the seasons.

And the houses people build nowadays! The old strong farmhouses in our Pennsylvania community still stand, but I see bulldozers sweep them down as though bombs had fallen, and in their place upon the raw and bleeding earth machines have built little metal boxes a few feet apart, and they are called homes and twenty thousand families crowd into them. When I saw them I knew that I wanted my children to know how to build a real house.

We went to Vermont one spring to see maple sugaring by helping to make it, and while we were there my revolt took sensible shape in a plan. Land covered with forest was cheap on the mountainside, a little more than two dollars an acre. We bought some high acres far from the road, and the next summer upon an old clearing where a farmhouse had stood a century ago, the boys began housebuilding under the direction of a Vermonter who knew how to do his job well. Thereafter each summer the boys went to the mountain and worked. Foundation, walls of stones mortised in cement, a beamed roof, two big fireplaces, windows and doors, a well-laid stone floor, these slowly came into being. The work was finished by a fine German workman whose passion for perfection was irritant and stimulus to the young Americans but joy to me, for I despise shoddiness of handwork, believing it to be accompanied always by shoddiness of mind and soul.

Slowly, slowly the learning went on, and at last the house was done, and here we are in our mountain house. Water has to be carried from the brook, lamps have to be cleaned and filled with oil, there will never be a telephone, I cook our meals on the fireplace and think it the best way of cooking in the world. Around us the forest folk come and go, squirrels and deer and sometimes bear, and we always watch for Brother Porcupine who will eat his way through anything, especially enjoying rubber tires. The house has cost us a third of what the new metal boxes in Pennsylvania cost, and the boys now know how to build for themselves and the girls know how to keep house anywhere and still be civilized. As for me, I have this big window, the fir trees and the mountains, and blessed relief from Pennsylvania ragweed.

Next to people, I remember landscapes, and though at this moment I look at green forests in Vermont, I can remember as clearly as what I see the northern Chinese town to which I went after my marriage. The decision to marry was the result of one of those human coincidences which cannot be explained except to say in the words of the wise man of Ecclesiastes that there is "a time to marry." When this time comes in the life of any healthy and normal creature, marriage is inevitable, whether it be arranged by parents or by the individual, and to the most likely person who happens to be in the environment. My parents did not approve my marriage and while they maintained an amazing silence on the subject, for they were an articulate pair and silence was not usual, nevertheless I discerned their disapproval because they were united in silence, and this was also unusual. Since I was on more intimate terms with my mother than with my father, I took her aside one day and asked her why they disapproved. She replied that they felt that this young man, while himself a good sort of person doubtless, would not, however, fit into our rather intellectual family. His interests were obviously not intellectual, she said, and when I reminded her that at least he was the graduate of an American college she retorted that it was an agricultural college and this was not what our family considered education.

"You two are behaving like Chinese parents," I said. "You think whomever I marry has to suit the family first."

"No," she declared, "it is you we think of. We know you better than you imagine, and how can you be happy unless you live with someone who understands what you are talking about?"

I was as wilful as any other member of our wilful family, however, and so I persisted in my plans and in a few months was married, with very simple ceremony, in the garden of our mission house and soon there-after I was settled in my own first home, a little four-room Chinese house of grey brick and black tile within the walled town of Nan-hsüchou, in Anhwei province, many miles north of my childhood province of Kiangsu.

It was a complete change of scene. I had never lived in North China before, and the very landscape was strange to me. Instead of our green valleys and the lovely blue hills beside the wide Yangtse River I now looked from my windows upon a high embankment where stood the city wall, foursquare, with a brick tower at each corner, and surrounded by a moat. Huge wooden gates braced with iron were locked against bandits and wandering soldiers at night and opened in the morning. Outside the walls and beyond the moat, the countryside stretched as flat as any desert, broken only by what appeared to be heaps of mud but which were actually villages whose houses were built of the pale sand-colored earth of the region. In winter there was no green of any kind. Earth and houses were all of one color and even the people were of the same dun hue, for the fine sandy soil was dusted into their hair and skin by the incessant winds. The women seemed never to clean themselves, and this I found was purposeful, for if a woman was tidy, her hair brushed back and coiled smoothly and her garments any color but the universal sand color or faded blue cotton, then she was suspected of being a prostitute. Honest women took pride in being unkempt as a sign of not caring how they appeared to men and therefore virtuous. It was impossible to distinguish between the rich and the poor, for a rich lady wore her satin coat underneath the dull cotton one and was no better to look at than any farm woman. It took me some time to adjust to what seemed to me downright ugliness in my landscape, and I remember being discouraged by the sameness around me and com-plaining that there was no use in taking a walk, for one could go ten miles beyond the city gates and still everything looked exactly the same.

But it has always been my weakness or my strength, and to this day I do not know which it is, to be easily diverted by and absorbed in whatever is around me, and I soon found plenty of amusement and occupation. I discovered that I liked housekeeping and gardening, and to arrange the simple furniture about the four rooms, to hang curtains of yellow Chinese silk at the windows, to paint some pictures for the walls, to design bookshelves and grow flowers were all enjoyable activi-ties. I was glad that I lived in a little Chinese house with a black-tiled roof instead of a foreign style mission house. It had no upstairs and the garden seemed part of the house. The climate was too dry for the many flowers in my mother's southern garden, but chrysanthemums grew well in autumn and the golden Shantung roses in May and June.

In the spring the whole landscape suddenly grew beautiful. The bare willow trees around the villages put forth soft green leaves and the wheat turned green in the fields and the blossoms of the fruit trees were rose-colored and white. Most beautiful of all were the mirages. I had never lived in mirage country before, and when the earth was still cold but the air was warm and dry and bright, wherever I looked I could see mirages of lakes and trees and hills between me and the horizon. A fairy atmosphere surrounded me, and I felt half in a dream. The enchantment of moonlight, too, upon the city wall and the calm waters of the moat outside is still in my memory, half unreal, and it was in this little northern town that I first felt the strange beauty of Chinese streets at night. The dusty streets were wide and unpaved, the usual streets of northern Chinese towns, and they were lined with low one-story buildings of brick or earth, little shops and industries, blacksmiths and tinsmiths, bakeries and hot-water shops, dry goods and sweetmeat shops, all the life of a people confined geographically and therefore mentally and spiritually to an old and remote area. I walked the dim streets, gazing into the open doors where families gathered around their supper tables, lit only by thick candles or a bean oil lamp, and I felt closer to the Chinese people than I had since childhood.

It was in a way a solitary life, for what my parents had feared proved to be true, and my inner life was lived alone. There were only two other white people in the compound, a missionary couple much older than I, and with them no companionship was to be had, especially as they were in delicate health and for long periods of time were absent and then we were the only white people there. I remember as I say this that we did have for a short time an American doctor and his young wife, but the poor wife hated the Chinese and would never stir from her house. Though they lived next door, she never visited us or anyone, and we all took it for granted that she could not be herself so long as she remained in the alien country. It was not long before they returned to America to stay.

Now when I remember that American doctor I think of one experience we shared together. I had often to help him in one way or another, and one night, long after midnight, I heard a knocking on my door. When I opened it, there stood the doctor, a tall thin American figure with a lighted lantern in one hand and in the other his bag.

"I've had a call to go to a young woman who may be dying in childbirth," he said. "I'll have to operate and I need someone to give the anaesthetic. But especially I need someone to explain things to them."

His Chinese was limited and an operation was a dangerous risk if the people could not understand what he was doing. I had never given an anaesthetic but he could tell me what to do. I put on my coat and went with him and we walked through the silent streets on that bitter cold night to a cluster of small houses crowded with people. Everybody there was awake, it seemed, and smoky oil lamps were lit and faces stared at us out of the darkness. All was silence, too, and I knew that such silence was not good. It meant that the people did not trust the foreign doctor. I followed him to the very back of the alleyway and there a young husband met us and with him an old woman, his mother, and various relatives.

He was distracted with terror, for, as he soon explained to me, a wife was expensive for a man in his situation, and he had only been married a year. If she died, the whole business of another wife, a wedding, and so on, had to be undertaken afresh. Moreover, his parents were old and they wanted the assurance of a grandson before they died. I expressed my understanding and sympathy, and asked that the doctor be allowed to see the patient. He led the way and we all crowded into a small un-ventilated room, where upon a big wooden bed, behind heavy curtains, a young woman lay near her death. The agitated midwife stood by her, declaring that no one could save the woman, and that the child was already dead. When I asked her how she knew this she fumbled about in the straw on the floor and produced the child's arm which she had pulled off in her efforts to assist the birth.

"You see the child is dead," I told the young husband.

He nodded.

"Then it is only a question of saving your wife," I went on.

"Only that," he agreed.

"You also understand that she will certainly die if this foreign doctor does nothing," I said next.

"I do understand," he said.

This was not enough, and I asked all the relatives, who stood silent and watchful, if they also understood. They nodded. Last of all I asked the mother-in-law if she understood that she was not to blame the for-eign doctor if it was too late to save the young wife. She too agreed that he could not be blamed. With so many witnesses it was safe to proceed, and the doctor, who had been chafing at the necessary delay, handed me his bag and told me to sterilize the instruments while he prepared the patient.

Sterilize them! I had not the faintest idea how to do that. But I saw I was not expected to ask questions, and so I went into the courtyard and found a few bricks and built a fire of some straw and charcoal between them. Then I put a tin can of water on the bricks and sat down to wait for it to boil. Around me in the cold darkness stood the family, fearful of what was to happen. There was no use in trying to explain germs to them at that moment, and so I merely said that we wanted to get the instruments clean with boiling water, and this they understood. The water boiled quickly and I dropped them in and let them boil and then took them, tin can and all, into the stuffy bedroom again where the doctor was ready. The unconscious woman lay across the bed, her head to the wall, and he gave me my instructions.

"Pour off some of the water into a basin," he said, as though I were a nurse in the hospital and I tried to obey like one as best I could.

He looked around the little room impatiently. "Can't you get these people out?" he demanded.

"We can't get them all out," I said. "We must have witnesses."

After some argument the relatives did go out, however, except the husband and the mother-in-law.

"Now," my doctor said to me, "get back to the bed and put this cotton lightly over the patient's nose and begin dropping chloroform from this bottle."

"How shall I know when she has too much?" I asked, trying not to be afraid.

"Watch her breathing," he ordered. "And don't ask me anything. I have enough to do. I have never seen such a mess."

He worked in silence then, the husband and the mother leaning to see what we did. I concentrated only on the woman's breathing. Was it weaker? Surely it was more faint. I could not spare a hand to try to feel her pulse. Once the breathing stopped.

"She's dead," I whispered.

The doctor reached for a hypodermic and stabbed her arm and she began to breathe again unwillingly.

The ordeal came to an end somehow and there was the little dead child.

"A boy!" the mother-in-law wailed.

"Never mind," I said. "She will get well and bear you another."

It was a rash promise, but it was fulfilled a year later. The incredible strength of the Chinese woman pulled the young wife through that night. We stayed until she came out of the anaesthetic and then we let the husband feed her a bowl of hot water with red sugar melted into it. By morning she ate a raw egg in rice gruel. It was enough. If a person can eat, the Chinese believe, he will not die.

And yet I was never really lonely. The Chinese were delightful and of a kind new to me. Their language fortunately was still Mandarin, and I had only to make a few changes of pronunciation and tone to understand and be understood perfectly, and soon I was rich in friends. As usual the people were ready to be friends, intensely curious about our ways, and since my little house was so accessible a fairly steady stream of visitors came and went, and I was pressed with invitations to birthday feasts and weddings and family affairs. I enjoyed it all and soon was deep in the lives of my neighbors, as they were in mine. I played with their babies and talked with the young women of my own generation and they told me their problems with their mothers-in-law and other relatives and as usual I felt profoundly the currents of human life.

Since the man in the house was an agriculturist, it was natural that I accompanied him on his trips into the country. I must confess that I had often wondered secretly what a young American could teach the Chinese farmers who had been farming for generations on the same land and by the most skilful use of fertilizers and irrigation were still able to produce extraordinary yields and this without modern machinery. Whole families lived in simple comfort upon farms averaging less than five acres and certainly I had known of no Western agriculture that could compete with this. I knew better than to reveal my skepticism, however, for I had been well trained in human relationships, among which it is important indeed that, if she is wise, a woman does not reveal her skepticisms to man. Therefore I walked with what I hoped was my usual amiability from farm to farm, and while the man talked with farmers I amused myself with the women and the children, except when language broke down between the American and the Chinese men and I had to be called in as interpreter. It became more and more apparent as time went on that it would be difficult to find concrete ways of helping the farmers of the region, who had learned to cope with drought and high dry winds and long cold winters, and it was disturbing to any American man, I am sure, to find that he had more to learn than to teach.

No such danger faced me. I could merely enjoy and feel no special duty, for being nothing more now than a wife, I had no conscience whatever. Nothing was demanded of me, or almost nothing, and so I busied myself in house and garden, I began to keep bees for their honey, and I experimented with jams and jellies made from the abundant dates of our region and the dark red haws that are a cross between damson plums and crab apples. I was in and out of neighbors' houses, as they were in and out of mine, and I enjoyed again the wonderful deep sense of the richness of friendships. More than once I almost began to write, but each time I put it off, deciding to wait yet a little longer until mind and soul were fully grown.

Strangest of all, the vivid intellectual and political turmoil of the country did not reach us here. We lived as serenely as though the nation were not in revolution. Without exception none of my friends knew how to read or write and felt no need of either accomplishment. Yet so learned were they in the way of life that I loved to listen to their talk. An ancient people stores its wisdom in succeeding generations, and when families live together, young and old, each understands the other. Moreover, I delighted especially in the humor of my Chinese friends and in their freedom from inhibitions. These made life a comedy, for one never knew what the day might bring forth. One morning, for example, we found that thieves had broken into the Christian schoolmaster's house and had stolen the school funds.

"Didn't you get up?" our elder missionary demanded.

Astonishment broke upon the fat placid face of the schoolmaster. "What—I?" he retorted. "I am a scholar, and naturally I have no crude courage. I told my wife to get up, but by the time she had put on her outer garments the robbers were gone."

No one in our town blamed him, for physical courage was not admired and certainly not expected of learned men. "Of the thirty-six ways of escape," a Chinese proverb preaches, "the best is to run away." It has been part of the revolution in China to repudiate this proverb and to lift up the soldier from the traditional position in society given him by Confucius and make him into something more nearly resembling the Western soldier, who is given the honor and glory that make easy heroes of our military men. Which conception is right? I can only say that in old Asia where the soldier was given no honor and war was without glory, there arose a culture which emphasized learning and wisdom and which produced no great and soul-racking world wars.

When my mind returns to the years I lived in that small northern town, I see people not in masses but individual and beloved. Madame Chang remains as one of the greatest women I have ever known. She lived just down our street, the matriarch of a large family, a tall and ample figure, dressed in a full skirt and a knee-length coat, as old-fashioned as a family portrait, her hair drawn tightly back from her round kind face. She was a Christian, at least she was a church member and a sincere one, but even the elder missionary took no credit for this. She had been a leader among the Buddhists before she became a Christian, and she was still a Buddhist. She joined the Christian church, she once told me, as a kindness to the foreigners, who were strangers in the town and whom she wished to encourage when she perceived that their works were good. Madame Chang was a widow, and like so many strong good women, she had been married to a weak and lazy man. He died when she was still young and the Buddhist priests in the temple told her that he had not gone to heaven but had been detained in purgatory. It was her duty, they told her, to release him by prayers and gifts to the temple, and for some years she had spent herself on the project of getting the poor man out of his misery. Bit by bit, the priests assured her, he was being freed, until he was held only by his left foot. Christianity then came to her aid to the extent of convincing her that the priests were hoaxing her, and wherever her husband was she let him remain thereafter. Strangely enough, this story of purgatory, common enough to dishonest Buddhist priests, I later heard in Ireland from a Catholic priest as a joke.

Madame Chang was a jolly kind-hearted soul, and every good work in the town had her support. Whenever something new was begun, the universal demand was "Does Madame Chang approve it?" If so, then the people got solidly behind it. There were no barriers between her and other human beings, and sometimes when my own heart ached for reasons I could not reveal, it did me good just to lay my head down upon her broad soft shoulder and be still for a bit. Never did she ask me what was the matter, but in her wisdom I felt she knew.

My neighbor to the left, Madame Wu, was entirely different. She was a thin beautiful woman, past middle age but still beautiful, and she ruled her big household with an absolute authority. Gossip told me that she had driven to suicide her eldest daughter-in-law and this out of sheer jealousy because her eldest son, her favorite, had fallen in love with his wife after marriage. This enraged her, for she had purposely married him to a girl not beautiful so that her own hold over him would not be threatened, and she had made the young wife so miserable that the poor creature hung herself from a rafter one day in her husband's absence. The young husband had not spoken to his mother since except in the barest necessity of filial speech. If Madame Wu felt this, she gave no sign of it. She was as proud as ever and she chose another wife for her son. Yet she was a friend to me, and from her I learned much about the ancient and time-honored ways of a family such as hers. She had exquisite clothes, garments of hand-woven satins and silks and many kinds of furs from the North. She even had a coat lined with fine Russian sable, which had belonged to her grandmother. She taught me a great deal, giving me instruction in correct local manners among other things, and from her I learned much Chinese poetry. She too could not read, but she had been a precocious child, an only daughter, and her father had taught her poetry.

We had many beggars in our town, professional beggars usually, and they lived not so much on charity as on the Buddhists who for the sake of their souls would perform deeds of merit, among which was to give money to the poor. I was annoyed especially by the number of idle young men among these beggars, and one day upon my entering a side street to visit the house of a friend, a particularly impudent and bumptious beggar boy of about seventeen demanded alms. I stopped and looked at him hard.

"Why are you a beggar?" I asked.

He was taken aback by this and hung his head and mumbled that he had to eat.

"Why don't you work?" I asked next.

"Who would give me work?" he retorted.

"I will," I said firmly. "Follow me into our gate and I will give you a hoe and you can hoe out the weeds in my garden."

This I did, amused to observe his sad face and reluctant hands as he took the hoe.

"How long am I to work before I am paid?" he asked.

"Work until noon and I will give you money enough to buy yourself two bowls of noodles for your dinner," I told him. "Work until the end of the day and I will give you a day's wage. Come back tomorrow and I will give you another day's wage at nightfall."

I left him and returned at noon to find a meager effort the result of his morning's work. Nevertheless I gave him the coins for his noodles and bade him come back when he had eaten.

He did not come back. I never saw him again until about six months later, when I happened to meet him in another street on the opposite side of the town where I seldom went. He put out his hand to beg, and when he saw who I was horror spread over his brown face. Without one word he darted away and after this time I truly never saw him again.

One Christmas Eve I heard a childish voice at our back door, and opening it, I found there on the doorstep a little boy of perhaps eight, thin and starved, and clad only in a cotton shirt. He was a pretty boy, unusually so, and he looked at me with huge dark eyes.

"Why are you here?" I asked.

"They told me it was your feast day and I thought you might have some scraps for me to eat," he said plaintively.

"Where are you parents?" I asked.

"I have none," he said.

"You must have a family," I remonstrated.

"I have no one," he said in his pathetic voice. "My father and mother and I were walking south to escape the northern famine and they fell ill and died and so I am alone."

It was true that there was a famine in the North that year and the boy looked honest. At any rate, my heart was soft with Christmas sentiment, and so I brought him in and bathed him and put warm clothes on him and fed him. Then I made up a cot in the small study and put him to bed. Nothing was hidden in our life, and of course the two servants we employed soon spread the news about the orphan and the next morning my first visitor was Madame Chang. She heard the story and then she inspected the small boy. He looked back at her in apparent innocence, answering her questions while she stared at him thoughtfully. After a while she sent him to the kitchen and she cogitated and then spoke.

"I distrust this child," she said. "I think someone is taking advantage of Christmas and your good heart. What do you plan to do with him?"

"I haven't thought," I confessed. "I suppose I'll just keep him here, send him to school and so on."

She shook her head. "Keep him but not here," she advised. "Let him go and live with the mission farmer."

Outside the city there was a small farm where the man in the house was experimenting with seed selection and a farmer lived there in our employ. I respected Madame Chang too much not to obey her, and we took our orphan to the farm, giving directions about his care, that he was to be sent each day to the village school and that he could learn to help about the place. Alas, after three months or so of this life, although he grew fat and cheerful, our pretty orphan ran away and we never saw him again either. The farmer was cheerfully philosophical about it. "That small one could never work," he remarked. "Eat and sleep and play he could do very well, but ask him to take the broom and sweep the threshold and he runs away."

The farmer was a kind man and his wife was a motherly woman who had taken the orphan as one of her own brood and she mourned over him, but he was gone, I suppose to join the band of beggars or thieves who had sent him to me in the first place.

Those were the years, too, when I travelled far and wide over the back country where sedan chairs were the only way for a woman to go. I went of course with the man in the house who was restless, I think, about studying Chinese and liked to escape his books. At any rate we travelled, he on bicycle and I in the usual sedan chair. It was enclosed and down the front hung a curtain of heavy blue cotton cloth. I rode with the curtain up while we went along open roads, but as we neared villages and towns I let it fall in order to escape the curiosity of crowds who had never seen a white man or woman. Even so, I did not count on some one who might pass me, walking or donkeyback, and who, reaching a town ahead of us, would cry out on the streets or in a teashop that a strange sight was soon to arrive. More than once when we reached the gates of a walled village or town a crowd would be there waiting, and in such an intense state of curiosity that they could not keep from pulling the curtain aside to stare at me. At first, trying to be like a Chinese lady, I fastened the curtain. Then reflecting that I was not Chinese, and that I had better satisfy their curiosity since it was friendly enough, I put the curtain aside and let them stare. Staring and pressing about me they would follow me to the inn and only an irate innkeeper could make them leave.

"What are you gaping at?" he would bawl at them. "Is it anything but a man and a woman with eyes and arms and legs? Are not all around the four seas one family under Heaven?"

He would make a great ado of pushing them out, but actually he was as curious as they, and soon they were all back again. When I went to my room and shut the wooden door, they would bend down to the ground where for six inches or so there was no door and stare at me upside down. If the windows were papered, they licked their fingers wet and melted holes in the soft rice paper and applied an eye to watch me. Only once was I frightened and that was when our baggage did not arrive and the man went back to find it and left me alone. As soon as they saw he was gone the crowd began to batter at the barred door, and I was uneasy because I had noticed a number of rough young men among them. I drew a heavy wooden chair against the door and sat down in it with my feet drawn up so that they could not see me, and waited until the baggage arrived.

Out of these travels still other friends were found, and as time went on and I became familiar with new places, I used to visit in families where no white person had even been, proud old families who had lived in remote walled towns and in the same houses for many hundreds of years, and sitting with the womenfolk, young and old, I listened to them talk and learned about their lives. One such house I remember especially in a fine old city, small and totally untouched by modern times. The family was surnamed Li, and I became friends with the wife of the youngest son, a woman about my own age.

She was intensely curious about me and about the life I lived, and yet she never spoke a word in the presence of her husband's mother and her elder sisters-in-law. I always noticed her sweet and gentle face, however, and always smiled at her. One day she came to my room alone and begged me to go to the part of the vast compound where she lived. We went through small lanes and hidden ways, for obviously she did not want anybody to know that she was monopolizing me, and at last we reached the little courtyard and the rooms where she and her husband lived. No one was there and she seized my hand and led me into her bedroom and barred the door. It was an old-fashioned Chinese bedroom, such as I had seen many times, the enormous bed, hung with embroidered curtains of red satin, filling one entire end of the room, tables and chairs placed against the wall, and the usual pigskin chests, varnished red and locked with huge brass locks.

"Sit on the bed so we can talk," she begged.

She stepped up on the footstool, for the bed was high, and patted the red satin mattress, and I sat down beside her. Immediately she took my right hand in both hers with friendly affection, and then she began her questions.

"Tell me," she said earnestly, "is it true your husband speaks to you in the presence of other people?"

"Quite true," I said.

"Not shameful?" she persisted.

"We do not consider it so," I assured her.

"Ah," she sighed enviously. "I dare not speak to mine except at night here. If I am with the family and he comes in then I must leave the room, otherwise it would be shameful. How many years do you think I have been married?"

"Not many," I said, smiling. "You look so young."

"Two," she said, holding up two slender fingers. "I have been here two years, yet I have never once spoken to my father-in-law. I bow to him if we meet and then I must leave the room. He does not notice me."

"I have never met my father-in-law nor my mother-in-law," I told her. "They live across the sea in America."

She looked astonished. "Then how was your marriage arranged?"

We talked a long time then about the differences between our peoples, and she showed a lively intelligence. Without the slightest help she had thought a great deal, although apparently her young husband was fond of her and sometimes answered her questions. She adored him, I could see, and she was only sorrowful because they could be together so little, for when he came home at night from the family business, duty compelled him to spend hours with his parents and it was always late when he came to bed, and she was afraid to ask him for too much talk. And yet there was no one else, except the bondsmaids and servants who were more ignorant than she, for custom forbade her to speak to the elder women unless she was spoken to. This rigorousness of family decorum was of course not to be found except in the oldest and richest and most conservative families. Among the poorer people and certainly among those who were more modern there was much freedom. Eventually even my friend would have more freedom, for when her mother-in-law died and her elder sister-in-law became the head of the inner family, her own position would improve until someday she herself might be the head, with daughters-in-law of her own. I am sure it was hard to wait, and she listened enchanted to what I told her about American women.

The longer I lived in our northern city, however, the more deeply impressed I was, not by the rich folk but by the farmers and their families, who lived in the villages outside the city wall. They were the ones who bore the brunt of life, who made the least money and did the most work. They were the most real, the closest to the earth, to birth and death, to laughter and to weeping. To visit the farm families became my own search for reality, and among them I found the human being as he most nearly is. They were not all good, by any means, nor honest, and it was inevitable that the very reality of their lives made them sometimes cruel. A farm woman could strangle her own newborn girl baby if she were desperate enough at the thought of another mouth added to the family, but she wept while she did it and the weeping was raw sorrow, not simply at what she did, but far deeper, over the necessity she felt to do it.

"Better to kill the child," this was what she thought.

Once in a small gathering of friends, and not all of them poor or farm folk, we fell to talking of killing girl babies. There were eleven women present and all except two confessed that at least one girl child had been killed in each home. They still wept when they spoke of it, and most of them had not done the deed themselves, and indeed they declared that they could not have done it, but that their husbands or mothers-in-law had ordered the midwife to do it because there were too many girls in the family already. The excuse was that a girl when she marries becomes part of another family, and poor families could not afford to rear too many children who brought nothing to the family and indeed took from it to go to another family when they married. Yet daughters when they lived were tenderly loved and death had to be done at birth or it was not done at all. A few hours, a first glimpse at a little newborn face, could move the hardest woman to realize that she could not destroy her child. Orders were given before the birth, so that the instant a midwife perceived the sex of the child, were it a girl, she could put her thumb to its throat.

I have heard proud young Chinese abroad declare that such things never happened in their country, and when I hear such talk, I hold my peace. They did happen, for I saw it and heard of it, but these young modern Chinese do not know why it happened, and if they cannot

146

understand the life of their own people and some of the tragedy behind it then let them say what they will. In the same way I have heard them deny that Chinese women have had bound feet in recent decades. Perhaps, living only in the foreign cities of Shanghai or Tientsin or under the Manchu influence of Peking they really have not seen bound feet. But I, living only a few hours from Peking in a town on the railroad, within my adult life have seen girl children with bound feet and most of the women, in both city and country, had bound feet. Our Madame Chang had bound feet, and though they were not small, being six inches long instead of the traditional three, yet she had suffered enough and when she walked it was as though she went on pegs. Madame Wu had always to lean on two bondsmaids when she came to see me, and her feet were only three inches long and she wore beautiful little satin shoes. Yet the granddaughters of Madame Chang and Madame Wu were not having their feet bound because they were going to school. Madame Chang put it in practical terms when she said one day, "I am glad for every girl who does not have her feet bound, for I spent my nights in weeping when I was a girl before my feet grew numb. Yet if she is not bound-footed she must be educated, otherwise she will not get a husband. A small-footed girl can get an old-fashioned husband and a big-footed girl, if educated, can get a new-fashioned husband, but small feet or schooling she must have, one or the other."

It is true that in certain areas of China there never were bound feet. I remember once travelling in the province of Fukien in South China and discovering there that the countrywomen went freely about with natural feet. They were beautiful strong women, and it was the wise local custom to marry sons to countrywomen so as to bring clean new blood into the family. These daughters-in-law were not ladies of leisure. Instead they did all the work of the family, very much as though they were maids, and the whole family depended upon them and they were always stronger than their husbands. I remember visiting in the family of a friend who lived in Amoy and although it was a scholar family we were waited upon at dinner by a handsome country girl with bare brown feet thrust into cotton shoes. She smiled when her mother-in-law introduced her to us as her daughter-in-law, and she busied herself, managing everything well, joining in the conversation and yet never sitting down with us.

And among the people in my childhood region in mid-China the farm women seldom had bound feet. It was only the city families who bound their daughters' feet. But there we were on the main road of new China, and few of my generation were binding the feet of their girl children. One hears many stories of how this custom grew up in

China, all of them mostly myth. It was in my time merely a matter of custom and beauty, exactly as the young Chinese are fond of saying, as westerners used to bind the waists of their women in corsets or as young Western women today preposterously exaggerate their breasts. People do strange things for what they consider beauty.

And speaking of cruelty, this is perhaps the place to mention the cruelty to animals which shocks so many foreigners when they visit China. There is indeed a vast difference between the way in which animals are treated in China and the way in which they are treated in the West. Animals are not petted and fondled and made much of by the Chinese. On the contrary, Chinese visitors in the United States are usually shocked and disgusted by the affection with which animals are treated, an emotion which the Chinese feel should be reserved for human beings. I believe in kindness toward animals and human beings and I used to wonder why my Chinese friends, whom I knew to be merciful and considerate toward people, could be quite indifferent to suffering animals. The cause, I discovered as I grew older, lay in the permeation of Chinese thought by Buddhist theory. Though most Chinese were not religious and therefore not Buddhist, yet the doctrine of the reincarnation of the human soul influenced their thinking, and the essence of that theory is that an evil human being after death becomes an animal in his next incarnation. Therefore every animal was once a wicked human being. While the average Chinese might deny direct belief in this theory, yet the pervading belief led him to feel contempt for animals.

Another seeming cruelty among the Chinese, also very shocking to Westerners, was that if a person fell into a danger, as for example if he fell into the water and would be drowned if not pulled out, no other Chinese, or only a very rare one, would stretch out his hand to the drowning one. Cruel? Yes, but again the pervading atmosphere of Buddhism through the centuries had persuaded the people generally to believe that fate pursued the sufferer, that his hour had come for death. If one saved him, thus defying fate, the rescuer must assume the responsibilities of the one saved. A man, however kind, might hesitate if by saving a person who had fallen into the danger of death, he had thereafter to care for this person and even perhaps his whole family because he had made himself responsible for giving new life to one who was supposed to die.

Time went on in our quiet northern town, and at last we, too, became embroiled in the national troubles. War lords had the country firmly in their rude clutches by now and in our own region battles began to break out between them. It was never called war but always "attacking the bandits." This is, each war lord would claim that he was the real ruler and the other one was the "bandit chief." At least once or twice a year bullets would fly over our town in brief but alarming scuffles, and the little hospital would be filled with wounded soldiers from both sides. We learned when the bullets whistled over the roof to run for the inner corners of a room and stand there until the battle moved on and certainly never to remain near windows. At sundown the battle usually ended, or if we were lucky enough to have a rainstorm come up, the soldiers on both sides prudently called a truce and returned to their encampments outside the city wall so that they would not get their uniforms wet. The city fathers never let either side camp in the city. When a battle threatened, the main gates were barred and the wounded were brought in through a small wicket gate.

Those old-fashioned wars were often amusing rather than dangerous, provided one stayed out of the range of gunshot, and since war lords themselves did not enjoy a strenuous battle they made various excuses for truce. Actually they preferred treachery and strategy to open warfare, and sometimes over a dinner table when the terms of a truce were to be discussed, there was a surprise assassination of the guests, and so was ended the danger of more war for the time being, at least. I learned to take such skirmishes as part of life, and used precaution without being afraid.

One further change came to my life, and it was the building of a new house. My little four-room Chinese home was needed for expansion of the boys' school and the mission bought a piece of land outside the city and we were told to design a modest house and build it. I wanted a Chinese house all on one floor but this I was forbidden by the mission authorities. No, it must be a two-story house after the Western fashion, and although I disliked exceedingly the idea of this monstrosity on the flat northern landscape, there was no recourse. I planned a story-and-a-half structure, very simple, but still with stairs, and when it was finished my city friends and country neighbors came to see the foreign house. They were fascinated and terrified by the stairs. They went up fairly easily but looking down that steep decline they could not risk it.

"This is the way I shall do it," Madame Chang declared, and she sat herself without more ado on the top step and gravely bumped her way down the steps on her seat, her padded winter garments protecting her nicely. And after her came all the other ladies without the slightest self-consciousness, until the last one was safely on the first floor. The most delightful quality the Chinese had, I do believe, was the total lack of self-consciousness in all they did. It did not occur to them to wonder or to care what anybody else thought. It was only in Western-educated Chinese that I began to see self-consciousness, allied with a pitiful false shame of their own people. How sorry I felt for them then, for indeed they ought to have been proud of a nation so civilized by the centuries that its people could behave without self-consciousness! Only royalty in England can equal them in the West, with perhaps the recent addition of Sir Winston Churchill himself.

The years passed tranquilly in our town in spite of the sporadic skirmishes between war lords and my days were absorbed in small human events. There is much humor in Chinese life when it is fully shared, and this comes from the sense of drama which is natural to almost every Chinese. The least quarrel, a festival or a birthday, provided rich entertainment, and a birth, a death or a wedding was enough for days of talk and enjoyment. The raw humor of peasants and the jollity of merchants and their families were never entirely overcome even by occasional and inevitable tragedy. How can I ever forget the trials of old Mr. Hsü, our town's rich man, whose life was enlivened and beset by his four wives, and the clamor with which they surrounded him! When he travelled on the train to Pengp'u he dared not do what he wished, which was to take only his youngest and therefore his favorite concubine with him. She was a pretty woman in her late twenties, the only one still slender enough to wear the long, tight and very fashionable Shanghai dress. Each journey he began with the determination that he would take only the youngest woman with him, but he was never allowed the luxury. It was impossible to keep anything secret, and so each woman complained until he had unwillingly agreed to take all four. For economy's sake, however, he distributed them through the train, the third and the youngest concubine with him in second class, the second in third class and his wife and the first concubine in fourth class. Alas, he still had no peace, for the three who were in the lower classes were continually around him, demanding the same food and tidbits that he bought for his favorite. The harassment of Mr. Hsü made town talk, embellished with local witticisms.

Suicides among young women were not uncommon and I shall never forget the one next door. She was my friend, a young woman of my own age, and so I knew that she was not happy with her husband or his family. She was a sensitive intelligent girl who longed to go to school, and much of our time together was spent with books, for she had an insatiable thirst for knowledge. I had been afraid that she might end her own life, for she had no escape, and gradually she had given up hope. I was sent for one bright sunny day at midmorning, and when I reached her room, the family had only just cut the rope by which she had hung herself. I took her hand and it was still soft and warm. She lay there on the tiled floor, limp as a child, her face not marred, and I could not believe she was dead. I begged them to let me try first aid, but her mother-in-law would not allow such foreign ways. The Buddhist funeral priests had already arrived and the death chant had begun. I met hostile looks when I persisted and Madame Chang, who had come soon after I did, hurried me away.

My chief intramural interest, if one may so speak of our compound, was the girls' school for which I was responsible, and I invited as head teacher one of my old girlhood friends from Chinkiang. She was an able teacher, young and enthusiastic, and I hoped for much accomplishment from her. Alas, as so often happens in China, although she liked the job and the friendly community and especially her eager pupils, she was defeated by the northern food. The Chinese are strangely insular in the matter of food, probably because of the importance that they attach to eating, and she could not make the change in diet from the rice of mid-China to the wheaten bread and millet of the North. She lost weight and vitality, not because she did not digest the new diet, but because it was too strange to eat bread instead of rice, and at last I yielded and acknowledged defeat.

All during these years I lived deeply and narrowly in one community where an age-old peace had never been broken in spite of the World War raging in Europe. True, Mrs. Liu, a tall thin woman with a very yellow face, was in much suffering because her husband, a "good-for-nothing," as she frankly called him, had gone to France as a laborer during the World War and she had then heard through another friend, whose husband had also gone to France as a laborer, that her "good-for-nothing" was living with a French woman. Mrs. Liu was torn between grief and pride.

"To think," she cried, the tears streaming down her face, "that my old good-for-nothing should have got himself a foreign woman! But what sort of woman, I ask you? Anyone can see that my old piece-of-baggage is no use. Why, I was even glad when he came home last year from Shanghai and said he was going for a soldier! And now he has got a foreign woman! What if he brings her home? How can we feed her? What do French women eat?"

The term "good-for-nothing," I discovered, was the usual name for a husband in our region, where women prided themselves on their virtue. "My *yao-yieh*," or "my good-for-nothing"—the women began most of their sentences with these words. It was true that generally speaking the men were inferior to the women, and this I suppose was because boys were so spoiled in Chinese homes, whereas the girls knew from the first that they had their own way to make and would get very little spoiling indeed. Whatever the reason, the Chinese woman usually emerges the stronger character wherever she is, and out of this fact comes a rich vernacular humor which American men and women could understand without the slightest difficulty. Chinese women are witty and brave and resourceful, and they have learned to live freely behind their restrictions. They are the most realistic and least sentimental of human beings, capable of absolute devotion to those they love and of implacable hatred, not always concealed, toward those whom they hate. The Communists could never have taken China, I believe, if they had not prudently given so much advantage to Chinese women. I remember seeing a few years ago the manuscript account of two young American fliers who had been forced down within Communist territory in China and were later released. During the weeks they spent in a Communist village, they observed with interest and pity how ardently the women supported the new regime and this, they said, was merely because the Communists gave the women help with their children, a meager amount of medicine and food, and yet it was enough to touch the hearts of those who had never been given help before. "How much better we Americans could have done it," the young fliers commented, "had we only known!"

The quiet and intensely interesting years in my northern town came rather abruptly to an end one day when the man in the house announced that there was a vacancy in the University of Nanking and that he intended to apply for it. He had been floundering, as I well knew, unable to find a way of applying Western farm methods to an old and established agriculture. It would be better, he now said, to join a group somewhere rather than to work alone. He could teach agricultural students in a university and let them make the practical application.

I was sad to leave my northern town where I had been so warmly befriended, and yet in a way I was glad to get back into the midst of modern China. I had almost lost touch even with the literary revolution except to know that it was still going on. True, Nanking was not the center of change, and certainly then I could not foresee that in less than ten years it would be the capital of Chiang Kai-chek's revolutionary new government. When I went there to live, it was still an ancient and conservative city and, by its own tradition, was even the stronghold of a school of old-fashioned scholars who opposed the "common language" of the young Western-trained intellectuals' school, the "riksha-coolie-talk school," as Lin Shu liked to call it. Nevertheless, Nanking was also a center of historical Chinese life, the capital for a long time of the fabulous Ming dynasty, and now it had two Christian colleges, one for men, one for women, and the Chinese National University also.

In my northern home town there were feasts and farewells and exchanges of gifts and considerable weeping and many promises to visit before finally I closed the new brick house, in which I had supposed I would spend the rest of my life, and took the train southward.

Island Beach, New Jersey

Our old Coast Guard house stands bleak and unimproved on the New Jersey shore. I came here today in the early morning, bringing nothing with me except a little food. A few worn dresses hang in the closet from one year's end to the other, a couple of bathing suits and some sandals, and depending on the season I get into dress or bathing suit and go down to the sea. On the other side of the narrow tongue of sandy soil is the wide bay where my American children played safely through their summer months when they were little, an old rowboat securely tethered to the rough dock for the center of imagination. They fell out of it into the shallow water and climbed back into it a hundred times a day, they crabbed and fished and rowed as far as the rope would go. Then suddenly they outgrew the bay and we moved our quarters to the Coast Guard house on the oceanside, and the bay was useful only for serious crabbing and later for the first outboard motor.

To the sea I go with love and terror, for actually I am afraid of water and I know why. I crossed the Pacific too often and too young, and I am never deceived by calm under sunshine or even under the moon. The madness is there, hidden in the depths of unknown caverns. And yet I go back to the sea again and again, although I do not want to stay long and there are certain times of the year when I would not be near it for any reason.

The beach is wide and deserted today except for a few fishermen who do not turn their heads to see who passes. It is as private here as any lonely coral isle could be, white sand, blue sky and a sea more blue. The children have gone out to sail, the house is empty and quiet, and memory flows unchecked as I sit alone by the seaward window.

. . . I had been in Nanking only once before I went to live there and that had been as a girl when I visited a school friend. My memories of it were vague and overlaid with later experiences, and now I saw the city with fresh eyes. It lies seven miles from the Yangtse River, a vast walled area, and its city wall is one of the handsomest in China, made of large brick as strong as stone, and so wide at the top that several automobiles can travel abreast. This wall is twenty-five miles in circumference, and I was to know it later for various reasons, one of which was that during the famines which befell North China periodically the refugees flooded into Nanking and lacking other space built their matting huts on top of the city wall where the winter winds were the most bitter. One of the few angry discussions I ever had with a Chinese friend was with a young woman of Nanking who had been graduated from the University of Chicago, where she specialized in social service. We had a famine that first winter in Nanking, a very bad one, and I tried to do my share in getting food and clothing for the thousands of wretched people huddled on the city wall. Thus I went to Mrs. Yang, only that was not her name. She was a young and very pretty woman—pretty, that is, in a sort of hard smart modern fashion. Her satin dresses were Chinese, but cut tight to her slender figure, and her hair was short. Her house was a two-story, Western brick building, furnished in semi-foreign fashion. In the neat little living room with flowered carpet, curtained windows, formal modern landscapes in gilt frames on the wall, I told her of the plight of the refugees on the city wall. She would not believe that conditions were as I portrayed them for her, nor could I persuade her to climb the city wall and see for herself. The street in which she lived was the most modern in the old city and she never went far from it.

"I saw such things in Chicago slums," she said complacently, "but I am sure that they are not here."

Nor would she stir herself to find out the truth. In my memory she is embalmed as the typical Western-educated Chinese who is no longer Chinese. She had created a little tight nice world of her own, whose citizens were all like herself. They lived in neat little brick houses, their husbands had university jobs and their children went to an exclusive kindergarten. Beyond this they did not want to know. Perhaps they were afraid to know. China had its vast and frightening aspects.

The city wall was more than a place for refugees, however. In the spring when they had gone back to their land, it became a pleasant place to walk and I could gaze out over the countryside and the mountains. One mountain stood high and clear against the sky, Tze-ch'ing Shan or Purple Mountain, and it became a resort of delight as I came to know my city better. Temples were hidden in the mountain, beautiful shaded spots of repose, and near there, too, were the tombs of the Ming Emperors, approached by avenues of huge stone beasts and men on guard. There were many stories still told about the Mings. No one, it was said, knew where the emperors were actually buried, for at the time of an Imperial funeral, nine processions, all exactly alike, proceeded at the same time from the nine gates of the city. Stories were told also of fabulous treasures buried in the tombs but I doubted that. Too many tombs had been looted during the centuries, and probably all that was left was the human dust, and that much disturbed.

I cannot but linger on Purple Mountain, even at this distance of time and space, for many of my happiest hours were spent there. Its crest rose to a peak, and I climbed it alone one day in July and reaching the cliff I looked over it. There on the northern flank of the mountain, before my astonished eyes spread a field of royal-blue wild monkshood, all in flower. I went to the mountain top each year after that to see such beauty, and I shall never forget the sight.

Bamboos grew upon the southern side of the mountain and pines and trees of every kind, and among them were pleasant stone-flagged walks which the priests had made for pilgrims. I loved the ineffable peace of the temples, and although I did not worship the gods there or anywhere, I liked to sit in the quiet of their presence, or perhaps only in the presence of lost prayers, still lingering in the fragrance of the incense that burned unceasingly before the images, a symbol of yearning human hope.

The countryside was surpassingly beautiful around Nanking and I reveled in it after the flat northern landscape, for I am one of those whom any city confines unbearably and am compelled to escape, although in Nanking there was much to enjoy even inside the walls. The site of the old Porcelain Pagoda, for example, which had been one of the wonders of ancient China, was a beautiful spot, and one could still find bits of the bright enameled tiles of which it had been built, many-colored, but mainly green. The Porcelain Pagoda is said to have been the most beautiful of all the pagodas in China. It was built in the early part of the fifteenth century by Yung-lo, the third Ming Emperor, as a thank offering to his Empress. Only nine of its originally planned thirteen stories were ever completed and even so the building took nineteen years. It was nearly three hundred feet high and nearly one hundred feet in diameter at its base, and it tapered gracefully as it rose. One hundred and forty lamps lit the brilliantly colored tiles by night, and when the sun fell upon it by day, it was truly a spectacle. Of course popular superstition surrounded such a fabulous building and all sorts of magic qualities were attributed to it. The lamps were said to illumine the thirty-three heavens above and to prevent disaster to all around. The pagoda had been destroyed in 1856 by the Tai-p'ing revolutionaries because they feared that its strange geomantic powers would work against them, and so all I could see of it in reality was the base and the bits of broken tile gleaming in the wild grass.

Near the site of the Porcelain Pagoda was a small but beautiful temple famous for its great bronze bell. This was the Temple of the Three Sisters, and the resonant echo of the bell was the result, an old priest told me, of the flesh and blood of the three young girls. They were the daughters of the bellmaker who, in spite of all efforts, could not persuade the metal to give forth a pure tone. The whole family was in distress, for the Emperor had commissioned the bell. One night the bellmaker's three daughters dreamed that a goddess came down and told them that if they would leap into the molten metal the next time the father melted the bell to cast it again, the tone would come out a deep pure music. Without telling their father they determined to sacrifice themselves, and when he melted the bell, they leaped into the cauldron without his knowledge. What was his wonder, when the bell was recast, to hear it give forth a magic voice! It is a story I have heard of other temple bells and so often that there must once have been such devoted daughters somewhere, if not at the Temple of the Three Sisters in Nanking.

And I remember Lotus Lake outside the city wall, where I was to spend so many happy afternoons and evenings. There in summer at the end of a long hot day I would go with a friend or two and engage a little boat, in which we sat as long as we liked while the boatman rowed us through the watery lanes of the lotus plants. The great rosy blossoms lay open upon the surface of the lake until the sun set and they slowly closed, their fragrance lingering sweetly upon the air. In the dusk the boatman would reach under the huge heavy leaves and pluck off lotus pods for us secretly, for the concession for lotus seed was rented out, such seeds being a delicacy used for feast dishes. In the moonlight we pulled the pithy pods apart and peeled the seeds hidden in them, nuts as big as almonds. If we were really hungry the boatman's wife would cook a dish of noodles for us, and while we ate we listened to the sounds of singing over the water, a pretty courtesan, perhaps a "flower girl," strumming her lute for her lover.

I remember, too, The Drum Tower, a handsome and ancient edifice near to the house that had been allotted to us for a home. The Drum Tower was a vast square building, painted red, upon which stood the squat tiered tower. A wide high tunnel made the building a gateway through which the main street to the river ran, and in those shadowy depths beggars took shelter in winter, and in summer the melon vendors sat there to keep their melons cool.

But indeed the old city was full of beauty and there is much to remember, too much to tell. I was grateful when I found that my windows opened to Purple Mountain, and I chose for my own an attic room from which I could look over the compound wall upon the near view of vegetable gardens and a cluster of brick farmhouses and a large fish pond. Beyond these, on the left, were the curved roofs of the university and beyond them a pagoda and the city wall and then the mountain. The city was full of trees and gardens, and this was because it had been designed from the first, centuries ago, to contain within its walls sufficient space so that if enemies attacked, the gates could be locked and the besieged could live indefinitely upon the land inside.

Within my own wall was a grey brick house surrounded by plenty of lawn, a bamboo grove and a vegetable garden, while the servants' quarters were in one corner at the back of the house. I set myself joyfully to make a flower garden and especially a rose garden, for the lovely Chinese tea roses had refused to grow in the dry northern climate. The gardener, who had been on the place before, begged to be kept on, which I was willing to do, and he led me about the place explaining its difficulties. When we came to the bamboo grove he gave me grave looks and sighed.

"There is something very strange about these bamboos, Learned Mother," he said.

"Indeed," I replied with interest. "What is peculiar?"

"They never have sprouts," he replied sadly. "Each spring I look for the sprouts and, alas, there are none."

"That is strange," I agreed. "I have lived in China since I was very small and never did I hear of bamboos with no sprouts in the spring. We must get up early in the morning when the season comes again and perhaps we shall find them. I like to eat bamboo sprouts in the spring."

He gave me the flicker of an eye and nodded, and thereafter we had no trouble at all about sprouts. Each spring they came up thickly and inevitably, and the cook made delicious dishes from them. As for the gardener, he stayed with me faithfully for the next years until a revolutionary army drove all white people from the city and then he disappeared and I never saw him again. With him, I was told, disappeared various valuables, and I suppose that he paid himself back for the bamboo sprouts he no longer ate. But I was fond of him for he made me laugh very often, rascal and wild-witted fellow that he was, and his wife, a small harassed woman, was my devoted friend. She was older than he, and nothing that either of us could do could prevent him from gambling his wages away, so that I often gave her secret money to keep her children from starving. They lived in a hut outside the wall, for he did not want the trouble of his many children trampling the flower beds, and much to his own and his wife's misery, they averaged more than a child a year. Indeed, as the poor little bedraggled mother said to me once, "It is mercy that we women must have nine months to make a child, for if it were only a day, I should have a new one every day, that man being what he is."

During the long hot summers there was always a new and ailing baby to keep alive somehow, and the mother's milk never was enough and each morning I made up bottles of formula and the mother came for them. Each year I remonstrated with the gardener and urged self-control, and he agreed with all that I said, but the new baby arrived as promptly as ever. At last I could only look my reproach, for words were useless, and one day he came in and said he had a favor to ask of me.

"Please, Learned Mother," he said plaintively, "find me a job on the opposite side of the city so that I cannot come home."

I knew too well what this meant.

"Which is it this time?" I inquired. "Boy or girl?"

"Both," he said in a whisper.

"Twins!" I gasped.

He nodded his miserable head, speechless.

It was another world, familiar and yet new. My parents were not too far away, only two hours by rail, and I went home as often as I could to see them. My mother was plainly fading, though she came of a long-lived family and was not yet old, and I was increasingly anxious about her.

My child was born that first year in Nanking, too, and after that I was not so free to come and go as I had been. I did not mind, for to have a child was a miracle to me and I did not dream of the dark future in store for us both. Mercifully I was to have nearly four years of happy ignorance about her. During that same year my mother died, not suddenly, but slowly and unwillingly, and I am glad that she never knew what lay ahead for me. But let me tell of the year of birth and death.

It was 1921 and I was in full touch again with what was going on in China. Japanese militarists had made great profit from the World War, for in 1915 Japan began the conquest of China in earnest. While the Western Powers were busy with the war, she made the infamous demands which would have reduced China almost to a colony, until the nine-power Washington conference, in 1922, was to return the province of Shantung to China and restored a measure of her independence. It soon became evident, however, that unless China could organize herself somehow and establish a unified government, she would eventually be swallowed up by Japan. Responsible Chinese were anxious, as one irresponsible war lord after another continued to borrow money from Japan and to give national resources as surety.

I began almost immediately to teach English literature in the National University but my students were distracted from their studies because of their rage, equally given to the Japanese aggressors and to their own indifferent and ignorant war lords. In Nanking itself we lived under a war lord who was only slightly better than those in the North, and his lack of energy in betraying his country was due to opium rather than to patriotism. It was a strange double sort of life which reminds me of the way we live now at this moment in the United States. While the President and his cabinet tell us that we may at any moment be annihilated, and while we realize the validity of the warning yet we all go on living and planning the details of our days exactly as though no threat hung over our heads. We know, we realize, we are not apathetic, but the monstrous potentiality of our times is too much for us. We cannot act as though the bomb might fall, or else we could not live at all.

So it was in those days in Nanking, when it was clear to everyone and especially I think to the young Chinese intellectuals what horrors lay ahead, and yet we went our daily way. The seasons changed, my garden bloomed, the markets were filled with fine foods and flowers and crowded with buyers, we did our work carefully and well, we went to the hills for picnics and weekends, the city seemed happy, the people were content and prosperous, our war lord was not oppressive, and yet we all knew that at any moment it might and perhaps it must end, because no one knew what to do to prevent the future before it became inevitable.

My friends now were entirely different from the ones in my northern town. They were my neighbors, young couples, both Chinese and American, who were ultramodern in their education and outlook, and my students who came from all over China. Some came, too, from Korea and it was in them that I discovered the source of the deepest hatred against Japan. These young Koreans were the sons and daughters of Korean families who had not been able to endure Japanese rule in their own land, and had therefore left the country, some to come to China, others to go to Manchuria and still others to Russia to rear their children. From their parents the young Koreans had learned rebellion, and so I first began to understand the causes whose results have led straight and inevitably to the Korea of today.

Three dates are monuments in my memory of the next decade. In October of that year of 1921 my mother died, after a last long illness. She had apparently recovered from sprue, but actually she had never recovered. The mucous membranes of her intestines were scarred, I suppose, and she could not absorb sufficient nourishment to maintain her health, whatever her diet. I wanted to take her to the United States but she was convinced that she could not survive the incurable seasickness which no remedy could allay and she would not cross the ocean. More than the conviction, I think she felt it was too late to lead another life than the one she had so long lived. She could not begin again, even in her own country, and so she quietly began to die and, although the dying took months, its end was soon clear and inevitable. She did not want to die, that was plain, too, but there was no help for it. I was with her almost constantly. But I could not hide from myself that she was doomed, and I tried to face a world in which I could never see her face again. I had learned to live my own life and yet it was rooted in my deep relationship with her. The relationship was sometimes irksome because of the very fact that I loved her so well and understood her and recognized in myself certain qualities which were hers. There were even moments, the parting being inescapable, when I longed for it to be over and in the past. This is the cruelty of youth, and there is no one who is not guilty of it sometimes. I look now at my own children and reflect that I must neither love nor be loved too much if I want them to enjoy their freedom while I am alive and not anticipate it before my death. Yet there must be enough love, too, for growth.

When on a grey October afternoon the nurse told us, my father and my sister and me, that my mother was dying it was I alone who could not go to her bedside. Had she been conscious, I would have compelled myself and indeed might have wanted to go and see her last conscious looks and hear her last words. But she was in coma, and whether I went or not she would never know, and so I let them enter her bedroom without me and I stood in the hall outside and gazed out of the window at a landscape dimmed by tears. When I think of her dying I still see that landscape, the bamboos swaying below the window, the valley beyond, the small farmhouses and the tawny fields, the late gleaners moving slowly across them, women and children in their peasant blue, and beyond them again the distant mountains. Those were long minutes in which I felt my very flesh being torn from hers. I longed to go to her and I could not. My father opened the door at last and said in a strange calm voice that she was gone and then he walked wearily down the hall and the stairs to his own study, and a few minutes later my sister came, but I cannot remember beyond that.

The next day a neighbor missionary coaxed me to go in and see her before the coffin lid was closed.

"She looks beautiful," the neighbor said in a tender voice. "You'll be sorry if you don't take a last look at your mother."

I went in unwillingly, nevertheless, and glanced at the waxen figure which I could scarcely recognize and then rushed away. And I wish, even at the length of these years, that I had not to remember that waxen doll, who was only someone strange.

The funeral was the next day, a grey autumnal day, dripping rain, and the little procession made its way down the hill and across the valley to the small walled cemetery of the white people. Oh, those sad cemeteries of the white people in alien lands! We used to walk about those very paths, my mother and I, when we came to bring flowers to my dead baby brother, buried there years before, and I knew by heart the verses on the tombstones. The earliest graves were more than a hundred years old, and beneath their green moss lay the dust of three white sailors, nationality unknown. I still remember the verse upon their common tombstone:

> *Whoe'er thou art who passeth by,*
> *As thou art now so once was I.*
> *As I am now, so must thou be,*
> *Therefore prepare to follow me.*

What my mother always saw, however, were the many graves of babies and small children and the many graves of women who died in childbirth. I remember her refusing to look at the tall shaft on the grave of a famous English missionary, who lay buried in a pleasant plot, surrounded by three of his successive wives and several of their children.

"The old reprobate!" she had said indignantly.

But here we brought her, too, to lie, and I was only glad that at least her grave was dug in an empty corner, where the sun shone down and wild purple violets clung in the crannies of the high brick wall.

Elsewhere I have described that day, and I cannot live it again, although it is as strangely clear against the years as though I had but just returned to the empty house.

When I went back to Nanking and to my new home there, I was filled with the need to keep my mother alive, and so I began to write about her. I thought and said it was for my own children, that they might have a portrait of her, since they were too young to remember her as she had been when alive. I did not know that this portrait, so carefully made from my exact memory, was to be my first book. I did not even think of it as a book until years later. It was for my children, and when it was written I put it in a box and sealed it and placed it in a high wall closet to wait until they were old enough to read it for themselves. I did not dream, either, that because I put it so securely away it was to escape the revolution which broke over our heads a few years later so that it was almost the only possession that survived. It went to America with me eventually and was put away again in my farmhouse to wait still longer, for by then I knew that my eldest child would never be able to read it, and I have told her story in a little book, *The Child Who Never Grew*. When a family need arose, after still more years, I thought of my mother and how she would have wanted to help and, as though she had said so, I remembered her portrait and dedicated it to the cause and it was published as a book under the title *The Exile*. It was the seventh of my published books, but actually it was the first one to be written.

When it was done I found I wanted to keep on writing, and the summer after my mother's death, while I was in Kuling with my sister and my child, I remember quite clearly one August afternoon that I said suddenly, "This very day I am going to begin to write. I am ready for it at last."

Though it was the hour sacred to the semi-tropical siesta, an hour which, however, I always devoted to reading, I sat down as I was, in my robe of blue Chinese silk, and I cannot tell why I remember such foolish detail, but that is always the way I see whatever I am thinking about, and I wrote a little essay, light enough in its touch but expressing some of the experiences of my world at that time. I typed it as best I could and that means badly for I have never mastered a machine, and sent it off to the *Atlantic Monthly,* which I suppose is the usual goal of the beginner. When this was done I enjoyed a delightful exhilaration. At last I had begun to do what I had always known I would do as soon as I felt rich enough in human experience. And after the essay was accepted and published, I had a letter from the *Forum,* asking for an article.

Since neither of these essays has ever been reprinted in any of my books, I include them here not only as part of the record but also as pictures of China in those days. The year was 1922, and I was thirty years old. It was high time, indeed.

And here is the essay, just as it appeared in the *Atlantic:*

IN CHINA, TOO

It is rather alarming, even sitting in one's armchair on the opposite side of the world, to observe the youth of America and England through the various newspapers and periodicals of the times. Especially when one's days have been spent, placidly enough, among the ultra-conservative parents and grandparents of a remote spot in the Far East, where the covert glance of a man for a maid is an outrage, and the said maid is at once fastened yet more securely behind barred courtyard doors!

Dancing on six inches or so of floorspace, the discussion of knees and necks and petting parties, the menace of the movies and the divorce question, are a far cry from this tranquil corner of my cool, wide veranda. I look through the shady screen of drooping mimosas and bamboos, upon the quiet street of a small town in the far interior of China. High brick walls almost hide the curving roofs of the staid, respectable neighbor homes about me. All I can see of the flapper age of maiden within is when a curtained sedan chair stops behind the spirit wall protecting each great carved gateway. If one watches keenly enough from the corner of one's eye, one may see a slender figure in peach-colored, brocaded silk, with tiny embroidered shoes, and smooth jet hair decorated with seedpearls, slip shyly through the gate. Fragile, long-nailed fingers stained a deep rose, a satin-smooth, painted cheek, and dark, downcast eyes—an instant, then the curtains are drawn, and the chair-bearers go trotting down the street.

Sometimes it is a ponderous dowager, in plum-colored satin, with proud drooping eyelids, opium-stained teeth, and a long bamboo pipe, silver-tipped, which she uses as a cane. She leans heavily on two girl slaves, and is supported into the chair. If her eyes fall on one, their glance passes haughtily through to the space beyond. What! Notice a foreign devil! A flash of ruby and the curtains are drawn close, and the chair-bearers trot off again—albeit not blithely, under the royal weight.

I never see, on this narrow, cobbled street, the barbarous sights whereof I read in the modern magazines. Yet all day long, people are passing. In the early morning, blue-coated farmers, and sometimes their sturdy, barefoot wives, come to town, carrying on either end of their shoulder-poles great round baskets of fresh, dewy vegetables, or huge bundles of dried grass for fuel; caravans of tiny, neat-footed donkeys patter past, with enormous, cylindrical bags of flour or rice crossed upon their backs, swayed down from excessive burdens borne to early. Sometimes their nostrils have been slit, that they may pant more rapidly under the weight of their cruel loads.

Wheelbarrows squeak shrilly along; the more loudly the better, for each wheelbarrow man cultivates his barrow's squeak assiduously for good luck's sake. They are brawny men, with swelling muscles, bare to the waist, their backs dripping and brown in the heat of the morning sun; a length of blue cotton is thrown lengthwise across their shoulders. Sometimes the barrow's load is a substantial country mother, in to shop or to visit a town relative, herself on one side of the wheel, and her bedding, a couple of cocks, a bundle of garlic, a basket of cakes, an immense oil-paper umbrella, and an odd child or two, on the other side. Sometimes an unearthly squalling racks the air, and it is a wheelbarrow with a stout middle-aged hog strapped firmly on either side of the wheel, with his legs waving violently, and squealing in the utmost agitation and outrage. A wheelbarrow, in short, may carry anything, from a lean itinerant missionary, with a six weeks' supply of bedding, food, and tracts, to a double basket of squawking fowls—geese, perhaps, with yards of neck protruding from the loosely woven reeds, and viewing the passing landscape excitedly.

Smiling, snag-toothed old men hobble along my street, with wrinkled brown faces, and sparse white queues braided up with a good deal of black string. They pass the time of day with each other by solicitous inquiries as to when the last meal was enjoyed—a curious outgrowth of a land of frequent famines.

Everywhere are fat brown babies tumbling about in the dust, for the most part naked and glistening in the warm sun, and grubbing among the cobbles and gutters. They ought to die, when one considers the amount and quality of the dirt they constantly consume from grimy fingers and unspeakable faces, not to speak of immensely long cucumbers and great turnips, gobbled rinds and all. But apparently they live to grow fat; although I have occasionally called one by his name of Little Two, to be answered with a broad grin that he is Little Three, Little Two having died of an excess of watermelons the previous summer. But where one drops out, two spring up to fill his place.

They play about promiscuously in the grime, until, in a few miraculously short years, the boys turn out in long gowns, and the girls in embroidered coats, with smooth black bands of hair about demure faces. They have apparently forgotten their playtime together, and ignore each other with the most perfect good breeding. The little girls go into seclusion with apparent docility, until such time as the great red bridal chair shall call them forth to the rule of a mother-in-law; and the boys turn to school or an apprenticeship, depending upon the family means and social position.

All a very placid and well-regulated existence! Yet I am vaguely troubled by a sort of undercurrent of changes; as, for instance, yesterday, when little Hsü Pao-ying came to visit me. I have known her since she was a mite, with a fat, solemn dumpling of a face, with no nose to speak of. At that time, her feast-day garb was a pair of ridiculously small red-cotton trousers and a little coat to match; a pair of shoes made to resemble improbable tigers, and a cap like an embroidered doughnut, with a tiny pigtail done up in cerise yarn sticking through the hole. Her parents are of the good old conservative type, not believing in overmuch book-knowledge for a girl, and with an eye to a good husband and mother-in-law for the child. An older married sister, advanced in views through a five years' residence in Shanghai, had teased them into sending Pao-ying to a boarding-school in the nearest city. When the child left last for school, last autumn, she was a tractable, meek, sweet-faced little thing, rather frightened at the prospect of leaving home. She had the patient air which all little Chinese girls have who are enduring foot-binding. I have never heard her volunteer a remark, and in my presence she had always been particularly awed and reverential—an attitude I have ever found very pleasing in the young.

Yesterday she came in a delicate blue satin of a more fashionable cut than I had ever seen; her feet were unbound and in little clumping, square, black leather foreign shoes. She was evidently very proud of them; they looked like shoes for a very rough little American boy, and had steel taps on the heels. They stuck out most oddly from her exquisite brocaded skirt.

After we had exchanged polite remarks, and had taken our first sip of tea, she was so evidently conscious of her feet that I could not but comment on her unusual footgear.

"It is the very latest fashion," she replied with great satisfaction. "You know that, of course, in the big cities like Peking and Shanghai, the really fashionable girls do not bind their feet any more. At the boarding-school they don't either; and so, when I came home, I cried for three days, without food, until for peace they unbound my feet so that I might wear these beautiful American shoes. My feet are still too small, but I stuff cotton in the toes."

Here was change, indeed! I fell back astounded in my chair. There she sat, slim, exquisite, and complacent, but no longer one to be condescended to, and not at all reverential. I felt slightly dashed. And in the course of the afternoon's conversation, I noticed several other things: a little superior smile at her honored mother's lack of worldly experience, as the present generation sees it; a petulant wish that her honorable father would smoke cigarettes, as everyone else did, instead of that absurd, old-fashioned water-pipe; a hint of a suffragist meeting attended, in the city where she had been at school for the year. One year ago, oh, my soul! and Pao-ying had been a shy little thing, with eyes eternally cast down, and never a word to say unless pressed to answer a question, and then so faint a voice! And now this young person chattering away of school and cigarettes, and what not!

"What do you know of suffrage, pray?" I asked in great amusement.

"Oh, a great deal, teacher," she cried eagerly. "I know that only in this country are women so helpless; why, in other countries, I have heard, they do everything they like! They may go out and take walks and play games, and never bind their feet. It is even said they walk with men,"—here a delicate flush—"but of course I do not believe that. Although this year, teacher, for the first time, we had men at the Commencement exercises—but only old ones. I looked when nobody saw me, and they were very old. Some of the girls at school are very wicked, and say they will not marry unless they are allowed to see their husbands first. But, of course, that is very bold!"

She shook her head virtuously. Then she looked up at me from under her eyelashes and asked shyly:—

"Of course, in your honorable country, the girls do not walk and talk with young men?"

I cleared my throat at that, and hesitated an instant. I thought of the magazine I had just been reading.

"Well, my dear," I said, "times and countries change, and I have not been back there for many years."

"I should like to know," she said wistfully. "Of course, one must not be bold; but really one's parents are too stupid about anything a little different from what they used to do. I am sure that, just because they never did, is no reason why it is wrong."

And this young sprig of modern Chinese womanhood looked very indignant and injured, as she uttered this heresy against all Chinese tradition. O eternal and unchangeable youth, the world over!

After she had gone, I sat in my old easy-chair and looked upon the quiet cobbled street, and thought of her and of those for whom she stood. Her grandmother and mother had been my friends—well-born, cultured ladies, and accounted well educated in their day. They sewed and embroidered exquisitely, and were skilled in the preparation of sweetmeats.

"How do I spend my days?" one of them had once said in answer to a question. "I rise late. My maid brings me the lacquered bowl of perfumed water for my bath. I eat a slight repast of sweetmeats. My hairdressing, gowning, the artistic painting of my face and finger nails, consume the time until the noon meal. In the afternoon, I embroider at the portrait of Li P'o, upon which I am working. That, and a little gossip with the other women and drinking of tea, and it is time for the evening meal. After that, I visit friends, or they come to me and we gamble a little, and it is time to retire."

Her granddaughter is up betimes at boarding-school, and goes through a stiff morning's work in science, history, literature, languages, and mathematics, with sewing, music, and gymnasium in the afternoon. To be sure, she has lost the delicate, swaying grace and the beautiful courtesy of her grandmother. She walks with sturdy feet well planted, and clips her words: she has her grandmother's eyes; but they look one calmly and widely in the face.

I am rather breathless over it all, having had my main outlook on life the last quarter of a century from this quiet corner of my veranda in a little interior city of China. We are really very conservative here yet, the rare visitors from an outside world tell us. Vague rumors of coeducation, of men and women dining together in restaurants, of moving pictures, and even imported dances, float in from the port cities. I know that I sometimes see the inhabitants of such places pass through the abominably ugly railway-station, which has just been foisted upon our old-fashioned little old town; and they look scandalous women to me, with their wide, short trousers and short sleeves and tight coats; but I suppose I am behind the times. I confess that I like my old Chinese friends better, with their courteous speech and gracious manners. I dislike the acquired abruptness of these young creatures. I dislike the eternal cigarettes, and the blasé, self-sufficient expression on young faces, which I am accustomed to seeing timid and reverential.

But—and but again—how much of my displeasure is dislike of the irreverence of my own pedantic old self, and discomfort at having my opinions, fixed by years, questioned and even flouted? How much of it, I wonder, is middle-aged stiff-neckedness? What if, after all, these young upstarts are the beginnings of a new growth out of the decadent soil of an old civilization insufficient for this day and time? The universe of space and time is not comprised within this old street, with its secluded, shaded courtyards, and spirit walls guarding dragon-carved gateways.

If these young things let the sunlight into the courtyards, and tear down the spirit walls in unbelief, and even desecrate these marvelously wrought dragons with modern paint and plaster—if, I say, it is done in the name of a new era of general enlightenment and clear thinking, and of a struggle for better things and conditions in this sleepy, unhygienic, ignorant old town and country, to the winds, then, with my slow, conservative soul and love of old-time reverence and manners!

For the world is marching on!

And my second article, in the *Forum,* follows below:

BEAUTY IN CHINA

It is only an American, born and reared in an alien country, who can appreciate fully the amazing beauty of the American woods in autumn. Inexplicably, no one had prepared me for it. I had lived all my days in a calm Chinese landscape, lovely in its way with delicate, swaying bamboos, curved temple roofs mirrored in lotus pools. It was gently colorful, too, in blues and greens, with a semi-tropic effulgence of sunshine, and a piercing starriness of night. But when summer was gone, and chrysanthemums had glowed and faded, the colors were put away for the most part, until the next spring. The trees dropped their leaves softly, turning the while to a quiet, neutral brown, without any great ado about it, and almost overnight we were in decent and sober winter garb. The earth took on a dull monotony of hue, which the little thatched farmhouses of adobe did not relieve. Even the people retired into enormous padded garments of dark blue and black. Thus, when after a loitering journey eastward, I stepped into sweet English country, I was entranced with its mauve and tawny shades of late summer. Could its hedgerows be lovelier, even in primrose time! There was a dreamy stillness about it which lifted cares away and left one quite content with quiet, well-tilled fields and ancient grey stone cottages, with their slow smoke drifting imperceptibly upwards in the motionless air. An exquisite rest lay over the earth in England as of one lying down to well-earned sleep.

In such a mood as this I crossed the Atlantic, and was thrown straight into New York. Who except one accustomed to the leisurely traffic of trams and rikshaws and wheelbarrows can realize the astounding activity of New York! Where one dodged one vehicle, a thousand sprang up to take its place, and crossing the street was a wild adventure, compared to which bandits in China are a mild affair. There was the bewildering clatter of elevated railways to dizzy one's mind, and subterranean roars from the bowels of the universe, apparently. I was fascinated with the yawning earth, which swallowed up people by the hundreds in one spot, only to vomit them up, restless as ever, miles away. Personally, I could not commit myself to the subway, and clinging to a trolley strap, thought regretfully at times of jogging peacefully along on a wheelbarrow, watching the lazy ducks swimming in the ponds by the roadside and stooping to pluck a wild flower for babies tumbling brown and naked in the dust.

But if New York shook me out of my quiescent dreaming, even New York did not prepare me for the shock of the American woods.

A week later I found myself walking through a wood in Virginia. How can I put the excitement of it into words! No one had told me how paganly gorgeous it would be. Oh, of course they had said, "the leaves turn in the fall, you know," but how does that prepare one? I had thought of pale yellows and tans and faint rose reds. Instead, I found myself in a living blaze of color—robust, violent, vivid beyond belief.

I shall never forget one tall tree trunk wrapped about with a vine of flaming scarlet, standing outlined, a fiery sentinel, against a dark rocky cliff.

There was a maple walk which might have been the pathway to the golden streets of the New Jerusalem. Wandering anywhere, above one's head were interlaced boughs, bursting with orange and red, crimson and seal brown, and yellow of purest quality. One walked on a carpet of hues which an emperor's wealth could not buy in a Peking rug. Even the quite tiny things, small vines and plantlets that must have been meek little things in summer, expressed themselves in the most outrageous and unrestrained colors.

Well! There can be nothing like it on this earth. Do the Americans realize it every year, I wonder? I shall not soon be astounded at anything now, I believe. Not at Aurora Borealis, which I have yet to see confirmed, not at Vesuvius, and I have my doubts even about that day when the skies shall roll away to the tune of Gabriel's trump. I don't believe there can come to a human being a more intoxicating revelation of beauty than that which fell upon me, straight from quiet, sombre things, when I walked for the first time in my life in American woods in autumn.

Thus it was that I fell to thinking again about beauty. It has long been my pleasure to note particularly bits of loveliness about the world, and to see how differently the peoples of the earth have expressed themselves in ways of unconscious beauty. I do not mean by that the great sights which tourists run to see. Seldom are the people of a country really to be found there.

I found France not in the Louvre, but in an old woman in a blue gown and white kerchief, kneeling to beat clothes beside a tinkling stream. Such a patient, enduring, loyal figure, I thought; suddenly she lifted her head and bewitched me with the eternal spirit of humor and coquetry in laughing, restless eyes, forever young and vivid with life in a wrinkled old face.

The Swiss is not truly expressed in the majestic pageant of the Alps, white and remote against blue skies. I found him, painstaking and slow, in his frugal plot of ground, carefully nailing his pear tree against the wall and counting the clusters of grapes on a vine trained to run as little to leaves as possible. Everything about him was neat and compact, and in its way, pretty. I doubt he looked twice a year at the Jungfrau, towering eternal above his minute possessions.

Strange how I never thus think of the peoples of the earth without my thoughts leaving me and twisting about the world until they come to my adopted country, China!

How many folk have greeted me as they stepped from the first brief train journey from Shanghai, "Ah, China is not beautiful like Japan, is it!"

I smile, and bide my time. For I know the beauty of China.

Japan is exquisite. Not only in the lovely porcelains; the brilliant, graceful kimonos; the pattering, charming children. These are for every man to see. Not only in the tiny terraced fields climbing up the hillsides, the clean, fragile buildings, the microscopic fairyland of life as it appears to the casual eye.

The great beauty of Japan is in the spots that you and I, if we be mere passersby, never really glimpse.

It is the beauty which moves the veriest coolie, after a day of crushing labor, to throw aside his carrying pole, and after a bit of fish and rice, to dig and plant in his garden the size of a pocket handkerchief. There he works, absorbed, delighted; his whole being resting in the joy of creating beauty for himself and his family, who cluster about him to admire. No one is without a garden. If fate has denied a poor man a foot of ground, he buys a big plot for a penny and slowly, after hours of labor pleasant and painstaking, he constructs a miniature park, with a rockery, a tiny summerhouse, a pool, with bits of moss for lawns and grass heads for trees and toy ferns tucked into crevices for shrubbery.

It is the quality of beauty, too, which moves a Japanese host to place in his guestroom each day for the delight of his guest one single exquisite note. From his precious store he selects today a watercolor, in black and white, of a bird clinging to a reed, painted with charming reserve. Tomorrow it will be a dull blue vase with one spray of snowy pear bloom arranged in such a way as to be a living invitation to meditation. Sometimes it is a piece of old tapestry, with a quaint procession of lantern bearers marching across its faded length.

I hear a deal of talk about Japan these days. There are those who begrudge them the possession of even quite ordinary human qualities. As for me, after hearing such tales, I reserve judgment until someone can reconcile these two qualities for me: utter depravity and the gentle love of all beauty which is to be found almost universally in rich and poor alike in Japan. Where there is such a willingness to spend oneself for beauty, often without any thought of money value, must not a little truth be hid? If it be true at all that beauty is truth?

Now the dainty loveliness which is so apparent in Japan is certainly not to be seen spread about in China. I really cannot blame those friends of mine who at first glance proclaim her ugliness. Doubtless it has been the economic urge which has driven the poor to think first and last and always of their stomachs and the wherewithal to fill them completely.

Certainly there is an appalling lack of beauty in the lives of the ordinary folk.

Said I to my coolie gardener one day as he was digging and delving upon my perennial flower border: "Now, wouldn't you like some of these flower seeds to plant in the plot in front of your house?"

He eyed me distrustfully and hoed vigorously. "Poor people have no use for flowers," he answered briefly. "These things are for the rich to play with."

"Yes, but it won't cost you anything," I persisted. "See, I will give you several kinds, and if the land is poor, you may take fertilizer from the compost heap, and I will give you the time to take care of them for the good of your soul."

He shook his head. He is a conservative creature. None of his ancestors had planted flowers for pleasure and he couldn't imagine himself at it. Besides, what would he do with the flowers when he had them?

He stooped to throw out a stone. "I'll plant cabbage," he said briefly.

The poorer Chinese does without doubt place a financial value on all his possessions. In one interior spot where I had lived for a time, I asked a farmer's wife how they spent or saved the money surplus of a good year's crops.

She smiled at the recollection. "We eat more!" she exclaimed, ecstatically.

In lieu of a trustworthy savings bank, they deposited their bits of reserve fund in the safest place possible in a land of banditry and transformed it into extra flesh. At least no one could rob them of that! And heaven knows their bones were the better for it.

In wandering through Chinese cities one is struck with their ugliness —the lack of sanitation, the congestion, the foul streets, the filthy and diseased beggars showing their vile stock-in-trade and whining parasitically, the mangy dogs skulking about. A glance into the small shops and homes depresses one with the strictly utilitarian aspect of life. Bare tables, stools apparently designed for discomfort, boxes, beds, and rubbish, the primitive cooking apparatus—all are crowded into an unbelievably small space, and the result is one of utter lack of repose or of any attempt after spiritual values to be expressed in beauty.

The other day I stood on a mountain top in Kiangsi. I looked over a hundred miles of lovely Chinese country. Streams glittered in the sunshine; the Yangtse wound its leisurely way along, a huge yellow roadway to the sea; clusters of trees cuddled cosily about little thatched villages; the rice fields were clear jade green and laid as neatly as patterns in a puzzle. It seemed a scene of peace and beauty.

Yet I knew my country well enough to know that if I could have dropped into the midst of that fair land I should have found the streams polluted, the river's edge crowded with little wretched, mat-covered boats, the only homes of millions of miserable, underfed waterfolk. The villages under the trees would be crowded and filthy with flies and garbage rotting in the sun, and the ubiquitous yellow curs would have snarled at my coming. There, with all that sweet air free for all, the homes would be small and windowless and as dark within as caverns. The children would be dirty and unkempt, and their noses would be unspeakable, for they always are! Not a flower anywhere, not a single spot of beauty made by man to relieve the dreariness of life. Even the bits of ground in front of the cottages would be beaten into threshing floors, hard and glaring in the sunlight. Poverty? Partly, of course, but often laziness and ignorance, too.

Where then, is the beauty of China? Not on the surface of things, anyway. But I bide my time. For it is here.

Some of the rarest bits of beauty in the world I have found in this old country, so reserved, so indolent for centuries, so careless of what the world thinks of her.

For China does not express herself in show places. Even in Peking, that bourne of all tourists to the Far East, the things that one sees are not show places. The Forbidden City, the Temple of Heaven, the Lama Temple—these and a host of the others were built up slowly out of the life of the people, for the people themselves, with no thought originally of tourist eyes and dollars. Indeed, for decades, no amount of money could purchase a glimpse of them.

The Chinese have naturally little idea of exhibition and advertising. Go into any one of the great silk shops in Hangchow and you will find a decorous, dark, quiet interior, with shelves and shelves of neat packages folded away, each with its price tag symmetrically arranged. There are no pedestals with gorgeous satins folded cunningly to catch the light and entice the buyer. But a clerk comes forward, and when you have made known your wishes, he selects carelessly half a dozen packages from the shelves and tears off the paper wrappers. Suddenly before your eyes bursts the splendor of stuffs whereof kings' robes are made. Brocaded satins and velvets, silk of marvellous brilliance and delicacy of shades are massed before you in a bewildering confusion. It is like a crowd of magnificently hued butterflies released from dull cocoons. You make your choice and the glory is all shut away again into the dark.

That is China.

Her beauties are those of old things, old places carefully fashioned with the loftiest thought and artistic endeavor of generations of aristocrats, and now like their owners, falling gently into decay.

Behind this high wall, which looms so grey and foreboding upon the streets, one may step, if one has the proper key, into a gracious courtyard, paved with great square old tiles, worn away by the feet of a hundred centuries. There is a gnarled pine tree, a pool of goldfish, a carven stone seat whereon is seated a white-haired grandfather, dignified and calm as an old Buddha in his gown of cream-colored silk. In his pale, withered hand he holds a long pipe of polished black wood, tipped with silver. If you are his friend, he will rise with deep bows and escort you with a most perfect courtesy into the guest hall. There in a high chair of a carved teak you may sip his famous tea and marvel at the old paintings hung in silken scrolls upon the walls, and meditate upon the handwrought beams of the ceiling, thirty feet above. Beauty, beauty everywhere, stately and reserved with age.

I mind me of a great dark guest hall in a temple, which faces out upon a tiny sunny courtyard, where a peony terrace is built up of faded grey brick. Here every spring the great pink shoots push up, and when I go there in May, the sunlight is pouring down upon the deeply tinted peonies, glowing in reds and dusky pinks, and in the center creamy ones with golden hearts. The terrace is cleverly placed so that the guests must needs look upon it from the dimness of the interior. What words could be spoken, what thought shaped in such a place, save those of purest beauty!

There are old paintings, old embroideries, potteries and porcelains and brasses, hidden away preciously by families who owned them before America was thought of; indeed, perhaps they are of an age with Pharoah's treasures—who knows?

It is one of the sad things of the present change in China that either poverty or careless, ignorant youth is learning the money value of things which are really too valuable for any sale; things which because of their sheer beauty are too great to belong to any individual and which should be reverently possessed by the nation. But their time of understanding is not yet.

Indeed, not the least of the crimes committed against China by foreign countries has been the despoiling by eager curio seekers and globe trotters and business firms of her stores of beauty. It has really been the robbing of the ignorant, for she has not known that what she thought to sell for thirty pieces of silver could not truly be sold at all.

Moreover, one shudders at the crude stage through which so many of the modern young Chinese seem to be passing. It is inevitable, of course, that in their distrust and repudiation of the past, they should apparently cast off the matchless art of old China and should rush out to buy and hang upon their walls many of the cheap vulgarities of the

West. Indeed, to those of us who see the passing of much that was characteristic of the country we have loved it has become a poignant question; who is to preserve the ancient beauties of China? For instance, with all the degradation that has unquestionably followed in the wake of idolatry, must we, along with all the discard, lose the exquisite curves of temple architecture?

Yet I am at times comforted. There must come out of all those beauty-loving ancestors a few to whom the pursuit of beauty is a master passion, and who will pass it on to calmer times.

I went the other day to the studio of a famous modern Chinese artist. My heart sank lower and lower as I passed the copies of posters, of old-fashioned Gibson girls, of lurid suns setting into the vilely colored ocean—dozens of perpetrations in oils. But away in one corner I found a little watercolor. It was only of a village street, misty blue in the sudden rain of a summer evening. Slanting lines of pale silver fell across it. Dim candle-light shone out of the windows of snug homes, and a lonely man's figure under a paper umbrella walked along, casting a wavering shadow over the glinting wet stones.

I turned to the artist and said, "This is the best of all."

His face lighted.

"Do you think so? I, too. It is a picture of my village street as I have seen it many times. But," regretfully, "I painted it for pleasure. It will not sell."

If I really have a fault to find with the beauty of China, however, it is that it is too secluded, too reserved. It does not permeate enough to the uttermost parts of the people to whom it belongs. It has been kept too much in isolated family or religious groups. The knowledge of the value of beauty has been withheld from many who have suffered from the lack. The poorer and more ignorant classes have been allowed for centuries to grow up and to die in utter indifference to all the subtle and necessary influences which flow from the essentially beautiful. The opportunity to pursue beauty has been too much the prerogative of the wealthy and leisured. Consequently the poor man thinks of it only as one of the pastimes of the rich and hence impossible for him.

What the average Chinese needs is an eye educated to see the beauty which lies waiting to be freed about him everywhere. When once he grasps the significance of beauty and realizes that it does not lie at all in the hideous lithograph for which he must pay the prohibitive price of forty cents; that it does not lie, solely, even, in the priceless possessions of the rich; but that it is in his dooryard, waiting to be released from careless filth and indolent untidiness, a new spirit will walk abroad in the land.

Anyway, I know that man cannot live by bread alone and that is what thousands of these folk have been trying to do here, submerged under unspeakably difficult economic conditions. To see the beauty in fresh air and natural loveliness, to know the joy of sunshine streaming on clear water and the graciousness of flowers,—these beauties free for all are what we need sorely.

I said this to my old Chinese teacher the other day, and he replied with a proverb which runs something like this: "When a man's barns are filled and his appetite appeased, then may he take heart to think upon the things of the spirit."

Which, I suppose, is true.

Yet I am sure the gardener has had a good supper last night when, as I sat musing under the bamboos, he was working cheerfully away on the lawn. Startled by an unaccustomed light, I glanced up and was smitten afresh with the sunset sky.

"Oh, look!" I called.

"Where—where?" he cried, seizing the hoe.

"There, at the wonderful color!"

"Oh, that!" he exclaimed in great disgust, stooping to the weeds again. "I thought when you called out so, that it must be a centipede crawling on you!"

To tell the truth, I don't believe that a love of beauty is based altogether on a well-fed interior. Plenty of gourmands are only gourmands still. Besides, if the proverb were true altogether, how could I explain deaf old Mrs. Wang, poorest of poor little widows, who sews hard all day to make a bowl of rice, and yet who manages someway to have a flower the whole summer long in a broken bottle on her table and who wept with delight when I pressed upon her a little green vase?

Or the tiny tobacco shop, whose cheerful, toothless old proprietor is always coddling along a plant of some sort in an earthen pot? Or the farmer outside my compound who lets a mass of hollyhocks stand as they please about his house? Or the little "wild" children of the street who press their faces against my gate sometimes and beg for a posy?

No, the love of beauty waits to be born in the heart of every child, I think. Sometimes the hard exigencies of life kill it, and it is still forever. But sometimes it lives and grows strong in the silent, meditative soul of a man or a woman, who finds that it is not enough to live in a palace and to dine even with kings. Such know that after all they are eternally unsatisfied, until in some way they find beauty, where is hidden God.

I had no illusions about the importance of these two little essays, they were trifles, but their acceptance induced a mood of happiness and I began to write in earnest on what was to have been my first big novel. It was natural to me to tell no one about the novel. This was not secretiveness, for if there had been any one to tell I would surely have told, but I had no friends on this level. Friends aplenty I had and have always had, but I learned long ago to meet them where they are. And I had no friends or relatives to whom I could speak about my writing, and it did not occur to me that this was strange or even a deprivation. I was long ago used to living in many mansions.

Meanwhile I was also enjoying quite a different sort of life. First of all were my house and garden. Though I can live anywhere, be either rich or poor with equal acceptance, I have to have a setting, and if there is not one, I make it. I subdued, therefore, the too large and somewhat graceless grey brick house where I lived, and within the limits of a small amount of money, I did as my mother had taught me to do and created as much beauty as I could. The garden furnished plenty of flowers, and well-designed furniture of cheap materials could be cushioned with the inexpensive but beautiful Chinese stuffs. Wicker and rattan I had wearied of, but the Chinese about that time were weaving cash string, a thin robe made of grass, upon strong bamboo frames, and such chairs were comfortable and substantial. Old Chinese blackwood tables could be bought cheaply, and there were always delicate and beautiful bowls and vases in the chinashops. One day in a silkshop I found yards of faded silk going at a bargain price and I bought it for curtains and dyed it in different colors. Matting rugs upon the floor gave good effect and sunshine and flowers did the rest. I enjoyed the whole process and have often thought to myself that if I had not wanted to write books I would have liked to build houses and decorate them. But then I like to cook, too, and my children know that if I did not want to write books above all else, I would be a cook in a big family, perhaps in an orphanage, and make delicious dishes for everybody. But there are many persons I would like to have been—for example, again, a sculptor—had I not wanted to write books. I am fortunate that I had not to make the decision. At that I once wrote a novel about a woman sculptor, entitled *This Proud Heart,* and there, I suppose, in the curious way writers have, I fulfilled a dream.

My life in my northern town had been simple indeed compared to the one I now led. I taught classes not only in the Christian university but also in the provincial one, and had therefore two entirely different groups of students. The young men in the Christian university were the sons of Christians and had scholarships or they were the sons of the rich who could afford to pay substantial tuition fees. All of them understood English at least fairly well and usually they came from port cities and were somewhat cosmopolitan and certainly conservative in their family backgrounds. The students in the National University, on the other hand, were nearly all poor and they knew little English and they paid no tuition. Most of them had not much to eat and they wore a sort of blue cotton garb later known as the Sun Yat-sen uniform. In winter they were bitterly cold, and so was I, for we had no heat in the buildings and when window panes were broken they were not replaced, whereas in the Christian university everything was in good order and we had central heat and much comfort. Yet I enjoyed my work in the provincial university far more, because there my students were desperate for learning and they waited eagerly for my arrival and tried to keep me from leaving at the end of our classes. Their English was almost unintelligible and had I not spoken Chinese I could not have taught them. Yet they yearned to speak English, and so we struggled along. They were young men and women, thinking and questioning and alive, and I learned far more from them than from the suave and acquiescent men students in the Christian university. I came away frozen with cold in my body but warm in my heart and stimulated in mind because between me and those eager young students, so thinly clad and badly fed, there were no barriers. They wanted to talk about everything in the world, and we talked. Even now I get letters from some who have escaped Communism, though most of them are dead in the wars and revolutions that have swept over us all.

In those days Sun Yat-sen was still alive and still working to bring unity to the country, but he was in retreat in the South. In Nanking we lived under the war lord, Sun Chuan-fang, a temperamental man younger than most of the war lords who divided the country into fragments, and in some ways less oppressive, but still he was a war lord. We were not disturbed, however, unless our war lord undertook a battle with some neighboring war lord, and the period of what is called, historically, fragmentation, seemed natural enough to the Chinese and to me. China, as I have said, always went into fragmentation under war lords in the periods between dynasties, and the people were patient as usual and waited for things to work themselves out. Without being religious, the ordinary Chinese had a vague faith in Heaven and believed that nothing could succeed without its will. This meant that whoever finally assumed the leadership of the nation would be the best one under Heaven's design. Meanwhile family life went on, the center and the core of the nation as it had always been, and our war lord did not interfere with our affairs.

My own interest has never been in politics but in the thoughts of men and women and so I continued to be deeply concerned with the literary revolution. By 1920 the spoken language had become the accepted written language of the new times. The question was, could real works of literature be written in the vernacular? Older scholars still insisted that it could never express allusive meanings as did the wen-li, or classical style of writing. The young scholars, Western-trained, had to prove that it could. Hitherto it had been used only for magazine and newspaper writing. Here again Hu Shih was the leader of the new school, for he now began to write his monumental work, *Outline of the History of Chinese Philosophy*. It was never finished, alas, but the first volume proved again that the Chinese spoken language could also be a beautifully clear and graceful written language, flexible and alive, expressing the most profound meaning and thought.

Once Hu Shih had shown the value of the new written language, young Chinese writers rushed to follow his example, and a mass of experimental material got into print. Most of it was bad, I must confess, and there were reasons enough for this dismal fact. The young Chinese who called themselves modern were burning with unclarified emotions, rebellious and ambitious, but actually they still had nothing to say. They had cut themselves off too abruptly from their traditional roots and had been trained too quickly and superficially in Western cultures. It was inevitable that when they began to write they wrote imitatively, and since they refused to imitate their own literary figures of the great Chinese past, they imitated the Western writers, who were foreign to them in spite of their determination to be modern, or Western. There were no modern Chinese in fact, there were only Westernized Chinese. How wearisome it was in those days to open one much-praised Chinese novel after another only to discover that it was all but plagiarized from a Western one! What a disappointment to go to the new modern theater to see an eagerly anticipated play by a famous young Chinese playwright and discover that it was a Eugene O'Neill play, scarcely disguised by Chinese names!

Since there was little original work, it was inevitable that much of the outpouring of the new writers soon became literary criticism of each other and of Western books, and shallow stuff that was, too. Goethe's *Sorrows of Werther* was the novel which seemed to suit the mood of most of the young Chinese and in my effort to understand them I read hundreds of Chinese "Sorrows." It became ridiculous, and yet so serious were these young men and women that one dared not laugh. It even became the fashion to ape the Western poets in person and one handsome and rather distinguished and certainly much beloved young poet was proud to be called "The Chinese Shelley." He used to sit in my living room and talk by the hour and wave his beautiful hands in exquisite and descriptive gestures until now when I think of him, I see first his hands. He was a northern Chinese, tall and classically beautiful in looks, and his hands were big and perfectly shaped and smooth as a woman's hands, and guiltless, I am sure, of any real manual labor. For our young Chinese scholars maintained the old traditions in one respect at least. They did no physical work whatever. Our Chinese Shelley died young, I am sad to say, for he had a sort of power of his own, and could he have outgrown the Shelley phase he might have become himself. But in his desire to have wings he was among the first to take to airplanes and he died in an accident.

The sickening romanticism purified itself gradually, however, and the strongest minds began to return to their own people. Chou Shu-jen, or "Lu Hsün," as he called himself, was perhaps the first to perceive that although his inspiration might come through Western literature, yet he could escape imitativeness only if he applied his newly found emotions to his own people. Thus he began to write sketches and stories and finally novels about the simple everyday people. Kuo Mo-jou became my own favorite and in spite of a cynicism that was sometimes only destructive. I think of that brilliant mind, whose habit was the utmost candor and whose passion was truth, and I wonder how he can live as he does nowadays under the Communist government in his country. Is he silenced, I wonder, or has he succumbed, as others have, to writing the extravaganzas of convulsive and surely compelled adoration of the new Magi? And I can scarcely believe that Ting Ling and Ping Hsin are changed, those two intrepid and fearless women writers, who used to make me so proud. But who can tell me? It is another world and one that I do not know. It is useless now to put down the names of all the brave young Chinese men and women who led the awakening minds of their compatriots, and who are either dead or in a living death, cut off from our knowledge by the present division of the globe. What I remember is that they provided for me the clearest mirror of the world we then shared, and through them and their books I understood what otherwise might have been inexplicable.

It was revealing that their books were short. Even their novels were short as though they had no time to make long books. Each fresh rush of emotion, each new perception, was hurried into a book, and there was scarcely time to write one before another pressed. Publishing houses sprang up and the bookstalls in my city were crowded with the cheap little paper-backed volumes. I could buy a basketful for a dollar or so and read for days, and this generous fare has made me impatient ever since of expensive books. I am never better pleased than when I know a book of mine can be bought for fifty cents or, better still, for twenty-five. No people can be educated or even cultivated until books are cheap enough for everybody to buy.

There was one interesting aspect of the literary revolution which has had lasting effect upon the Chinese modern mind. In the effort to repudiate all Confucian tradition, these young modern writers became rigorously candid, and they repudiated utterly the old moralistic essays of the past. I suppose that the revolt against Confucius which became part of the first trend toward Communism, began in this invincible determination of the young to refuse all pretense of being moral because their elders seemed to them such hypocrites. They began to reveal themselves in the most intimate moods of their minds, and they reveled in descriptions and declarations of themselves, their feelings and their actions, which shocked to the soul their parents and older relatives. Yet it was a therapeutic process. So long had they been taught and trained in the moralistic patterns of the past, that it was almost as though they now felt compelled to tear off their clothes and walk the streets naked. It is interesting to compare their violent denial of Confucius with the Communist rejection of religion, for indeed Confucius, though he was a philosopher and no priest, had shaped Chinese society and posterity in an ethic religious and moral in its effect. It will be a long time, I fear, before the balance is restored, and Chinese will again realize how much they owe to Confucius, their greatest figure. Yet it must not be supposed that this revolt was against ethics or morals, as such—quite the reverse. Confucianism had become almost entirely superficial after many centuries, its morals too often mere pretense, and the angry young revolted against these qualities in their elders and in their revolt they threw Confucius out the window, too. The corruption and hypocrisy of the orthodox church in Russia were similarly the understandable reasons for the violence of that revolt against religion. For the soul of man is born fresh in every child, and there is an age in every creature, unless he is debased too young, when for a time he sees clearly the difference between truth and falsehood, and hypocrisy infuriates him. He cannot forgive those who should be true and instead are liars. This fury, I believe, is the first cause for revolutions throughout history.

I must speak here of the extraordinary place of newspapers in the literary revolution. When I was a child, we had only English newspapers to read, printed in Shanghai. My father read *The Chinese Imperial Gazette* when he could get it, but it contained little except court news. Beyond that he read the wall newspapers, which were simply bulletins pasted on the walls near the city gates. Now, however, newspapers modeled on Western ones sprang up in every large city, and since the spoken language was also the recognized written language, they were easy to read. The effect of this was that literate men began to read newspapers, and would talk about the news to others who could not read. It became quite usual in a crowded teashop for one man to read a newspaper aloud to a score or more of men who had never learned how to read. Indeed, until the literary revolution made it worth while, reading was a luxury pastime and a practical man had no need for such an esoteric skill. Now that newspapers were printed in the vernacular, however, so that what was read could also be understood, every man wanted to be able to read, and the desire for this means to knowledge spread even to women. I was moved to the heart in those days to see old women as well as young striving to learn a few characters in order to feel, and to say, that they could read. The newspapers often were unreliable and biased, but at least one could get a Chinese point of view on events and interests. Some of these newspapers were put out by the writers themselves, just as many of the young publishing companies were merely groups of writers, but they were none the less valuable for that. The writers were, I remember, forever organizing themselves into societies and clubs and it seemed to me they wasted their energies in disagreement in their newspapers and magazines. Yet I could feel a rising feeling of larger unity among them, in spite of their dissensions, and I was afraid. Total revolution was more clearly ahead than ever and I could not discern its form. Indeed the disturbance in young Chinese minds, articulate in the new publications, was sure to rush headlong into some sort of violence and older people were becoming more and more bewildered as they watched their sons and daughters whom they could no longer control. If a father could not quote Confucius without seeing his son flare into contempt, then where could he turn for help?

The public scorn of the young was not only for their own traditions. The first blind and romantic attachment to Western literary figures died away after the end of the First World War and a general disillusionment arose. Of what value were even the Western cultures, young Chinese asked in newspaper editorials and arguments, if Western peoples clashed in murderous and devastating wars as cruel and uncivilized as the battles of savages? Not in Europe, they now declared, were to be found the ideals the Chinese people sought, but if not in Europe then where?

As if in reply, the Russian revolution burst at the end of the First World War upon a wave of crude and dangerous idealism. In Russia, as the young Chinese watched, young intellectuals, like themselves, declared the peasants their allies, and with the force of combined revolt, they overthrew the traditional government in the hope of shaping a new culture and life. "Feudalism," the pet devil, too, of the Chinese modern writers and thinkers, had been ended, and with it, the Russian Communists declared, "capitalistic imperialism." How weary did I grow of those words, shouted by children on the streets as they used to shout "foreign devil" when a white man or woman passed! *"Ta Tao Ti Kuo Chu I,"* "Down With Imperialism!" The children thought it was a curse, and the young people inflamed themselves with the hatred it contained. What it meant I daresay few of them knew, but they had a vague idea that all the poor in Russia were now rich and that the rich were doing the dirty work in city streets and country fields.

They were confirmed in this belief, for, ever since the Bolsheviks had come into power in Russia, there had been hundreds of pitiful White Russian refugees streaming southward in China and settling into the port cities. Even when I had lived in Nanhsüchou I had known them. Sometimes there was a knock on the door and when I went to open it I saw on the threshold a sad little group of men and women, perhaps children, too, aristocrats of Russia, who were exiles. They were bewildered and lost and yet even while they begged they showed a proud discontent with what they were given. "Have you no better shoes than this?" they inquired or they examined disconsolately a dress or a suit. All their lives they had been served and cared for and now it was an evil dream that their great houses and easy comforts were gone forever.

The young Chinese exulted thus to see the rich white people brought so low, but old Chinese were usually kind, comprehending, it may be, the portent of what they saw. I remember once, in the northern country where I was visiting in a wealthy home, very ancient and famous, that the old grandmother one day led me outside the great carved gateway and showing me a deep ditch she said:

"There I have twice had to hide, once with my parents when the peasants on our land turned against us, and again when my own children were small."

Her old forefinger with its long curved fingernail did not tremble as she continued to point. "And there," she went on, "yet again will my children's children hide, for the poor are always against the rich."

Ah well, so those White Russian aristocrats filtered down through the Chinese cities. They lived in poverty and they sickened and died and their beautiful daughters became dancing partners hired in cheap cafés in Shanghai and Tientsin and the young Chinese modern men learned from them to tango and foxtrot while the tall handsome White Russian boys became chauffeurs and bodyguards for the war lords and the wealthy Chinese merchants, protecting their lives and keeping their children from being kidnapped when they went to expensive private schools. Meanwhile, Chinese revolutionists were saying the Red Russians were the only people in the world who had been brave enough to rise up and take the land from landlords and corrupt rulers, to overthrow the old superstitious religions and in place of God to set up Science. The modern young minds in China in those days admired Russia extravagantly and it began to be uncomfortable to be a plain American who did not like what she heard of Communism and its doings.

There was some reason, I confess, for this urge of interest in the Russian revolution, although those of us who knew history remembered only too well the ancient desire of Russia toward China. The young Chinese, however, were as impatient with the lessons of history as our young Americans are, and they heeded only what was taking place in their lifetime and therefore within their own knowledge. Like the Gaderene swine, they could not be prevented from rushing to their own destruction.

This brings me to the second monumental date of that decade between 1920 and 1930. Again it is the date of a death. In the year 1925 Sun Yat-sen died in Peking of cancer of the liver. He had gone there in the hope that at last he could unify the country with the help of a successful war lord, Feng Yü-hsiang, that burly, gigantic, half-humorous figure who had conquered, at least temporarily, the other northern war lords, and then suddenly declaring himself for a republican form of government, had invited the revolutionary leader to come and help him. Alas, before the meeting could bear fruit, Sun Yet-sen was dead.

The story of this man has been told many times, and it is not needful, surely, to tell it here again. In his way Sun Yat-sen had been to me as distinct a figure as the Old Empress once was, but the romantic elements were entirely different. Sun was a typical product of Christian schools, although he was not an average man, at least in the vital energy of his unselfish idealism. Yet no great man appears as a solitary star, unrelated to what has gone before, and alone Sun Yat-sen could never have achieved what he did in his brief lifetime. He was the crest of a wave of revolution, and such a wave is always the rise of a deep ground swell of human events, and Christian missionaries themselves continued to increase that ground swell, without knowing what they did. They were men and women of single mind and one purpose, and when after a hundred years Christianity still seemed to take no root in the vastness of Chinese life they cast about to discover why this was. The cause of their failure, they decided, was not so much in the strength of other religions as in the whole Chinese culture which was so strong, so closely knit, so solidly united that it had to be attacked at its very foundations. Attack it they did, therefore, and in much the same way that the modern

Communists are attacking it again. The missionaries set up schools and they taught the Chinese children that their own religions were superstitions, and that their elders were not to be obeyed before the Christian God, for this God was the one true God. They enforced these teachings with the practical benefits of Western life, such as hospitals, modern medicine, famine relief, unbound feet for girls, free choice of mates in marriage. The impact of these ideas was terrific and radical.

Like the missionaries, Sun Yat-sen was both a Christian and a realist. That is, he prayed and sometimes got what he wanted. When he did not, he went to work for himself. What he owed to the foreign religion was very much, nevertheless. It was more than an education, it was a fierce dedication to the benefit of his own people through modern reforms. He did not begin as a rebel, but as a Christian who wished to serve. He saw misery and injustice everywhere about him, and he wanted to change what others said was unchangeable. He trained himself as a doctor and a surgeon and established a successful practice. Then the intolerable slowness of his task overcame him. In a lifetime of incessant labor he could help but a few people among the millions who needed help. Only a good and modern government, he concluded, could change his country. He gave up his profession then and spent his life in the simple determination to overthrow the Manchu government and help his people set up another better one, under which China could be strong.

To look back now upon this singlehearted man is to feel pity and sorrow and an unwilling admiration. He was a man who won the affection of all who knew him, a man of goodness and unshakeable integrity, qualities remarkable enough in a corrupt age. There was never a wind of evil rumor about Sun Yat-sen. No one suspected him of accumulating riches for himself. Chinese gave him money everywhere he went in order that he could help their country, and no one doubted his honesty. He gathered men to him, particularly the young modern intellectuals who had nowhere to find employment, since their traditional place in government administration was no longer open to them, for, since the first graduates of mission schools were not educated in the traditional subjects of literature and philosophy and history, and government posts were denied them, it was natural that they flocked to Sun Yat-sen, whose purpose was to overthrow the government itself and establish a republic, modelled after the United States. If he were successful, the Western-educated youth would fill its posts.

And Sun Yat-sen welcomed them, at home and abroad. One of his gifts was that of impassioned speech. He was a born orator, for he believed always that what he said was true, that what he dreamed was possible. All over China he set up cells of revolution among the young intellectuals, and he remained their leader through years of struggle and disappointment and defeat that ended too soon in death. The story of his life is that of a consecrated, tragic and lonely man, a failure, it must be said, for the orator and the revolutionary leader is seldom and perhaps never the organizer and the man to make his own dreams come true.

While I write these words the autumn rain falls quietly over my Pennsylvania hills. The lake is grey and by its edge under the yellowing willows the heron stands in his accustomed place upon one leg, head drooping. Years have passed, yet clearly as though it were this morning I remember the day upon which Sun Yat-sen died. He was not so great a man as Gandhi, and sometimes I thought that his people had forgotten him. But when he died they remembered him and all that he had dreamed for them which he had not been able to bring to pass, and they mourned for him. Who now would take his place? There was no one. He became a Lenin for the Chinese revolution. People told each other stories about him, how he had suffered, how he had been always poor for their sakes, and they read the newspapers that detailed his last hours. He had gasped out those tragic words—"I thought I would come here to set up our national unity and peace. Instead I have been seized by a stupid disease and now I am past all cure. . . . To live or die makes no difference to me as a person but not to achieve all that I have struggled for through so many years grieves me to the very heart. . . . I have tried to be a messenger of God—to help my people get equality—and freedom. You who live, strive—to put into practice—"

In China the last words of a good man are precious. They are carved upon wood and written into the records. But a foreign doctor had begged Sun Yat-sen to rest and he fell asleep for a while. When he woke in the early evening his hands and feet were cold. Yet he lived through the night still clinging to his dream. They heard him murmuring, "Peace—struggle—save my country—" He died in the morning. His young wife was with him, and upon her his last look rested.

We read those last words again and again and wept and we forgot that he had not been able to do all that he dreamed. What he had done was to give himself, and his figure remained a symbol of hope. Yet, now, while I gaze out over the American landscape, I cannot but ponder the quality of his influence. His goodness and his integrity stand unimpaired, but we know that those qualities, essential as they are, were not enough. He had too little knowledge even of his own country. In spite of his devotion to his people he was basically an uneducated man and his ignorance did them hurt. He had no understanding of history and therefore no judgment for his times. When Soviet Russia alone offered her friendship, he declared that it was to Russia the Chinese people must henceforth look.

For after the First World War the Western nations lost prestige in China, partly because the Chinese considered major war a proof of moral disintegration, and further because they suffered directly from the effects. Imperial Japan, who had allied herself with the so-called democracies, took over Germany's possessions in China and proceeded to establish herself upon the Chinese mainland. So outraged did the Chinese people become that the Chinese delegate at Geneva did not dare to sign the Treaty of Versailles. By 1920 the Russian Communists had consolidated their hold on Russian territory and then they made a clever and farsighted move. They offered to renounce extraterritorial rights in China, and henceforth to treat China as a respected equal. Adolph Joffe came as the Russian envoy to Peking to announce the news, and while the foreign ambassadors ignored him, the Chinese common people and intellectuals alike welcomed him with feasts and friendship. Meanwhile no Western power had paid any heed to Sun Yat-sen's appeals for help. In 1921 he ceased asking and instead he met Joffe in Shanghai and there formally he accepted the aid of Soviet Russia. China would not have a Communist government, Sun said, for he did not believe that Communism, in the Soviet sense, was suited to his people. But the Nationalist party would accept the help of the Soviet, would allow a Chinese Communist party to be strengthened and would accept its co-operation. This party had already been formed among young intellectuals and also among Chinese students in France. With the aid of Russian advisors the Kuomintang, or Nationalist party, was now completely reorganized on the Communist pattern, with the same discipline, the same techniques of propaganda, and the same ruthless political commissars. We heard no more talk of democracy or of a republic. Instead it was accepted that a one-party rule must be set up in China and that a long period of training, or "tutelage for the people," would be established.

I remember how deeply concerned I was when I read such news in the Chinese papers. The English papers said very little and I saw no mention of it in the American magazines and weeklies that came from the United States. I did not know why I was afraid, except that I had always felt the powerful shadow of Russia. I had never forgotten our visit there before the revolution when the inevitable shape of events was already ominous, nor had I forgotten my father's prophecy, that out of Russia would come what he called the "the Antichrist." I did not know what that meant, either, but the words carried a terror of their own. And now Russia was to be the friend, and not my own country, America! How desperately I longed in those days to have a voice, to be able to cry out and tell my own people what was happening, and yet what would I have said? And who would have listened?

It is interesting to know that at that very moment there was a certain young man, the son of a well-to-do peasant, who was working as an assistant in the library of Ch'en Tu-hsiu's university, in Peking. His name was Mao Tse-tung. And in Paris Chou En-lai was a member of the first Chinese Communist group of students. A third man, Chu Teh, the son of a wealthy landlord and an officer in a war lord's army, was in Germany learning modern military science, and there he too became a Communist. As for me and my house, in spite of my fears, we had two more years of strange peace after the death of Sun Yat-sen.

I do not know why I did not plunge wholeheartedly into my own writing during these years, except that the very events which were taking place prevented me from the dispassionate view which is necessary to a writer. These events were not only in my outside world but also within my home. After my child's birth there was a brief visit to the United States for certain medical care not then to be had in China. I spent some weeks in a hospital and a few more recuperating weeks in the idyllic quiet of a simple farm in northern New York before I hurried back again to China. After my mother's death, it was necessary, too, to arrange for my father, then seventy years old, to come and live with me. This meant a great deal more than mere living, for he had no idea of retirement and his work had to be moved with him. The breaking up of our old home with all its associations and furnishings was a sad task, and the new life for my father had to be most delicately and carefully arranged, for it did not occur to him that he might not be the head of any house in which he lived. The illusion was not lessened by the unfortunate fact that he did not like his son-in-law, and made no bones of letting me know it by considerable private I-told-you-so conversation, which only my deepening affection for him and sense of humor made endurable. I had been reared with the Chinese sense of duty to my parents, however, and this helped me very much. One does not argue with one's older generation nor does one say words or behave in any way to make a parent unhappy. I can remember only once when I allowed my occasional impatience to escape me. One hot summer's afternoon, when the sun had set, I opened the windows to allow the cool air of an approaching but still distant typhoon to make the house comfortable before we had to close all doors and windows against the storm. As soon as I opened one window my father quietly followed and closed it, and upon discovering this I turned and said a few reproachful words. His mild reply was that he felt chilled as he rested upon a couch and then I heard him repeat the old words he used to speak to my mother when her robust temper got the better of her. "Oh, don't talk that way!" I did not let him get beyond the "don't," for all my conscience rose against me. I flew to him and embraced him and begged him to forgive me and promised that the windows would be closed. It is a small thing, and yet to this day, I wish it had never happened. Life is so pitifully short, the years with parents especially so short, that not one second should be misused.

My house seemed filled with problems in those days, for beyond the growing fears about my child I had the necessity also of helping her father to find his own place and work. It was still not easy to know how to teach agriculture to Chinese, and it was not enough merely to teach American agriculture from American textbooks. Yet what else was there to teach? It seemed obvious to me that one could not teach what one did not know, and I suggested, one worrisome evening when there seemed no solution to this problem, that perhaps the wisest plan would be to discover first the facts about Chinese farming and rural life. No questionnaires had ever been used on the subject of Chinese farm economy, and yet the Department of Agriculture at the Christian university was full of students who had come to learn. I, who had grown up among Chinese farms and country people, realized how much there was to learn and how remote our young Chinese intellectuals were from their own rural life. The sons of farmers did not come to universities, and the students were at best only the sons of landowners. Actually they were nearly all the sons of rich merchants or college professors or scholars. They not only knew nothing about their own country people, they did not even know how to talk with them or address them. My blood used to boil when a callow young intellectual would address a dignified old peasant with the equivalent of "Hey, you—" The contempt of the intellectual for the man who worked with his hands was far stronger in our young Chinese intellectuals and radicals than it had been in the days of their fathers. I felt a passionate desire to show them that the peasants were worthy of respect, that peasants were not ignorant even though they could not read and write, for in their knowledge of life and in their wisdom and philosophy they excelled at least the modern intellectual and doubtless many of the old scholars as well.

This desire moved me to help as much as I could with the project which gradually shaped itself. Chinese students were given questionnaires on rural life, which they took to Chinese farmers, and when the replies came in, the material was assembled and organized and its findings put down in a small book on Chinese farm economy. When this book was published by the University of Chicago, it drew the attention of the Institute of Pacific Relations and was the beginning of a wider and more significant study of Chinese rural life.

Before that time came, however, much was to happen. Living quietly in beautiful old Nanking, I had a deep and unspoken premonition that so peaceful an existence could not continue. Rumors floated across the ocean by traveler and by books and magazines that the Western world itself had been jarred and shaken by the catastrophe of the World War. The old stable American life I had barely glimpsed in my brief college years was no more what it had been. Americans had withdrawn from a world too alarming to share and they had made a desperate effort to return to what they thought of as normal life. It was they themselves, alas, who could never again be normal, although they had withdrawn from the League of Nations almost entirely except for some of the technical and humanitarian parts of it. My brother, for example, was spending half of each year in Geneva as an advisor on the shaping of an international public health service. His own experience in the field of national public health had been successful and notable. Through him I learned much of what was going on in the League, even after it was crippled by the resignation of the United States. He believed with Woodrow Wilson that the withdrawal was at worst a disaster and at best only a postponement of what must one day be established, if only as a matter of common sense, in a council of cooperating nations. All this interested me intensely. I knew so little of my native land that I was always fascinated by the gleanings I could gather and I pursued shamelessly the few Americans I knew, who were able to understand the complexities of the United States. Yet my daily concern was still with China, I kept myself informed of every movement that went on, and more and more clearly I discerned the rising ground swell of a new phase of the long-continued revolution. It is strange to remember that in spite of increasing dread I busied myself as though the daily life I lived were to be eternal. I planted my flower beds with lilies and larkspur and snapdragons, and in the autumn I spent hours over such chrysanthemums as filled my heart with pride. The gardenia bushes were my summer delight, and early in the mornings the fragrance of their white flowers, opening gemlike against the rich dark green of the leaves, could actually wake me from sleep. How often did I look from my open windows then to see other women who shared my treasure! My Chinese neighbors, half ashamed, could not resist the temptation to steal in through the gate before I came downstairs and pick a few blossoms apiece for their hair. The scent of gardenia seemed to intoxicate them with pleasure, and though they knew I did not mind their coming, they were careful, not knowing that I watched, to pluck the flowers that grew under the leaves, so that on the surface the shrubs seemed still in full bloom. In silence they plucked, each one thrusting three or four flowers into her knot of smoothly oiled black hair, and then as noiselessly as they had come in they stole away again, and this went on year after year. They knew, of course, that I knew, but they knew, too, that not for anything would I let them know I knew, and so the amenities were observed.

Yet I suppose I did realize somehow that the beautiful quiet life could not go on forever, for I was restless within. I went no more to Kuling, enduring the torrid heat of the summer months because I wanted to be among the people, to catch what went on, to continue my friendships and my teaching. The colleges closed, but in the evenings I taught English literature to a group of young men in business and in the arts, and from them I learned much of what such men were thinking. They too were moved by the same subtle dread and we spoke in hushed voices as we sat outdoors to catch the first breath of the night winds. The lawn was on two levels, but we sat on the upper one so that we could see over the compound wall. I remember forever the stars of those soft dark summer nights, so mellow and huge and golden. We sat in a circle as though in a heavenly theater and waited for the moon in its time, and it came up enormous and stately over the pagoda beyond the wall, and whatever we were talking about we fell silent to watch that majestice appearance.

Ah, but a hundred small memories sweep over me, none somehow having anything to do with myself, for I did not live within myself in those days, there being in me nothing but sorrow, perhaps, and that must be avoided. But I remember the roses blooming by the hundreds because the gardener emptied the night soil into their roots every day, human night soil that is the finest fertilizer in the world. It pains me to this day to know that the wonderful treasures of night soil from our great cities are not used. I visited a few years ago an exhibition in Grand Central Station in New York and saw there a model of the underground of the city. What horror to discover that the invaluable wastes were all sorted out into clear water and residues, the water to be drained into the river, and the precious solids, the materials for nutrients of the earth, carried out to sea in barges and there thrown away! I came away quite distracted by such folly.

In the midst of one of those waiting summers in Nanking, I remember, too, a strange foul odor which rose over the compound wall and I supposed it to be night soil applied too fresh. But no, it persisted night and day until at last I inquired of a neighbor and was told that a man's body lay dead and rotting among the rushes on the edge of a pond. He had been a woman's lover while her husband was away, and when the husband came back he was discovered. The husband killed both wife and lover but he buried his wife and threw the lover's body into the rushes. There it lay and no one took it away, although the lover's family knew it was there. The crime merited the punishment in those days when men and women still had to obey the ancient laws of the family. The dogs, I suppose, did the scavenging then, for after a few days the stench was no more. And one has to understand how stern that justice was and how frightened young men were of such a fate, how much more frightened than newspaper headlines and television trials seem to make them nowadays.

In the autumn the other white people who had gone away for the summer returned again and the universities opened and the students came back in a flood of youth and earnestness. In those days the young were not gay, certainly not the ones who went to the colleges. They felt the weight of the future upon them, I think, and they were too earnest and too argumentative. If one wanted gaiety one had to find it in the streets and in the fields, and there I did find it. I loved to go outside the city and spend hours and days among the country people who did not fear the future because they had been through so much in the past. And especially did I still love, too, the city streets at night, the old winding cobbled streets of Nanking, lined with little shops all open and revealing by glimmering candlelight or flickering oil lamps the solid family life of the people within. In summer when the evening meal was over they moved bamboo couches and chairs out upon the street, there to gossip and drink tea and at last to sleep under the sky. Each little shop had it own kind of merchandise. There were no department or consolidated stores. Every family had its own business, and if there were foreign wares they were usually Japanese. The growing power of Japan was manifest in the many varieties of industrial goods to be seen everywhere through China in those days.

In spite of the infamous demands and rising oppression of Japan the Chinese people themselves were slow to anger, and were not easily roused even by the slogans and passionate anti-Japanese speeches of the students and young intellectuals. Had the military leaders and great industrialists who were then in control of the Japanese government been wise enough or informed enough they would have understood that by trade and patience they could have assumed a unique place in the development of a new and modern China. Instead they chose the already obsolete methods of war for empire and so lost all they had gained or might have gained. It was a mistake of judgment which resulted in Japan's defeat in the Second World War, and her future now seems merely the choice between disasters. It is sorry reflection to remember how easily all might have been averted had England and the United States joined to stop the first aggressions of Japan in Asia, and yet even those aggressions were the fruit of earlier ones when England was not yet ready to think of the inevitable and rapidly advancing end of her own colonial empire.

Meanwhile my life, as usual, was maintained on several levels. In my home I was a housewife and nothing more, or so I felt. To my father I was only his daughter, as much as I had been when I was a child myself, while to my children I was mother. Among the white community I tried to take my place as neighbor and friend. Yet I was increasingly conscious of the years of separation from my own people. My childhood had not been theirs, nor theirs mine, and I think at this time that I felt toward them a real envy, for under the life of everyday I knew that the old cleavage was deepening. My worlds were dividing, and the time would come when I would have to make a final choice between them. This was true in spite of the fact that my reality, the warm and affectionate relationship between human beings that alone makes life, was still with my Chinese friends and neighbors, and, in a different way, also with my students. When something was too much for me, it was to Chinese friends I went for encouragement and friendship. The decencies kept us from self-revelation, but Chinese are wise in comprehending without many words what is inevitable and inescapable and therefore only to be borne. In their homes, or when they came to my home, I found healing in their very presence, in the humane and gentle kindliness which was their natural atmosphere.

It was a comfort to me, too, when they came to me for something of the same comfort. In the midst of a certain sorrow of my own, it did give me comfort, for example, when a dear neighbor, not a highly educated one, and not one of those who had been abroad, but a sensible good woman, turned to me when her little son died. We had lived next door to each other, she and I, for a long time. She had been in the northern country with me, her husband a teacher in the boys' school, and later, by invitation, they had come also to the University of Nanking. For a long time the couple had no children, and then to their joy they had a little son. He was a beautiful baby, and I shared him, enjoying with my friend his growth and health and intelligence. One day a messenger came running into my gate to say the baby was dead. I could not believe it, I had seen him only that morning in his bath, and I dropped whatever I was doing and ran down the street. The moment I opened the door of the small grey brick house, I knew the dreadful news was true. There sat the parents, side by side on the wicker couch, and upon their knees lay the little boy in his red cotton suit, his crownless hat upon his head, all limp and lifeless.

How could I keep from weeping with them? In the midst of our sorrow I heard the story. He had had a touch of dysentery a week before and my friend, his mother, had been taking him to the mission hospital for injections. He had recovered easily and today had been the day for the last injection. After his noon feeding she had taken him to the clinic. A strange doctor, not the usual one, had come out of the office to give the injection.

"I noticed," she sobbed, "that the needle bottle was full of medicine. Usually there was only a little in it. I told the doctor that it was too much, and he was angry with me and said he knew what he was doing and that I was only an ignorant woman. I had to let him put the needle in my baby's thigh. Ai-ya—the child went stiff and was dead in a few minutes!"

"Was it the American doctor?" I asked.

"No, a Chinese," she sobbed.

We all wept again, but this tells of the deepening division in my worlds—though my heart ached, I was glad that the doctor had been Chinese, and not American. I continued to be glad for that as my friends came to stay with me for a few days so that they could recover themselves enough to face their own lonely house, but I was angry again at the intellectual, the Chinese doctor, who had told the mother rudely that she was only an ignorant woman and then in the pride of his superiority, as he had thought, he had killed her child. It was typical of the contempt of his class for their fellow countrymen, and I write it down here to be remembered, because this attitude was responsible for what Lin Yutang later, in a moment of complete honesty, once called "the failure of a generation."

And still another Chinese friend I remember especially, among all the ones I loved and still do love, although I have no means now of communication with them. For I dare not write to them nowadays, since a letter from an American might endanger their lives in the strange Communist China I do not know. And no letter ever comes from them any more, to tell me how the children grow and which is being married and which married ones are having grandchildren. One wintry morning, then, somewhere in those years of uneasy peace after the death of Sun Yat-sen, I heard a knock at my door. I opened it and saw a woman standing there, a ragged dusty figure whom I could not recognize. She came from the North, that I could see, for her half-bound feet and baggy trousers, her old-fashioned knee-length padded jacket and rusty disheveled hair could only belong to a northern peasant.

"Wise Mother," she said, "do you not remember me?"

"No," I said, "but please come in."

She came in then and sat on the edge of a chair and told me who she was. In the North I had had for a while a rascal of a young fellow for a gardener. He knew nothing and worked as little, and we soon parted company. He was her husband, she now told me, but he had run away and left her when the famine came down. It was a famine year, I knew, and we were expecting refugees before many months, but this woman had come early. And she was pregnant, that I could now see.

"Have you no children?" I asked.

She patted her belly. "Only this one. The others all died of the ten-day-madness—five of them."

This ten-day-madness was simply the convulsions of tetanus, a disease from which many Chinese babies died within the first fortnight of their lives. It was the result of infection at birth, and yet was easily prevented. I had spent a good deal of effort in teaching young Chinese women how to boil the scissors and the bits of cloth or cotton which they used for the children when born. In the North, however, scissors were not used. Instead a child's cord was cut with a strip of reed or leaf, peeled from the inside. By some sort of experience the women had learned not to use metal and the reed could be clean or not, depending upon its handling.

"I came to you," the woman said, adding with touching and I must say annoying naïveté, "I have no one else."

I cannot pretend that I was at all happy about this naïveté or that I was in the least flattered by her confidence. Where could I put a pregnant peasant woman in my already too complex household? She could not live outside the compound, for a woman alone and without relatives would only be molested by any idle man in the neighborhood, and we had plenty of such in these times of war lords and unrest and wandering soldiers. The old peaceful security of my own childhood was entirely gone and even my children could not wander about the countryside as I had once done.

My guest must have seen what was going on in my mind, for she said humbly, "There is a little house behind your garden, Wise Mother. I saw it when I came in the gate. I could live there until the child is born, not troubling you or anyone except for a handful of rice, and then when I am able I will find work."

The little house was a hen house and in no way fit for a human being and I told her so. Besides, there was another room, used for storage but quite good, and it could be prepared for her. "But you had better have your child in the hospital," I concluded. "Then you will have good care."

Mrs. Lu—there is no reason why I should not tell her true name, for she is dead now, good soul, and there are as many Lus in China as there are Smiths in America—was a sweetly stubborn woman, as I was to discover. She wanted the chicken house, where she could be alone, and she would not, under any persuasion, go to a foreign hospital. She had had so many children, she insisted, that she knew exactly what to do and she wanted no one with her when the baby was born. I yielded at last, for she would not yield, and the hen house was cleaned and white-washed, the two windows scrubbed free of dust and cobwebs and the floor relaid with fresh clean brick. I put a bed and a table and a chair or two in the little room and curtained the windows so that men would not look in at night and gave her a strong padlock for the door. With a little money I gave her she bought herself a pottery charcoal brazier, to be used for both heat and cooking, an earthen teapot and two bowls and a pair of chopsticks, and a small store of food. Thereafter Mrs. Lu was part of the compound and she remained almost unseen while she waited for the child. Meanwhile, troubled that she would not go to the hospital or even have our good amah with her, I made up a small sterile kit for her, containing bandages, scissors, and a bottle of iodine.

One crisp December morning the amah came with good news. Mrs. Lu had come out of her little house long enough to tell her that the baby had arrived during the night. I ordered the usual nourishing food and liquids for the mother, first a bowl of hot water strongly mixed with red sugar, and followed in an hour or so by chicken soup and noodles. This was accepted northern practice, the red sugar supposedly replenishing the blood, and the chicken and noodles insuring a good supply of milk. Then I went to visit mother and baby. It was a pretty sight. The little room was clean and warm, for Mrs. Lu had made everything tidy after the event, and she was lying in bed, her large flat face rapturous, and, wrapped in the clean baby blankets I had given her was a small very fat boy. She had put on him the usual Chinese arrangements for diapers and then he was encased in the blankets. All seemed in order and I gave her a birth gift for congratulations of two silver dollars wrapped in red paper. She was so grateful that she made me uncomfortable and I left as soon as I could.

The next day while I was at breakfast the amah came in to tell me that the baby was dying. I could not believe it.

"Didn't she use the boiled scissors to cut his cord?" I asked.

"Oh, yes, Wise Mother," the amah said. "But his belly is burned."

What mystery was this? I went out at once to the little house and found the baby very ill indeed. Mrs. Lu unwrapped the swaddling garments and there upon his tiny belly I saw burns around his navel. They were iodine burns.

"But I told you not to pour the iodine on the baby," I exclaimed.

"Ah, so you said, Wise Mother," Mrs. Lu moaned. "But I thought, if the medicine is good, why not use it all?"

I said I would take the baby at once to the hospital but this Mrs. Lu would not hear of, nor would she have the foreign doctor touch the child, not for a moment. But she let me take him to my own house and there I did the best I could for him. After a few days in my bedroom his robust peasant ancestry came to his aid, he decided to live, and I could return him to his mother. Before he was a month old his father, the runaway husband, appeared at the gate and the family was united again. I found a job for him on the university farms and Mrs. Lu rented a small earthen house, two little rooms, just over the compound wall.

Once again the baby came near death before he was a year old. It was after the summer, and Mrs. Lu walked in with him one day weeping and declaring that the child was doomed to die for some past sin in another incarnation. She turned him over to display his naked bottom and there I saw broken blisters and raw flesh.

"How is it he is burned again?" I inquired, astounded.

"He is not burned, Wise Mother," Mrs. Lu said. "I said to myself that now he is so big I should not use the water cloths you gave me but lay him on a bed of sand as we do in the north country, so that when he wets, there is no washing. But here there is no sand as we have in the North and so I laid him on ashes from the stove."

Ashes? Of course the urine had combined with the wood ashes to make lye. Again I took Little Meatball, as his milk name was, and after a few weeks of nursing he was well again.

All this is of no importance in itself, but it is very important because of the last of the three dates which I remember as monuments of the events in that decade between 1920 and 1930, and which changed my world. This third date was March 27, 1927.

While thus my life continued within my house, I was continually mindful of what was happening outside. It was difficult sometimes to know exactly what was going on except from the Chinese newspapers which printed brief undigested items which had somehow to be connected by pondering and guessing and then connected again with the grapevine of students' confidences and complaints. In Peking the huge blustering peasant war lord Feng Yu-hsiang, with whom Sun Yat-sen had hoped to make alliance before his death, had been defeated by the despotic war lord of Manchuria, Chang Tso-lin. Yet we all knew the Chang regime could not last, and it was tolerated only because everybody waited to see what the new Kuomintang revolution, then shaping up in Canton, was going to do. It was rumored and then confirmed not only that the Nationalist party had been reorganized, that Communists were now allowed to be members and that Russian advisors were being employed, but the new party was very different, we heard, from the old one. It was organized under military discipline and carried on with all the spirit of a crusade. When the time was ripe, we heard, this army would march north against the war lords and conquer them and unify China. We were troubled but not frightened, for it was questionable, and certainly the white people thought it so, whether the "Cantonese," as they liked to call the Kuomintang then, could win against the tough and reckless old war lords in the rest of the country who were doggedly pursuing the historic Chinese techniques of fighting each other until a final victor could and would set up a new dynasty. The students and intellectuals, however, passionately believed in the new revolution and worked for it, while the vast mass of people in both city and country simply waited for what was to happen, not indifferent but passive until the traditional steps were accomplished.

Though Sun Yat-sen was dead, in a powerful way he was more than ever the leader. He had, after his *rapprochement* with Soviet Russia in 1921, sent a gifted young soldier to Moscow for further military and revolutionary training. This man was Chiang Kai-shek. He had returned and had set up the new military college of Whampoa. There the officers of the future army were being trained. This Sun Yat-sen had planned, convinced at last that only by military means could China be unified. By his death, then, Sun Yat-sen accomplished far more than by his life. Alive, he had made many mistakes and had often alienated even those among his own people, but dead, he could be made perfect, and this the Kuomintang proceeded to do. His last words, his famous will and his portrait were printed everywhere, and the very sight of his pictured face inspired the students to fresh patriotism and revolutionary fervor. A little more than two months after his death, for example, an incident occurred in Shanghai that was worth a dozen victorious battles to the new leader, Chiang Kai-shek. There had been a strike in a Japanese-owned mill and the police in the International Settlement had arrested some of the strikers. A huge crowd of students from many schools gathered together in a demonstration one day soon after, to protest the arrest, and they refused to heed the warnings of the police. They would not disband when ordered to do so. Finally the police fired and several students were killed. Instantly resentment spread over the whole country. There were demonstrations everywhere, and boycotts were set up against Japanese and British in one city after another from south to north. Hong Kong was entirely boycotted and so many angry Chinese of all classes left that English colonial possession that its life was literally hamstrung until the anti-foreign fever died down again. Few foreigners could read Chinese newspapers but those who could were really terrified, and many white people were recalled by their consuls from the interior where they could not be protected.

My own sympathies were entirely with the Chinese, for though the police were within their rights as foreign-controlled police, yet it should have been remembered that they were in China and that the traditional Chinese attitude toward law was entirely different from that of the West. In China law was only for criminals, to punish them for their crimes. A person who was not a criminal could not be reached by law. Therefore when the police shot down innocent people even after due warning, and especially young students and intellectuals, who were traditionally recognized as valuable and upper-class persons, it was the police who had committed the crime of murder, the people said, and not the innocent young people who were only trying to be "patriotic." The incident was sadly typical of the differing points of view of my two worlds. There were many such differences and their number and ferocity were to rise to such volume that they fed directly into the Second World War, with its continuing war in Korea.

The May 30th Incident, as it came to be called, was a wonderful aid to the Kuomintang revolutionists. The war lord government in Peking was everywhere denounced as "running dogs of imperialism," and the revolutionaries in the South, building upon the anger of the people, planned their expedition for the next year much earlier than they might otherwise have been able to do. In 1926 began that triumphant northern march, Chiang Kai-shek leading it and flanked by Communist Russian advisors, both political and military. They found no resistance. The war lords of the southern provinces made a pretense of resisting, then fell to bargaining and then to yielding and "joining" the revolution. In the second summer after Sun Yat-sen's death the revolutionary forces had reached the very heart of China, and had occupied those three vital industrial cities of the middle Yangtse, Hankow, Wuhan and Hanyang. It was far more than military victory. As soon as a region fell the Communist organizers, under Russian direction, spread through the country and organized the peasants against the landlords and the workers in the great factories of the cities against their employers. I say Communist and yet I do not believe that Communism itself was meaningful in those days to the Chinese revolutionists. They had been told by their dead leader that Soviet Russia was their friend and that since the revolution in Russia had been successful in overthrowing an ancient and tyrannical government and organizing a new one—whose tyrannies, alas, were too little known anywhere and to the Chinese unknown—they, the Chinese revolutionists, must be guided by the Russians. The driving force in the Chinese, however, was not political unrest, which was only secondary, and not even class conflict. It was a passionate determination to get rid of the foreigners who had fastened themselves upon China through trade and religion and war, and set up a government for the reform and modernization of their country.

I pause here to reflect. Over and over again in recent years Americans have said to me with real sadness that they cannot understand why the Chinese hate us "when we have done so much for them." Actually, of course, we have done nothing for them. They did not ask us to send missionaries nor did they seek our trade. There has been individual kindness on both sides. Americans have sent relief in times of famine and war. I am sure the Chinese would have done the same for us, had our positions been reversed. Individual Americans, usually missionaries, have lived kind and unselfish lives in China, but again they came of their own will and they were appreciated. Individual Chinese have risked their lives and sometimes lost them for missionaries and other white folk in time of revolt or war.

The Chinese attitude toward the whole business of the missionary may best be exemplified from a little incident I once saw take place in my father's church in an interior city. He was preaching earnestly and somewhat long, and the congregation was growing restless. One by one they rose and went away. There is nothing in Chinese custom which forbids a person to leave an audience. He saunters away from the temple, the public storyteller or the theater when he feels like it and a sermon is an entirely foreign notion. My father was disturbed, however, and a kindly old lady on the front seat, seeing this, was moved to turn her head and address the people thus: "Do not offend this good foreigner! He is making a pilgrimage in our country so that he may acquire merit in heaven. Let us help him to save his soul!" This reversal so astonished my father, and yet he so perfectly understood its sincerity, that he begged the pardon of the assembly and instantly stopped his sermon.

It did not occur to the Chinese, actually, that missionaries were in China for any purpose except their own, and being an incomparably tolerant people, accustomed to individualism, they interfered only when the missionary was personally objectionable. Moreover, it must constantly be remembered that while Americans took no part in the wars and Unequal Treaties, beyond having a punitive force in Peking at the time of the Boxer outbreak and keeping war vessels in interior Chinese waters, yet whenever any other country, usually England, forced a new treaty, we demanded that its benefits be extended also to us. The famous Open Door Policy of the United States was useful to China but certainly it was as useful also to us. In short, it would be hypocritical for us to claim anything but self-interest, enlightened though it might be, and the Chinese, who are accustomed to all sorts of self-interest and hypocrisy, even in the subtlest forms, are not and never have been deceived about anybody, including the Americans. We have therefore no honest claim to gratitude from them. It is true that we have always liked the Chinese people unless and until they are Communists, but for this we are scarcely to be thanked since it is impossible not to like them when one understands them. They are almost universally liked and likeable.

An interlude in these years was one that I spent in the United States, and I had almost forgotten to mention it for it seems to have no relevance to my life. It was necessary, nevertheless, for the sake of my child. In 1925, the year in which Sun Yat-sen died, I went to the United States and took my child to one doctor after another, and when I was told of the hopelessness of her case, I felt it wise to plunge into some sort of absorbing mental effort that would leave me no time to think of myself. The child's father had also been granted a year's leave of absence and he decided to spend it at Cornell University. Thither we went, the three of us. We found a small house, very cheap, and I, too, decided to study, and for my Master's degree.

It was not altogether an empty year. First I learned to know what poverty can mean in a society as individualistic as that of the American people. In China I had earned my own living by teaching but now I did not earn it. This meant that I had to contrive to live on the single salary of the man, in order that I could study while he did, and this meant an economy so severe that only the most rigid care could pay our meager bills. For example, I bought eggs enough for two a day, one for the child and one for the man. Once a week I bought a small piece of meat. Instead of buying vegetables and fruit at the grocery, I paid a farmer to bring me a cartload of potatoes, onions, carrots and apples and these I piled in the cellar to provide the winter's food, except for a quart of milk a day and a loaf of bread. The only other expenditure was a small sum paid to a kindly neighbor woman to stay with my child two or three times a week for an hour, when I had to be at classes. Fortunately the professor under whom I majored in the English essay and novel was wise enough not to demand that I attend many classes. He left me to my own research, and this I could do at night. Once the child was in bed, and her father at his own books in the next room, I was free. Then I walked a mile through the woods, along a path that ran at the edge of a gorge and a rushing stream to the university where I went at once to the library. The joys of that library! I worked alone in the stacks, free to read as many books as I liked, free to think and to write. Sometime in the night I left off, unwillingly even then, and walked home again by moonlight or by lantern. No one was ever seen or heard at that hour, and I walked alone, the damp mist from the deep cold gorge wet upon my face and hair.

Even my stringent economy, however, was not enough for life, and after Christmas I saw that something had to be done to earn some money. I had no warm coat, for one thing, and besides I knew I must take back a few necessities to China in the summer. So, casting about in my mind, I thought of a story I had written on the ship coming over. We had taken the cold northern route to Vancouver because it was the shortest and whenever my child slept I had not gone on deck but had found a corner in the dining saloon. There with my notebook and pen I had begun a story, my first, and had finished it before we landed. I thought it sentimental and not good, and I had done nothing with it. Now, however, driven by anxiety, I got it out and tightened it up and copied it. Since it was the story of a Chinese family whose son brings home an American wife, I sent it to *Asia Magazine* and waited. It was a marvel of good fortune that I did not wait long, for almost at once, as such things go, I had a letter of acceptance from the editor, then Mr. Louis Froelick, and the promise of a payment of one hundred dollars. That sum seemed as good as a thousand. The problem was, should I buy the coat with part of it or use it all to pay school fees and bills? I decided to let the coat wait, and to start another story, a sequel, carrying on the first.

Meanwhile, the weather was bitterly cold. The landscape around Ithaca was a strange one to me and very dreary and I felt chilled in heart as well as in body. The hills there are not sheltering, but long and rolling and they are cut by deep dark gorges which conceal rivers and lakes. I was depressed especially by the lakes, which looked bottomless, and indeed there were ghostly stories about young men and women who had gone out together in canoes or rowboats and had been drowned, their craft overturned, and their bodies never recovered. Indian legends enhanced the horror of the grey waters, and I was never happy there.

Yet, in honesty, I must admit that perhaps part of my sadness came from my own circumstances.

Nevertheless, Ithaca contributed at least one glorious memory. It was the year of the total eclipse of the sun. Partial eclipses of sun and moon I had seen in China more than a few times, and they could scarcely be forgotten, because the people were terrified by them, and, believing that the source of light was being swallowed by a heavenly dragon, they rushed into the streets beating gongs and tin pans to frighten the dragon away. In Ithaca the eclipse was magnificent not only in beauty but in dignity. I watched it from a hilltop. Fortunately the day was gloriously clear, it was winter, and I looked over miles of snow-covered landscape, feeling an expectancy beyond any I had ever known. I love the theater, and the moment before the curtain goes up is always an experience, but this time the drama was of the universe, and the solemnity immense. Soon a shadow crept over the land, a mild but ever deepening twilight; strong waves of darkness streaked with light seemed to make the earth shiver, until at last the sun was entirely obscured and the stars shone out of a black sky. Upon my hilltop I felt as lonely as the last human being might feel were the sun to burn itself to ash and leave the earth in darkness forever. How glorious was the reassurance when slowly the light returned again to the full brightness of the day! I have never forgotten that hour and its meaning.

The second story went slowly, burdened as I was with schoolwork and housekeeping and caring for the child, and I began to despair of being able to finish it. I cast about then for another way to make some money and remembered certain money prizes which the university offered. Quite cold-bloodedly I asked which was the largest and found that it was awarded, as I now remember it, for the best essay upon some international subject. My professor told me, however, that it was always won by a graduate student in the history department and he discouraged me from trying for it.

I did not tell him then that I had decided to try for it anyway. It was for two hundred dollars, and this sum of money would see me safely through the year, even though I bought my coat. There were a few weeks between terms when I could work on the essay, and I chose as my subject the impact of the West upon Chinese life and civilization. My essay grew into a small book before it was finally finished. All manuscripts were handed in without names so that the judges could be impartial. Our names, of course, were given to the office. A fortnight passed and I began to think I had failed. Then someone told me that he had heard that a Chinese had won the prize, for only a Chinese could have written the winning essay. A weak hope rose in my bosom but I repressed it, for there were several brilliant Chinese students at Cornell. In a few days, however, I received a letter telling me that I had won the award, and what a pleasure that was, especially when after my next class I went to my doubting professor and showed him the letter!

Ah well, it is not often that need and grant meet so neatly and at a time when a certain human spirit had fallen very low in hope and joy. My heart recovered itself, and I finished my story in good mood and sent it to *Asia Magazine* and again it was accepted. Now I was quite rich, and I bought my warm coat, a soft dark green one that lasted me until I lost it in the revolution, of which I shall tell hereafter. And I got back my faith in myself, which was all but gone in the sorry circumstances of my life, and I went to China in the summer, not only with what I needed in material goods but also with a second child, my first little adopted daughter, a tiny creature of three months whom the orphanage had given up the more readily because she had not gained an ounce since she was born. Nothing, they told me, agreed with her, and so I said, "Give her to me," and they did, and as soon as she felt herself with her mother, she began to eat and grow fat. How easily happiness can be made, and when it is made how wonderfully it works!

One other small thing I did in that year in Ithaca. I discovered that the Asian students in Cornell were usually isolated and lonely. Only a few of the more attractive and brilliant ones found American friends. Many of them, mostly Chinese, lived to themselves, absorbed in their books and too poor to spend anything on fun. It was serious, I felt, that they learned nothing at all about American life. For that matter, the Americans, too, were missing a rich chance to learn something about the Chinese, for even then I was beginning to perceive that unless there could be understanding between East and West there would someday be terrible conflict between them. I spent time, therefore, in trying to persuade the women of Ithaca through their clubs and organizations to open their homes to Chinese students and see to it that the young people who had come from so far could go home again with knowledge of even one American town and its citizens. I did not make much headway. The ladies were kind but they were absorbed in their own affairs, and some of them were reluctant, alas, to let Chinese mingle with their sons and daughters. They could not foresee that such sons and daughters would mingle anyway, through war, if not through peace.

Summer came, we took ship again, and returned to China. It was still home.

The long Indian summer in which I have been writing has broken overnight. We do not have typhoons here as we used to have in China but we have hurricanes and blizzards and northeasters and the effect is almost the same, and yet not quite. There is still nothing as terrifying as a typhoon, unless it be a Western cyclone, a sight that I have never seen. This is a northeaster. Somewhere out at sea a whirligig of a wind began and enlarged itself to include our region, and so this morning, too early in November for our climate, which is, as someone has said, "the far thin edge of the tropics," I see a thick soft snow spread over the landscape. In the court beneath my window the little Italian statue of a boy who stands above the pool holding a big shell in his arms bravely bears a burden of snow on his shoulders. Beside him the coonberry bush is stripped of its dying leaves but the bright red berries are redder than ever against the snow. The usual events of a winter's day lie ahead. Breakfast is made in a hurry so that skis can be found and shovels brought out for clearing the paths, and at the farm the snowplow is hitched to the tractor.

Breakfast over I cross the court into my workroom and beyond it the flowers in the greenhouses shine through the glass doors like gems in the white twilight of the snow lying on the roofs. Against the exquisite shadow the carnations and roses glow and snapdragons glitter like candles. The chrysanthemums, bronze and red, are embers. The greenhouses are my avocation, and when a story halts and its people refuse to speak, an hour's work among the plants will often melt the most stubborn material into something alive and responsive.

My life, flung so far around the world, has in a way been unified in my gardens. The scarlet coonberry bush is a remembrance of the red berries of the Indian bamboo which grew thickly about the terrace of the house in Nanking, and they, too, were beautiful under the light snows of those past years. Chinese artists for centuries have loved to paint red berries under snow, and, whatever the government under which they now live, perhaps this ancient love is permanent, with all that it signifies.

Easily today my mind goes back to those other days. The winter after my return to China, the fateful year of 1926-1927, had been a usual one, mild as most of our winters were in the Yangtse Valley, and yet we had enough snow to enhance the green bamboos and leafless branches of the elms and the prickly oranges that made a hedge to hide the compound wall. Yet it was, I recall, a strange uneasy winter. The revolutionary forces had dug in around The Three Cities and we waited for the spring when they would march again. Newspapers were cautious and I was reluctant to trust the rumors which came by word of mouth. White people were hopeful or distrustful, depending upon their feeling for the Chinese people. The missionaries were guarded but ready to welcome whatever came if they were allowed to continue their work undisturbed. My sister was married and her little family was in far Hunan, and the Communists had settled across the lake from her home. Nobody knew exactly what the Communists were. Bandits and brigands had joined their ranks, but bandits and brigands were an inevitable part of all war lord regimes. What we heard about the Communists was what we had always heard about the bandits and brigands. Which was which? No one knew.

The spring was slow that year of 1927, and this in spite of the mild winter. The la-mei trees bloomed after the Chinese New Year, and they had never been more fragrant or more beautiful. Those fairy cups of clear and waxlike yellow blooming upon the bare and angular branches were always my delight. There is no perfume equal to theirs, and yet I have never seen them in any other country than in China. They were scarcely gone, I remember, when word came from my sister that she and her family were leaving their home and coming for refuge to my house in Nanking. In a few days they were with us and unharmed, for nothing had actually happened, except that they had heard disquieting stories of the anti-foreign behavior of the revolutionary troops, who were on the march again, and planning to come down the river.

I was glad that we were all together, my father and my sister and I and our families, while the strange waiting went on. The Three Cities were a long way off, and there was still time to watch and try to guess what we should do. My father, always tranquil, refused to believe that the new revolutionists would also be anti-foreign, for by this time he refused to believe anything evil of any Chinese, and had become far more Chinese than American. Yet I remembered. In spite of all my friends, I remembered the refugee days in Shanghai and the sudden look of hate upon the man's face whose queue I had once pulled when I was a naughty and impatient child, and other such looks, fleeting enough, but which nevertheless had not escaped me. Most of all, I remembered the many reasons why the Chinese should hate the white man and I feared that if hatred were now to flare again none of us could escape. And all this went on underneath the everyday life of coming and going, of pleasant communication between my pupils and me, and between friends and neighbors. Nobody said anything to make us afraid. There was no animosity even on the streets.

The Chinese New Year came in due season and guests filled the house.

I served tea and many kinds of cakes and sweets, and our children exchanged gifts. Ah, it was so exactly like every other year that it was hard to believe that the comfortable house was not the safe and pleasant place it had always been! The servants, I remember, were even more considerate and helpful than usual, and my Chinese women friends were tender in their goodness to my children. The festival season passed, and after it the days and weeks until the last of March.

When I remember the fateful morning of March 27, 1927, I see it in a scene, as though I had nothing to do with it. A little group of white people stands, uncertain and alone, on the early green lawn of a grey brick house, three men, two women, three small children. The wind blows damp and chill over the compound wall. The sky is dark with clouds. They hold their coats about them, shivering, and they stare at each other.

"Where can we hide?" This is what they are whispering.

One of those women is me, two of the children are mine. The other woman is my sister. The two younger men are our husbands, and the tall dignified old gentleman is our father. The nightmare of my life has come true. We are in danger of our lives because we are white people in a Chinese city. Though all our lives have been spent in friendly ways, it counts for nothing today. Today we suffer for those we have never known, the aggressors, the imperialists, the white men of Europe and England who fought the wars and seized the booty and claimed the territory, the men who made the Unequal Treaties, the men who insisted upon extraterritorial rights, the empire builders. Oh, I was always afraid of those white men because they were the ones who made us all hated in Asia! The weight of history falls heavy upon us now, upon my kind old father, who has been only good to every Chinese he has ever met, upon our little children, who have known no country except this one where now they stand in danger of death.

"Where shall we hide?" we keep asking, and we cannot answer.

The pleasant house which until now has been our home can shelter us no more. The rooms stand as we left them a few minutes ago, the big stove still burning in the hall and spreading its heartening warmth, the breakfast table set, the food half eaten. I was just pouring the coffee when our neighbor, the faithful tailor, came running in to tell us that the revolutionists, who in the night had captured the city, were now killing the white people. He stood there at the table where we were all sitting, happy that the battle was over, and he wrung his hands and the tears ran down his cheeks while he talked.

"Do not delay, there is no time—Teacher Williams lies dead already in the street outside the gate!"

Dr. Williams? He was the vice-president of the Christian university!

My father had breakfasted early and was gone to his classes at the seminary, but only just gone, so immediately the houseboy runs to bring him back. My sister and I know only too well now that death is possible, and we get up quickly and find the children's coats and caps and our own coats and we all hasten outside the house that is no longer a shelter, and here we stand in the chill wet winds.

Where can we hide?

The servants gather around us, half fearful for their own sakes. They know that if they are found with us they too may be killed. Nobody knows the ferocity of the revolutionists. We have heard such stories.

"There is no use in hiding in our quarters," the amah says. "They will find you there." She falls to her knees and puts her arms around my child and sobs aloud.

Oh, where can we go? There is nowhere. We hear the sound of howling voices in the distant streets and we look at each other and clasp the children's hands. My old father's lips move and I know he is praying. But there is nowhere to go.

Suddenly the back gate squeaks on its hinges, the little back gate in the corner of the compound wall, and we all turn our heads. It is Mrs. Lu, who lives in a cluster of little mud houses just over the wall in a pocket of an alley off the street that runs in front of the house. She comes hobbling toward us on her badly bound feet, her loose trousers hanging over her ankles. Her hair is uncombed as usual, rusty brown locks hanging down her cheeks, and her kind stupid face is all concern and alarm and love.

"Wise Mother," she gasps, "you and your family, come and hide in my little half-room! Nobody will look for you there. Who would harm a woman like me? My good-for-nothing has left me again and I and my son are alone. Come—come—there is no time!"

She pulls at me, she embraces all the children at once, and we follow her blindly, half running, leaving the gate open behind us. There are no houses very near, we have lived in one of the open spaces of the city, and we run across two or three acres of grassland and old graves and between some neat vegetable gardens until on the far side of our wall we reach the handful of mud houses, in one of which Mrs. Lu lives. The people are waiting for us there, the kind poor people, and they receive us, her friends and neighbors, and they hurry us into the dark little half-room which is her home. It is indeed only half a room, barely big enough for the board bed, a small square table and two benches. There is no window, only a hole under the thatched roof. It is almost entirely dark. Into this narrow place we all crowd ourselves and Mrs. Lu closes the door.

"I will come back," she whispers. "And if the children cry, do not be afraid. We have so many children here, those wild soldiers will not know if it is your child or ours that cries."

She goes away and we are left in the strange silence. Our children do not cry. No one speaks. We are all trying to realize what is happening. It has been too quick. Then my father looks out of the little hole under the roof. We can see a light, a glow from a reddening sky.

"They are burning the seminary," my father says. It is where he goes every day to teach and to do his work of translating the New Testament from Greek into Chinese. Nobody answers him. We are quiet again.

This is what I see, this is what I remember.

And yet, strange and unexpected as it was, it was all familiar. Sitting there on the edge of the bed beside my sister, each of us holding a child, I told myself that I had always known it would happen. The wild winds had been sown and the whirlwinds were gathering, and it was only chance that I had been born in the age of whirlwinds, chance alone that I was reaping what I had not sown. Call it chance, too, that I was born of the white race, but I could not escape that, either. I sat in silence, pondering over these things, as I knew each of us in his own way was pondering, my old father with all his years spent now and gone, my young sister and her little boy, and I with my own eternal child, and the little daughter I had adopted and brought from America, the two Americans my sister and I had married. None of us could escape the history of the centuries before any of us had been born, and with which we had nothing to do. We had not, I think, ever committed even a mild unkindness against a Chinese, and certainly we had devoted ourselves to justice for them, we had taken sides against our own race again and again for their sakes, sensitive always to injustices which others had committed and were still committing. But nothing mattered today, neither the kindness nor the cruelty. We were in hiding for our lives because we were white.

I remember thinking on two levels. One was the world and the centuries of history, and I felt nothing but sympathy for the Chinese who knew only the evil of the white man and none of the good. Were I a young Chinese, had I been taught only what the white man had done to my country, I too would have wanted to be rid of him forever. I could not blame them. But on the other level I was thinking of this very moment, and of the children. My father would meet his fate with calm and with peace. I had no fear for him. He had lived his life. The two young men must handle themselves as best they could when the last minutes came. My sister and I were strong enough, too, to bear ourselves proudly and without showing fear. But what of the little children? My helpless child was only seven, my little adopted daughter only three, my sister's little boy also three. These could not be left. Somehow we two mothers must contrive to see them dead before we ourselves must die.

For by now the mobs had risen and outside the little hut we heard the firing of guns and the howls of the crowd. There is always a crowd in any city, in any country, when order breaks down. There are the thieves and the looters and the fire lovers and the men who are afraid to kill in times of peace but who let their lust for blood blaze out when there is no peace. We began to hear screams and loud laughter, yells and sounds of blows. We heard the heavy front door of our house beaten in and then the shout of greedy joy when the crowd burst into the hall.

I could see it as clearly as though I stood there watching. I saw the rooms as we had left them, the rooms I had made and loved, my home, as warm and pretty a place as I could contrive, the yellow curtains at the windows, the dull blue Chinese rugs on the floors, the Chinese furniture and the few comfortable chairs, the flowers on the tables. I had nursed for weeks the bulbs of the white sacred lilies and they were in full bloom, scenting the house. A coal fire burned in the grate under the mantelpiece in the living room. And upstairs were the bedrooms and the children's nursery, and in the attic was my own special place, where I did my work. And I remembered that on my desk in that attic room was the finished manuscript of my first novel.

It was all gone. The crowd was surging through the rooms, snatching everything they could take, quarreling over garments and bedding and rugs and all else that had been mine. And I, by some irony which almost made me smile, was sitting here on a board bed in a hut wearing my oldest clothes and not even my good American coat. I had planned, this day, to clean the attic thoroughly now that my novel was done.

Hour after hour went by. No one came near us for a long time and we made no sound. Even the children were silent, not crying, not whispering, simply clinging to us as we held them. It was strange to be left thus alone, for we had not been alone at all for days. As the revolutionary armies drew near to the city and battle became inevitable, our war lord had declared that he would fight, and he had locked the city gates and prepared his soldiers. I had foreseen a siege and so as in other such times I had laid in canned foods and dried Chinese foods and fruits and grains. We had a little chicken yard and the children would have eggs, and I had bought some cases of American canned milk, some Australian tinned butter.

The battle had begun three days ago and only the children had slept since the first guns were fired, for all of us knew that this battle was not like any other. The Communists had organized the forces and they were the leaders. Even Chiang Kai-shek was with the Communists, we were told. These were not only Chinese, therefore. Something new and dangerous had been added. The Communists were building upon hate, the hate for the foreigner, the injustice of the past. Never before had the old hatreds been organized.

As usual in times of war, the city Chinese had flocked to our house. I do not know whether other houses like mine were full of them, but every room in our house was overflowing with Chinese. With us were our Chinese friends, their families, and their friends. Everyone was welcome at such a time. They brought what food they had and we had all shared our resources during the three days. But downstairs the big cellars, inevitable in the semitropical houses, were filled with unknown people from the streets. We did not keep them out. If there was any safety to be found with us, we were only glad, and until now there had always been safety with the foreigners, for the Unequeal Treaties protected the Chinese friends of the white man, too. I had always hated those treaties, and never for myself would I ever willingly accept their protection, yet actually I was helpless against them. Wrong as they were and now bearing the bitter fruit of a hatred accumulated through generations of Chinese, I had been protected by them in spite of myself, but at least I had shared my safety. I remember the night before, I had laughed and told my sister that the cellars were so full of people I felt as though the floors were heaving. The people tried to be quiet but the subdued noise gathered and mounted to the very roof in a stilled roar. I had sent tea and bread loaves downstairs lest they were hungry.

We had gone upstairs to bed at last longing for the morning as we went, for the rumor was that the battle would end before dawn. In the morning, we had told ourselves, we would be at peace again. There would be new rulers, for by now it was obvious that our old war lord must be defeated. All the youth and the idealism and the patriotism were on the other side. I knew, for that matter, that my own students and most of my friends, certainly the young ones, were on the side of the revolutionists. Our war lord's soldiers were only mercenaries, and they would desert as soon as defeat was plain. But we were used to battles and changing rulers, and we were only hoping that the new ones would be better than the old. Almost anything would be better than the war lords, each greedy for himself and a sore burden for the patient people.

That night I slept from exhaustion and was wakened early, not by noise, but by a silence so deep that at first I was bewildered. It was barely dawn, I could see only the outlines of familiar furniture and the grey rectangle of the window. The guns were stopped, the booming of the old-fashioned cannon was ended. A solid silence filled the room. But what silence? There was not even the sound of a human being. No child cried, and the rumble of voices from the cellar was dead.

I got up and dressed myself and went downstairs. The rooms which I had left full of our friends and friends of friends were empty. There was no sign of a bedding roll or a garment. I opened the cellar door and went downstairs. No one was there, not a soul. The place was clean, nothing left behind. Only in the kitchen the cook was stirring about dubiously, red-eyed and pale-cheeked.

"What has happened?" I asked.

"They have all gone," he said. "Everyone went away in the night."

"Why?" I asked.

"They are afraid," he said.

But it did not occur to me even then that they were afraid to be found with us. I did not dream that the white people could shelter no one again, not even ourselves.

In the crowded hut we sat the hours through while the noises mounted outside. One foreign house after another went up in flames and we said nothing. The door opened at last and Mrs. Lu crept in with a teapot and some bowls.

"Your house is not burned," she whispered to me while she poured the tea. "The wild people are looting, but they have not burned your house."

"It doesn't matter," I whispered back.

She whispered again. "The cook and the amah and the gardener—they are pretending to loot but they are taking the things for you. I and the neighbors here—we have taken too, but it is for you. You understand that it is not for ourselves?"

She patted my cheek. "You helped me when I had no home. Twice you saved my son's life."

It may sound strange but at this moment I felt such a peace come over me that I remember it still. Here was a human being who was only good. At the risk of her life she was saving ours. What comfort to know that there was this human being!

Yet did she realize her own danger? "You know that if we are found they will kill you, too?" I asked whispering.

"Let them try," she said robustly under her breath. "Just let them touch me, the wild beasts! Not knowing the difference between good people and bad!"

She hugged my child. "Little precious," she whispered tenderly, and went away again.

The day dragged on, and the madness continued unabated. Once again the door opened. This time it was my friend's husband, the one who had lost her baby by the hypodermic. He came in to whisper that many Chinese were working for the white people. They had gone to the Communist Commander-in-Chief, they were waiting upon him, they would beseech him to spare us.

"Take courage," he told us. "We are trying to save you." He hesitated, I remember, and then he said. "I have been a long time finding you because Mrs. Lu trusts nobody. She would not tell even me where you were until a few minutes ago. One does not know now who is friend and who is enemy—these Communists!"

He went away and the hours passed. Again the door opened and a kind Chinese face peered in, an old woman who lived in the cluster of huts, a stranger to me then. She came in with bowls of hot soup and noodles and set them on the table.

"Eat," she said in a loud whisper. "Eat, good foreign devils, and let down your hearts. They will not find you. Nobody here will tell where you are. We are all true. Even our children will not tell. And if your children cry let them. If I hear your child cry I will smack my grandchild and make him cry outside the door so that no one knows who cries. All children cry the same noise—"

She went away, nodding and smiling to reassure us, and we fed the children and again the day dragged on.

Alas, the madness grew. We could not hide from ourselves that the uproar and the frenzy were worsening, and with the night ahead and the darkness our chances were small. What, I wondered, was happening to the other white people in the city? Many would have friends as we had, but many perhaps were already dead for lack of such a hiding place as ours. For the first time in my life I realized fully what I was, a white woman, and no matter how wide my sympathies with my adopted people, nothing could change the fact of my birth and my ancestry. In a way, I suppose, I changed my world then and there, in that tiny dark hut. I could not escape what I was.

No one opened the door now, not even Mrs. Lu. I knew that this was not disloyalty but protection of us. The soldiers must be very near, so that she dared not make the slightest move to betray our presence. We could hear the rude voices, the hoarse chanting of the Communist songs and the endless crackling of the burning houses, the rumbling of falling walls.

Sometime in the afternoon, before twilight fell, the door did open once more. It was the young Chinese again, the husband of my friend, he who had come in the morning. He entered now and fell at once on his knees and before us he made the ancient kotow.

"We can do nothing," he told us, the tears wet upon his cheeks. "We are helpless. We have been told that all will be killed before nightfall. Forgive us, forgive us, we have greatly harmed you, we sin against you."

He kotowed again and again and we begged him to get up, saying that we understood that he had done all he could for us and indeed had risked his own life. He was not alone in trying to help us. University professors and students and neighbors and friends, all were trying to save our lives.

"Thank you," we said, bowing to him as he bowed to us. He went away and now indeed we were alone. Each of us in his own way tried to face what lay ahead. It was impossible to speak. My sister and I sat clasping each other's hands, and then realizing that she had her husband, I turned to my father. He sat on a bench, his face calm, his spirit unmoved. I had never loved him as much or admired him more. As for the children, they were small and they would never know. As for me, I would see that they went ahead of me.

In this strange speechless waiting the afternoon wore on, the dreadful wild noise unabated. It grew dark in the hut. It was five o'clock when we were last able to see our watches. Then I took off the little gold watch I wore and slipped it under the pillow on Mrs. Lu's bed. At least she would have that. Loud feet passed and repassed the door and at every instant we expected to hear it burst open and it would be the end of this day. In the midst of this desperate waiting suddenly we heard a frightful noise, a thunder, rumbling over the roof. What was it? It came again and again. It could only be cannon. But what cannon? The Chinese had no such cannon as this, deafening us, roaring above the human shouts and cries. Again and again it came and again and again.

Foreign cannon—the warships in the river! Suddenly everyone thought of the same thing. Of course, what else? We had not imagined such a possibility. The river was seven miles away, but the powerful weapons were dropping their loads not far from where we were hidden.

The booming lasted for what seemed a long time but was only a few minutes. When it was over we heard no sound whatever. The shouting had ceased, the footsteps were gone. Only the falling of a burning beam from some house, or the crumbling of a wall, broke the sudden silence.

What now, we asked ourselves? How I wished Mrs. Lu would come in! But no one came. We remained alone in the silence for two hours or more, so we guessed, but it was hard to know in the darkness how slowly the time went. And what did the silence mean?

The door opened at last and by the light of the flame of a torch flying in the night wind, we saw again our Chinese friend. He was surrounded by soldiers, Communist soldiers we could see by their uniforms. He stepped across the threshold and stood in the doorway. He did not bow or show any formal politeness.

"You are all to go to the university buildings," he commanded harshly. "All white people are to gather there by command of the new General."

In the light of the torch I saw his lips move and his eyebrows lift. His harshness meant nothing except protection. "Forgive me," his lips were silently saying.

I rose at once, understanding, and taking a child by each hand I led the way out of the hut. In the shadows outside I saw Mrs. Lu among the watching people. She was crying and the torchlight shone on her wet cheeks. But all the others made no sign, and we spoke to no one, lest by recognition we mark them as our friends and bring suffering on them later when we were gone. Out of the little cluster of houses we went, and along the narrow paths between the vegetable fields, all their cabbages and onions ruined by the feet of the mob, and then over the grassy gravelands to the road which led to the university. In the darkness my helpless child grew impatient and pushed against the young soldier who was ahead. He turned on her with a frightful snarl, his bayonet pointed.

"Please," I cried, as once my mother had cried for me. "She is only a child. I ask pardon for her."

We went sullenly on then, and thus led we entered the campus and marched between enemy guards to enter the big university building where other white people were already waiting. But as we passed, the light of the flaming torches fell on the faces and I looked to see what sort of men the revolutionists were. They were all young, every face was young, and I saw among them not one face I knew. They were ignorant faces, drunken faces, red and wild-eyed, and perhaps they were drunk with wine, but perhaps only with triumph and with hate. They glared back at us, and they grinned with a dreadful laughter, for what they saw was the downfall and the humiliation of the white people who had for so long been their oppressors. I knew, I knew what they felt, and I could not hate them and so I returned to my old thoughts. The winds had been sown and these were the whirlwinds, so long foreseen, inevitable, inescapable, and it was only accident of time that here was I.

We went upstairs and into the big room and there we found the other white people, men, women and children, some safe, some wounded by gunshots, some hurt by manhandling and rough usage, and when we had been welcomed we heard the varying stories of the tragic dead. All these alive had been rescued by heroic Chinese who had worked steadily to save the lives of the white people without thought of their own danger and future punishment for taking our part. It was a wonderful and joyful meeting, and never had I felt so near to my own people. Never, either, had I loved the Chinese so well or honored them so much. Somewhere and sometime, I was sure that my two great peoples would come together in understanding and enduring friendship and so the dreadful day closed in exhilaration of spirit. We bedded the children down in overcoats and quilts that the Chinese had gathered and at last we slept.

What remains to be told? We stayed there that night and all the next day, still not knowing whether we were to be released or held for an unknown purpose, but there was nothing lonely about our imprisonment. One by one through the night and the next day the few remaining white people who had not yet been found were brought to join our number. We knew now the dead, and among them was a gentle old Catholic priest, an Italian, who had been a teacher at the Chinese university where I too had taught. There we had often talked together while we waited for our classes to gather.

But what kept us from being lonely or isolated was the steady flow of Chinese friends who continued to brave the harsh revolutionary guards to bring us food and changes of clothing and toothbrushes and money and combs and warm clothes and everything they could think of for our comfort. They came weeping and heartbroken and we had to cheer them up and thank them over and over and assure them that we bore no one ill will for what had happened. And indeed this was true, for we had all been heartened and warmed by the friendship they had shown us.

Still we did not know what was to happen, although we heard rumors that the commanders on the foreign warships were negotiating for our release. Late in the afternoon of that second day, however, we were told to gather ourselves together and come out of the building. We were to march to the Bund, there to be taken off on the warships. When we reached the gate we found that several broken-down carriages had been provided for the old people and women with little children, and so I with other mothers climbed in and drove off down the familiar streets. How strange, how strange it was, and still it seems strange to me, even after all these years, and I remember it all as though there were no years between. The streets were lined with watching silent people, but the scene, so familiar, had changed overnight. Would I ever see the city again? I did not know, and yet I could not imagine never coming back.

The miles were slow, but at last we reached the river's edge and there we were met by American sailors, who took us aboard the gunboats. And almost at once we learned that we had had a second narrow escape, this time at the hands of our own countrymen. Here is the story. The American Consul, John Davis, an old friend of mine, whose father had been a missionary and a friend of my father's, was on board the man-of-war, whence the American Commander was directing our escape. The Communist military officers in the city had been given a time ultimatum for our arrival, and if we failed to appear by the set hour, six o'clock I think it was, the city would be bombarded in earnest, not at all like the firing of the day before which had been carefully planned for the empty spaces within the city wall, so that only two or three people were killed. At six o'clock we were still not in sight and the American Commander was about to order the bombardment to begin. But John Davis, knowing that exact hours meant nothing to Chinese, begged for a fifteen-minute delay, and when, at the end of that time, we were still not in sight, for yet another brief delay. Still we were not in sight and the American officer was ready to give orders, when a third time John Davis besought him to wait only a few minutes more. Within those minutes the first of our ragged caravan appeared at the river's edge. Had the cannon fired, undoubtedly we would have been killed by our own fire. As it was, we went aboard the ships safely.

All my life I had seen those gunboats on the river, and I had wished that they were not there. I had felt they should not be there, foreign warships in Chinese interior waters. Now such a ship was saving me and mine and taking us to a refuge. I was glad not to die, but I wished that I had not needed to justify, against my will, what still I knew to be wrong. There was no use quibbling now, however, and I turned toward my own countrymen. They were only the sailors, young and crude, from aboard the destroyer, but I longed for a friendly word from them. Alas, they were not friendly to anyone. I suppose they were tired, I suppose they were disgusted with us because we had not left Nanking when the Consul warned us, months earlier, of the dangers from the revolutionary Chinese army. Certainly those young American sailors could not understand our being in China at all, and it was only weariness that we were there to be cared for. At any rate, they were harsh and some of them even contemptuous, and I shrank away from them and felt lonely indeed. Yet I had to accept their help for the sake of the children, and so on the ship at last we gathered about a bare table where plates and forks and spoons were heaped, and a sailor ladled out some sort of stew. Everybody ate except me and I could not eat. It was more than mere exhaustion. The exhilaration of spirit was gone. The Chinese who had been our friends were far away, and here were only these rough young men who did not smile, even when they looked at the children.

In the night we had one more catastrophe. Into a cabin designed for six sailors, fourteen women and all their children were crowded. Some of the women had come from the mission hospital with newborn babies, and they were given the best berths. Others slept on the floor. I was given a berth for my children, and I put them to bed in the same clothes they had worn, the only ones they had, and I sat down beside them to rest for a moment. Then I saw that my helpless child was feverish and somewhere I borrowed a thermometer and took her temperature. She was fretful and bit the glass to pieces and I had to be sure that she swallowed none of it. It was just then that I noticed a greenish look on other faces and suddenly my younger child vomited and other children began to vomit. In a few minutes women and children were in violent nausea, except me, and a missionary doctor, called to attend them, staggered into the cabin, himself violently ill, to report that everybody was ill. The stew, it seemed, had been made from old tinned meat, long held in reserve, and it had caused ptomaine poisoning.

What a night that was! I ran back and forth with various vessels, emptying and washing and holding them again to be refilled. We had only one toilet, but fortunately it was a flush toilet and so somehow we managed. Once when I went in, loaded with pots, I found a friend, a woman who had been my neighbor, earnestly searching the toilet contents. She had swallowed her wedding ring the day before when a Communist soldier had tried to take it from her and now she was trying to recover it. It was part of the absurd nightmare of that night that she did recover it, thanks to her determination.

When the worst was over and it became apparent that nobody was going to die and when my own children were asleep at last, it was near dawn and the destroyer was racing down the river toward Shanghai. Then I sat down on the edge of the berth again and wished that I had something to read, anything to take my mind away from this pit of horror and to keep me from thinking of an unknown tomorrow. There was not a book in sight. Some sixth sense made me put my hand under the berth, however, and there in an open canvas bag I felt the outlines of a book. I pulled it out and by the light of the sturdy oil lamp on the wall I read the title. It was *Moby Dick,* and I had not read it before.

Never say the gods are not kind! While the others slept away their fever and their pain, I sat in good health and restored calm and read for the rest of the night.

I had a curious sense of pleasant recklessness when I stepped off the ship at Shanghai. There is something to be said for losing one's possessions, after nothing can be done about it. I had loved my Nanking home and the little treasures it had contained, the lovely garden I had made, my life with friends and students. Well, that was over. I had nothing at all now except the old clothes I stood in. I should have felt sad, and I was quite shocked to realize that I did not feel sad at all. On the contrary, I had a lively sense of adventure merely at being alive and free, even of possessions. No one expected anything of me. I had no obligations, no duties, no tasks. I was nothing but a refugee, someone totally different from the busy young woman I had been. I did not even care that the manuscript of my novel was lost. Since everything else was gone, why not that?

I cannot advise the deliberate wooing of such a mood, for what it meant was that my roots were abruptly pulled up, and never again was I to put them down so deeply. Anyone who has lost all his habitual environment by sudden violence will know what I mean, and those who have not, cannot possibly understand, and so there is no use in trying to explain. Simply the fact was that nothing was ever as valuable to me again, nothing, that is, in the way of place or beloved objects, for I knew now that anything material can be destroyed. On the other hand, people were more than ever important and human relationships more valuable. My mind was crowded with all the different people I had met in the last forty-eight hours, from the moment our tailor had come to warn us and my loved Mrs. Lu had come running across the fields to save us, down to the last surly young sailor. Surly they remained, too, for not one of those sailors showed the slightest responsibility for the poisoning nor any pity for a child.

When the destroyer docked I stared at the crowds on the Shanghai Bund who had gathered to stare at us, and felt neither shame nor concern. Plenty of Chinese were there who did not conceal their pleasure at seeing a crowd of white people as dirty and weary refugees, but others were there, too, who were kind and good and wanted to give us food and shelter. I had already learned that any crowd will contain the same contrast, wherever it gathers. Room had been found for us all, and so indifferent was I that I cannot now remember where we went or even how long we stayed, except that it was not long. We bathed and put on fresh garments collected for us, and then I felt that Shanghai was even more intolerable than usual and that I must go away.

I wanted to go somewhere into high mountains, where there were few people, and if possible no one that I knew, and where I could review all that had happened to me and see what it meant that I had been pulled up by the roots. What did one do with roots that were no good any more, and were roots necessary, after all? If not, why put them down again? These were questions that had to be answered and I said to my family:

"Let's leave. Let's go to Japan, into those mountains above Nagasaki and the sea. We could rent a little Japanese house."

I cannot remember how it was done except that the mission head let us draw on salary for funds, nor do I remember how we got the house nor any of the other means whereby I achieved just that end. But, we found space in a crowded little Japanese ship and we crossed the sea to Nagasaki, on the island of Kyushu, Japan. In those days Nagasaki was a clean and charming place, familiar to me, for we had visited it often as we came and went across the Pacific. There, too, my eldest sister had been taken ill to die upon a ship at six months of age, when my parents were taking her home to China after a holiday, long before I was born.

What comfort it was to walk on quiet clean streets again, to go to the small inn and settle into peaceful rooms, to have a Japanese bath, long and soaking and hot, a delicious Japanese meal and then sleep, hours of sleep! I remember how I savored every moment of such restoration. And when we woke we walked the streets among friendly courteous people, and we watched the evening mists gather over the mountains that seemed almost to push the houses into the sea. Up in those mountains was hidden the little Japanese town where I hoped we could find a home for a while until we knew what we wanted to do.

It was all so easy, so safe, so free from strain. A Japanese cabman drove us up the winding roads into the mountains and we took rooms at an inn until we could find a house and settle into it, and that inn I remember because of the hot springs in the baths, wonderful clear warm water, medicinal and soothing. The mountainside was pierced with such springs, little curls of steam rising from the rocks, and Japanese woodcutters and tourists cooked their eggs in the steam and heated their rice and vegetables, and I packed picnic baskets and did the same for the children.

My sister and her family went on to Kobe, for she expected a child and needed to be near a doctor, and my father, enlivened by his unaccustomed freedom from work, decided to go to Korea by himself and so there were only the four of us in Unzen. I tired quickly, as usual, of living in a hotel, and within a few days we moved to a little Japanese house across the valley and on another mountain. It was made of wood, as all such houses are, and it was deep in a pine forest. The house itself was one big room whose whole front could be slid back into boards at either side, and behind it were three cubbyhole bedrooms, and a tiny room with a large oval wooden tub for a bath. On the narrow back porch a rough table provided my kitchen, and upon it stood a charcoal stove which was only a pottery jar under a grate, and there I cooked my meals.

In this simple space I found healing. The scent of the pines pervaded the air, and the stillness of the forest was peace itself. I did not want a servant nor any stranger in the house, and indeed there was nothing to do except to prepare the meals and sweep the floors with a bamboo broom and when this was done to wash our few garments in the brook. The nights were long and still and in the morning I was waked by the soft rustling and whispering of the crabwomen. When I had washed and dressed I went out and found five or six old souls, in worn cotton kimonos, very clean, and sitting in a row on the edge of the floor of our living room as it opened directly into the trees. They had been too kind to wake me, but once they saw me they held up their baskets of fresh crabs and fish so that I might make my choice for the day. I tried to buy from one and the other, in justice to all, and they made no complaint, but they always came together and went away together, leaving me with a grass string of frantic crabs or pulsing fish in my hand. Rice, boiled dry and flaky, and a green of some sort was enough for a meal and we grew healthy and clear-eyed on the fare.

Sometimes we made sandwiches of bread I baked once a week and then we went off for the day, to climb a mountain or explore a valley, and often we found ourselves part of a procession of tourists, picnickers and people on walking tours, for the Japanese love their mountains and beauty spots and are indefatigable about picnics. I must have been very happy and idle for I cannot remember anything else about our months in the mountains of Japan, except once when I was taking my daily bath in the wooden tub, my glance happened to fall upon a familiar knothole in the wooden wall and I saw it not green, as usual, with the immediate forest, but filled with an unblinking black eye. I stared at this eye for an instant, and then put my forefinger into the knothole, whereupon it withdrew. I pondered upon the sex of the eye's owner, but could come to no conclusion. When I had finished my bath and had dressed and come out again, however, I found that the eye belonged to a young woman with six eggs which she wished to sell. She had heard the splashing of water in the tub and had merely wanted to know if I was at home.

I enjoyed doing my own housework, or supposed I did, but one morning before I got up I heard a loud familiar female voice from the back porch, and slipping into a kimono, I went out and found one of our faithful womenservants from Nanking. This hearty and indomitable creature had decided that it was her duty to find me, because, she said, she was sure that I needed her. She had gone to Shanghai, had inquired of friends where I was, and then with her own money she had bought a steerage ticket and found her way, not speaking a word of Japanese, to our mountain top. I have no idea how she accomplished all this, but when I saw her standing there on the back porch in her blue cotton jacket and trousers, her belongings tied up in a flowered kerchief and her round lively face all smiles, I suddenly knew that I did need her, and that I was glad to see her. We fell into each other's arms and within minutes she was managing everything as usual.

The story of this woman is too complex to tell here, and perhaps no one could understand it in detail who had not heard her tell it and explain all that had happened. Years later she became the material, in the very rough, for my novel *The Mother*. In those days, however, even I did not know her whole. The first time I saw her was when she was employed as an amah in a missionary's family. We had shared a summer cottage with that family once at Peitaiho, a seaside resort in North China, which somehow I have not mentioned, perhaps because I forget it unconsciously since it was the place where I first knew that my child could never grow. At any rate this woman, Li Sau-tse, and I shall have to write her name because of after events, decided that she wanted to work for me, because I could speak Chinese as well, she declared, as she could. I had refused to hire her, however, out of fairness to her mistress, and so the summer had ended. Besides, I needed no amah, having my own faithful one.

A few months later Li Sau-tse appeared in Nanking, determined to work for me. She had given up her job, she told me, and would not go back, and when I said that I needed only a table boy, my own having had to go home to care for his old parents, she said she would be a table boy. As table boy, then, she stayed. It became evident, in spite of her padded winter garments, as the days passed, that she was going to have a baby. Since she had long been a widow, this was astonishing and upsetting in our Chinese society. I felt compelled to mention the matter to her before much longer, whereupon she wept loudly and declared that she had been waylaid by a soldier in the kaoliang fields of the north country, and she had been forced, etc. It sounded doubtful, it looked doubtful, for she was a tall strong creature, able, I thought, to defend herself against anyone, but soldiers did sometimes do such things, as I knew, and so I accepted her story, whereupon she became immediately cheerful, and assured me that I need not trouble myself about anything, that she would attend to the child when it was born and bring it up outside the compound. I said she could keep it in the compound, and we let matters rest. A few weeks later when the house was full of important guests, some sort of an investigating group from America, she did not appear in the morning to serve breakfast. The other servants went around with pursed lips, and the amah suggested that I go myself to their quarters. I did, and upon opening the door of Li Sau-tse's little room, I stepped literally into a pool of blood. She had made an abortion for herself, but far too late, and the violent Chinese drug she had swallowed had produced a frightful hemorrhage. We got her to the hospital at once and there she stayed for weeks with blood poisoning. When she recovered, nothing could separate her from me. She declared that her life was mine, and although there were times when I wished it belonged to anyone else but me, for she was an opinionated, devoted, loud-voiced person, yet I knew her loyalty. When we had hidden in the little hut on the day of revolution, it was she who tried to save as many of our possessions as she could, risking her life, the lovable and ridiculous woman, upon such follies as kitchen cooking pots and umbrellas and pillows, and leaving to the rabble my fine old French china and the silver my ancestors had brought from Holland.

At any rate, there she was in Japan with us, as madly devoted as ever, and insisting upon doing everything, so that I was compelled to idleness, and, since she had no one to talk to except me, I had to listen to her long monologues on the Japanese, who, she declared, were much better than the Chinese.

"In China I heard nothing except how bad the Japanese are," she would say, "but here I see they are good, and much better than we Chinese are. Look, Wise Mother, when two Chinese riksha men bump together, what do they do? They curse and howl and one calls the other's mother dirty names, but when two riksha men bump together here in Japan, what happens? They stop, they bow to each other, they are not angry, each says he is wrong, and then they go their way. Is this not better than the Chinese?"

I always agreed with her as the easiest way to silence.

Yet somehow the atmosphere of the little house changed after this good soul came. She was one of those women—and there are such men too—who battle whatever they do. Thus when Li Sau-tse cleaned a room, she not only made it clean but in the process she opposed every article of furniture, she attacked it and compelled it to be clean, and the floor was nothing short of an enemy. A spider web in the beams of the ceiling demanded ferocity to exterminate it and mutterings and threats, and before she had been with me a week the local police had visited us three times. She had done nothing wrong but in her zeal to civilize my habitation she had burned the dead pine needles at the door and thus smoke had ascended and the police came to investigate a possible forest fire. Again they came because they discovered that she had no passport, and it was true that in her innocence she had not thought of it and had somehow managed to bustle her way through the authorities. The third time they came because she had sullied the stream with bits of garbage, and the farmers below us complained.

By this time my sister's baby was born and she and her family needed a place to stay, and so after a little time together in the small house, I decided upon a sight-seeing journey. It was not to be a tourist journey. In the first place I was too poor to go in luxury, and in the second place I wanted to see the Japanese as they travelled, and that was not in first-class coaches. One fine morning my children and I set out, therefore, on a pleasure trip, and such it proved to be. We took a train, any train, and all through the lovely autumn days we sat with travelling companions who were Japanese, kind and courteous and interested and interesting. When we were hungry we bought little lunch boxes at a station, cold rice and pickle and a bit of fish daintily packed in a clean wooden box with a pair of new bamboo chopsticks, and bottles of hot pasteurized milk for the children and persimmons and pears and small red apples for dessert. Sometime before darkness we got off the train, just anywhere, and found a Japanese inn, clean and welcoming, and there we stayed the night, sleeping after a hot bath as I had not slept since I was a child.

It was like a dream to wake in the night and lie there under the soft quilts upon the *tatami* mats, and gaze into the dim moonlight of the garden. There was always a garden and we always drew back the paper-paned sliding doors, so that the soft damp air of outside filled the little room where we slept. To gaze awhile at the misty branches of the trees and the vague outlines of the rocks, to hear the tinkle of a small water-fall and then fall asleep again was pure peace. And in the morning we waked at the minute sounds of the maid, bringing in the breakfast trays of rice congee and fish and pickled radishes. In all the weeks of our journey we had not a single misadventure or one unkindness. I remember the wonderful controlled beauty of Japan, not only in such places as the island of Miyajima, where the beauty was sophisticated and planned, but I remember especially the everyday beauty of the little inns and villages, and above all, I remember the kindness of the people. Their self-discipline was exquisite and it broke only when a man was drunk. Then to my surprise, instead of growing mellow and humorous as the Chinese do when drunk, the Japanese turned wild and ferocious. I learned not to go abroad on Saturday nights, even on the country roads, when the farmers, usually so well-mannered, were coming home from market singing and roistering after they had spent part of their profits on hard Japanese liquor.

Green Hills Farm

In these days while I have been writing of the months I once spent in the mountains above Nagasaki, there has been a little figure wearing kimonos of dove grey or soft plum color with wide embroidered obis of dull blue or gold stealing about the rooms of our old Pennsylvania farmhouse. She is from Japan, a gentle friend, visiting our country again after twenty-seven years away. Long ago she came here as an honor student from a Tokyo university, who had won an award to a scholarship to Wellesley, but after her American college years were over she went home again to Japan, married and lived the life of a Japanese wife and mother, struggling against poverty all the while, and trying to keep alive the life of mind and heart stimulated and broadened by her years in America. She went through the war years, lost her home in the bombings of Tokyo, survived with her family nevertheless, and was one of the keenest observers of the Occupation. Its faults she saw, but she feels, she has told us, her voice so mild, her English precise and beautiful, that the Americans brought to her country something glorious and unforgettable, a warmth and an outgoing which the repressed Japanese needed.

We have listened to her in long evenings by the fire, trying to see the postwar Japan she portrays, and seeing it at least in her own slender and exquisite person and in her sad and lovely face, whereupon are carved the lines of a terrifying and tragic patience, which is also of Japan.

It is quite by chance that my Japanese friend's visit has coincided with the moment when I had reached Japan in this book, a fortunate chance, for in this woman I see both the old and the new of Japan, the narrow isle, the broader way. She sees no great hope now for her country, situated midway between East and West and coveted by both. How, she asks without expecting an answer, can Japan survive? She belongs with Asia, with the peoples of India and China and Indonesia and the Philip-

224

pines, and from them she was cut off by her own militarists, and now again by the new alliance to the United States, which the Japanese fear and yet dare not reject.

I ventured the remark one evening, "How tragic that your militarists insisted upon a war of conquest in Asia! Actually, your country had a position in China, at least, which was far above that of any country. Wherever I went in those days, into whatever little interior city and town of China, I saw Japanese goods, exports from less than a penny in value to more than a thousand dollars. The Chinese had vast quantities of raw material they wanted to sell to Japan and Japan needed raw material desperately. Indeed, the whole of Asia wanted to sell Japan raw material, and the Japanese had a strategic opportunity, because they could manufacture so cheaply and so well."

"We know now," the little figure from Japan sighed. "But at the time we were completely deceived by our militarists. And we are so frightened lest we are being deceived again. The people have no way to know the truth and we have no one we can trust."

It is the predicament of all peoples that we have no way to know the truth and no one whom we can wholly trust. Even in those years so long ago I could feel the doubt of the Japanese people as I travelled through their country. The shape of the future was already clearly drawn. The army was being increased, families were having to give up their sons, Japanese were encouraged to move to China and above all to Manchuria. Industrialists were making plans with the militarists in the old dangerous combination, and everywhere I felt the reluctance of the people, who had no way of finding the truth because they had no way of reaching the other peoples.

Yet I could not stay in Japan to follow that fate. We began to hope that white people could safely return again to China, for the Nationalists, under the new leadership of General Chiang Kai-shek, were setting up a government in Nanking, my home city, and it was only a matter of months, we were told, until order would be restored enough for our return. For, as all now know, Chiang Kai-shek separated himself from the Communists in 1927. While we were hiding in Mrs. Lu's hut, he was already in Shanghai negotiating with Chinese and Western bankers and other influential men. He had disliked the increasing arrogance of the Russian Communists, and was determined to drive them out of China, and put an end to Chinese Communism. To this end he declared himself friendly to the West, and invited foreigners to return to Nanking, which was to be the capital.

It was good news, and yet I felt sad to leave Japan, where I had found shelter and peace and friendliness. I should like to set up a monument here to the people of Japan, a modest monument, for I have not the means of making anything more. I should like to say that living among them as I did, without pretensions and in real poverty, I found them finer than any people I have ever known, in their own particular way. Other peoples have been more articulate, more demonstrative, more aggressively kind, but the Japanese were so delicate in their understanding of sorrow, so restrained and yet so profound in their sympathy, so exactly right in the measure of their comfort, which never demanded and never expressed itself, but simply was there. They did not fear long silences when one could not speak. Silences were not hastily filled with needless talk. Mere presence was enough. This same quality of silence has been a part of our evenings here at the farm with our Japanese friend. She can sit quite at ease without speaking, not because she has nothing to say, but because she waits to discover what one of us might wish to say. She responds upon our own level, her remarks gentle and penetrating. Often she presents some new and even original idea but in the same quiet voice. This can be a very soothing atmosphere.

And I am forever grateful for the beauty of Japan, for the wooded mountains, rising so sharply above the most beautiful coastline in the world. I remember warmly the twisted pines and the rocks and the incoming curling tides. The people built their houses as a part of the landscape, the roof lines conforming to the planes of rock and coast and mountain, and within the houses I found the same treasurable discipline of beauty and restraint. I know no other country where beauty is so restrained that poured into one clear mold it emerges in the form of an ecstasy. And I admire above all the fortitude of the Japanese upon their dangerous islands. For they never know when fierce earthquakes will destroy their homes or typhoons attack them or tidal waves sweep over their coastal villages. They live literally in the presence of death and this they know and yet they are calm.

Never did I conceive it possible that the Japanese people could be an enemy to me nor I to them. War was an agony to be endured while one remembered that the ones who made war, who committed crimes and atrocities, were not the Japanese people, but those who deceived them. I remember the day after Pearl Harbor was bombed that I sat in my office in New York, and Yasuo Kuniyoshi, the great Japanese artist, was announced. He came in and I rose at once to receive him.

"Sit down, please," I said.

He sat down in a chair opposite me, speechless, the tears running down his cheeks. He did not wipe them away, he did not move, he simply sat there gazing at me, the tears running down his cheeks and splashing on his coat.

"Our two countries—" he whispered at last, and could not go on.

"I know," I said. "But let us remember that our two peoples are not enemies, no matter what happens."

There was nothing more said. He wiped his eyes after a few minutes, we clasped hands and he went away. We were continuing friends, understanding each other, whatever the day's news was.

One other such person I knew, months later, perhaps even years later, for I have never been able to measure time, and this person was an American woman, quite average at that. It was in Los Angeles, where I had gone to make some speeches for war relief. The Japanese-Americans had already been sent to the detention camps, and some sort of argument was going on about the confiscation of their property. Suddenly one day I received a hurry call from the American Civil Liberties Union to go and testify on behalf of the Japanese-Americans before a State senatorial committee then meeting in Los Angeles. Without delay I put on my hat and went to the hall. There I was called almost immediately, and I argued that it would be gross injustice to confiscate the property of persons whose guilt had not even been proved. And when, I asked, had it become legal in the United States to confiscate property? I came from Pennsylvania where there were many German-Americans. Indeed, the center of the secret Nazi Bund had only recently been discovered in a town less than five miles away from our home, and a neighbor's barn was burnt because she had said something publicly against Hitler. While it was burning she received a telephone call, and an unknown voice had said, "This'll learn you to talk about the *Führer!*" Yet there had been no talk about confiscating the property of German-Americans, and no thought of doing so. To discriminate thus even between enemies was not just, I said.

When my testimony was finished a middle-aged plain-looking woman asked to testify also on behalf of the Japanese-Americans. She was allowed to do so, and she said very simply that she did not think it was fitting for Americans to take peoples' houses and land just because they were Japanese in ancestry. She said that some of her neighbors had told her she ought not to speak for the Japanese because her son was at that moment fighting them in the Pacific.

"But," she said, her face honest and good, and her eyes clear, "I tell them that my Sam ain't fightin' the same Japanese. I know Mr. and Mrs. Omura and they've always been kind good people and nice neighbors, and I don't think we ought to take their property. They'll need it when they come back. Anyway, it's theirs."

A scattered hand clapping followed her testimony, and two or three others got up and dared to endorse what she had said. I don't know that any of us had influence enough to impress the row of hard old faces behind the table, but at any rate the Japanese-Americans were not robbed, and later their sons proved their loyalty by fighting and dying for America in alien Italy, while in the concentration camps their families lived with dignity and grace, creating gardens in the desert and works of art out of sagebrush, roots and stones.

I did once make another little monument of a sort, too, to the Japanese people. It was carved from a day spent in Kobe, a day which threatened to be lonely and sad because I was then lonely and sad, and which instead was an experience which I have placed among the most treasured of my life. I put it into a small book for children, entitled *One Bright Day,* which was exactly what it was.

Ah well, I needed a memory crammed with tenderness and beauty when I went back to China that next winter. We were still not allowed to return to Nanking, after all, and so we had to find quarters somehow in Shanghai, a city more repulsive than ever that year, filled as it was with refugees of every sort, and it was the more repulsive because of the war lords and the rich people and their families living in magnificence in the French and British concessions. They rolled along the streets in huge cars chauffeured by sad-faced White Russians, and when they came out of cars to enter expensive English and French shops they were guarded by tall young White Russians, in uniforms. These were, as I have said, the sons of nobility and intellectuals driven from Soviet Russia, and their sisters were trying to earn their living as hostesses in the new night clubs. Sometimes in despair, for there was no future for them, Russian girls even became the concubines of the war lords, and joined the heterogeneous households of women and children. It became fashionable for a war lord who had made his peace with the revolutionaries at a price and had retired to Shanghai to take a beautiful White Russian girl as a concubine, and soon the wealthy merchants and bankers began to do the same thing.

One of the most repulsive aspects of Shanghai life grew out of the promiscuity among the decadent Chinese intellectuals. The city had many rootless young Chinese, educated abroad, who did not want to involve themselves in anything more trying than art and literature, the artists from the Latin Quarter in Paris, the postgraduates from Cambridge and Oxford in England, the Johns Hopkins-trained surgeons who did not practice, the Columbia Ph.D.s who could not bear life in "the interior," the graduates of Harvard and Yale who kept their hands soft and spent their time in literary clubs and poetry-making, who published little decadent magazines in English and pretended that the common Chinese did not exist. In such groups there were also a few American women who had come to China for adventure, women who took Chinese lovers and about whom the Chinese lovers boasted, so that what an American might fondly think was secret was in reality everywhere known. There were always, too, American hostesses in well-to-do homes of American business tycoons, who thought they were seeing "new China" when they invited such mixed groups to their homes, but were in reality only seeing the expatriates, who knew little indeed of their own country.

There was nothing healthy or good about Shanghai life. Its Chinese city was filthy and crowded, and the foreign concessions were hiding places for criminals of all countries, behind their façades of wealth and magnificence. Upon the streets the beggars and the struggling people pushed and hurried. If I had to draw a cartoon of Shanghai at that period, I would draw a wretched riksha puller, his vehicle piled with five or six factory workers on their way home after work, being threatened by a tall English policeman, or a turbaned Sikh in the British Concession, while he made way for a car full of satin-clothed people of any nationality that one might mention, but usually Chinese. I am not one of those who think the poor are always right, for I know they are often stupid and wrong, and the rich are not wrong merely because they are rich. Yet that is what I see when I think of Shanghai.

A friend recently sent me a copy of a letter which I wrote from Shanghai to her in White Plains, New York, on December 26 of that year 1927. I include it here because of the prophecy it contains, a prophecy I wrote twenty-six years ago. I do not claim to be a prophet, at that. If I had any advantage over other white people in those days, it came from a life centered in China and the Chinese instead of in the constricted foreign circle of my own race. The few foreigners who had lived as I had certainly knew at least as much as I could know. Here is the letter:

1056 Ave. Joffre
Shanghai
Dec. 26, 1927

Dear ———
Your letters to others I happened to see last night and today being the day after Christmas and the children still absorbed in their toys, I am moved by an unaccustomed sense of leisure to write you solely in the selfish hope that you will write to me.

Your letters mirror a delightfully placid existence in your American home. I feel in some ways like a poor little girl looking into a shop window full of unattainable pleasures. Like the same little poor girl, however, I have my compensations. Living in China these days is like being the spectator at a tremendous melodrama, with the Communists as villain and the Nanking government as the fair damsel in distress. The crisis is fast approaching and the spectators, as well as the heroine, are beginning to look frantically about for the hero, who, as yet, has not appeared, and may not even yet be born! Meanwhile the villain is waxing bold and furious and no one can foretell the end. . . .

As for China itself, it is very difficult to speak of the future here. We stand by from day to day. If this were any other country one would say such a condition of chaos could not possibly continue, but in China anything can continue indefinitely so long as people gather together enough food to keep from starvation. Tremendous crops and poor transportation have combined this year to make rice in central China unusually cheap and therefore chaos is the more philosophically endured.

You will have read of the Nationalists' endeavor to get rid of the Soviet. They have returned the Russian Consul and all the Red Russians they could get hold of. Many Russians have been treated most brutally in Hankow and Canton. I hate Bolshevism, but I hate brutality, too. Everyone has been shocked by the brutality of the Chinese in this affair.

The hardest thing about living in China these days, however, is the spirit of disillusionment and despair which is everywhere growing. The best Chinese are so sad over the failure of the Nationalists, already apparent, that it is heart-breaking. The Nationalists are using the old militarist methods—heavy, illegal taxes, corruptly spent. Same old thing! Chiang Kai-shek could retire a rich man, we hear, and whether true or not, the gossip implies disillusionment.

All this is hard to bear. The leaders in the Nationalist party are returned students, for the most part. It is a shock to those who have believed that in modern education lay the salvation of China. The hopefulness in the whole thing is, however, that this despair and disillusionment may be the beginning of sober self-realization and facing the fact that the roots of China's troubles are in the moral weakness of her upper classes, and in the helplessness of the peasants. Full humility and facing of truth is the only hope I see for this country. Many are realizing it. But here in Shanghai I am appalled by the wanton extravagance and carelessness of Chinese rich people. I feel as though I were living at the capital of Louis of France before the French revolution broke. The streets are crowded with hungry, sullen, half-starved people and among them roll the sedans and limousines of the wealthy Chinese, spending fabulous sums on pleasure, food, and clothes, wholly oblivious to others. This cannot go on forever. Personally I feel that unless something happens to change it, we are in for a *real* revolution here, in comparison to which all this so far will be a mere game of ball on a summer's afternoon. Then it will be a real uprising of the ignorant and poor, against those who own anything. When it will come, no one can tell. Good crops put it off awhile. But the people are very restive and angry now. . . .

Shanghai is swarming, too, with destitute White Russians. They keep pouring down from the north, anxious for money or work or anything. They do the most menial labor, and are oftentimes the most pathetic of creatures. The night watchman at a Chinese house near us was once a professor of literature at a Russian university—a cultured gentleman. One's heart gets so surcharged with the sorrows of the world here sometimes that one breaks. . . .

As ever,
PEARL

As for my own bit of the city, it was a small third-floor apartment in a fairly comfortable house which I shared with two other American families. Of those months I spent in Shanghai there is not one incident worth telling except a pleasant day after Christmas. Somewhere during that time I wrote a story and it was sold by my agent in the United States. Yes, I had an agent by then, because it took so many months to wait for rejections. A month perhaps, to write a story and type it, a month to send it to New York where all magazine editors and publishers seemed to live, two or three months for a lagging decision to reject, another month for the rejection to reach me, made me foresee an eternity of waiting. One day when I was walking past Kelly and Walsh's bookstore, I went in and among some secondhand books I found a dingy little book called *The Writer's Guide*. It was published in London, but I searched the index and found the names of two literary agents who had offices also in New York.

I wrote to them both. One of them replied after two months that he could not consider material from me because "no one was interested in Chinese subjects." The other, David Lloyd, replied that he would like to see my material. I sent him my two stories once printed in *Asia Magazine,* with the suggestion that they might make a novel. As a matter of fact, Brentano's had already written me about the first one, asking me to enlarge it into a novel, but upon reflection I had decided that the story was too slight to enlarge and they had declined the second story as a possibility for combination. For a long time no further word came from Mr. Lloyd, and I all but forgot the stories.

But some other small story was sold, somewhere, I don't remember where. That Shanghai Christmas was the most dismal and wretched I had ever had, and added to the general sadness of my situation, I received not one gift which had any meaning. I am not one to care for gifts, nor to be ungrateful, I hope, for thoughtfulness, but that year I needed just one real gift.

The day after that dark Christmas I decided upon what, for me, amounted to a crime. I decided to spend my little store of money, and thus entirely selfish, I sallied forth on a grey December day and bought Christmas gifts for myself.

I wish that I could say that I felt afterwards a sense of shame but even now I feel nothing but satisfaction. For those few objects of beauty which my dollars could purchase had such a restorative influence upon my soul that from then on my courage was renewed. And of that winter in Shanghai I can remember nothing else, wilfully of course, for there was plenty in our crowded house.

No, wait—I do remember Li Sau-tse and her romance, which in its small way was contemporaneously connected with the romance of Chiang Kai-shek and Soong May-ling, then a young Shanghai debutante.

The redoubtable Li Sau-tse had of course accompanied us from Japan and she had established herself in the basement kitchen of our three-family house and proceeded to cook our meals. With the three amahs, she declared, she could manage, although she might in the future want a table boy, but it would be one of her own choosing. We were willing to be managed and gave no more thought to the table boy. One morning, however, we heard a violent noise in the basement where Li Sau-tse lived, a man's voice protesting loudly. A man? Our servants were all women. I sent an amah for Li Sau-tse and after a few minutes she came up breathless and red-faced while the man's voice continued to bellow from below.

"Li Sau-tse," I exclaimed, "what is going on?"

She explained. Since these were modern times, she had fallen in love with the table boy of a neighbor the winter before and there had been some amorous passages and promises. Then the man had disappeared.

"It was those Communists," she declared. "When they came and you all left, my man went crazy. Everything was upset, you understand. There were no law and custom any more. In this time another woman seized him from me, and he could not be found. So I went to Japan to serve you. But yesterday when I was at the market to buy your vegetables, I saw the woman, older than I am and uglier. He was with her and I seized him before her eyes and brought him here and locked him in my room. We are going to be married."

"Bring him here," I said. "I will talk with him and see whether he wishes to marry you. We cannot have this noise in the house."

232

She looked unwilling but she went away and returned soon with a tall good-looking young man.

"How is this?" I asked him as severely as I could.

He was quite willing to tell me how it had happened. "It is difficult for me now that we are having a revolution," he said. "Two women want me for a husband. They are both widows, it is true, but such women are shameless nowadays."

"Do you want either of them for a wife?" I asked.

"Either would do," he said quite honestly. "And I would like a wife, although to get a virgin still costs money. A widow can be had for nothing. I am willing."

"But which?" I urged.

"Li Sau-tse is as good as the other," he replied. "Yet I do not wish to be locked up."

Li Sau-tse, who was supposed to be in the kitchen, now thrust her head in the door to bawl at him, "If I do not lock you up, you good-for-nothing, you will go back to the other woman!"

The man grinned rather nicely. "Let's get married," he suggested.

This was all entirely unorthodox, but it was symbolic of the upset times, at least in coastal China. Marriages were being made independently, divorces were easy, a mere newspaper notice was enough, and the incident in my own house made me realize suddenly that the old China was really gone.

So they were married, we gave the wedding feast, and for a few days all went well. Li Sau-tse managed the table boy who was now her husband as she managed everyone, and since she had the best heart in the world, I let it go. Alas, the other woman's charms became brighter in the bridegroom's memory as he continued to live under Li Sau-tse's oppressive love, and one night he told her he wanted to leave. She locked him up immediately, and we were wakened at dawn with his shouting and thumping on the door.

Once more I summoned the strong-minded bride. "You cannot keep a grown man locked up," I protested.

She looked grim and folded her arms across her full bosom. "Do you know what he wants?" she demanded. "He wants the other woman, too —both of us!"

"Many Chinese men have more than one wife," I reminded her.

"No," she said impressively, "not since the revolution. And he is only a common man. He is not Chiang Kai-shek."

While this kitchen romance had been going on, the much more important one had been taking place in the new national government. Chiang Kai-shek had been pursuing his courtship of Soong May-ling, and although it was supposed to be private, everybody knew everything. They knew that old Mother Soong objected, as a stout Methodist Christian, to his already, reportedly, having three wives. The young lady herself, reared in America, also objected, one heard, to this old-fashioned competition. She insisted that she must be the only wife. Her elder sister had made the same demand of Sun Yat-sen. The three earlier Madame Chiangs were not only to be put away but divorced, gossip said, although Chiang Kai-shek it seemed, was reluctant to be so severe, and public opinion was with the older ladies who were blameless and loyal. Compromise was being talked of, however, not by the Soong family, but by the interested nation. It was this compromise which disgusted Li Sau-tse. A Chiang Kai-shek could have what he wanted, the old and the new, but not her common fellow. The upshot of it nevertheless, was that she released her bridegroom upon my insistence, and he fled instantly and she went about weeping for several days. Suddenly, when she had given up hope of ever seeing him again, he returned one day without explanation, and from then on was an exemplary husband.

It was a happy ending, and quite unexpected. When last I saw Li Sau-tse she was the proud mother of a child, not her own, for the terrible abortion had made motherhood impossible for her, to her great grief. In necessity she returned to the ways of old China. She chose a nice ugly concubine for her husband, and the obliging girl promptly produced a fine baby boy whom Li Sau-tse instantly appropriated for her own. She adored him and kept him beautifully dressed, exhibited him with maternal conceit and boasted of his intelligence. At the age of six months, she declared, if she whistled in a certain insinuating way he would immediately make water, and she was prepared to prove it to anybody at any time and anywhere.

As for Chiang Kai-shek, whose high romance coincided with this simple one, he was obliged to sacrifice his wives, or so we were told, and there was a great wedding, very fashionable and Christian, and Soong May-ling became the First Lady of the land. They made a handsome pair, he so straight and soldierly in his bearing, and she proud and beautiful. I said to a Chinese gentleman after the wedding, "What do the people think of this marriage?"

He looked at me astonished, "Does it matter? A man's marriages are his own business."

Ah well, it was a man's point of view!

Meanwhile, far more important than romance was what was happening now in the nation. Chiang Kai-shek was in Nanking consolidating his government. It was a time of weighing and testing to see which elements in the revolution would follow the right wing which he led. The Three Cities upriver were uncertain, then they decided for him and we were all hopeful. The Communist party was firmly expelled from the Kuomintang and was forbidden even to exist in China. All Soviet advisors were sent back to Russia. Moreover, the Nationalist army forced its way triumphantly to Peking and drove out Chang Tso-lin, the last war lord in that seat of empire, and victory was announced.

This was all very satisfactory for the white people, at least, who felt Chiang Kai-shek was the best leader on the horizon, and certainly one who would not demand too much from them. They wished to do their part, and so they gave up some of the smaller of their advantages. The Concessions at Hankow and the lesser ports were returned to the Chinese, although the really important ones were kept, as were the extra-territorial rights. This was compromise and both sides so understood it.

The Communists, however, were not so easily vanquished. Part of the Fourth Army, under the leadership of Chu Teh, mutinied against Chiang in Kiangsi, and was immediately organized into the Red army, dangerous because it provided a nucleus around which all discontented persons could gather. Still more dangerous was the fact that while most of the intellectuals, the Western-trained scholars, left the Reds and flocked about Chiang Kai-shek who promised them government jobs, the peasants had nowhere to turn. Those who had been organized for the first time by the Communists, remained for the most part with the Communists, for to peasants Chiang Kai-shek had made no promises. This division between peasant and intellectual was the first threat to the new government. Never in Chinese history has any government succeeded if there is division between peasant and intellectual.

But this I did not comprehend immediately. The American Consul had granted us permission to return to Nanking and I had to think of making a home again. Our house, I heard, had been vacated at last after having various occupants and fortunately it had not been burned. But it had been used recently as a government cholera base and it would have to be thoroughly cleaned and disinfected. My kind Chinese friends helped me again, they whose little son had been killed by the overdose through hypodermic. I have not used their surname because it might be dangerous in these strange days under the Communists if I write it down, even though now I am thousands of miles away and an ocean lies between us, and all the years besides. Let me call them Chao, because it is not their name. At any rate, they invited me and my little family to stay in their house as long as we needed to do so, while I made the other house home again.

We went back, the first American family to return, although my unconquerable old father had returned alone some months before and had been living quietly with a Chinese family in the city. How strange it was to ride again into the city gates which had been shut so finally behind us when we left, homeless and possessing nothing! I saw no visible change, the carriage was as dirty and decrepit as ever, the horse as disconsolate after the revolution as before, and the streets were as crowded and filthy. Nothing else was changed, either, not the great city wall, nor the monumental gates, the pagodas and the temples and above all the soaring crest of Purple Mountain.

I say nothing was changed and yet the carriage had not passed through the city gate before I felt a change. It was in the people. The city was crowded with new people who looked at us with curious and unfriendly stares. I saw familiar faces, too, the peanut vendor who had always stood at the corner of The Drum Tower was still there, the gatekeeper at the Li Family Gardens, an occasional riksha puller, passers on the street. But they did not smile nor did I. It was too early yet to know if old friends could be recognized.

And so we went jogging along with our few bags to the Chao house, a modest place in a valley below the university buildings, and there we found Mr. and Mrs. Chao and their recently born baby girl and their old parents waiting for us. They were in the tiny living room, and I felt that they were still uneasy and had not dared to come outside to greet us. But they were kind and as warm as ever otherwise, and Mrs. Chao led us to two small rooms set aside for us.

We stayed there a month, and I shall never forget the unfailing daily courtesy of this Chinese family. If they were inconvenienced or in danger from our presence they never let me know. If my two children were troublesome, I heard nothing of it, except that one day my amah told me that the elder child had thrown mud into the jar of soy sauce, that prized possession of every family. Mrs. Chao, being an old-fashioned housewife, made her own soy sauce and it always stood for a whole year fermenting in the yard under the eaves of the house, the jar covered with a wooden lid.

"Do not speak of it," the amah said. "She made me promise not to tell you. But I do tell you because it will be necessary to show her some special kindness in return when the opportunity comes."

The opportunity came a few days later when I happened to see in the glass-covered foreign china closet of Mrs. Chao's living room a fine large platter which had belonged to my set of Haviland china. There it was, quite obvious, and when I first noticed it, I almost cried out, "Oh, where did you find my platter?"

236

Remembering my amah's warning, however, I kept silent, and as the days passed, I found other possessions which had once been in my house, a set of teapoys, a sewing machine, a victrola and records, and so on.

"Where did she get them?" I asked my amah in the privacy of our own rooms.

"She got them honestly by buying them at the thieves' market," the amah said. "That is where the looters sold the foreigners' goods when the Communists came in."

"Isn't it strange she doesn't ask me if I want them back?" I inquired. I had thought that I understood my Chinese friends, but this was a new experience.

The amah looked surprised. "But you lost them," she reminded me. "They do not belong to you any more. And she is your friend—why should they not belong to her?"

I could not explain why this seemed wrong reasoning, and yet it did. I was more American than I thought. "I don't mind anything except my Haviland platter," I said stubbornly. "I do want that back."

"Remember the soy sauce, please," my amah advised. "If you are patient," she added, "someday you may be able to have the plate again without losing friendship."

I knew the amah was right. To lose friendship is a human disaster, and so I held my peace and pretended not to see the platter. Meanwhile every day I spent in my own house, superintending repairs, and when I was not satisfied with the work, getting down on the floor myself to scrub and sand and disinfect every crack between the boards. All the walls had to be whitewashed and every bit of woodwork and stone scrubbed with lysol. The house smelled hideously but at last it was clean and safe to live in again, and I began to gather some furniture and to hang new curtains.

Some of the household objects which our good servants had saved for us were returned from their hiding places in friends' houses, enough so that here and there were remembrances of what had been before. And speaking of this, I must speak, too, of the manuscript of *The Exile,* which I had put into a wall closet. There it had been overlooked by the mobs but discovered later by students of mine who had gone to my house to salvage my books. They saved many books and these now stand upon the shelves of the library here in my American home, their pages torn and their backs soiled, but they are precious to me. I even have ten of the old Dickens volumes which I read so often as a child. Among these books when they were returned to me I found my manuscript quite safe and indeed still in the box in which I had left it, and not a page was missing.

And it was next to the last day, I think, before we left the Chao house, when absent-mindedly I let my eyes rest on the Haviland platter. I was not thinking of it any more, but unguardedly my eyes had fallen upon it and Mrs. Chao noticed. She said in her sweet calm voice, "I bought that big platter of yours so that I might have a dish upon which to place a whole fish. But it is too flat—the sauce runs off."

"You have been so kind to us," I said, trying to seem indifferent. "Let me buy you a big fish plate in the china shops in South City."

"Do not trouble yourself," she said. "Are we not friends?"

It was true that our friendship was deeper than ever. We had enjoyed the month together, and not by the slightest sign had the Chinese family showed the least weariness, although there must have been times when our presence was a burden indeed. I doubt that any but a Chinese family could have been so unfailing in courtesy, for no other people, perhaps, are so trained in the art of human relationships.

We moved at last to our own house, leaving gifts behind us, and among the gifts was a fine big fish dish which my amah had gone to South City to buy for me. The day after we moved, Mrs. Chao's amah came up the hill with my Haviland platter.

"My mistress asks me to thank you especially for the fish dish," she said as she stood before me. "She asks me to say that since she now has the fish dish, she would like to present you with this plate."

With both hands she presented to me my plate, wrapped in red paper, and I received it with both hands as a valuable gift, and certainly as one which I had never seen before.

"You see," my amah said, later, "if relationships are conducted with honor, the reward is sure."

"Thank you for teaching me," I said.

My friendship with Mrs. Chao continued throughout the years, we discussed the most intimate details in one family crisis or another, yet never did we violate the courtesy of the platter that had been mine, then was hers, and now was mine again. It was an incident, slight in itself, and yet for me it has been unforgettable. Through my Chinese youth I had learned that the proper conduct of human relationships is the most important lesson of life. Now the learning was crystallized. I perceived a technique as well as a text. The technique is mutual consideration and deference, applied with patience and in the certain conviction that there is reason in every man and woman, a cause for all that is said and done. Such cause must be known and understood before judgment can be made and action proceed. Great lessons are learned usually in simple and everyday ways. So it was in the case of the Haviland platter and the fish dish, exchanged between my Chinese friend and me. At this distance of years I have forgotten the hardships of that return to the despoiled house in Nanking. What I remember is the lesson of friendship. That is a permanent possession.

I am an inveterate homemaker, it is at once my pleasure, my recreation, and my handicap. Were I a man, my books would have been written in leisure, protected by a wife and a secretary and various household officials. As it is, being a woman, my work has had to be done between bouts of homemaking. Thus to establish again my Nanking house and garden took solid months. I am not a perfectionist, I do not like floors that cannot be walked upon or books that cannot be left about, or untouchable tables and chairs. But a strong sense of design, and a love of ordered beauty are essentials of life not only for my family, as a duty, but for myself as a background. I cannot live anyhow. In one room, if it is all I have, I am compelled as instinctively as a bee to create order and produce a home. I cannot settle myself to writing books unless I have first made this background of life as complete as I can. The necessity is a curse and a blessing, separately and together, but so it is.

Before I could look about me, then, to see what was happening, I had to settle my house and establish the routines. My father came back to his own rooms, my children were happy in their nurseries, the kitchen was in order, the servants re-engaged, all except the incorrigible gardener who went with the Communists, and to all appearances my life was as it had been before, except that it was not and never could be again. We were living in another world, not the old world of our war lord and our ancient city. As soon as I bestirred myself to go out of my house I saw that a government was here which was like none I had known. It was the Nationalist government of China, and its head was Chiang Kai-shek, a spruce sharply straight figure whom we seldom saw. But he was already a presence in the city, a force, a personality. I heard him talked about on the streets as well as in the homes of my friends. Once, for example, there was to be a procession for a visiting prince from Europe, and vast preparations were made, even to the extent of tearing down hundreds of the mat huts in which the beggars lived along the foot of the city wall, clustered together like wasps' nests. But the old shops and slums could not be torn down and so walls of mats, thirty feet high, were built to hide the worst of the ancient buildings from the eyes of the foreign prince. Oh, how ashamed the young Chinese Western-trained men and women were, in those days, of their country and the people whom they loved so much, and how touching and pitiful was this shame! Well, on the morning of the day of the procession I went out early to escape the crowd. I needed a length of raw silk to make a curtain for the dining room. The common people were already gathering for the show, and on my way back I was caught in the crowd and had to stand until they moved. Next to me was a vendor of small bread loaves. He held his basket on his arm, and over the loaves was the usual filthy grey rag to keep the dust and flies away. As usual, too, he talked. Everybody always talked to anybody on the streets, and it was one of the delights of living in China.

"This old Chiang Kai-shek," the vendor declared, "he is winning all the battles with bandit war lords. As soon as the foreign prince is gone he will fight in the North."

"Will he win?" I inquired.

"It depends on the weather," the vendor replied judiciously. He was an ancient man, a few sparse white hairs stood out on his withered chin and his eyes were rheumy with trachoma.

"The weather?" I repeated.

"Certainly the weather," he replied. "This Chiang is a river-god, reincarnated in a human body. How do I know? He was born by a river in Fukien. Before he was born that river flooded every year. Since he was born it has not flooded once. Therefore if the sun shines he always loses in battles. If it is a rainy day, he always wins. We shall have to wait and see what Heaven decrees."

Chiang Kai-shek had already become a legend, then! There were more legends and stories every day, not only about him but about his new young wife, too. The people of Nanking, like other Chinese, were lively in humor and curiosity, and they were well aware of the problems which a Chinese military man, who had never visited the West and who was still essentially old-fashioned in his outlook, would have with a spirited and beautiful young woman who, because she had lived in America since she was nine years old, was considered a foreigner by her countrymen. She could not speak good Chinese and she did not know Chinese history. She was Western in her habits and in the way she looked and moved. Worst of all, in Chinese opinion, she was dominating and outspoken, and their sympathy was therefore with her husband. Servants from inside the Presidential Mansion described incidents exciting and amusing, and the whole city relished the situation of a strong man, old-fashioned, married to a strong woman, new-fashioned. Bets were made as to who would win on anticipated occasions. Would the lady be allowed to attend the sessions of the executives in the government? Bets were almost even and only slightly in Chiang's favor. The guards had been ordered not to admit the lady but when the final moment came and she stood face to face with them would they dare to refuse her? She would be too clever to arrive with her husband. She would come later, when he was busy, and then, unsupported, would they have the courage to tell her what he had commanded? Which did they fear the more, the male or the female tiger?

It was impossible not to be amused, and in this particular incident it would not be fair to conceal the outcome. Those who bet on Chiang Kai-shek won. After that, the bets were always in his favor. He lost once again, however, years later, when the lady wanted to visit the United States. An eyewitness, whose name cannot matter, told me that one day the great man came out of his personal rooms looking pettish.

"Such trouble," he said in effect. "Every day it is the same thing. She wants to go to America."

My friend looked sympathetic but said nothing. One does not interfere between tigers.

That morning, the great man went on, she had produced a new argument. The President of the United States, she told him, allowed Mrs. Roosevelt to go anywhere she pleased. This was because the President of the United States was a modern man. At this very moment, she said, Mrs. Roosevelt was disporting herself in England, having a wonderful time. Whereas she, surely no less low in position than Mrs. Roosevelt as the First Lady of another great republic, could not go anywhere abroad to have a good time! The great man then told her to go, but he made more than one word out of it.

My friend ended his story with relish. The great man, he said, had afterwards been astounded at the regal tour of his lady, especially when she was even invited to address the Congress of the United States, since he had supposed she meant only to make of it a pleasure trip and shopping tour. But it may be that even a queen is only a woman in the chamber she shares with the king. Who knows?

My fears for the new government came one day to a climax. We had heard much talk of the new city that was to be made from our old Southern Capital. We were proud that Nanking had been chosen as the capital of the new government, in spite of the grumbling of the foreign legations who had been so long and comfortably established in Peking, the seat of Empire. A clear break with the past was good, we felt. Moreover, the last true Chinese dynasty, the Ming, had made its capital in Nanking and outside the city there still stood the ancient stone monuments. It was true that later in their dynasty the Ming rulers had moved the capital to Peking, but this only provided a precedent for Chiang Kai-shek when he had conquered all the war lords who still lingered in various parts of the northern country, if he should after all decide upon Peking. Meanwhile Nanking, we were told, was to be made into a

modern city with wide streets and electricity and telephones and automobiles and great department stores. New public buildings would be
built, and motion picture theaters and government houses, and there
was even to be a modern sanitation system and city water. We listened
and wondered. Our city was as old-fashioned as ancient Jerusalem. Its
cobbled streets were narrow and winding and if a riksha and a sedan
chair had to pass, the people were obliged to flatten themselves against the
walls of the houses. Gutters ran on both sides of the cobbles and into
them the householders poured the waste water of kitchen and wash-
tubs. A faint reek of urine usually hung in the air, particularly in rainy
season, for while the women and girls used decent wooden buckets in
the privacy of their bedrooms the common man stepped lightheartedly
out of his front door and stood against the wall, and babies were held
over the gutters at regular intervals. And what about the shops? The
heaps of vegetables and fruits and fish and meats were piled to the
very edge of the streets and any space left was taken by the tables of
fortunetellers and secondhand booksellers' stalls. What was to happen to
all these necessary aspects of daily life? We did not know.

I heard rumors, but then one could always hear rumors in a Chinese
city lacking daily newspapers and regular reporters. I could not imagine
how a modern city could be made from our old capital. Then one day
I understood. Our tailor, he who first had come to tell us of the Communists' entry into the city, and he who, by the way, and I may as well
say it here, was later the tragic hero of my short story "The Frill,"
came to tell me that "they" were pushing down the homes of the people
with a monstrous machine. "They" by this time meant the new government.

"Please explain," I said, unbelieving.

"I cannot explain," he replied. "It is being done."

I put on my jacket and went out to see for myself. We lived not far
from the main road into the city and a few minutes' walk brought me
to the spot. There I saw the monster machine, something I had never
seen before nor heard of, and therefore which I could not name. A
man rode upon it, a young Chinese man, not a workingman but a
Western-educated man, and he was guiding it slowly along one side
of the street and then the other. What was he doing? He was pushing
down the houses. Those old one-story houses, made of hand-shaped
brick and cemented together with lime plaster, had stood well enough
for shelter through hundreds of years, but they had been built long before such a machine had been conceived in the mind of Western man,
and they could not withstand the assault. They crumbled into ruins.

Had this been in my earlier world, I would have stopped the man

242

and asked him what he did and why. But this was another world, and I did not ask. I was a foreigner, I knew it now, and I dared not ask. I stood among the Chinese people, watching, silent, stricken. And the young man said not a word, not even when an old grandmother who had lived in a house since she was born, began to cry wildly and aloud. I asked her son in a whisper if the families were paid for the loss of their homes, and he whispered back they had been promised pay, but none of them trusted promises. I never knew whether they were paid. I think it likely that some were paid and some were not, depending upon the personal honesty of those through whom the government dealt with individual owners. But no money could pay for the homes that were gone, with all their inherited traditions and memories.

I went back to my own resurrected home with a heavy heart indeed, for I knew that from that day on the new government was doomed in the end to fail. Why? Because it had failed already in understanding the people whom it purposed to govern, and when a government does not rule for the benefit of those ruled, sooner or later it always fails, and history teaches that lesson to every generation, whether or not its rulers can or will understand. And the Communists in China gained their first victory that day, even though they were then in apparent flight. True, the people did not know who the Communists were, true that the name was still only a name, but when the young Nationalists sowed these first wild seeds of the winds of resentment in the hearts of their own people, they prepared for the whirlwinds which would compel the people to turn to their enemy merely because it was the enemy of those whom they resented. It is a natural human impulse, individual as well as general, that when one hates, the hatred becomes a benefit to the enemy of the hated one. Thus before the new government was even well established, it had alienated the people.

And yet, cursed as I always am with the necessity to see two sides of a question, I felt deeply for the young Nationalists and especially for those who had been educated in the United States. They came back so eagerly to their own country, proud of their honors and their degrees, sincerely patriotic, too, but in the years while they had been away they had forgotten what their country was, enormous, illiterate, mediaeval, or as they loved to call it, "feudal." To me who had always lived there it was beautiful in spite of its ancient filth, its illiteracy, its age. Nay, it was beautiful because of its age, and the vast accumulation of its wisdom. A people so reasonable, so ready to change when they understood the need, could easily have been persuaded and led, but they were the last people on earth to be forced. Chinese were born, it seemed to me, with an accumulated wisdom, a natural sophistication, an intelligent naïveté, and unless they were transplanted too young, these qualities ripened in them. To talk even with a farmer and his family, none of whom could read or write, was often to hear a philosophy at once sane and humorous. If ever I am homesick for China, now that I am home in my own country, it is when I discover here no philosophy. Our people have opinions and creeds and prejudices and ideas but as yet no philosophy. That, perhaps, can only come to a people with thousands of years. And the sad and frightening fact was that the young and uprooted Chinese, who had been trained in Western universities or in missionary schools and other modern schools in China, had lost the Chinese philosophy. They belonged neither to East nor to West, and they were pitiful, for they were dedicated to the improvement of their own country, and yet they could not understand that it was impossible for them to save their countrymen because they themselves were lost. They still did not know how to speak to their countrymen. I cringed when I heard an earnest young Chinese, the milk of his American doctorate still wet behind his ears, haranguing a Chinese crowd on a street in our city or in a village where I chanced to be that day. He was so thin, so intense, so filled with missionary zeal as he talked about sanitation, or better farming, or the new government, or foreign imperialism, or the Unequal Treaties, or whatever cause lay upon his soul, and he did not know that with every word he spoke he was destroying his own hopes. Why? Because he spoke to the wise old people as though they were serfs, stupid and ignorant, and he was angry with them in his heart because they stood before him unmoved and they laughed when the sweat ran down his poor young cheeks. He was so angry that he could scarcely keep from weeping, and I am sure that he would have been glad if lightning had struck them dead. But Heaven never helped him, and the rain continued to fall and the sun to shine upon them as well as upon him and by such divine injustice the best of reformers are confounded.

And I, having learned my lesson of silence, could only go away feeling more sorry for the young man on the machine than for the people, because the people were strong and he was not and in the end I never doubted that the people would win. Later I put the making of the new city into a short story called "The New Road," and the touching and earnest young man and all the thousands like him went into another entitled "Shanghai Scene."

In these days, too, a strange change was taking place upon the flank of our beautiful Purple Mountain. From my distant attic window I could see what looked like a white scar daily growing larger among the pines and the bamboos. It was the tomb of Sun Yat-sen, for the new government had decided that Sun's embalmed body was to be brought from the North and laid to rest in the southern capital. The cornerstone had been laid on the first anniversary of his death. I went out to look at the mausoleum now and then during the years of its making, and watched it progress from a dislocation of rocks and earth to a monument so hybrid that people did not know whether to repudiate it as something foreign, or be proud of it because it was partly Chinese. A gatehouse, or sort of p'ailou, stood at the foot, and from there a vast flight of white marble steps led up to the mountain. I climbed those steps so many times during the next decade that I thought I could never forget how many there are, yet I have forgotten, for my feet since then have carried me to many other countries and to far places. At the top of the marble flight was the memorial hall and behind it the tomb itself. The blue-tiled roof curved upward in the old temple style and the marble terrace in front of the building was impressive, for from the balustrades one could look over many miles of countryside. To the right was the winding city wall and within it were the roofs of houses, laid closely together.

The climax of that building was on a hot summer's day—the day of Sun Yat-sen's funeral, in 1929, four years after his death. Preparations had been going on for months, and among the more difficult was the necessary, if temporary, reconciliation between Madame Sun Yat-sen, the widow, and the rest of her family, which now included Chiang Kai-shek himself, for Madame Sun was pro-Communist, as she believed her husband had been. Would she come to the funeral or would she not? She did come, and everybody was relieved. To bury The Leader without having his wife present to honor the occasion would have been unthinkable. Yet even so there were many stories among the people and rumors that though she came, she would not speak to any of the family. Nevertheless, the preparations went on.

And my two guests during those days of the pomp of Sun Yat-sen's funeral were Dr. Alfred Sze, the Chinese Ambassador in Washington and father of Mai-mai Sze, who has become well known in the United States, and Dr. Taylor, the missionary physician who had embalmed the body of Sun Yat-sen.

Dr. Sze was a tall handsome man, polished in the cultures of East and West alike, and he could scarcely conceal his dismay at the discomforts of Nanking. I had been asked to entertain him because our house was more comfortable than some, and yet we, too, had no electricity or running water or any of the modern conveniences to which Dr. Sze had become so used in his years abroad. The glimpses he gave me of my own country were extremely enlightening and entertaining, and I in turn tried to modify his discouragement about his own. But what I remember most clearly was a brisk after-dinner conversation between me and the unquenchable Li Sau-tse, still managing our household in spite of her relatively reduced position as kitchen help.

"It is a pity," she said in her loud practical voice, "that so pretty a man as this guest of ours was fed too many chicken feet when he was little."

"How do you know he was fed chicken feet?" I inquired.

She was cleaning up in the kitchen as usual, the cook, after the manner of overlords, having departed, leaving the dirty work to her.

"Don't you see how his hands tremble all the time?" she inquired.

"True," I replied. Dr. Sze's hands did tremble in a slight nervous palsy.

"That," Li Sau-tse declared, "is because he was fed too many chicken feet when he was little."

"Indeed," I observed. I knew better than to contradict her. She would cheerfully spend hours to prove that I was wrong, did I disagree, and the time was late.

As for Dr. Taylor, I remember only his anxiety lest Sun Yat-sen's embalmed body might not hold together in the June heat. There was much consternation because the people wanted to see their dead hero, and this meant that the coffin had to be open for a matter of hours. Could the sacred body endure the ravages of the air? Nevertheless, in spite of Dr. Taylor's agitation, the coffin was opened for a few hours and Sun Yat-sen did hold together except for his hands, but gloves were put on those, and so all went well.

My own memories of the funeral itself are from the modest viewpoint of a bystander, but that, after all, is perhaps the most interesting. I stood among the crowd which gathered for miles along the road upon which the *cortège* was to pass, and was pressed on one side by an odoriferous beggar and on the other by a stout and lively country housewife. I peered between clustered heads in front and was pushed by unknown persons from behind while the stately procession passed. Boy Scouts and Girl Scouts in uniform, exhausted with waiting, the sweat running down their faces, students and young people, representatives from all organizations, soldiers and bands, the endless procession went on. Finally I saw the dignitaries from other countries, the handsome and impeccably garbed British, looking cool in spite of their morning clothes and tall silk hats, the Europeans with their brightly striped ribbons and honors across their bosoms, the tall turbaned men from India, the small Japanese men in Western clothes too big for them, the businesslike Americans looking more like clerks than officials. They passed in silence and order and last of all the great casket, draped in flags and silks, passed in slow pomp, followed by the family and the Chinese honoraries.

We had stood for hours, and now we got what conveyance we could and drove outside the city wall to stand again through the funeral. The rather small mausoleum was crowded with dignitaries, and again I chose my place at the foot of the marble steps among the vast crowd. I do not remember what the program was, except that there were speeches in various languages, presentations of wreaths, singing of songs, all conveyed to us through loud-speakers, the first I had ever seen. What I do remember is that the program broke down somewhere about the middle, and we waited and waited. I wondered what had happened, and in spite of all, I fell into my old habit of identification with the Chinese and worried lest some mistake should spoil the occasion before the foreigners. As though my thoughts were premonition, over the loud-speakers came a Chinese whisper, loud and urgent and perfectly audible.

"Hurry up—hurry up—the foreigners must not laugh at us!"

Whoever was delaying matters hurried, and in a few minutes the program went on again. Meanwhile I did not look at any Chinese, pretending that I had not understood the whisper. I suppose most foreigners did not understand, since most of them spoke little or no Chinese.

When the program was over and nearly all the people had gone away, I climbed the marble steps and went into the reception room of the mausoleum. At that moment Chiang Kai-shek came out of an inner chamber. He wore the Nationalist uniform, upon his breast a row of honors and medals, and, his eyes straight ahead, he strode across the marble floor and stood in the wide doorway, looking out over the valleys. I stood near, watching his face, so strangely like that of a tiger, the high forehead sloping, the ears flaring backward, the wide mouth seeming always ready to smile and yet always cruel. But his eyes were the most arresting feature. They were large, intensely black, and utterly fearless. It was not the fearlessness of composure or of intelligence, but the fearlessness, again, of the tiger, who sees no reason to be afraid of any other beast because of its own power.

He stood a long time in the blazing afternoon light, and I stood in the shadows, very near, and did not move. What, I still wonder, was he thinking of and what does he remember now, exiled upon that island whose people to this day do not think of themselves as part of China or the Chinese?

I have no memories of peace under Chiang Kai-shek. He had severe problems to meet and he was not equipped by his education to solve them. He was a soldier and he had the mind of a soldier, and neither by nature nor experience, either, was he fitted to be a civilian ruler of a republic. I read that today the Old Tiger gets up early and says his prayers. They say he likes to walk quietly along the roads of Formosa, his wife at his side. Well, he is getting old. I hear that he reads poetry and he meditates. If so, he is following the tradition of the war lords. Old Wu Pei-fu, as arrant a war lord as ever lived, in his declining years used not only to read poetry but to try to write it, and he yearned in the wistful fashion of so many aging Chinese militarists to be remembered by posterity not as a man of battles and wars, but as a human being, wise and kind. Deep in the hearts of the Chinese people the ancient ways still hold. It cannot be otherwise, for people do not change in a day or a night from what they have been for centuries. And long ago Confucius decreed that the ways of peace are the honorable ways, that the superior man does not fight and kill, but governs himself first and then his household and at last his nation.

I remember no peace, for those were the years when Chiang Kai-shek's army was pursuing the Communists across the country and into the far Northwest. The pursuit stretched far but it began in our own city and I saw it even in my classes. More often than I care to remember there were vacant seats in the schoolroom, and when I inquired where my missing pupils were, the others made significant looks and gestures which told me that the unfortunate ones were under arrest as Communists. Sometimes I tried to save them from death, if not from jail, and sometimes I could but usually I could not. I suppose that there were Communists among them, but they were very young and perhaps they could have been brought back again. If so, they were given no chance. It was easier to kill them. But many of them were not Communists, as I very well know. They were arrested for reading liberal magazines, for associating, perhaps accidentally and without knowing it, with a classmate who was a Communist, or for criticizing the new government. Thousands of young men and women who were not Communists were thus killed all over China in the name of Communism, and we were all helpless unless we knew the name of the individual student soon enough to intercede in his behalf. I will not dwell on that sad time, for the bones of those young men and women are already dust. But I learned then that the same cruelties can be committed by any man who has the will to crush those who oppose him, or who even appear to oppose him, if power is his ambition and his satisfaction, and I learned then that the noblest end is lost if the means are not worthy of it. With every injustice thus committed, the Nationalist government was further weakened and as early as 1930, behind closed doors and in the villages, the people were singing their secret songs of revolt. They were not Communists, but they were against injustice, knowing that a government built upon

248

injustice to its people cannot stand, whether it be Communist or Nationalist, or any other.

And so in silence and with bland faces the people in our city and in the countryside watched the brave young officials, the Western-trained specialists and earnest intellectuals, the students and the ardent reformers, go the way of all flesh. Law in China was traditionally for the criminal and not for the good citizen, and certainly not for the government official, and so traditionally the new officials and intellectuals broke the very laws they made. They did not even obey the new speed laws for automobiles, for they were grown haughty and domineering and there were already whispers of widespread graft. The old evils were still with us. I had an example in my own classes, in the handsome son of a high government family. He came every day in an American car, chauffeured by a White Russian. The tall youth wore a uniform and he had a "Lieutenant" before his name, and he arrived every day after the others, his bright spurs clanking as he walked. When the end of the term came he did not appear for his examination and I failed him on the semester's work, especially as he had not handed in class assignments on time or at all. He was hotly indignant.

"Do you not know that I am a lieutenant in the Nationalist army of the Chinese Republic?" he demanded.

"As far as I am concerned, you are merely one of the students in this university who happens to be also in one of my classes," I replied.

"My father is—"

"That makes no difference to me," I said, and proceeded to give him a briefing on democracy in a modern state, while I tried not to laugh at the proud and incredulous young face.

He was one of many. And somehow the Chinese people could not forgive the new officials because they were so much like the old. They had hoped for more than a new government. They had hoped for a new world.

In the midst of these years I made a swift journey to the United States to put my invalid child into a permanent school. The decision had been hastened because I foresaw a future in China so uncertain in terms of wars and revolutions that the only safety for a helpless child was in a life shelter. It was during those few months in the United States, in 1929, that I heard my first novel, *East Wind: West Wind,* had been accepted for publication. I had sent that slender manuscript off to David Lloyd in New York a year before, and then so much had happened that I had all but forgotten it. I was visiting in a friend's house in Buffalo when a cablegram from David Lloyd reached me, forwarded from China, and telling me that the book had been taken by the John Day Company, and that I was asked to come to the company office to discuss some revisions. This news came one morning when I was feeling very desolate at the prospect of a future of separation from my child, and while it did not compensate, nevertheless it brightened life in its own way. I am told that both agency and publisher were astounded at the calmness with which I replied, and at the fact that I waited weeks before going to New York. I suppose my habitual casualness about time is the result of having lived so long in a timeless country.

In time, however, I did go to New York and there I met David Lloyd whom I had never seen, and went with him to the offices of the John Day Company, where I waited patiently upon a long Pennsylvania Dutch bench which stood in the vestibule and which, incidentally, now stands in our dining room as a keepsake. The president of the John Day Company was late in coming back to work after lunch that day. When he did come I was interested to hear that it was he who had decided to publish my little book, since his editorial staff was equally divided for and against it and he had cast the deciding vote, not, he told me quite frankly, because he thought it a very good book, since he did not, but because he believed that he saw evidences there of a writer who might continue to grow. I had already been told by David Lloyd that my manuscript had been sent to every publisher in New York and that had the John Day Company not accepted it, he would have withdrawn it. I was therefore in a properly humble frame of mind, but long ago Mr. Kung had already seen to that, and I was neither downcast nor uplifted. Almost immediately I returned to China.

The house in Nanking was empty without my little elder daughter and not all the friends and family could fill it. This, I decided, was the time to begin really to write. So one morning I put my attic room in order and faced my big Chinese desk to the mountain, and there each morning when the household was in running order for the day I sat myself down to my typewriter and began to write *The Good Earth*. My story had long been clear in my mind. Indeed, it had shaped itself firmly and swiftly from the events of my life, and its energy was the anger I felt for the sake of the peasants and the common folk of China, whom I loved and admired, and still do. For the scene of my book I chose the north country, and for the rich southern City, Nanking. My material was therefore close at hand, and the people I knew as I knew myself.

In all my books I have made such mixture. Years later, for example, I put into *Kinfolk* bits of the same northern country. Uncle Tao's tumor, which he kept so proudly in a glass bottle for everyone to see, grew first and actually in the stout body of Madame Chang. She too mustered the courage to have it cut out, and she too put it into a bottle of alcohol and kept it on the table in her main hall for everybody to see. "Are your characters real people?" A hundred times and again I am asked that question and of course they are real people, created from the dust of memory and breathed upon by love. Yet not one of them lived outside my books exactly as they do within them.

How long the days were, in the separation from my child, although I crammed them full! In the afternoon I taught my classes in the new government university, and when I came home at four o'clock there were always guests for tea, young Chinese intellectuals, old Chinese friends, young Americans and English from the Language School which had been opened in Nanking by cooperating mission boards. Still the days were too long, for there were the evenings and the weekends and the long hot summers when schools were closed, and I did not care to go to Kuling any more. In the summers I had even more time, for my father always spent the two hottest months of summer with my sister's family in the mountains, and the house was emptier than ever. It was then that I decided to begin my translation of the great Chinese novel *Shui Hu Chüan,* which later I called *All Men Are Brothers.* The Chinese title is meaningless in English, although allusive enough in Chinese, where robbers and pirates have always gathered about the watery margins of river and lakes, and the Chinese words refer to them. Four years I worked on the translation of that mighty book, spending upon it the hours when I could not write my own books and when I did not teach. It was a profound experience, for though the book was written five centuries ago, the pageant of Chinese life was still the same, and in the Communists, fleeing now into the Northwest, I saw the wild rebels and malcontents who had risen against government in the old days of Empire.

The same? No, there was now something much more dangerous. Those early bandits were not organized under a sinister new banner. They had been only Chinese rebels, angry against other Chinese who ruled them unjustly, and they had a rough sense of justice which made them help a good man and destroy a tyrant, whether he were an official or a village bully. But I knew by now that the Communists were part of a world movement, and when the Chinese malcontents and rebels allied themselves with Russian Communism it was something that we had never seen before.

Yet I was still only a bystander. No foreigner had any influence in those days among the young intellectuals except the advisors who were hired from abroad, for example, Bertrand Russell from England who came with Dora Black and put our young men and women into a furor of upset, and soon they were all talking free love, by which they meant the right to choose their own husbands and wives, until my elderly Chinese friends, their parents, were appalled.

"Is this what it means to be a republic?" Thus my old neighbor, Madame Wu, inquired of me at least twice every time we met, and I could not reply, for I did not myself know then what it meant to live in a republic.

Paul Monroe and John Dewey came to help in the organizing of the new public schools, and they did sound work in planning for a university in every province, a high school, or middle school as we called it, in every county, and a grade school in every city. It was still impossible to speak of compulsory education, for there were few teachers ready to teach in modern schools. For another generation, at least, seventy-five percent of China's children must go without schools. Now, after having seen years of public schools in my own country I sometimes question, however heretical that is, whether a compulsory school system is all that our fathers planned it to be. The task of the teacher in the United States is very hard. I see classrooms of lounging unwilling adolescents, and schoolrooms where noisy and troublesome children must be taught, whether they wish or not, the elements of learning. And most difficult of all, I see bricklayers and truck drivers and mechanics, good men but certainly ignorant, get more pay than the teachers themselves or than most brainworkers can command, and then I do not blame the American children for their confusion. Perhaps indeed it is true, as a certain young adolescent remarked to me the other day, that there is no use in going to college when one can make much more money than a college professor by stopping his education after high school and undertaking a career as a truck driver. In China the brainworker, the intellectual, always commanded the highest salaries, for there knowledge was valued, not only for its own sake, but because it is the source of wisdom in the conduct of life, and for this technical knowledge was not considered enough.

As a bystander, therefore, I watched my Chinese world change before my eyes. Government bureaus by the dozen were established, manned by clever young Chinese who could speak English or French or German better than they spoke Chinese. I remember sitting beside one such young man at a great dinner one night. He asked me what I had been doing that day by way of diversion, and I told him that I had ridden horseback out into the country to a distant village to see the ancient stone lions of the Liang dynasty. It had been a beautiful autumn day, the air golden and still. The Chinese countryside is never lovelier than in autumn, after the rice has been cut and the gleaners, in their blue cotton garments and carrying their bamboo baskets, go out over the stubbled fields to pick up the grain that has been left. Behind them in turn come the inevitable flocks of white geese to find the single grains that the gleaners leave. I had ridden happily and alone along the earthen paths that followed the ancient stone paved roads and so I had come to the Liang Lion Village, and there had dismounted. It was a gay place after the harvest; young women were playing with the children on the threshing floors, now swept clean, and old women were spinning in the doorways. I had not been there before, but I had long known of the stone lions from Western books on Chinese sculpture, and so I recognized them at the end of the village street, although they were at the moment covered with the village wash. From under ragged blue coats and trousers the noble beasts looked out with the patient gentle air of life endured for centuries. The villagers knew very well that they were Liang sculptures, and they gave me a lively and fairly accurate account of their history.

This I relayed that evening to my dinner companion. He was a spruce young man in a well-cut Western business suit. I could see that his mind was on other matters while I talked, for he drank tea, drummed his fingers on the table, coughed and moved restlessly in his chair. When I had finished he said decisively, "There are no Liang stone lions near Nanking."

I was startled at his rejection of history, and I protested mildly. "Western scholars have long admired the stone animals, and you will find photographs and data—"

"There are no Liang stone lions near Nanking," he said again more loudly than before.

Already I had learned that we had minds among us which could not be informed, and so I held my peace. Now when I think of the young men who manned the bureaus of our new government I think always of that incident, and I offer it here as example, if not proof, of the dangers of ignorance. As for the Liang lions, I am sure they still stand there as they have for hundreds of years and I am sure, too, that the village women still hang their faded garments upon their stone shoulders and haunches, and this though Mao Tse-tung reigns today in Peking, even as Chiang Kai-shek reigned in those days in Nanking.

Reigned? Well, something like it, for he was having a hard time to preside as a president of a republic. He knew nothing about modern democratic government, or perhaps any government except a military one. He was used to men who came when he said come and who went when he said go. The education of a military man is the same the world over, and our President was a military man. He had, however, a number of wilful civilians in his cabinet and they often opposed him manfully. When he could not thunder them down he began to kill them. Such a protest was aroused by this highhandedness that he paused, in some astonishment, to discover that evidently a president is not an emperor. He earnestly wanted to be modern, I do believe, in spite of not having the education for it, for certainly his year in Moscow and his other years in a military school in Japan did not educate him for democracy. It is to his credit that he modified his ruthlessness then to imprisonment, and at last even to a fairly pleasant imprisonment. There was a hot springs resort not far from Nanking, where he had made a house for himself and his wife. This house he turned over to be a place of confinement for the members of his cabinet who disagreed with him. There they went and there they stayed until they saw reason, and I remember passing sometimes when I was riding outside the city wall and asking the villagers who was now in prison. They always knew. As for younger offenders, there were either none who dared to oppose our President or he disposed of them in ways less polite.

I do not propose to blame him now for these doings. He had risen to a place of great power suddenly and without previous preparation, and it was inevitable that he behaved in the only ways that he knew, which were the traditional ways of the military conqueror who kills his enemies if they will not bargain with him, and tradition had not really been changed very much even by the Communist advisors whom Chiang Kai-shek had once obeyed and then rejected. Modern communism itself is not new, perhaps, shaped as it is by the tyrannies and cruelties of ancient Russian rulers. Chiang Kai-shek sincerely did the best he knew, but he did not know enough. I do not know whether ignorance can be called a crime. If so, then many in this world are guilty, and I see them here in my own country, too, in high places.

Meanwhile I was writing *The Good Earth*. This I did in three months, typing the manuscript twice myself in that time. When it was finished I felt very doubtful indeed of its value, but to whom could I turn for judgment? My brother was in China that year on a mission from the Milbank Memorial Fund in New York, to look into the Mass Education Movement headed by James Yen, with a view to giving a large grant to that admirable work. He had only a few days to spend with me, and during that time I mentioned shyly indeed that I had written a novel. He was kind as always, he expressed interest, but not enough for me to feel I could ask him to take his valuable time to read my manuscript and tell me if it were any good. My old father certainly could not tell me, and there was no one else. So I tied up the pages and mailed them off to New York myself, and prepared to wait while I busied myself with other work.

At this period of my life and of China's history I was keenly aware of the Chinese peasant, his wonderful strength and goodness, his amusing and often alarming shrewdness and wisdom, his cynicism and his simplicity, his direct approach to life which is the habit of a deep and natural sophistication. It seemed to me that the Chinese peasant, who comprised eighty-five percent of China's population, was so superior a human group, that it was a loss to humanity that he was also voiceless because he was illiterate. And it was this group, so charming, so virile, so genuinely civilized in spite of illiteracy and certain primitive conditions of life that might very well be merely the result of enforced mental isolation from the currents of modern thinking and discovery, whom the young moderns, rootless and ruthless, proposed to "educate." Nothing in Communist theory enrages me more than Trotsky's callous remark that the peasants are the "packhorses" of a nation. Who made them packhorses? And to what heights may not these "packhorses" rise if they are considered human beings instead of beasts of burden? For in all my years in China I never ceased to feel intolerable pain and anger when I looked into the thin intelligent face of some Chinese peasant twisted into sheer physical agony because on his back he bore a burden too much even for a beast. I have seen his slender legs quiver under the weight of a two-hundred-pound bag of rice, or under the huge wardrobe trunk of some travelling foreign tourist. Edwin Markham's poem "The Man with the Hoe," discovered late by me, gave me a wonderful catharsis of the spirit. Here was an American who could have understood the whole problem of Asia. And my continuing regret concerning Asian leaders is that so few of them have understood the quality of their own peasants, and therefore few have valued this mighty and common man of the earth. And among them the Communists are the most guilty, for with all their talk, I do not see that they have valued this man, either, and their condescension to him makes my soul sick. Yesterday in New York a young Chinese woman sat in my small living room and told me breathlessly of the great and marvellous changes that the Communists are making in China. And in her words, too, I caught the old stink of condescension.

My mind could not rest after I had finished *The Good Earth* and almost immediately I began to write another novel, *The Mother,* in which I portrayed the life of a Chinese peasant woman, but more than that, I hoped, it was the life of such a woman anywhere, who has been given no fulfillment except her own experience and understanding. Everywhere in the world there are such women and by the million. I had supposed in those days that certainly they were not in my own country, but when I came here to live I found her here, too, in many a farmhouse not far from where I write these pages, and certainly in the Deep South where she is often Negro, or on the deserts of the Western states, where she must travel miles to meet another human creature, or shut away in the mountains of New England. That woman in China, however, was too remote from the book readers in my own country, and certainly from the minds of the critics and reviewers for them to understand her—a strange thing, I thought, until I remembered how alien to me are the warped and twisted people in the novels of William Faulkner. I never saw such people in China, but I take it for granted that he lives among them here since they make the stuff of his famous books. But abroad, in France, and in Italy and in other countries where the peasant woman is strong and alive, my readers knew her and my book was understood. It is one of the compensations of the writer that somewhere there is always the reader who understands. I remember an honest critic in New York said once of my book *Pavilion of Women* that he did not "get" what it was about. Why should he, how could he? But from all over the world women have written to me and comforted me for their understanding of that book. Yet it would not be fair of me if I did not record here that, when I had finished *The Mother,* I was far from pleased with it and I threw it in the wastebasket beside my desk. There it lay and it was only chance that it was not thrown away permanently. The houseboy happened to be away for a few days and the baskets were not emptied, since one servant did not presume to do the work of another lest it appear he envied him the job, and before the houseboy returned, I had retrieved my manuscript to examine it again and see whether I was wrong. Eventually it was a book, although I put it away for several years before I offered it doubtfully to my publishers.

That houseboy, by the way, had a curious habit of triumphing over fate and gods. He was a tall pallid melancholy silent fellow, a dogged pessimist at all times. One day he appeared so phenomenally pallid that his yellow countenance was actually a pale moss green and I inquired if he were ill. He was not, he said, but his wife had typhoid fever and he had to care for her and the baby and got no sleep. I was properly terrified since he handled dishes and silver and waited on the table and helped the cook. I begged him to take his wife to the hospital, but he refused, saying that nobody went to a foreign hospital unless he expected to die. I knew better than to press the matter since if the woman did die, I would be held responsible for having insisted, and so I merely said that he had better stay at home and care for his wife until she was better. He reflected upon this for a while, standing stock-still before me, his disconsolate head drooping, and at last he said that he would take her to the hospital, since there was no one to look after the child anyway in the daytime, and he could not care for both wife and child even though he stayed at home, since he had not slept for six nights. So to the hospital she went, and after apparent recovery one day she took a turn for the worse. The houseboy came to tell me that she was dying, as he had feared she would if he put her in the foreign hospital, and that he wanted to take her home now. Since the message was that she was near death, I begged him to leave her in peace, but no, his mind was made up, we were all helpless and he took her home in a riksha, unconscious, saying that he would let me know when he could come back to work. I half expected never to see him again, since it was quite probable that in his habitually debilitated condition he would have the disease himself.

In two weeks or so, to my astonishment, he returned, looking rested and fatter than I had ever seen him and certainly less melancholy. His wife, he said in triumph over me and all my kind, had recovered. As soon as he got her home he laid her on the bed and stayed in the room with her and the child for five days, feeding her broth and rice gruel and keeping her warm. "They washed her too much in the hospital," he explained. "They were washing her life away. I did not wash her at all, and she got well and now she is doing everything as usual."

I expressed my pleasure and said no more. Far too often I have seen doctors confounded and science defied by just such love and determination.

The year of 1931 was a monumental one in many ways for me. In that year my dear old father died in the eightieth year of his life. In that year the Yangtse River swelled with unusual rains and flooded our whole countryside, a sight no one living had ever seen before, and in that year the Japanese empire builders seized Manchuria, and all thinking Chinese and a few white people comprehended the full portent of this act of aggression. Mr. Lung, the old Chinese scholar who was working with me on my translation of *Shui Hu Chüan,* said to me often and anxiously, "Can it be possible that the Americans and the English do not understand what it means that Japan has taken Manchuria? There will be a Second World War."

I said that neither English or Americans could understand this.

For me, of course, the most moving event was my father's death. His story I have told elsewhere, and, therefore, I will not repeat it here. During the last two years his tall ascetic frame had grown more and more frail, his nature more completely the saint, and I feared, observing these changes, that he had not many more years to live. That summer, however, he went to my sister in Kuling as usual, and spent a happy two months with his old friends and with her little family. It was when he was preparing to come back to me again that he was suddenly seized by his old enemy, the dysentery. He weakened rapidly and in a few days was gone. I could not even get to his funeral, for the river was flooding at a frightening speed and all ships were delayed. With my father's death the last of my childhood life was gone, and I was from then on living in the new world of struggle and confusion. His steady faith that all things work together for good was removed from my house.

Once upon a platform in Sweden, I was comforted by hearing Per Hällstrom, in his citation, mention the biographies of my father and mother. Actually I did not tell my father's story until years after he died, when I wrote *Fighting Angel; Portrait of a Soul*. I wrote that book because some of my American readers were so bemused by my mother's story in *The Exile*—for by then the manuscript I had written for my children was published—that they thought I did not love my father. On the contrary, I had learned to love him with warmth and reverence when I grew old enough to understand and value him. His soul can perhaps be best expressed in two quotations I placed at the beginning of my book about him:

ANGEL—One of an order of spiritual beings, attendants and messengers of God, usually spoken of as employed by him in ordering the affairs of the universe, and particularly of mankind. They are commonly regarded as bodiless intelligences.

Century Dictionary

Who maketh his angels spirits
And his ministers a flame of fire.

The Epistle to the Hebrews

And that monstrous flood of 1931—how strange it was to see the yellow waters climbing over the walls of the Bund seven miles from the city, and then come creeping and crawling through the streets and spreading into the fertile fields outside the city wall! The road to the mountain was built high enough above the fields so that the water did not cover it, and I rode out to Purple Mountain often to gaze upon a landscape which had become a muddy sea. Our own people now were refugees, a strange experience, and we had to set ourselves to the task of local relief, a heavy one until the waters receded again. Land people became boat people, and farmers who had always got their living from the soil now housed their families on boats and lived on fish and crabs, and all this with the utmost calm and good nature, blaming no one for the disaster. True, I heard some mutterings that had Chiang Kai-shek not been a river-god in his previous life, we could scarcely have so great a flood, but by this time our President had established such a reputation that few dared to complain in public any more, and such discontent as there was took the form of street ballads and impromptu songs, which blind musicians sang to the accompaniment of their two-stringed violins, or jokes which were whispered behind hands from mouth to ear. Incidentally, everybody feared a blind man, for it was thought that the blind had divining powers to compensate for their darkened eyes, and no one dared to rebuke one blind. It must be said that a blind man sometimes made the most of such a reputation and was often indeed a very mischievous creature.

In spite of the wickedness of that flood and the enormous damage it did, I could not but enjoy its wild beauty. The colors of the sky were reflected upon it, and to sit as sometimes I did upon the crest of Purple Mountain and survey the scene was to be lifted up to strange heights indeed. To the right the huge and noble city wall was mirrored in the water. Lotus Lake where we often spent our summer evenings in a pleasure boat was merely an arm of the new sea, and when the sun set behind the distant hills, the whole sea was illumined, its muddiness forgot, transfigured into rose and gold. When I came down from the mountain I had to take a boat to where my horse waited, tied against a tree at a solitary farmhouse built high enough to live in, and the boatman was a waterman who lived even in dry times upon the canal which ran outside the city. That boat was in normal years a coal barge, and though profitable now as a ferry, it was as black and dirty as ever, and so was the boatman. He grew thirsty on the way and he dipped his pottery bowl into the water and drank the floodwater just as it was, filthy with dead animals and every vile effluvium of the countryside.

"Are you not afraid you will fall ill?" I inquired.

He was a hearty fellow and he gave a hearty laugh. "You would fall ill if you drank it," he assured me in a loud cheerful voice. "But it is safe for me. The river-gods know that I trust them for my living and they would not let me die from drinking their waters."

I said nothing, smiled, and let him think I was impressed, for I had learned long ago how vain is preachment. And who knows what an accumulation of germs had done for him? Germs war one against another within the battlefield of the human body, we are told, and the result is immunity—that is, provided the body is not killed first.

259

And speaking of Lotus Lake, it was there and in that same flood year that Charles and Anne Lindbergh arrived in their plane all the way from the United States, to help in relief. What an event that was, and how the people crowded our streets and roadsides to see the brave young couple who had come so far! As usual, I stood among the crowds to see what was to be seen, and I watched the faces of the Chinese and listened to their talk as the two Americans came walking by, Lindbergh looking very tall and his wife small and gentle and kind. Yet it is not the Chinese that I remember when I recall that scene, but a little American boy of eight or ten, who stood near me, his face white with excitement and his blue eyes blazing. Lindbergh was his hero, as anyone could see, and in all his world there were for the moment only the two, his hero and himself. At exactly the planned moment, when Lindbergh was within a foot of him the little boy shouted in a mighty voice, "Hello, Lindy!" Lindbergh looked down blankly into the boy's face and went on without speaking. He was, I suppose, absorbed in his own thoughts and observations, and doubtless the boy's voice did not reach his conscious mind, but how could a child know that? What I remember is the stricken look on the face of an American child in an alien land, whose American god had not answered him. Ah well, I suppose we are all guilty some time or other of inflicting such wounds upon the innocent!

The Lindberghs did in fact perform a great service to those of us who were devoting ourselves to flood relief. They flew their plane over the entire area and mapped out the isolated villages and thereby many lives were saved. And they all but lost their own lives at that, for when they left it was from the swollen Yangtse River and their plane nearly capsized, or so we heard. Our hearts stopped, for few are the human beings who have ever fallen into that river and survived.

My further memories of the Lindberghs, however, center about a dinner our American Consul gave them upon the evening after their arrival, where I was a guest invited to meet them. Lindbergh was restless and absorbed, his mind single upon the task he had come to perform, and most of the evening he spent poring over a map of the Yangtse river bed. But Mrs. Lindbergh was charming and sensitively aware of every current of thought and trend of talk in the room, and I sat watching her mobile face, so changeful and yet so controlled. Whenever I read one of her rare books even now I see her face as it was that night and I hear her voice, and though it was long before the great tragedy of her lost child fell upon her, yet somehow there was already tragedy in her face and bearing.

During the floodtime that year, I had a message from another American, Will Rogers. He telegraphed from Shanghai that he would like to come and see me, and if I had no idea then of his significance in the American scene, I knew enough about him to await his coming with expectation. The flood, alas, prevented his arrival and so I did not see him then, but two years later when I was in New York he and Mrs. Rogers came to have tea with me at the old Murray Hill Hotel, and they stayed a long time, and how warmly I enjoyed being alone with them, for by then I knew what he was and how much he had done for me in praising *The Good Earth,* and in words he afterwards wrote and said about me, which still make me blush when I think of them because they were all too kind. There was something honest and homespun and yet alert and shrewd in the best sense about Will Rogers so that instinctively one trusted him, not only for honesty, but common sense. And he made me laugh so much that I still thank him most of all for laughter. In those days to be able to laugh was wonderful for me, and I was learning it again, and Will Rogers had the genius of making me laugh because what he said was truly funny, and not contrived or sarcastic. Blessed be his memory!

And I remember, too, the visit of yet another American in that flood year, but it was earlier, before the flood had reached its height, and traffic was still clear between our city and the coast. That American was Lewis Gannett, and I remember thinking that it was the first time I had ever seen a live critic. He looked kind, a pleasant, very American man, and I have always been glad that he met my father, for afterwards when he reviewed *Fighting Angel* in the New York *Herald Tribune* he recalled my father and was able to write of him as "that Lincolnesque figure." And so he was.

I ought to say that in the spring of this same year of 1931, on March 2, before my father died and the floods came, *The Good Earth* was published. I remember when the first copy of it reached me and I felt shy about it, since nobody knew of its being, or knowing had forgotten it, and I went to my father's room and showed the book to him, not expecting much, to be sure, since he read no novels. He was very kind about it, he complimented me upon the appearance of the book and inquired when I had had time to write it, and then a few days later he returned it to me saying mildly that he had glanced at it but had not felt equal to reading it.

"I don't think I can undertake it," he said. So much for the book in that distant world of mine.

No, there is a little more. I remember, although I have forgotten it these many years, that my first letter from the United States about the book was from a worthy Christian, an official in a mission board, who sent me several pages of blistering rebuke because I had been so frank about human life. He used another and dirtier word, but let it go at that. And, reared as I had been in the naturalism of Chinese life, I did not know for a long time what he meant, but now I know. The worlds in which I have lived and grown have made me what must be called a controversial figure, as I have been told often enough, and this is because inescapably, by experience and nature, I see the other side of every human being. If he be good, then there is that other side, and if he be evil, there is again another side, and if the ability to comprehend the reasonableness of both seems confounding to those who are content with one dimension, to others as to me, it is an endless source of interest and amusement and opportunity for love and life. We have no enemies, we for whom the globe is home, for we hate no one, and where there is no hate, it is not possible to escape love.

The flood did not help the people to like the new government any better. They were too reasonable to blame Chiang Kai-shek for an act of Heaven, and yet, as other peoples do, they felt resentment at the general hard times, and, irritable and impatient, they muttered that something could be done and must be done to make life more bearable. Beyond the local disaster of the flood, there was also the gnawing awareness of the greed of the Japanese militarists, now firmly entrenched in Manchuria, and when next they moved into the vital province of Jehol, these aggressions taking place in the years 1931-1933, the Nationalist government still did nothing. The Chinese Foreign Office merely busied itself with complaining against the Western Powers and the old Unequal Treaties and the Concessions, and such complaints kept the people angry and restless, for they saw themselves friendless in the world. Finally Japan virtually took over North China, basing her attacks from Shanghai, where large sections of the city were burned and ruined. No one knew when or whether they planned to advance up the Yangtse.

The American Consul now advised all American families in Nanking to send their women and children away, and, mindful of the ever-rising anti-foreign feeling, I took my little younger daughter and went to Peking. I had always wanted to stay there for a time and I hoped, too, to do some research into ancient editions of *Shui Hu Chüan*, with the hope of finding old illustrations of which I had heard. Those months seem, at this distance, only an incident, one of the pleasant interludes which somehow always seemed possible for me to find in the vastness of Chinese life, and I was entirely happy for the time being, absorbed in history and sight-seeing and meeting men and women of many nations. Peking has been written about so much and described so often that it is idle to repeat here what may be found elsewhere. For me, however, the experience was recreative, focusing my mind again upon the deep roots of China's past and giving me perspective upon the rapidly changing present. It was in Peking, too, that I became convinced that sooner or later I must leave China and return permanently to my own country, for such wars and upheavals lay ahead that no white people would be allowed to remain. It was becoming obvious that Chiang Kai-shek's policy of "internal unification before external attack" was doomed to failure, for while Japan continued her aggressions with all the strength of her army, led by officers trained in Germany, Chiang Kai-shek was still fighting against the Communists, who had simply retreated strategically to the Northwest where he could not reach them. He was right of course in believing that Communism was the basic enemy to the Chinese way of life, but what he did not understand was that by ignoring the terrifying growth of Japanese domination he was alienating his own people, who did not yet gauge the dangers of Communism, especially when the Communists in this case were themselves Chinese, but who did very well perceive the danger of their own weakness and Japan's increasing strength. Chiang thus was losing even more of his people's support, and years later when he needed them very much to rally to his side against the Communists, they were already lost.

As for the Communists whom he was pursuing at all costs, they, too, behaved stupidly while under Russian advice. The Russian Communists, before they left China, had advised the Chinese Communists and especially their military leader, Chu Teh, to capture the cities where, they said, the factory workers or "true proletariat" would gather to their aid. But few Chinese cities had factories, there was no proletariat in the orthodox Communist sense, and moreover the Chinese people, still under their doughty old war lords, had no intention of being captured by Chu Teh, whom they did not know. When he attacked Changsha and Canton and then Amoy, the people helped their local armies and destroyed huge numbers of the Communists, who in the end were completely routed so that they were compelled to hide in inaccessible mountains. There in a famous meeting place, Chingkangshan, Chu Teh, the militarist, much depressed at his losses, met Mao Tse-tung, the civilian and son of a well-to-do peasant, and together they reorganized the Chinese Communist party, this time without help and advice from Soviet Russia, who indeed had by now withdrawn from the scene, dismayed by Chu's defeats after Chiang Kai-shek's repudiation. The reorganized Chinese Communist party under Mao and Chu proceeded then to entrench itself in the peasantry, for as Chu said, "The people are the sea, we are the fish, and as long as we can swim in that sea, we can survive."

All this was contradictory to orthodox Communism as defined by Soviet Russians, and it is interesting now to remember that they for a long time repudiated Mao Tse-tung wholeheartedly. The rejection, however, was only gain for the Chinese Communists who were thus thrown upon the knowledge and experience of their own people, and they determined to do all they could to win the favor of the peasants. This they did by announcing as their enemies those whom the peasants traditionally considered their enemies, namely, landlords, tax gatherers, moneylenders and middlemen. The peasants were won by such a policy and they helped the Communists in every way they could, telling them when the Nationalist soldiers were coming and generally defeating the purposes of Chiang Kai-shek, without really knowing what they did. The peasant anywhere is a direct and literal-minded human being and he helps those who help him, an axiom the young intellectuals who guided the affairs of the Nationalist government never did understand. By now I saw what everybody could see, that neither Nationalist nor Communist could win at present, since neither had the necessary support of both peasant and scholar in the ancient and invincible combination, and therefore that a long struggle lay ahead, especially as at the same time Japan was bent upon conquest while China was thus divided.

Whether Communist or Nationalist would finally win, I believed, depended upon which one first recognized the menace of Japan. Unfortunately it was the Communists who were the first to do this and who virtually compelled Chiang to fight Japan, although their own declaration of war upon Japan was ridiculous in its weakness and was obviously only propaganda. Nevertheless in forcing Chiang to realize the danger with Japan they had an immense advantage, which after the Second World War remained with them in the renewed struggle with the Nationalists, still under the leadership of Chiang Kai-shek. Against this advantage no Western influence could prevail, or could have prevailed, unless Chiang Kai-shek could have changed his habits and his policies completely. This of course was too much to ask of him. He had grown old in his ways, and no one could reach his mind any more, not only because it was fixed, but because it was his fatal weakness to surround himself with people who dared not tell him the truth. A Chinese friend told me that he had heard it said in Nanking, after the Second World War, when the inflation was at its absurd and dangerous height, that Chiang Kai-shek even then did not know the reality of the situation and when he was told cautiously by some visitor in secret about the rise of inflation he declared that he would go out and see for himself, whereupon he ordered a meal at a public restaurant. But his coterie were terrified and sent word ahead that the prices were to be the same as before the war and that the restaurant keeper would be reimbursed. The great man therefore dined complacently at prewar prices, convinced that what he had been told was false. Whether this is a true story or not, it was believed by Chinese and the effect was the same upon the people. This is not to accuse Chiang alone of wilful ignorance. It is impossible for any man in so high a place to know the truth about anything. There are always those about him whose interest it is to hide the facts since, when a regime falls, many fall with it.

The Chinese Communists now, therefore, had cleverly made full use of Chiang's internal policy, and as they had capitalized upon the peasants' hatred of landlords they next proceeded to capitalize upon the hatred of the Chinese people for the Japanese aggressors. They adopted as their new watchword, "Chinese do not fight Chinese," meaning that they were willing to be unified with the Nationalists in order to fight the common enemy and knowing, I am sure, all the while that the Nationalists would not yield to them.

It was tragic in those days to watch the decay of the new government, but it was impossible not to see it, for while the nation was torn in dissension and struggle, the people bewildered and angry at what was going on, the intellectuals and party members were still only quarreling among themselves over such paper work as a constitution and new laws and what form labor unions should take, all good concerns but irrelevant in the face of immediate and tragic danger. It was, in its way, a manner of fiddling while Rome burned, and yet our young men were not Neros, but very earnest and well-meaning ignoramuses. Meanwhile Chiang Kai-shek, also irritated and desperate, was trying to establish some sort of order, not only among his own government officials, but among rebellious war lords whom he could not actually conquer and with whom therefore he had to bargain, and they were not men of honor, for as they saw his position weakening they demanded new bargains. Dissidence had risen to such a point that the wild and wilful man, Feng Yü-hsiang, still the most spectacular among the war lords, had in 1930 withdrawn from all bargaining, and had set up a rival government in Peking, further to confound the agitated President.

While I was in Peking, then, two years later, it became clear that unless I wanted to spend my life in a turmoil which I could neither prevent nor help, I would have to change my country, and with it my world. I dreaded the change, for I deeply loved China, and her people to me were as my own. I remember how long I pondered in those days of the Peking spring. The dust storms of the northern deserts blew down over the city, and the winds were cold and dry, and yet I spent my afternoons, when my morning's work was done in the excellent National Library, in wandering about the city and renewing my knowledge of the past. It was a good place in which to make the decision of whether I should leave China, for nowhere is China greater and more manifest in beauty than in Peking. I felt the nobility of the wide streets, designed for a princely people, and the palaces and tombs remained as splendid monuments. Yet the monuments were falling into decay, and I remember my sadness one day when I visited the very palace where the Old Empress had liked best to live. It was under guard, for the new government, as we still called it, was conscious of its national treasures and the great imperial buildings of the past were all under military guard.

On this day I had lingered long in The Forbidden City, the idle soldiers staring at me curiously, and at last one of them beckoned me to follow him around the corner of a palace. Thinking that he wanted to show me something I had not yet seen, I followed. But when I reached the place where he stood, he put up his hand and pulled down a magnificent porcelain tile from the edge of a low roof, a tile of the old imperial yellow, stamped with a dragon.

"One silver dollar," he said in Chinese.

I shook my head, trying to decide whether I would accuse him or be silent and go away. I went away. What use was it to make the accusation? He did not feel the idealism which alone would have made him perform his duty. Idealism? There was the weakness. The new government never gave its people an idealism to live by, and the Chinese, like all of us, cannot live on bread alone. Mere nationalism was not enough. There had to be something to live for. There had, above all, to be a leader whom they could reverence. The judgments of people are often cruel, and perhaps no man could have been strong enough or great enough to organize China in time to save her from her troubles. Be that as it may, Chiang Kai-shek was not strong enough nor great enough and now the people knew it. Others have pointed out that the Chinese do not object to a dictator, if he is strong enough as a man to command their respect. It is true that their conception of democracy is totally different from that of the Americans, for their conception of a nation is different. The head of the Chinese government, whether emperor or president or Communist dictator, stands in the position of the father of the people. As a father he must be worthy of their honor and obedience, a brave figure, wise, inflexible and yet reasonable, strong to command and to enforce his commands, yet just and free from pettiness of temper tantrums and hostilities. If in addition to all else he has also a sense of humor, then his hold is absolute, but always by the will of the people. If he fails in these qualities, they desert him and seek another. He must also be a good provider as the father of his people, for the Chinese proverb has it, "When the price of rice is beyond the ability of the common man to pay, then Heaven decrees a change of rulers."

In short, the Chinese people do not at all mind the role of voluntary subject if their ruler is a man whose powers they respect and admire, but they will not follow a lesser man, and especially one who cannot keep order in his own party. Twenty years ago, alas, the Chinese people began to reject Chiang Kai-shek, not suddenly nor spectacularly, but none the less absolutely. The failure to recognize this fact was the primary failure of later American policy. Had we recognized it in time we might have prevented the appearance of a Communist leader who was able to seize power because he was comparatively unknown, or at least untried. The whole process was in accord with the tradition of Chinese history. A decaying dynasty fell with the inadequacy of the rulers and new rulers arose to whom the people gave allegiance until it was proved that they too were unworthy. Corruption and dissolution began when it was apparent that Chiang could not hold the people. This corruption was not the cause of the people's defection nor even of the downfall of the Nationalists, although it has often been said that it was. The truth is that any declining government falls into corruption, and the very fact is a proof of its approaching end. There was no idealism left, no hope of a better life for the people, and this despair gave China to the Communists. All other causes were lesser and concomitant.

This became plain to me that spring in Peking, when the Japanese were threatening every major port in North and Central China, and yet never had I loved China so well. I moved among my friends with renewed pleasure, visiting some I had not known before, and others whom I had always known. Thus I remember a notable luncheon party in the home of Owen Lattimore, who had just returned from a long journey into Mongolia and Manchuria and from whom I earnestly wished to hear of the effects of Japanese conquest. He and his wife and small son were living in a charming Chinese house, where that day we dined with his Mongol friends upon Mongol meats, eaten from a low table while we sat on the floor. The Mongols and our host, too, smelled stoutly of goat's meat and milk curds, and I remember finding the aroma difficult, in spite of my admiration for the tall Mongol men and my enjoyment of their rollicking hearty laughter and ready wit. Owen Lattimore spoke their language fluently but he translated as easily and I was able to share in the conversation through English, for the Mongols did not speak Chinese, either. My interest in Mongols has continued to this day, for they are a brave and handsome people, and I have come to understand something more of their nature through my friendship with the Dilowa Hutukhtu, or the Living Buddha, a man of high place in the Tibetan religion, whom Owen Lattimore saved a few years ago from being killed in his own country by the invading Communists. The Dilowa, being a man of his own mind and of invincible spirit, had refused to obey the Communists when they came, and he was thrown in prison. Only the devotion of his people compelled the Communists to free him, but on the threat that if he opposed them again they would kill him. Owen Lattimore helped him to come to the United States, and with him brought two young Mongol princes and their families, also endangered by the Communists as reactionaries. Here the three Mongols have lived safely if not always happily, for prejudice from Americans ignorant of their race has occasionally made them uncomfortable. They overlook this with characteristic grace, however, and are only grateful for hospitality.

And one of my happiest days in Peking was spent with the great Chinese actor and female impersonator, Mei Lan-fang, in his beautiful house. He talked of many matters, and he sang and played upon his lute for me, and showed me his priceless collection of musical instruments. And his cook, one of the most famous in Peking, prepared delicious Mongol sweets for us, and dainty Chinese pastries, and Mei Lan-fang ate them with conscience-smitten enjoyment, for he was already getting plump, and the willowy heroines he impersonated were essential to the ancient Chinese opera. During the war with Japan he went to Shanghai, I heard, and there he refused to act or sing and even grew a beard and moustache, in order to make it impossible for him to play the part of a beautiful woman, and so be compelled to perform for the conquerors. When the war was over he returned to Peking and his great house and he shaved off his whiskers and once more began to delight audiences in his ageless fashion. Now he heads the actors' organization under the Communists, I am told, and I wonder if he, too, like other great dramatic and literary figures, is compelled to play the Communist party line. We have no more communication now, and I dare to write this about him only because he is great enough, I believe, to hold his own under any government. And by now he must be really old, but still beautiful upon the stage, I am sure, for his beauty was of inner grace.

Ah, when I think of Peking, my heart still dissolves, for the very soul of the Chinese people was there and it is no wonder that many a foreigner went to visit and stayed to live, and, now driven forth, is forever exiled. My joy was not in the cosmopolitan life of foreigners, however, although they were kind enough to me. My joy was to wander the streets alone, to linger in the palaces and the gardens, and sometimes to ride outside the city among the bare mountains and gaze at the Summer Palace, deserted and empty. My joy was to listen to the people talk, in that purest of Chinese Mandarin, the aristocrat of languages, and to watch them as they came and went, the proudest race upon the earth.

And as I write I do remember one thing more. That spring a little dramatic group among the foreigners gave a play for the English-speaking community. It was *The Barretts of Wimpole Street*. I do not remember the other actors but only the little frail creature, whose name I have forgotten, but who played the part of Elizabeth Barrett. She was a missionary, I was told, a shy virginal woman, not young, not old, whom nobody knew. But she had great dark sad eyes and a small olive-skinned face and heavy dark hair, and a soft stealing footstep. Upon the stage she became Elizabeth herself, the beloved of a poet, and before our amazed eyes she gave a performance so passionate, so true, so utterly astounding in the perfection of its sensitive comprehension of a poetic love, that I have never forgotten it. And indeed when later I saw our own great Katharine Cornell play the same part in a revival, I felt the little missionary had surpassed even her performance. Yet when the play was over that small creature shrank away again, and when she was tried in another play was quite mediocre, I was told. Something in that play and in that one character fitted, I suppose, the emotional need of her own life at the moment. Years later I wove the incident into a short story.

I did not decide quickly or easily to leave China, and in fact the decision was not final for two years. We had a sabbatical year in 1932 and were spending it in the United States, and those months, I felt, would give me time to know what the future should be. I seem not to remember much about the departure, but I did return from Peking to the house in Nanking and it was put in order for my absence, and farewells were said to all the Chinese friends and the faithful servants. I was detached enough not to grieve as I might have done in earlier years, and besides I had the joyful expectation of seeing my elder child, from whom I had been absent for nearly three years. She, too, would have her part in my decision to stay in the United States. I do not even remember the journey across the Pacific Ocean, except that my chief concern was a brief case containing my completed translation of *Shui Hu Chüan* together with the photographed copies of hundreds of illustrations from a very ancient text in Peking. I did not then know the difficulties and the cost of illustrations in books, and I hoped to use all the pictures, making the English translation as nearly as possible like the best Chinese version. Two or three times the precious brief case was mislaid in the various changes of the journey, and every time all else was stopped until it was found again.

I had been told that upon this visit to the United States I would find another world awaiting me and different from the one I had known so casually before, but such remarks had made no special impression upon me, since I could not imagine that future. My American publisher met my train in Montreal with a car and a list of questions to be decided, and it was not long before I saw that the year I had thought of as somewhat idle and certainly very free was to be neither. But it is of no interest even to myself to recall the events which are almost standardized for the author of a best seller, as *The Good Earth* had proved to be. The dinners, the cocktail parties, the invitations to see and be seen, to lecture, to give opinions on everything, were mildly interesting in themselves, but what deeply I searched for was not to be found in such activities. I wanted first of all to know my own people, for until I did, I knew that I could not put down roots in my country, and second, I hoped to find a circle of congenial friends in my own field of the arts.

To change countries is an overwhelming and it may be a crushing experience. I have accomplished it during the years that have passed since I left China, and my respect for all immigrants and my understanding of them have grown steadily. To move from an old established society, and the Chinese were that and have remained so in spite of the upheavals of revolution and temporary governments, into an effervescent and a fluid new society, such as the American still is and must remain for many future decades or perhaps centuries, is to do more than change countries—it is to change worlds and epochs. Moreover, I did not then understand what later I found to be true, that the naturally changing quality of our American culture, compelled by scientific discovery and invention to move so rapidly from a pioneer stage to high industrialism, was violently shaken by the First World War. The effect of that war is not yet fully comprehended or assessed, either materially or psychologically, but we are not only a changing people in the normal course of our national life, we are a changed people as a result of the World Wars.

I was ill-prepared for all this. My parents had left their own country in 1880, many years before I was born, and they had never lived long enough again in the United States to understand its development. My mother used to ponder the American papers and magazines that reached us, concerned over the waves of immigrants that came into America and how they were affecting the national life. But she could tell me no more than we read. I had had no home during college and thus I had never become a part of the American scene. True, the isolation had made me understand very well how it was that Chinese students could spend four years and sometimes seven in American universities without comprehending in the least the structure of our nation or the character of our people, and I had seen the disaster of not knowing the life of a country in which one lived or was educated. Many white people, indeed most, I suppose, lived in China, too, in a remote fashion without understanding either the culture or the customs, or even the language of the Chinese. I did not want to be such a person in my own country. Yet I soon saw that it would be very easy to live as an expatriate in the United States. In so large a land it would be easy merely to choose a pleasant spot to call my home and there to spend my life in various gentle interests. I did not want to do that, I wanted to be an American in the fullest sense of the word.

While I spent my first year, then, in a round of literary and social affairs, mainly in New York, my real interest was in the many kinds of people I saw, met or came to know. I soon perceived that there was no circle of literary people, in the European or even in the Chinese sense. The brilliant young group of literary revolutionists headed by Hu Shih and others certainly had no counterpart in my own country. One of my first acquaintances was Alexander Woollcott, a man who occupied then a peculiar place in American letters, eclectic rather than creative, and critical rather than original. He invited me to come to dine with him alone, and I was advised that I had better go, since in his way he was a little king. He lived in a charming apartment and I could scarcely resist his library, where I should have liked to spend the evening alone, had I dared to risk such discourtesy. As it was, I sat listening for two or three hours to his running comments on the American literary scene, in which I gathered that he had the place of leading critic. It was amusing and therefore delightful, and when I left I felt I knew him much better than he knew me, but that was perhaps the more important knowledge for us both. One after the other I met writers and critics, and I soon discovered that far from mingling in comradeship and interchange American writers tended to draw away from each other, and to work alone at places far from any center. When they came together they seemed cautious and prudent, reserved toward the very ones with whom I had imagined they would be free. There was little frankness of talk between them, and I often pondered this and wondered why it was so. It could not be jealousy, for many of them were far too great for so small a vice. It may have been their insecurity in our fluid society where the economics of a writer's life are dependent upon a changing public taste, which nevertheless at all times holds the intellectual in mild contempt mingled with fear. It may be, too, that the writers wisely know that their sources are not in each other but in the common life of the country, and this is so varied and so rich that there is enough for all. Yet I feel something is lost when creative minds cannot meet and discuss freely and easily the thoughts and questions upon which we brood. Brains need to sharpen brains, not with wit and wisecrack so much as in serious interchange.

Among second-rate and third-rate writers there was plenty of coming and going, but since that was the age of the speak-easy it was considerably muddied with liquor ill digested. I went once, that winter, to a speak-easy as an invited guest and saw my first dead-drunk man. The Chinese drink quantities of hot wine but with their food and so I had never seen drunk men in China. In Japan I had seen wildly drunken men coming home from the city after a weekend, but they were excited and not dead, and I had seen plenty of sailors from foreign war vessels on the Yangtse River drunken in my childhood city, but they too were far from dead. I thought at first, therefore, when I saw a man suddenly stiffen and then collapse in the cellar of a speak-easy in New York, that he had died, and I exclaimed because no one seemed to care. My host, Christopher Morley, laughed vastly at this, and explained the circumstance, ordinary enough, whereupon I ceased to be amused and went no more to such places. I have never learned to view with unconcern the loss of control over one's faculties. It is to me terrifying and repulsive, and I suppose this, too, goes back to the days of Mr. Kung, who instilled in me the old Confucian ethic that a superior person does not lose self-control, either in temper or drunkenness.

And yet I knew, too, that Li P'o, the beloved Chinese poet of the eighth century and the T'ang dynasty, was a drunkard. I had often visited the temple outside Nanking that is dedicated to him, and there had heard the priests tell of his life. From the cliffs beyond the temple one could see the famous spot upon the flowing yellow waters of the Yangtse where, it was said, one night when he was boating with his friends he was drowned because he leaned too far to grasp the image of the moon, reflected upon the current.

Of this poet a courtier spoke thus to the Emperor Hsüan Tsung, then regnant, "I have in my house the greatest poet that ever existed. I have not dared to speak to Your Majesty of him, because of his one defect, impossible to correct. He drinks and sometimes to excess. But his poems are beautiful. Judge them for yourself, Sire!"

And he thrust the manuscript into the Emperor's hand.

"Fetch me this poet and at once!" was the Emperor's reply, and from then on Li P'o was under royal patronage, drunk or sober. He lived surrounded by friends for the rest of his life. Ah me, those were pleasant times!

This year of my return, 1932, was the year of the Great Depression in the United States, and yet it is significant that I did not notice it. My fireside critic, when I said this, exclaimed, "Do you not remember the men on the streets selling apples? Do you not recall the beggars?" The fact is I had always lived where beggars were an accepted group in society, providing by their very existence a means for merit for other folk who wished to perform good deeds as a requisite for a career in heaven, and so I did not notice the beggars on the streets of New York, except to marvel how few they were. Had the great rich city been in China or India, the beggars would have been many times more. And I was used all my life to seeing vendors selling small stores of fruit on the streets of any city and so I did not notice the few apple peddlers in New York that year. The first real understanding I had of the Depression was the day that Franklin Roosevelt, the new President, closed the banks in order to reorganize the nation's finances, and then indeed I saw crowds of anxious frightened people. But even banks had not been of importance in my experience, and I did not comprehend the basic nature of their existence in our economic structure.

That day, I remember, was a morning bright and clear, the air clean from the sea as sometimes it can be in New York, and I had risen in good spirits to spend the hours ahead filled with interesting engagements and pleasurable excitements. After breakfast I walked on the streets, as I love to do, and soon I came upon a great throng of people pressing about a closed building. Why, I thought, should they be gathered there, and why were they all silent and anxious? I made myself part of the crowd as I had used to do in China, and soon I learned that they were afraid because they thought their savings might be gone, the bits of money they had accumulated from hard work, for these were working people, as I could see from their clothes and their hands. Their security, I thus discovered, was not in family and in human relations but in something as cold as a bank, and a bank could shut its doors upon them and upon what belonged to them. It was deep relief when later our financial system was revised so that, hopefully, such disaster can never happen again.

And I remember, when I think of crowds, my first motion picture and the palatial theater in which I saw it, or it seemed a palace to me, for I had seen a few motion pictures in Nanking since the revolution, mainly comedies by Charlie Chaplin and Harold Lloyd and I had enjoyed them vastly, but I saw them sitting on a hard backless wooden bench in a big mat shed. Around me were crowded Chinese audiences and part of my enjoyment lay in their running comments upon what they saw, their roars of laughter at the jokes, their lively horror at the kisses, the old ladies decently holding their sleeves before their eyes, and peeping from behind while they exclaimed with delighted repulsion at the disgusting sight of mouth upon mouth. So that was the way foreigners behaved! How pleasant then, the audience implied, to be a Chinese and a superior person!

My discomfort at first in American theaters, however, was not because of what I saw but of what I smelled. I had lived so long among Chinese and had eaten their food so consistently, since I preferred it to Western food, that my flesh had become like theirs. Like them I abhorred milk and butter and I ate little meat. Therefore among my own people I smelled a rank wild odor, not quite a stink, but certainly distressing and even alien to me at the time, compound as it was of milk and butter and beef. I remembered how my Chinese friends had used to complain of the way white folk smelled, and so they did. Sometimes before the picture was ended I was quite overpowered, especially if the air were heated, and then I had to leave the theater in spite of my earnest desire to see the finish of the story. It was only after a year or so of consuming American food, though still without milk to this day, that I was able to endure an evening among my own kind, and this is because now I smell like them. There is no validity whatever to the absurd theory that races smell differently from some inherent cause. Unwashed people of all races smell unwashed, and beyond that their odor depends upon their food. I remember that Mrs. Li, my neighbor in Nanking, complained very much to me when her son came back from his four years at Harvard because he smelled like a foreigner. It took a year or so to make him smell Chinese again.

Feasting and feting and pleasure there was aplenty for me, much kindness and generous praise, but what I remember are not these. I remember first an invitation in New York to view an exhibition of paintings by Negroes. I went from curiosity and what I saw confounded me. The paintings were of unimagined horrors. I saw sad dark faces, I saw dead bodies swinging from trees, I saw charred remains of houses and tragic children. I saw narrow slum streets and slouching poverty-stricken people, I saw patient ignorant faces. And in the crowd there to welcome me I saw the sensitive intelligent faces of educated Negro men and women. Of them I demanded an explanation of the pictures and they explained them to me. What I saw was what they had lived. I heard about prejudice and segregation and denial of opportunity

274

to these citizens of the United States because they were dark. I heard about lynching.

It was a blow from which I could not recover. To me America had always been the heavenly country, the land where all was clean and kind and free. I had seen white men cruel to dark people in other places, but those white men had not been Americans, and so I had somehow from childhood supposed that no Americans were cruel to people whose only difference was that they were dark of skin. And I had known so well the horrors and dangers of race prejudice! Had I not, because I was white, suffered from it even in my childhood? It seemed to me, as I listened now to the Negro men and women who explained to me the pictures, that I remembered all that I had purposely forgotten, how as a child I had heard other children call me a foreign devil because I was fair and they were yellow-skinned, and how they had called my blue eyes "wild beast eyes," and when I sat in a Chinese theater to watch a play or in the court of a temple to enjoy wandering minstrels and actors on a summer's day, how always the rascals and rogues in the plays had blue eyes and red hair and big noses and I was vaguely wounded because it meant that the Chinese thought my kind was evil. I remembered how since the revolution I had sometimes been spat upon in the streets by Chinese who did not know me except that I was a foreigner. Above all, I remembered the day when I had all but lost my life because I was a foreigner, though I had spent my life in China and spoke Chinese better than English. And above all I remembered that in the whole world it was still the white people who were the minority, for most of the world's people are dark.

Yet what broke my heart was not that I had suffered any of these things, but that my own people could commit such offenses against others, and that these others were their fellow citizens. Americans could do this! I stood there before the ghastly paintings that day and gazed at them, and listened to their meaning, and my heart simply filled up. I had to speak or to weep, and I suppose I did both. I cannot remember what I said, but somehow or other I found myself speaking to a group of people, white as well as colored, who had gathered about me, and to them, who were strangers to me, and yet all my own people, I poured out my heart. I tried to tell them that unless we Americans fulfilled our destiny, unless we practiced the great principles of human equality upon which our nation was based, those principles which are our only true superiority, we would one day have to suffer for the sins of white men everywhere in the world, we would have to bear the punishments of Asia upon the white man. And that we might prove our difference from those white men, whom we were not, we must begin here and now to show, by our actions to our own citizens who were not white, that we and they were one, that all were Americans alike, the citizens of a great nation, the members of one body.

Something like this I said, trying to make those Americans understand not only how none in Asia would believe us if at home we degraded people merely because of skin color, but also how we betrayed ourselves and our high calling as a free people if we did not accept all human beings as our equals. When I had finished speaking, I went away at once and remained alone for several days, not wanting to see anyone or to hear a human voice until I had faced and understood the full meaning and portent of this monstrous situation in my own country, a situation which involved us in the whole danger of the white man in Asia, though it was on the other side of the globe. Thereafter I read everything I could on the subject, and I came to know many Negroes, men and women, and I made up my mind that if ever I did return to my own country to live, I would make them my first concern. I know now that this primary disillusionment hastened my decision to return to China, and so to postpone the final question of whether I ought to leave Asia.

There was a final pleasant event. It was a visit to William Lyon Phelps and his wife in New Haven. There I went at Commencement to accept an honorary degree from Yale. It was a warm June day, and when I stepped from the train it was to find myself in a crowd of well-dressed and happy parents, relieved and eager to see their sons graduated at last. Not a porter was to be found to carry my rather heavy bag, and when I approached tentatively a large Negro, he brushed me off saying that he had too much to do. I picked up the bag and was staggering off with it when Dr. Phelps himself, in his cream-white suit, came hurrying to meet me with delightful cries of joy, for he had the gift of making every guest feel welcome. The stately porter, observing this, immediately dropped the innumerable bags he was carrying and hastened across the platform to snatch my own and to glare at me with reproachful eyes.

"Whyn't you tell me you was comin' to see Mist' Billy Phelps, lady?" he demanded. "I always tends to his company first."

I went off in triumph, Dr. Phelps hauling me along by the arm, and we got in his car, the porter delaying to see us go and to lift his cap. Thence down the street we went, Dr. Phelps talking without let and his car dashing and darting about most alarmingly until he pulled up with a jerk before the handsome red brick house which was his home. Inside his wife Annabel waited for us, as cool, as sweetly sharp as usual, and I was sent up to a big square bedroom where the bed was so high that I had to step up on a stool that night when I went to bed.

One never went to bed early, however, if one could help it, in that charming house. The big living room downstairs was also the library and there I spent a fine evening looking at rare books, and saw for the first time the autographs of my favorite English authors, most of them long dead. Thus I saw the handwriting of Charles Dickens and Robert Browning and Thackeray and Lord Byron and George Eliot, and Dr. Phelps recounted to me the wickedness of book thieves and how he had lost valuable books to various persons whom he had supposed honest. And this, he went on, in spite of his keeping a large tableful of books by the door to which anyone could help himself, only they were all modern books and so not precious, sent to him free, he admitted, by publishers who wanted his praise if possible, knowing how generous he was to praise. For William Phelps, if he was too kind to be a critic, was so because he had all but missed being a writer himself. He had the writer's temperament and understood very well what it is to make a book and see it destroyed in a moment by someone who is unable himself to write so much as a bit of fiction. Writers are usually poor critics, I do not doubt, certainly of themselves, but the vice versa of that is still more true. Yet William Phelps was shrewder than he seemed, and he could gauge very well the final measure of a book, and when he did not like it he ignored it altogether.

It was a glorious evening, I enjoyed all of it, and never did a brilliant restless witty man have a more perfect wife than his Annabel, who loved him and humored him and scolded him mildly and thought him all the while the most attractive man in the world, which he knew. At the dinner table he had mumbled grace at top speed, and had told with relish the anecdote of how his Annabel had complained once that she could not understand a word of what he said at grace, and how he had retorted, "I wasn't talking to you, my dear!" He ate at top speed, his nervous energy burning up the calories he consumed, and the rest of the evening was spent again at the books and in greeting a few friends who came in and went away again, then he resumed his talk at once exactly where he had left off until it was obviously time to go to bed, what with tomorrow's events ahead. And on that tomorrow how much I valued walking beside him in the procession and again how proud I was to stand and listen to his all too generous citation on the platform of the assembly hall—proud because I knew and valued his high spirit and his warm heart and all his vast humanity, clothed in the seeming simplicity which is the final sophistication. He could have talked with anyone from any country and found relish in the conversation, for his interests were as wide as the whole world. When he died a few years later, I lost one of my best American friends.

And still another last event of that year was the dinner given me by Chinese students from Columbia University. By this time I knew that some young Chinese intellectuals were not pleased at the success of *The Good Earth*. They reproached me for writing my first successful book about the peasants of China instead of about people like themselves, and while I was in the United States that year one of them even undertook to reproach me through the *New York Times*. His letter was so interesting and expressed so well the feelings of the intellectuals that I give it here below, in part, and do myself the justice of reprinting, too, my reply.

"Chinese pictorial art long ago attained its high stage of development, and the masterpieces of the Sung, the T'ang and even as early as the Chin dynasties have been, since their introduction to the West, a source of inspiration to Western artists and art connoisseurs, but Chinese paintings, except wall decorations and lacquer work, are always executed with ink and brush on silk or paper either in black and white or in various colors, and there has never been a painting in oil in China. The ancestral portrait, which is painted when the person is alive but is completed posthumously for the worshiping by future generations, is especially a subject of detailed convention and definite technique. The person represented must be shown full face, with both ears, in ceremonial dress, with the proper official rank indicated, and seated in the position prescribed by tradition.

"Once a Chinese mandarin sat for his portrait by an artist of the Western school. After the work was done he found his official button, which was on the top of his cap, was hidden and, moreover, his face was half black and half white! He was very angry and would never accept the artist's explanation and apology, so vast was the difference between their conceptions of correct portraiture and the use of perspective.

"It arouses in me almost the same feeling when I read Pearl S. Buck's novels of Chinese character. Her portrait of China may be quite faithful from her own point of view, but she certainly paints China with a half-black and half-white face, and the official button is missing! Furthermore, she seems to enjoy more depicting certain peculiarities and even defects than presenting ordinary human figures, each in its proper proportions. She capitalizes such points, intensifies them and sometimes 'dumps' too many and too much of their kind on one person, making that person almost impossible in real life. In this respect Pearl Buck is more of a caricature cartoonist than a portrait painter.

"I must admit that I never cared much to read Western writers on Chinese subjects and still less their novels about China. After repeated inquiries about Pearl Buck's works by many of my American and Canadian friends, I picked up *The Good Earth* and glanced over it in one evening. Very often I felt uneasy at her minute descriptions of certain peculiarities and defects of some lowly bred Chinese characters. They are, though not entirely unreal, very uncommon, indeed, in the Chinese life I know.

"She is especially fond of attacking the sore spot of human nature, namely sex. Some of her skillful suggestions make this commonplace affair extraordinarily thrilling to the reader. It is true that life is centred in sex, and it is also true that analytical studies of sex life show it as plain and necessary as food and drink, but nasty suggestions are worse than hideous exposition. This is why thin stockings and short skirts display more sex appeal even than a nude model. I do not wish to uphold any conventional standard of sex morality, but I do believe that the less the sexual emotion is stirred the better it is for individual and social life. A natural, sound and free sex expression is much to be desired for our younger generations but not the pathetic and unhealthy kind that is chiefly presented in Pearl Buck's works.

"In her works she portrays her own young life in China as much under the influence of Chinese coolies and amahs, who are usually from the poorest families of the lowest class north of the Yangtse-Kiang Valley. There are, of course, among them many honest and good country folk, hard working and faithfully serving as domestic helpers. Their idea of life is inevitably strange and their common knowledge is indeed very limited. They may form the majority of the Chinese population, but they are certainly not representative of the Chinese people."

My reply to this letter, requested by the *New York Times* and published in the same issue, January 15, 1933, was as follows, again in part:

"I am always interested in any Chinese opinion on my work, however individual it may be, and I have every sympathy with a sincere point of view, whatever it is. In that same spirit of sincerity I will take up some of Professor Kiang's points.

"In the first place let me say that he is distinctly right in saying that I have painted a picture of Chinese that is not the ordinary portrait, and not like those portraits which are usually not completed until after the death of the subject. Any one who knows those portraits must realize how far from the truth of life they are; the set pose, the arranged fold, the solemn, stately countenance, the official button. I have dealt in lights and shades, I have purposely omitted the official button, I do not ask the subject if he recognizes himself—lest he prefer the portrait with the official button! I only picture him as he is to me. Nor do I apologize. . . .

"But far more interesting to me than matters relating to my books, which are, after all, matters of individual opinion, and not of great importance, is the point of view expressed in Professor Kiang's letter. It is a point of view I know all too well, and which always makes me sad. When he says 'They'—meaning the common people of China—'may form the majority of the population in China, but they certainly are not representative of the Chinese people,' I cannot but ask, if the majority in any country does not represent the country, then who can?

"But I know what Professor Kiang would have: there are others like him. They want the Chinese people represented by the little handful of her intellectuals, and they want the vast, rich, somber, joyous Chinese life represented solely by history that is long past, by paintings of the dead, by a literature that is ancient and classic. These are valuable and assuredly a part of Chinese civilization, but they form only the official buttons. For shall the people be counted as nothing, the splendid common people of China, living their tremendous lusty life against the odds of a calamitous nature, a war-torn government, a small, indifferent aristocracy of intellectuals? For truth's sake I can never agree to it.

"I know from a thousand experiences this attitude which is manifest again in this article by Professor Kiang. I have seen it manifest in cruel acts against the working man, in contempt for the honest, illiterate farmer, in a total neglect of the interests of the proletariat, so that no common people in the world have suffered more at the hands of their own civil, military and intellectual leaders than have the Chinese people. The cleavage between the common people and the intellectuals in China is portentous, a gulf that seems impassable. I have lived with the common people, and for the past fifteen years I have lived among the intellectuals, and I know whereof I speak.

"Professor Kiang himself exemplifies this attitude of misunderstanding of his people when he speaks so contemptuously of 'coolies' and 'amahs.' If he understood 'coolies' he would know that to them it is a stinging name. 'Amah,' also, is merely a term for a servant. In my childhood home our gardener was a farmer whom we all respected, and we were never allowed to call him a 'coolie,' nor are my own children allowed to use the word in our home now. Our nurse we never called 'amah' but always 'foster-mother,' and she taught us nothing but good, and we loved her devotedly and obeyed her as we did our mother. It is true she was a country woman. But if her idea of life was 'inevitably strange' and 'her common knowledge limited' I never knew it. To me she was my foster-mother. Today in my home my children so love and respect another country woman, whom they also call, not 'amah' but by the same old sweet name, for this woman is not a mere servant but our loyal friend and true foster-mother to my children. I can never feel to her as Professor Kiang does.

"The point that some of China's intellectuals cannot seem to grasp is that they ought to be proud of their common people, that the common people are China's strength and glory. The time is past now for thinking the West can be deceived into believing that China's people look like ancestral portraits. Newspapers and travelers tell all about China's bandits and famines and civil wars. There is no incident in 'Sons' which has not been paralleled within my own knowledge in the last fifteen years. The mitigating thing in the whole picture is the quality of the common people, who bear with such noble fortitude the vicissitudes of their times. . . .

"But I have said enough. I will not touch on Professor Kiang's accusation of obscenity in my books. The narrowest sects of missionaries agree with him, and I suppose this fear of normal sex life is a result of some sort of training. I do not know. Suffice it to say that I have written as I have seen and heard.

"As to whether I am doing China a service or not in my books only time can tell. I have received many letters from people who tell me they have become interested in China for the first time after reading the books, that now Chinese seem human to them, and other like comments. For myself, I have no sense of mission or of doing any service. I write because it is my nature so to do, and I can write only what I know, and I know nothing but China, having always lived there. I have had few friends of my own race, almost none intimate, and so I write about the people I do know. They are the people in China I love best to live among, the everyday people, who care nothing for official buttons."

PEARL S. BUCK

On the following day the *New York Times* commented on this exchange as follows, on its editorial page, in part:

"Professor Kiang Kang-Hu gave his own case away by his 'ancestral portrait' illustration. Though painted when the subject is alive, it is completed posthumously and must be treated with a certain technique. The person represented must be shown in a prescribed posture—'full face with both ears'—and in ceremonial dress. Certain conventions must be followed—even if they prevent a faithful likeness and violate all rules of perspective and light and shade. In the case of a mandarin the 'official button' must be visible. Professor Kiang's criticism of Mrs. Buck's pictures of Chinese life is that the conventions have not been observed by her: that China has been painted 'with a half black and half white face,' and that the official button is missing.

"Mrs. Buck admits that she has not painted the conventional portrait. She used lights and shades in presenting the Chinese individual as she saw him in her life, both among the common people and the intellectuals. As to accuracy of detail, she is able to furnish abundant evidence from the region of China in which she spent many years from childhood up. Local custom varies so widely in China that no one can lay down a sweeping statement. She verified her localized accounts by reading them to her neighboring Chinese friends. Professor Kiang's criticism is that she depended too much upon Chinese 'coolies' and 'amahs,' rather than the 'handful of intellectuals,' as she characterized those who speak so contemptuously of the common people, from whom they are separated by a portentous gulf that seems to her impassable.

"To Mrs. Buck they who form the great majority of the population of China are rightly representative of the vast, rich, somber, joyous Chinese life, the splendid common people, living their tremendous lusty life against the odds of a calamitous nature, a war-torn government, a small indifferent aristocracy of intellectuals.

"They are China's strength and glory, bearing with notable fortitude the vicissitudes of their times. One does not have to read old texts, as Professor Kiang deems necessary, in order to understand and interpret the China of today. No conventionalized painting of the life there can persuade the West that the people really look like the ancestral portraits which Professor Kiang would have us accept as truly representative of the Celestial Empire. Mrs. Buck has enabled us to witness and appreciate the patience, frugality, industry and indomitable good humor of a suffering people, whose homes the governing intellectuals would hide from the sight of the world."

To return to the dinner with the students in New York—it was a delightful occasion, but my intuitive sixth sense, developed through years of living among the Chinese, warned me that it had a deeper purpose than mere courtesy. This purpose would be revealed in the final speech, of course, and so I waited in amused anticipation. In due time the last speaker arose, a handsome earnest young Chinese whose name I have forgotten, and after much flattery and congratulation the pith of the evening was revealed. They did not want the translation of *Shui Hu Chüan,* or *All Men Are Brothers,* to be published for westerners to read. And why? Because, the young man said, there are parts of it which describe a renegade priest eating human flesh, in his desperate hunger.

"The westerners will think we Chinese are uncivilized if they read this book," the handsome young man said, flushing very red.

It was difficult to refuse their request after so fine a dinner, and I replied as politely as I could, but firmly. I begged them to consider that the book was hundreds of years old, older than Shakespeare. Had the English wished to suppress *Macbeth,* for example, because of the witches, what a loss to literature everywhere in the world! Surely the greatness of China, and so on—

What made me sad was that here gathered about the long table in New York I saw the same young Chinese men who at home were earnestly and unconsciously destroying their own country and its culture. Yet they could not understand what they were doing, for they could not believe it when told. I had already learned that people can be taught only what they are able to learn. It was a lesson I needed to remember years later in my own country. By that time Dr. Kiang had died in a Communist prison in China and Communists were the rulers there.

I returned to China that year by way of Europe, lingering in England and the exquisite Lake Country. A lovely haze hangs over the memory of that prewar England, a succession of scenes and experiences. In quiet towns and old villages the Second World War seemed as impossible as once the First World War had seemed, and the countryside was steeped in beauty.

One day leaps forward to be remembered. The Sidney Webbs had invited me to luncheon and I had accepted. They were already old and living in the country, and though they had given me meticulous driving directions, I lost my way once or twice and was a little late. At last I turned into the probable lane, and there at the far end I saw two figures who surely could never have existed except in England. Upon a wooden bench, immobile and waiting, they sat together, Sidney Webb with his hands crossed upon the gold knob of his walking stick, his beard upthrust as he gazed steadfastly down the lane, and beside him Mrs. Webb very straight and rigid in a full-skirted grey cotton frock and a white mobcap, also gazing down the lane. When they saw my car they rose, side by side, waved vigorously and then walked ahead as guides, Mrs. Webb turning now and then to shake her head to prevent me from stopping the car to descend and then waving again to indicate that I was to follow. In a few minutes we reached a neat lawn and a modest-looking house. I stopped and got out and we shook hands.

"You lost your way," Mrs. Webb said in an accusing voice.

"I did," I replied, and apologized.

"Surely the instructions were clear?" she said, still severely.

I explained my habitual stupidity in the matter of directions, which they accepted without contradiction.

Everybody was waiting, two maids, a dog and another guest, an American man, and almost at once we were seated at the table, Mrs. Webb still in the mobcap, whose ruffle hung over her face to the extent of reminding one of the Marchioness and Dick Swiveller. Of that memorable day I actually remember only these, to me amazing, incidents. In the middle of the luncheon conversation which consisted of a duet between the Webbs while the two guests listened, the American, a rather stolid and humorless young man, new to England, startled us all by mishandling the siphon bottle of soda water and accidentally releasing a volume of fizzing water full into Sidney Webb's face. He was talking at the time, and the American was so aghast at what had happened that he could not instantly remove his finger from the siphon. Streams of water dripped down Sidney Webb's cheeks, wet his beard and fell into his plate. He gave one subdued gasp and then went straight on as though nothing was happening. Mrs. Webb, too, sternly ignored the incident, her attention to her food resolutely unshaken, while one maid snatched the bottle from the American and the other seized Sidney Webb's plate. Mrs. Webb then took over the conversation with courage while Sidney Webb wiped his face surreptitiously with his napkin, his interest fixed politely upon what she was saying. The American was speechless and so continued to the end of the meal.

After it was over, Mrs. Webb announced that we would take a walk, for her husband's health. He looked unwilling although he prepared to obey, and when we went out allowed the Americans to go ahead with his wife while he muttered to me that he did hate these walks. We went on, nevertheless, Mrs. Webb at a tremendous pace and stopping every few minutes to turn and beckon us on. After an hour of this we went back to the house and I prepared to take my leave. Mrs. Webb, however, was not quite ready to let me go. Still wearing the mobcap, she shot out her forefinger at me.

"Now why," she said in her most positive voice and fixing me with a gaze piercingly clear, "why didn't you put any homosexuality into your *Good Earth*? Because it's there, you know, among the men!"

I was too startled to reply more than feebly. "I never thought of it."

"Ah, you should think," Mrs. Webb said reproachfully.

I gathered myself together. "Really, Mrs. Webb, I have no information on the subject, I'm afraid. And if you ask my opinion, I should say that there is less homosexuality among the Chinese than among any other people."

"Now, now," Mrs. Webb said, still with the forefinger outstretched, "You've just told me you have no information."

"No, but just thinking aloud, Mrs. Webb," I went on, "Chinese families marry their sons so early, you know, and besides, there is never much homosexuality in countries where there is no real militarism, where the young men are not segregated young when their sex impulses are most strong, into camps and so on."

She capitulated suddenly, her forefinger retreating. "Perhaps you are right," she said abruptly.

I left, and the American with me, and at the end of the lane we paused to look back. The endearing old couple had walked after us and were sitting on the bench again, side by side, Sidney Webb's hands crossed on his gold-headed cane, and Mrs. Webb upright, the snowy ruffle of her mobcap fluttering in the breeze.

From English countryside I went once more to London, purposely to discover its Dickensian past, which first I had discovered long ago on the wide southern veranda of our bungalow on the Chinese hill. I remember one day, while wandering about the city, that I came upon The Old Curiosity Shop, exactly as I had imagined it, and I stood gazing at it for many minutes in a dream of pleasure, obstructing the sidewalk where I stood and creating a human eddy so that pedestrians were obliged to part on one side of me and come together again on the other side, which they did with dogged English patience. In the same way Charles Lamb came alive again, too, in the dim and narrow streets of the Inner Temple.

From London I went next to Sweden, and found a country so crisply modern that in many ways it made me think of the United States, except that being a smaller country it was better organized and governed. The advantages of a small country are enormous in times of peace, and even in times of war I suppose that Switzerland, and Sweden, too, have proved the positive possibility of a neutral and prosperous existence, provided that the country is not in the way of conquest. On the other hand, the swift rise of Hitler could never have taken place except in a small, relatively homogeneous country. Nowadays, when I view with frequent unease certain events in my own nation which remind me of Germany before the Second World War, I reassure myself merely by reflecting upon our size and variety It would take more than a mastermind to shape us into totalitarianism, I still believe. But I was uneasy enough at the end of the war, although Hitler had blown himself to bits, to inquire of an intelligent German woman who had seen the rise of the Nazi drama, to explain to me exactly how the whole brutalizing process had taken place in Germany and I put what she said into a book, which I called *How It Happens*. And the last lines of that book are these:

"A long silence fell between us.

" 'Have we finished our book?' I asked at last. She lifted her head and I met her grave grey eyes. She said,

" 'I want to tell one story, about an American girl who comes from a small town. I like her very much. She is full of good will, she has become a social worker, and she wants to help. She is so open-minded—that is what I like about Americans, they are so open-minded, even if they don't understand. This girl's boy friend was in Germany and on the day when the armistice with Japan was declared, she came to see me and she said, 'Now it's all over!' She was happy and glad, as we all were, that the terrible war was over. But the very next moment she said, 'Let's forget about it as quickly as possible!'

" 'Then I said. "No, let's never forget about it! Let's remember it forever. Let's learn how it happened so that it can never happen again!' "

" 'That is what I want to say to all Americans.' "

The Second World War, the rise of Hitler, the continuing evil influence of Fascism were undreamed of in those days, however, at least by me, and Sweden was a holiday. When I left there, I took my first journey by airplane, destination Amsterdam, and discovered that I am irrevocably ill when I am in the air, proving that I am what I have always known myself to be, an earth-bound creature with no heavenly aspirations. I lingered again in Holland, for my mother's ancestors had come from Utrecht, and then I went to France, through Belgium, and in France I remember again the fields of small white crosses of the American dead, and the mausoleums upon whose walls, as I have said, are engraved the tens of thousands of names of the lost youth of our country, and I reflected even then that if our country could be drawn into a European war at such cost what would be our loss if ever we were drawn into a war with Asia? It was impossible to ignore the portent, for I was now haunted by the similarity of the condition of the Negroes in my own country and that of peoples in colonial Asia. So many of the stories I had heard as I stood that day in New York before the Negro paintings were what I had already known on the other side of the world, and I saw how the minds of the Negroes, revealed in the paintings, were obsessed with the same deep injustices and cruelties that had burned in the minds and hearts even of the Chinese revolutionists. I determined before I returned to my own country to live, if I ever did, that I would travel to India and to Indo-China and Indonesia and see for myself the full measure of the feelings of the peoples there, in order that I might have a world view of the relations between the races of man.

My European journey ended in Italy, for after a stay in Venice I took ship to China again, by way of the Red Sea. Of that journey upon a handsome Italian ship little remains to remember. I spent my time, mostly in solitude, reviewing all that I had learned during the year in my own country, and preparing myself for the year ahead. If, I told myself, I had indeed only one more year in China, how should it be spent? Surely in nothing but learning and writing. And during the long hot days on deck while the ship ploughed its way through a placid sea to the coast of India, I conceived the idea of a series of novels, each of which should reveal some fundamental aspect of Chinese life, even perhaps of Asian life, if I could accumulate that knowledge. But China I knew to the core of heart and the last convolution of my brain, and what was happening in China could and might happen in any country of Asia, unless some unforeseen wisdom in the West could prevent it by understanding in time. Thus I planned my next novel, which I decided to center upon that key figure in Chinese history, the war lord. Surely I knew him, having lived under his rule for decades. This was the beginning of my next novel, *Sons*.

I went ashore at Bombay and again in Colombo but I made no effort then to see much of India, for I knew that I would come back. I was not returning this time only to China but to all of Asia. It was an Asia as ancient as ever, as mediaeval, and yet in its strange aspects, piercingly new.

Before I reached Shanghai, while I was still aboard the ship, I received an invitation from an American lady to meet the staff of the *China Critic* at a dinner at her house. This magazine was a weekly, put out by a very modern, Western-educated little group of Chinese literary figures, among whom was Lin Yutang. I had not then met him, but I knew his writings in Chinese as well as in English in the *China Critic*. He was an essayist, a wit, a humorist, never profound, his rivals said, yet I felt a shrewd accuracy in his pungent jokes and sharp thrusts. In those days he was criticizing Chiang Kai-shek and the Nationalist government with such alarming honesty and fearlessness that his friends besought him not to "twist the tiger's tail." He was always lighthearted, however, reckless with a laughing courage that no one seemed to take too seriously, and yet all were grateful because he said much that they only dared to feel.

I accepted the invitation for dinner, mainly to meet him, and passed one of those amazing evenings, where an exotic international intelligentsia poured forth a potpourri, not always fragrant, of wit and scandalous gossip. I listened as usual and said little and accepted a dinner invitation from Lin Yutang to come to his home and meet his wife. The only other guest was to be Hu Shih.

This second evening was even more interesting, for at his house I met Mrs. Lin Yutang, a warmhearted thoroughly Chinese lady, and with her their little daughters. The dinner was delicious, and while I enjoyed it I listened again, this time to interchange between the two notable but curiously contrasting Chinese gentlemen. The lack of understanding between the two men was already plain, Hu Shih being slightly scornful of the irrepressible younger man. He left early, and then Lin Yutang told me that he himself was writing a book about China. It was to be the famous *My Country and My People*.

I left the house late, excited by the idea of a book in English by a Chinese writer and one so fearless. Its influences, I felt, could be boundless, and I wrote to the John Day Company in New York at once, recommending their immediate attention to this Chinese author, unknown as yet to the West.

The grey house in Nanking stood as I had left it, and I must say that when I walked in the front door it looked empty to me. The servants had done their best and all was neat and clean, but somehow it was no longer home. I had changed more than I knew. Well, to be fair, I must make it home again, I thought—lay down the new rugs I had bought in Shanghai and open doors to a terrace, and even, if I were extravagant, put in central heating. If I had grown too easily used to the luxuries of American life, I would have a few of them here, so that the issue of leaving China would not be confused with the fact that living in America was perhaps physically more pleasant.

I know now that it was a habit of my woman's nature to plunge deep into housekeeping and gardening whenever I had mental and spiritual problems to face and solve. For the next months, therefore, I did no more than make the house pleasant, bring back my garden to its accustomed flourishing condition in fruit and flowers, renew my friendships with my neighbors and listen to all the news of the city and the nation that was poured into my ears.

The outlook was not good. I found an ever-deepening gulf between the white people and the Chinese. Both groups of the white people, businessmen and missionaries, were alike unhappy. The new government had set up a regime which, however justifiable its rules, antagonized even their white friends while it made the unfriendly furious. Mission schools were forced to comply with the government regulations of obeisance before the portrait of Sun Yat-sen, required to hang on every chapel or assembly hall wall. The famous *Will*, now a sacred document, had to be read aloud once a week, the audience standing. To the missionaries this smelled of worship before other gods, yet they had to comply or face the possibility of closing their schools. In the Christian churches the Chinese members were pressing for self-government and control of foreign funds, although among many missionaries there was still a hidden distrust of all Chinese—or at least a sense of responsibility toward their home churches, who had collected so painfully the money sent abroad for foreign missions.

In business circles there was the same hostility, for different reasons. Foreign businessmen and their firms knew that the Western nations did not want to take over China, or to conquer her in a political sense. What they wanted was more trade, special concessions perhaps, and guarantees of safety for their personnel. None would have wanted the responsibility of governing China and so assuming the burden of her confused affairs. Indeed, since the end of the First World War no Western power had the strength for such a feat. England was groaning even under the management of India. Colonialism for any nation was nearing its end as a profitable possession. Yet the Nationalist government continued to harp upon the aggressions of the past and to ignore entirely the new and dangerous aggressions of Japan, who, it was obvious, did want to take over China and annex her as she had annexed Korea. Had the Nationalist party, or Kuomintang, understood in those days the true position of the changing West and the real danger from rising Japan, the war with Japan would certainly, I believe, have been impossible, for by siding with the West and moving against Japan, the Nationalists could have prevented the attempts for the Asian empire planned by Japanese militarists and industrial interests in combination. The Nationalist government therefore must take the primary blame for what happened later. It should have been obvious that the end of Western aggression in China, and indeed in Asia, was already in sight. Britain was yielding her concessions, the special rights were under discussion for change, and it was only a matter of setting up adequate Chinese courts for the extraterritorial rights also to be abolished.

Soviet Russia, however, had earlier confused the Chinese leaders by voluntarily relinquishing her special rights, and at the end of the First World War the fact that the Germans had been forced to yield all special rights further influenced the new Chinese. Chiang Kai-shek would have none of Soviet Russia, of course, but he did display a special friendliness toward Germany, especially as Fascism rose to power there. It was obvious that Fascism appealed to him, and roused in him the old Chinese tradition of the despot, crystallized so long ago at the time of Christ under Ch'in Shih Huang, the First Emperor, a fascist ruler in the fullest sense. It was this Emperor who even at that early time had repudiated the benevolence of Confucius, the great philosopher and intellectual, and had ordered the burning of books, in order that Confucianism could be ended forever. The new and growing Chinese army was put under the advice of German military men, and we saw preference given to German white people over the rest of us. This meant that other Western powers were alienated and so they stood aloof as they watched Japan encroach further and further upon Chinese soil. Let the Japanese solve the massive problem of China, they said to one another. Thus when the war actually broke, China had not a single Western ally and Germany was on the side of Japan! The Nationalists had guessed wrongly.

It was plain by the beginning of the year 1934 that the Nationalist government, still called the "new government," could not endure. It had never faced the basic problems of the nation, and the peasants were still suffering under the old evils of landlordism and even higher taxes than they had endured before. Thus when I wandered about the countryside beyond the walls of Nanking, as I had used to do, everywhere the farmers and their wives complained that whereas under the old regime they had only one ruler to whom to pay taxes, now there were many little rulers, all demanding taxes, and they were worse off than ever. Democracy? They did not know its meaning, they said, although young men were always spouting the word at them. People's rights? What were they? There was nowhere they could appeal for their rights. The new roads? Yes, there were new roads but only for motorcars, and who had motorcars except the officials and a few rich men? When those cars roared past, every farmer, carrying his loads to the markets on his shoulders, had to get out of the way. There was no democracy, if by that one meant rights and benefits for the people, and how could a government succeed if it did not practice what it preached? Even the young relatives of the rulers rode through the streets like lords, scattering the people before them. In the old days they would not have been allowed thus to behave.

A thousand such complaints were poured into my ears, and it was impossible not to conclude that the new rulers had indeed failed to understand the necessities of the people. They had tried to stop the revolution without discovering its causes and removing them. They had declared that the Chinese people should believe in and practice a new nationalism and all the while they were allowing the Japanese aggressions to go unchecked. An explosion from the people must be the result, unless Japan attacked China first and I believed, after much listening and observation, that Japan would attack before the people could rebel. The Chinese are long-suffering and patient, and moreover there was no one to lead them in rebellion. The intellectuals were busy in the government, in their own pursuits, and anyone among the people who showed the slightest sign of unrest was instantly disposed of as a Communist. Yes, it was time for me to leave China forever, for sooner or later all white people would have to leave. History had mounted too high, a debacle was inevitable sometime in my life years. If I could have prevented its arrival in any way, I would have stayed to do it, but no one could prevent the inevitable, and any individual would be simply a straw. And I was a woman, at that.

There were personal reasons, too, why I should return to my own country. It is not necessary to recount them, for in the huge events that were changing my world, the personal was all but negligible. My invalid child, nevertheless, had become ill after I left, and it was obvious that for her sake I should live near enough to be with her from time to time. The grey house, too, had ceased to be a home for family life, in spite of my efforts, for the distances between the man and the woman there had long ago become insuperable. There were no differences—only a difference so vast that communication was impossible, in spite of honest effort over many years. It was the deep difference which my parents had perceived long before I did, and which had made my mother try to persuade me against the marriage. I had not heeded her and although sadly soon I had known her right, I had been too proud to reveal myself wrong. Now the difference had come to include the child who could not grow and what should be done for her, and there was no bridge left to build between. It was time for me to leave China.

Yet I had decided that before I finally went I would travel in the countries of Asia as far as I could go, and gain at least a swift view of the position of the colonial peoples at this critical moment of history. I began therefore to travel, first in parts of China that I had not seen, and then further to Indo-China and Siam, to India and Indonesia. I planned, in fact, a journey of exploration into empire, to see how the peoples did under colonialism and to discover, if I could, how the future lay, in timing, if not in event. When, for example, and how, would India get her freedom?

For me the journey could only be a business of looking and listening. I wanted to see no officials, even if I could have met them, and I wanted as little as possible to do with white people. Their point of view I knew already. I wanted to move about a country in my own half-lazy fashion, stopping where I liked, enjoying everything and learning as much as possible. It would be idle now to detail such a journey for many others have travelled in those countries and it has become quite a matter of course even for American officials to take the Grand Asian Tour.

What do I remember, then? I remember first the beautiful province of Fukien, in South China. It is a seacoast province, its undulating shores infested with pirates, their nests centuries old. The little steamer that carried me had a strong iron fence and a barred gate on the stairway between the upper decks where the white folk travelled and the lower decks where the rest of the world ate and slept. Fence and gate, the English captain told me, were made so that if pirates were hidden among the lower deck passengers, the white people could defend themselves from above. What, I asked, if the pirates set fire below?

The Captain shrugged. "We have the lifeboats."

I was glad to get ashore from that vessel and settle myself for a few days in a pleasant but certainly not immaculate Chinese inn. And from there, with Chinese friends, I travelled slowly by bus into the back country through the handsomest citrus groves in the world, the trees rich with oranges and pumeloes which the kindly farmers plucked for us as we passed. We went as far as the inner mountains, and there the bus stopped, for the mountains belonged to the Communists hiding there, or if one preferred, the "bandits." The bus driver was a daring, not to say a wild man, in spite of his calm face and miraculous sense of humor. The bus was an old American castoff, and every hour or two it broke down and we all got out and waited while the driver patched up the engine with bits of wire and string. It always started again, he shouted and we climbed in and went on. Once while he tinkered I observed that there was no hood to the engine.

"Where is the hood?" I asked.

He looked up, his face streaked with oil. "That lid," he said with contempt, "it was take—it—up, take—it—down, and for what? I took it off altogether."

The engine burst into loud snorts, he yelled, and we climbed in.

And travelling south through the rich province of Kwangtung, I learned for the first time how the heavy brown sugar was made which I had eaten since childhood as a delicacy. The cane is crushed by a press pulled by slow-moving water buffalo, and a stream of thin whitish-green sweet water pours from a spout into buckets. This water is boiled down very much as maple sugar water is boiled in Vermont, until it is thick and dark. Then it is poured into huge shallow tins and cut into squares like fudge. We ate quantities of it, hot and strong, and then we saw it cooled and crushed again into the coarse sugar we all knew.

And what a scene it was, the beautiful lush green countryside, the thatched roof of the circular mill, open on all sides, the buffalo yoked together or single, pulling the heavy wooden beam across their shoulders, the blue-coated peasants feeding the sugar cane into the press, and then the sugar boiling on the earthen stoves, and the children dancing about, licking their fingers, while wasps and bees droned in the warm air—it all comes back to me still, wrapped in a daze of sleepy content, the fragrance and the heat and the dancing children. They were far from the new capital, those people of the South, and when it was spoken of they were indifferent and cynical about it as about all governments. Only in the cities did I see the new and bitter slogans pasted on the walls of the buildings and the city gates, forever crying out against the "Western imperialists."

And so southward to Canton, and I am glad that I have seen more than once the old Canton before it was "improved," for in the old city I could walk the ancient narrow streets where the ivory dealers, the jade lapidaries, the gold and silversmiths, had their one-story shops. Each trade had its own street, in its own area, and one could watch an ivory carver use his delicate instruments to shape a tusk into the graceful flowing figure of a Kuan-yin, or make a huge ivory ball, containing within it eighteen other balls, each separate from the other, and each rolling free from every other, a magic I have never been able to comprehend, in spite of seeing it often with my own eyes. And the jade of every color, yellow, or rust red, blue, or green as spring rice, mottled as marble, or smooth and cold and white as mutton fat, every variety exquisite and put to exquisite use! I had seen triumphs of such art in the palaces of Peking, whole landscapes carved from a single huge lump of jade, but here in a Canton street I saw it actually done, a lifetime spent upon one work. The southern jades came usually from Burma, whereas the jade in Peking was brought by camel from Turkestan. It was a Chinese in the thirteenth century A.D. who discovered the mines in Burma, but not for a long time, in fact not until the latter part of the eighteenth century, did the Chinese jade lovers consider the Burmese gem as valuable as their own variety, and indeed there is a difference, the Burmese jade being a jadeite and the Turkestan a nephrite. But Chinese jade miners and Burmese alike believe that jade has miraculous qualities. The Kachins or Burmese hillmen locate the mines by a bamboo divining rod, set afire, and then, when jade is found, they perform the old rituals and ceremonies for opening the mines.

But why should I divert myself here to speak of jade? It is a subject for many books, from the moment of mining the boulders encrusted with earth and hard rock, their hollow hearts lined with the precious and various stone to the final setting of the stone as jewel or *objet d'art.* Jade became in China a divine gem in the time of Ch'in Shih Huang, for whom the first great Imperial Seal was made, and that seal was preserved throughout the dynasties, so that whoever was strong enough to gain it and to keep it became by that very sign the Heaven-ordained ruler. It was this seal that the old Empress Dowager carried with her whenever she fled into exile, knowing that so long as she held it, her people would not recognize another on the throne and I wonder where that seal is now. Indeed jade is a possession to be cherished by anyone who can find it or buy it or steal it. Chinese women ask for jade ornaments for their hair, for jade bracelets and rings, and old men keep in their closed palms a piece of cool jade, so smooth that it seems soft to the touch. Rich men buy jades instead of putting their money in banks, for jade grows more beautiful with age. When men die, their families put jade in the tombs with them to keep them from decay and the orifices of their bodies are stopped with jade for purity. The poorest courtesan has her bit of jade to hang in her ears or to use in a hairpin, and the most successful and popular actresses wear jade instead of diamonds, because jade is the more sumptuous jewel against a woman's flesh. And so enough of jade.

The journey westward into Asia was one of discovery and is now one of remembrance. I went to see what was to be seen, and though every land had its extraordinary and peculiar beauty, it was to see the people that I went.

In Indo-China I found the old familiar signs of colonialism, and the sign which is most unlovable, perhaps, is that colonial people grow too selfish and self-centered. Since they have no responsibility for governing themselves they take little responsibility for anything outside themselves and their families, and when some misfortune comes, they blame anyone except themselves. Otherwise this interesting and beautiful tri-state country of Indo-China was charming, and when it is free and responsible for its own welfare, it may become a tropical Switzerland. For Indo-China is really three small territories, or states, combined to make a nation. Vietnam is mainly Chinese, Cambodia is Indian, and Laos is Siamese. The three languages are quite separately spoken, and French is the common unifying tongue. There are no large cities except Saigon, which is very much French, and where the white community leads an active life in street cafés and night clubs, and where there is less segregation than in other colonial countries. On the streets I saw the mixed, the half-whites, French father and any woman for the mother, and their children as lovely as wild flowers but lost, growing by the wayside, belonging nowhere, intelligent, oversensitive, always wounded. Nevertheless I say still that there is actually less race prejudice among the French than among any Western people, and a beautiful French woman had Indo-Chinese lovers as easily as her own kind.

Colonialism degraded the French rulers, too, as it degrades everywhere, and the French in Indo-China were often unlovely in thought and behavior, inferior nearly aways to the ones at home in France. In spite of this, the Chinese have liked them better than other white men, because they do not act unjustly merely because of race difference. It was, however, an unworthy colonialism that I saw in Indo-China, without pretensions of nobility or goodness. Its purpose was altogether commercial and its goal was money, got anyhow and anywhere, and the only shrewder businessman than the Frenchman was the Chinese.

I went to Cambodia because I wanted to see Angkor Wat and I do not know to this day whether I am glad or sorry, for I hold that place in my memory so deeply that even now sometimes when I wake in the night to instinctive and unreasonable dread, I see the dead palaces, ruined and yet standing in the clutches of vast trees, rooting themselves not in the earth but like serpents entwining the stones. The very approaches are serpents and the balustrades of bridges are the thick bodies of stone cobras with poisonous heads uplifted and hoods flaring. I walked for hours through the desolate and empty palaces that none can explain, for they were lost so long in the jungle. They were built for the Khmer rulers, we are told, but why, and by whom? Tradition says that it was all done by slave labor, that stone upon stone the slaves piled up the palaces for their despotic kings, who treated them with such cruelty and callous inhumanity that at last the slaves rose in insurrection and destroyed their masters, and the deed must have been evilly done, for the reek of evil was everywhere, though slaves and masters alike are long dead. I am not given to superstition, yet there are certain places in old Asian countries where human beings have been born and have lived and died for so many generations that the very earth is saturated with their flesh and the air seems crowded with their continuing presence. Never have I had the same consciousness here in my own country, a new land, scarcely settled in terms of old Asia. But I felt that crowded air in Angkor, even though the jungle pressed about, and I knew that it was evil. The soft sweetish stink of death was everywhere, even the rooms in the hotel smelled of it, the sheets and pillows, the closets where my clothes hung, so that when I got away I put everything into the hot and tropical sunshine to burn out the reek of decay. It conveyed in its own way the old fearful threat, as potent today as a thousand years ago, that when men do evil to other men, when men deal unjustly and without mercy and count others lower than themselves and therefore of no worth, they create for themselves the certainty of downfall.

Yet there were strange and amusing incidents, too, as I continued my journey. In Bangkok, the capital of Siam, I had two experiences entirely new. At a Rotary Club dinner, where the speaker was a prince of the royal house, I sat through a meal as American as meat and potatoes could make it, and after it was over the Prince read a speech of such extraordinary dullness that I could not believe my ears. All through the dinner he had been sparkling in wit and laughter and we had been charmed. But what, I thought, was this speech? When he had finished it he lifted his head, which he had held doggedly to his page, and the sparkle was shining again in his voice and dark eyes.

"Excuse me," he said. "I have performed a duty. This speech was written in American headquarters and sent here from Chicago."

Mighty laughter then, and we all roared and applauded, and he sat down with as wicked and sophisticated a twinkle as a handsome face could create. And after this we were led down the corridor into a darkened theater room for the entertainment, also canned and shipped from the United States, and I saw my first Walt Disney film, *Three Little Pigs*.

But what I really remember about Bangkok, aside from a curious fruit called a durian, so hard that I used it as a permanent doorstop in my hotel room, was the life on the streets, the yellow-robed priests sauntering everywhere, the magnificence of ancient temples, rising in golden steps from a vast and solid base, exactly as modern buildings rise today in steel and glass, but not so high, and the beautiful smooth-faced women and little children, and the gentle-looking men. Small houseboats drifted slowly on the glassy opaque waters of the canals, the families who lived upon them clean and beautiful, and surely the Siamese are among the world's most handsome creatures, not large, but smooth-skinned, cream-colored flesh covering small smoothly shaped bones, the eyes large and oval and not slanted, dark brown instead of black, and the hair soft and smooth again and dark but not black. These were a free people. And they looked free, their heads lifted, frank and inclined to friendliness instead of hostility, and what lovely hands and feet and slim round bodies they had, men and women and children, all of them!

A few days ago I saw a little half-Siamese boy, born in the United States and therefore an American, a guest in my house, put his arms about his adoptive mother's neck, she a white American, and loving this child as dearly as though she had created his body within her own. Remembering his other country and all the Siamese ancestors behind him, I knew her blessed. The heritage is good.

India had always been part of the background of my life, but I had never seen it whole and for myself until now. Yet the stories that our Indian family doctor and his wife told me when I was a child had woven themselves into my growing dreams, and I had long read everything that I could find about that country. From my father I had learned of it through Buddhism and the life history of the Lord Buddha. I had seen the opposite face of India, too, in the tall turbaned Sikh policemen in the British Concession in Shanghai, who did not hesitate to beat a luckless Chinese riksha puller if he got in the way of traffic or disobeyed the imperious demands of the turbaned ones. India was not all of a piece! And through young Indians I had learned about the colonial empire of England, some of its evil and some of its good.

China and India are as unlike as two countries can well be. The life philosophies of the two peoples are different and this in spite of the fact that they share a universal attitude toward all mankind. Both peoples are peace-loving, but for different reasons, the Indians because their religions teach them that life is sacred and must never be destroyed, and the Chinese because they know from their superb common sense, inherited and congenital, that war is folly, and that a wise man prevails by his wisdom. Thus the Chinese have accepted even into their blood stream all their invaders, insofar as the invaders themselves have allowed it. The Jews, for example, for centuries took refuge in China, entering first through India and by the ancient trade routes from Asia Minor, and settled in the inner province of Honan, making their headquarters in K'aifeng-fu. Yet of the Jews as a separate people there is no trace left in China. The Chinese never persecuted them and instead by sheer kindliness and active commercial interchange they absorbed them and were the better for it. Often when I found in China an artist of unusual talent, or a mind more vivid than others among my students, the chances were good that he had Jewish blood in him. It is a creative strain. Once, I remember, a portfolio came from Peking to *Asia Magazine,* in New York, of drawings signed by various names. The editor chose for publication the ones he thought the best, and later he discovered that all but one were actually by the same artist, a young Chinese Jew. But the story of the Jews in China I have already told in my novel *Peony,* which in England is entitled *The Bondmaid.*

In India the Jews have not been absorbed. It is not India's way to absorb. Instead she has allowed peoples to remain separate, although a part of her whole. Thus the Parsis, that affluent and influential people, who came from Persia centuries ago, have remained intact, their religion still fire worship and their burial grounds the splendid Towers of Silence near the city of Bombay. And in the south of India there remain the black Jews, burned dark by the Indian sun shining upon them for so many generations that they have lost their own color.

The very word *color* reminds me of the variety of hue that is Indian life, as various as our own American human scene. In Kashmir, where the white barbarian invaders from Europe long ago penetrated India, the people are often fair. Auburn-haired, blue-eyed women are beauties there. A young Indian friend of mine has recently married a Kashmiri man who, though his hair is dark, has eyes of a clear green. The skin color of the Kashmiri is a lovely cream and the features are as classic as the Greek. But all the peoples of India must be reckoned as belonging to the Caucasian race, whatever the color of the skin in the South, though it be as black as any African's.

And India has an amazing way of appearing unexpectedly in other life, as for example, today in the life of South Africa, the Indians make a third group between the South Africans, and the black and white. For that matter there was our Indian family doctor, and why should there have been an Indian doctor in a Chinese port to tend an American family? And rumors of India persist, for they are a memorable people, dramatic and passionate and finding dramatic lives. Years ago an Irish maid, long with our family during the peripatetic life between New York and Green Hills Farm, happened to mention, when we were expecting an Indian guest, and this only after years of serving us, that she herself had once been in India. Upon my exclamation of surprise she said yes, that her father had been in the British Army, and that his family had gone out there to be with him. She had been only three or four years old and could remember very little.

Whereupon I asked, "How did your father like India?"

And she replied absently, her mind obviously upon sheets and towels. "He liked it well enough, mum, except burnin' them Hindus."

"Burning the Hindus?" I repeated, stupefied.

"Yes, mum," she said, still absently. "They took 'em prisoners by the wagonload and didn't know what to do with 'em. But it was narsty, burnin' 'em, mum."

I did not and still do not believe the story, and all my inquiries have since denied the validity of this tale, but it shows how rumor can become stark as reality. The British did commit cruelties, as all colonial masters must if they are to maintain their power over such powerful peoples as the Indian. Thus the famous remark of the English captain, who when he heard of the devastation committed by bombs upon Warsaw in the Second World War cried out in anguish that this European city had been treated as though it were nothing but a Pathan village in India. Pathan villages might, it seemed, be bombed when the inhabitants disobeyed their colonial masters, although, as the Englishman said solemnly in vindication, not until the inhabitants had been duly warned in time to leave their homes.

And then, after the war, a young American ex-GI became our gardener, and after months of pleasant work together over asparagus and roses and such, I discovered that he, too, had been in India and had mightily enjoyed the experience. He had volunteered in the Second World War for foreign service, and he was sent to Asia, his ship crossing the Atlantic first to Africa and thence around the Cape, because of the German submarines and the Japanese also, for by then the Japanese were already using the small one-man or two-man submarines, designed for suicide. Small enough to be cast from a ship, the submarines went down to seek for their target of an Allied ship. When it was found, man and submarine both crashed against it. Suicide is the right word, for if no target were found, the small craft used up its gasoline supply and the man within died anyway. And that also reveals an aspect of the eternal Japanese character.

Around the Cape of Good Hope our young Americans went during the first year of the war and then to Karachi. So there was where my gardener landed, he tells me, and for four years he lived in Lahore, Bombay, Calcutta and New Delhi. He was sensible enough to appreciate the opportunity and he learned to know Indians so well that he was invited to weekends in their homes.

"How did they entertain you?" I asked.

"They took us to American movies," he replied, seeing nothing strange in this. True, he added, sometimes he was taken also to see dancing girls. Wherever he was I am sure that he was a simple and good American, the son of a Pennsylvania farmer, friendly and accepting each Indian as a friend.

"I'd like to go back now that it's peaceful," he said the other day when we were working in the camellia house. "I'd like to see how things are going. I could manage all right living there."

You see how India has a way of permeating human life? And consider how India has managed, merely by maintaining her independence, and yes, by producing superior individuals, to influence the world in these few short years of freedom. They have put to good use the benefits the English gave and left, the knowledge of the West, the pure and exquisitely enunciated English tongue of men and women educated on both sides of the globe—witness Nehru and with him a host of men learning how to govern, and the first woman to be President of the General Assembly of the United Nations a woman of India, and the man in charge of the prisoner exchange in Korea an Indian general, who won trust from all. Even the blustering and accusations at home and abroad have not changed the quiet confidence of the new India, and this confidence, founded in unyielding idealism, permeates our world life.

I entered India, then, in 1934 and at Calcutta and went straight to the home of an Indian friend. Bombay is the great twin city on the other side of the continent, but Calcutta is not so spruce, nor so English. I reached there in the evening, and the sidewalks were all but impassable with the outstretched bodies of sleepers—the homeless, the vagrant, the wanderer. And I confess that it shocked me to see the depredations of the sacred cows, especially upon the stalls of the vegetable vendors, although the shrewdness of the Bengalis did often devise an outwitting even of the godly cows.

What did I go to India to see? Not the Taj Mahal, although I did see it and by moonlight, not Fatehpur Sikri, although I did see it, and not the glories of empire in New Delhi, although I did see them. I went to India to see and listen to two groups of people, the young intellectuals in the cities and the peasants in the villages. These I met in little rooms in the city, in little houses in the villages, and I heard their plans for freedom. Already the intellectuals believed that another World War was inevitable. They had been bitterly disappointed after the First World War by what they felt were the broken promises of England. The English, they declared, had no real purpose to restore India to the people. I could believe it, fresh as I was from China, where the period of "People's Tutelage" seemed endless and self-government further off every year. "When you are ready for independence," conquerors have always said to their subjects, et cetera! But who is to decide when that moment comes, and how can a people learn to govern themselves except by doing it? So the intellectuals in India were restless and embittered, and I sat through hours, watching their flashing dark eyes and hearing the endless flow of language, the purest English, into which they poured their feelings.

The plan then was that when the Second World War broke, India would rebel immediately against England and compel her, by this complication, to set her free. They would not be forced, as they declared they had been in the First World War, to fight at England's command.

"And then?" I asked.

"And then," young India said proudly, "we will ourselves decide whether we wish to fight at England's side—or against her."

What they did not reckon on, when the time came, was the savagery of Nazism and the aggressions of Japan in Asia. When they perceived that they must choose between the Axis and the English, they chose the English, aware that in spite of many injustices they were choosing between barbarism and civilization. They postponed their plans for freedom, Gandhi meanwhile doing his work within his own country until the war was over, and by then the wisest minds in England, understanding the new world, returned India to her people, in spite of all opposition from Englishmen and others who did not have sufficient understanding of Asia to know what wisdom was. Not even Churchill's prophecy of a blood bath, partly fulfilled at that, could prevent the inevitable. India had waited as long as she could, and peasant and intellectual were on the same side in the old invincible combination. It was Gandhi's strength that made him know very early that both peasant and intellectual must be won to work together for their country, his hold was equally strong upon both, and so he achieved his end, without war. Perhaps we Americans do not yet fully understand the great lesson that India has to teach in thus winning her freedom. Beside her mighty triumph of a bloodless revolution our War of Independence shrinks in size and concept. India has taught humanity a lesson, and it is to our peril if we do not learn it. The lesson? That war and killing achieve nothing but loss, and that a noble end is assured only if the means to attain it are of a piece with it and also noble.

The real indictment against colonialism, however, was to be found in the villages of India. There was rot at the top, too, in the thousands of young intellectuals trained in English schools for jobs that did not exist except in the limited Civil Service. The towns and cities were frothing with unhappy young men, cultured and well educated, who could find no jobs and were not allowed by the old superstructure of empire to create them. But the real proof of evil, I say again, was in the miserable villages. I thought I had seen poverty enough in China, yet when I saw the Indian villages I knew that the Chinese peasant was rich in comparison. Only the Russian peasant I had seen years before could compare with the Indian villager, although that Russian was a very different creature, and inferior in many ways. For the Indian peasant was like the Chinese in being a person innately civilized. The maturing culture of an organized human family life and profound philosophical religions had shaped his mind and soul, even though he could not read and write. And the children, the little children of the Indian villages, how they tore at my heart, thin, big-bellied, and all with huge sad dark eyes! I wondered that any Englishman could look at them and not accuse himself. Three hundred years of English occupation and rule, and could there be children like this? Yes, and millions of them! And the final indictment surely was that the life span in India was only twenty-seven years. Twenty-seven years! No wonder, then, that life was hastened, that a man married very young so that there could be children, as many as possible before he died. I loved England, remembering all the happy journeys there, but in India I saw an England I did not know. And I was forced to see that if the English, in many ways the finest people on earth, a people who blazed the way for all of us to achieve the right of men to rule themselves, if colonialism could so corrupt even these, then indeed none of us could dare to become the rulers of empire.

It seemed to me, as I lived with Indian friends, new and old, that all the ills of India could easily have been mended if there had been a government whose purpose was first of all to benefit the people rather than to live upon them. The desert-dry country, for example, the fruitless land between Bombay and Madras, was already famished although it was only February and the sun hot enough to fertilize any seed had there been water. And why was there not water? Why not sink artesian wells, or even dig shallow wells, since, I was told, the water table was high? But the enervated and exhausted people had not the strength to take such initiative after the years of colonialism. It was more than that. The worst result, perhaps, of the colonial system was to provide the subject people with an infinite excuse against work and so against helping themselves. "You are responsible for me," is always the sullen attitude of the subject to the ruler. "You have undertaken to feed me and clothe me and govern me. If I die it is your fault." There were always the British to blame, and certainly the blame was not always just. Yet essentially perhaps it was, for when the heart of a people is gone, their spirit dies with it.

In India, I found, any one who had Indian blood was Indian, although three-fourths of his blood might be white, and this policy added to the numbers of the discontented. In the first years of colonialism English women did not follow their men, and even until the end young men did not marry, or married late. It was inevitable that a large group of human beings existed, neither English nor Indian, yet uneasily belonging to both. They were almost invariably superior to the stock they came from, on both sides. The men were handsome, the women beautiful, and both were, more often than not, superior in intelligence. Scientists tell us nowadays that a mixed people, hybrid, if you like, are usually a superior people, even individually, as the hybrid rose and hybrid corn are superior in the vegetable world. We are told that the richest cultures, the most vital civilizations, come from the hybrid peoples, and surely the American is hybrid enough, drawing even his Caucasian blood from as far north as Sweden and Finland to as far south as Italy.

In Indonesia I found a curious difference in attitude toward the hybrid individual. There whoever had a drop of white blood was counted as white. This wise colonial policy made the stoutest Dutchmen of men of mixed blood, removing the discontented half-and-half of India. In Indonesia he had, if not a total equality, at least a surface one which salved his pride. Indeed, if the prudent Hollander developed a colonialism in any way superior to that of India or of Indo-China, he did this mainly through his relatively enlightened racial policy. True, Indonesian intellectuals, too, were chafing to be free even then, but the movement was calm, almost unnoticeable as yet among the people, whereas in India the ferment seemed ready to burst.

Between such serious study and observation, I took much pleasure in the different landscapes, in wandering as far as I could about the countryside of each nation I visited. I had my first taste of true jungle in Sumatra, although I had seen jungles too in Indo-China, but even from the air the jungle in Sumatra looks dangerous, the muddy rivers crawling through the livid green like sluggish serpents. And when the plane came down how sickish sweet was that humid air with something living and yet fetid! I am not one for jungles.

Looking back, I find that among the many impressions of the people of India, absorbed while I lived among them, and still clear in my mind, is their reverence for great men and women. Leadership in India can only be continued by those whom the followers consider to be good—that is, capable of renunciation, therefore not self-seeking. This one quality for them contains all others. A person able to renounce personal benefit for the sake of an idealistic end is by that very fact also honest, also high-minded, therefore also trustworthy. I felt that the people, even those who knew themselves venal and full of faults, searched for such persons. Gandhi had among his followers many faulty men and women, and he himself was not free from certain petty dominations, as those who lived with him continuously knew very well. Yet they devoted themselves to him because he had made the great renunciation of personal gain and benefit.

The devotion given nationally to Gandhi and finally even internationally is well known, but I found the same homage paid to local persons who in their measure were also leaders because of their selflessness. Thus I remember a certain Indian village where I had been invited to visit in the home of a family of some modern education, though not much, and some means, though not wealth. The house was mud-walled and the roof was of thatch. Inside were several rooms, however, the

303

floors smooth and polished with the usual mixture of cow dung and water. The active master of the house was not the head of the family, but a younger brother. This I discovered when I arrived, for before we entered the house, my host led me to a curious sort of cage standing well above the ground on four posts. Inside the cage, made of wire netting, I saw to my amazement an aging man, lying on his back, his head supported by a pillow.

"My eldest brother," my host explained. "He has had a stroke of paralysis, and though we beg him to live in the house, he chooses to live out here so that he may be ready to listen to the villagers when they come to him."

My host spoke fair English, but the elder brother spoke none, and we could only exchange greetings and look at each other with friendliness. What I saw was an intelligent, thin, pain-sharpened face, whose eyes were at once wise and piercing. The body was quite helpless, but it was scrupulously clean and the cotton garments were snow-white. We exchanged a few remarks, and then a group of villagers approached, not to see me but to talk with the elder brother, and so my host led me into the house to meet his young wife and children.

All during my stay I watched that cage, and seldom indeed did I see it except surrounded by people, and never, as long as daylight lasted, without at least one man squatting on the ground, talking earnestly and then listening. My host said,

"My brother has always been our wise man. Now he is our saint."

My host, I observed, had his own place, too, in the village life, for twice while we were eating our luncheon that day he rose from his corner of the room and went out, to answer a shout, apparently from a neighbor. When he came back he made the same explanation.

"I was called to kill a dangerous snake."

The luncheon was plain country fare, lentils, rice, spinach boiled very much, condiments. Before we ate, an old cousin brought in a brass ewer of water and a clean homespun towel for us to cleanse our hands with, a necessary preliminary to eating with the fingers. Chopsticks I had used all my life and preferred them to knife and fork, but after I had got used to eating with my right hand, I liked it as well. After all, what is so clean as one's own right hand, washed? And from babyhood the Indian children are taught that the right hand is for clean services, such as eating, and the left hand may perform the more lowly tasks.

Another cleanliness was that our food was served on fresh green banana leaves instead of plates. Well-cooked rice piled on a broad green leaf is a pleasant sight and stimulates the appetite. In any household where caste was observed the food was placed on such leaves or in dishes of fresh pottery, broken after we had finished with them. My host fulfilled the requirements of his caste by eating in the opposite corner of the room, and sitting on the floor with his back to us. By now I had learned to overcome my first feeling about a distance such as this. It was simply a private devotion to a religious feeling and not inhospitality.

Religion is ever-present in Indian life, in its best as well as in its worst aspects, for there, as elsewhere, fanaticism reaches into evil. I liked the simple acceptance of religious motive, however, and the perfect freedom to behave as one's religion moved the soul. Thus in my first Indian family, an intellectual and fairly well-to-do one, while I sat and talked with my hostess in her living room an Indian gentleman came in without speaking to us and moved gracefully to the far end of the room, his bare feet silent upon the floor. There he knelt, his head bowed, and so remained for perhaps a quarter of an hour. When I glanced at him curiously my hostess said in a manner entirely casual:

"It is my husband's eldest brother. He comes here during the day at his prayer times, since his own home is at some distance from his place of business."

When the prayer was over the brother went away again, and it was not until later that I met him, and then it was outside of prayer hours.

My life has been too crowded with travels and many people for me to put it all within the covers of one book, however, and indeed all my books have not been enough to tell the things I would like to tell. Years after I left India I wrote *Come, My Beloved* against its background. Strange, the Americans, except for a few, have not understood the real meaning of that book, but the Indian readers understand. We have not lived long enough, perhaps, to know universally that the price of achievement, whatever the goal, is an absolute. In my book I chose three Christian missionaries to prove it, for of all the people that I have ever known the missionary is, in his way, the most dedicated, the most single-hearted. He believes that God is the One, the Father of mankind and that all men are brothers. At least the Christian says he so believes and so he preaches. Then why has he failed to change the world in spite of his sacrifices? Alas, they have not been enough, and he has not been willing to pay the full price for faith. He pays only part, unable to accept utterly the full meaning of his creed. I see the same refusal here in my own country, over and over again, and not only among Christians. But the people of India know what it is to be willing to pay the last full measure of the cost of an idealism. They understand, and to them my book is not a puzzlement.

To China I returned with all that I had accumulated of knowledge and experience, and I stayed awhile, sorting over these treasures and pondering upon my own future. In Nanking again, a stone's throw from the Nationalist government, I still saw no change for the better, no vision, no understanding of the real problems to be solved, and the people were increasingly sullen. The Communists were soon to be locked in the far Northwest, the Long March taking place in 1935, but the war lords were still not conquered, not all bought and bargained with, and Japan was ominous indeed. All this and more—bad news from my child across the sea, and in my house the deepening difference, finally made up my mind. I would leave China, if not forever, nevertheless as the country of my youthful heart and childhood life. I would go back to the land of my ancestors and make another life. The decision brought me closer than I had ever been to those ancestors. Once they, too, had left the known to go across the sea to the unknown. In my case there was a reversal—I had grown up alien and made a strange land mine, and now I was to return to the land of my ancestors. The uprooting was the same, whatever the direction.

Before I left I went once more to Peking, simply to see it, simply to impress upon my memory the last scenes of what had been the heart of my childhood China. It was not a private return, for by that time too many people knew me and there were invitations I could not refuse. I do not remember them now—what I do remember is the blind musician I met one twilight evening in a lonely street. I was walking just for pleasure when I heard the melody of an accomplished hand upon the two-stringed Chinese violin, and there against the light of the hutung was the figure of a big man in a long grey cotton robe. His massive head was high, his dark eyes wide-open but blind, as I could see when he came near. He held his violin across his breast, and as he played upon two strings with his bow he strode along, too absorbed to feel my presence. I have never forgotten that man, nor his melody.

And I have not forgotten the hours in the old well-known inns, the Moslem inn where roast mutton was the dish, the Peking inns where one called for duck, and chose it alive and waited for the finished dishes. I made the rounds again too of the old palaces, and stayed very long one day in the rooms where once the Old Empress had lived. And a day's journey away from Peking, I walked upon the Great Wall of China, now so useless, although still the enemy was to come down from the North, and I spent another day near the Jade Pagoda so that I might remember it forever.

Thus I filled my cup full, perhaps for all my life, for who could know whether it would ever be possible to return even for a visit? War was certain, war with Japan if not a world war, and by now a world war lay upon the horizon, and much larger than a man's hand. In that war,

Japan, I knew, would not be on our side but with the enemy. Yet when the last moment came, the final departure from house and garden, I took nothing with me. I could take nothing. I felt compelled to leave it all exactly as it was, as though I might be coming back when summer was gone and as in other years I had come back. And thus, in the spring of 1934, I went to my own country.

IV

Green Hills Farm

FOR me my country was a new one, although I was an American by birth and ancestry. The first half of my life was spent, but the better half, the longer half, since there is much waste in the childhood years, yet remained to me. I was a mature person, healthy, alive to every new sight and sound and experience. My kinsmen had fought bravely in three wars, the War of Independence of 1775, the Civil War of 1861, the First World War of 1914. In each of these wars the purpose had been the same, an idealistic one, to make and keep the United States a united and a free nation. In peacetime my kin were professional men—preachers and teachers and lawyers and landowners. Culture was our family tradition, and education was taken as a matter of course. Parents held their children's noses to the grindstone of school, whether or no until the young ones learned to like it, and excellence was expected. All this simply meant that I came to my country without the burden of the individual in a classless society. I had no reason to worry about myself. I had always been able to do what I wanted to do, and this meant freedom from self—that is, freedom from fear of failure and also from conceit. I commend the mood, since it gives all one's time for observation and thought, work and enjoyment.

My first summer I spent in New York, and the result of it was that I learned that I could never understand my country unless I became a part of it somewhere else and not merely a city visitor. This meant a home, and home meant a house, and where does one live when there is a vast country from which to choose? The choice may be merely geographical, and I saw many places delightful enough in which to remain, the bare beauty of Western deserts, the enchanted high plains of Kansas, the mountainous states of the Rockies, the close hills of New England. I set aside the Deep South. I could not live where the colonial atmosphere prevailed, and where I would have always to look at signs to see where I belonged in railroad stations and restaurants. Besides, I planned at last for more children, for here, I thought, was a safe country for children, and I did not want the responsibility of having them in-

311

stilled with color prejudices which I knew would be dangerous to us in the world of the near future.

After some musing and travelling, I decided on a region where the landscapes were varied, where farm and industry lived side by side, where sea was near at hand, mountains not far away, and city and countryside were not enemies, a big rich state, a slice of the nation— Pennsylvania. And where in Pennsylvania? That was decided by the sort of house I wanted. It was to be old, for I was used to old places, I liked their solidity, their soberness, their size. The houses of my Chinese friends were ancient houses, the beams enormous, the walls thick, the gardens aged. I admired the white and green houses of New England and New York, but they seemed ephemeral. Wood burns too easily. In China the houses even of the poor had thick earthen walls. Only in Japan had I lived in a wooden house, and that was because of earth-quakes, averaging more than two thousand a year, if one counts the small ones. But they burned. No, stone if possible, please, for red brick I did not like after the quiet grey of the Chinese brick.

I found the stone houses in Pennsylvania, and farms were cheap then, at the end of the depression. Country was my place, although I enjoyed a city for some reasons, but not for living in and doing my work. So a farm, then, whether I farmed the land or not, a quiet place somewhere in a moderate landscape, a house on a hillside, a brook, trees and gentle hills. Extravagant landscapes are sights to be stored in the memory and to see again and again, but not to live with, I think.

How does one choose one's house? It is first built in the imagination. I saw mine very clearly, rough fieldstone, brown with glints of gold and red, a big chimney. It was not a tall narrow house, but a wide one, at least a century old, low-set against the earth, a wing perhaps leaning against the main building, many windows, a mild view toward forests and hills and the brook. There it was. It remained only to be found. One day in a crowded downtown New York street I saw the sign of a Strout Farm Agency and I sauntered in.

"Do you have any small farms in Pennsylvania for sale?" I asked, exactly as though I were buying a pair of gloves in a department store.

A yawning clerk pointed with his thumb to a pile of little folders on a table. I took the top one and saw a picture no bigger than a postage stamp, in the lower right-hand corner, of my house, exactly as I had planned, a wide main building and then a wing, all stone, big chimneys, set pleasantly on a hillside, a brook, trees, even an old three-arched bridge over the brook, forty-eight acres of land, forty-one hundred dollars.

"Thank you," I said. Then, holding my breath and pointing to my house, "Is this sold?"

The lazy clerk looked up something in a file. "No," he said indifferently.

"Thanks," I said.

I went away, impatient that it was too dark to set forth that day to claim the house. But at dawn next day I started, breakfasting somewhere along the way, and in a few hours I had reached my destination, missing the road a good many times at that. It was a summer's day, very green and still, the sky gently overcast for coming rain. I found the local Strout agent, a Pennsylvania Dutchman, and under his guidance we turned down a country road, dusty as any Chinese path, and soon we crossed the three-arched bridge.

"Dere it iss," he said.

He pointed toward the shallow hill. I looked, and there it was, exactly as it had been in the postage stamp picture. We turned to the right along a still narrower road, the old mill road, he said, that ran between the house and the enormous red barn. Then we stopped and got out. I had seen plenty of better houses and to this day I cannot tell why I insisted upon that one, although I have never regretted the choice. But I tried to be prudent, I paid the down fee, and said I would let him know in a couple of days. He grunted a Pennsylvania Dutch grunt, and said he would show me some more houses if I liked, and since I felt I should in common sense see as many houses as possible, I spent the rest of the day in looking at them, and with difficulty restrained myself from buying mine instantly. Then I went back to New York and could hardly bear to wait the necessary days until I could get back. Had it not been a weekend, I could not have waited. Three days later I owned the house.

Books have been written many times in the intervening years between then and now by people who have done just what I did, and I have enjoyed all the books, reading avidly to see what others did. The only difference is that they seem to grow caustic, little or much, over the many trials of making an old house into a home for living. But I had no such trials. Everything was pure joy for me, perhaps because this house was my own first possession, or perhaps because I should have been an architect. Of course, did I build a house it would not be like the one I bought. It would be functional, shaped to the landscape I might choose, in the way that Chinese houses are built, or more truly, the Japanese houses. Frank Lloyd Wright knows exactly what I mean, for he has used the same philosophy and has often found his inspiration in Japan and Korea. The older a people grows, the more it absorbs its own landscape and builds to it.

Yet there was something fit for me in the stone house I bought and have lived in ever since. I do not know what instinct led me to the part of Pennsylvania where my paternal ancestors first came, two hundred years ago. They left it, to be sure, after the War of Independence, and bought lands in the Shenandoah Valley in Virginia, but here my paternal family had its American beginning, nevertheless, and the knowledge was solid behind me. I believe in family, ancestors and all. The individual is a lonely creature otherwise in this changing world.

There were more than ancestors, there were traditions that came with my Pennsylvania house, and first of all the tradition of William Penn and his fair and just treatment of the red Indians. Rascality there sometimes was—I know it, for near my house is the storied Indian Walk where, a century and more ago, it was agreed between white man and red Indian that the white man could have as much land as his legs could cover in a day. The amiable Indian thought this meant honest walking with time out to rest and eat, but the shrewd white man trained himself to walk at a fierce pace and covered such territory in the day that the Indian was hotly indignant. "White man lun—lun—lun all day—" thus history records his remonstrance.

English Quaker and German Mennonite saw to it, however, that cheating and killing were kept at a minimum, and the tradition is still strong here that peoples are to be treated alike and with generosity, though of course generosity is always sensible rather than extravagant. Pennsylvania Dutchmen are not extravagant, and neither, I must say it, are the English-blooded Quakers. They live harmoniously together, firm in their belief in the value of money and land and good cows. Solidity is the habit in our region and Republicanism is our natural trend, yet when we like a man we can forsake all for him.

For myself I was pleased to discover that I had bought land belonging once to Richard Penn, William's brother. And it was interesting that twice when we pulled up a vast dead tree we found coins mingled with its earth, not of great value, but once Spanish coin, and again English. I liked the evidence that earlier people had lived here before me. It was even pleasant to discover a ghost belonging to our house. In China ghosts are nearly always women, the vapory souls of beautiful women, part fox, part fairy, who incarnate themselves again in living female bodies. Our ghost, however, is a Pennsylvania Dutchman, Old Harry, politely called, but usually Devil Harry, whose remains lie in the Lutheran churchyard of the nearest village. I have never seen our ghost, but our hired man insisted that Devil Harry walks every Christmas Eve

314

at midnight from the barn to the bridge and back again, and that anybody who knew what he looked like can see him plainly. Our Mennonite maid believed in him, and when a dish sprang from a cupboard and broke itself, or a door slammed on her finger, she cried out, "It's Old Devil Harry again!"

And the mason who built the walls of the new wing after the children came told me that Devil Harry was so obstreperous, being given at times to liquor, that one night when he came home drunk his own wife decided to make an end of him. He threw himself on the kitchen floor in a stupor, whereupon she tied the end of a rope around his neck and pushed it through the stove hole in the wooden ceiling into the bedroom above and then went upstairs and hauled him clear, as she thought, and tied the rope to the four-poster. After waiting a suitable length of time she went down again expecting to find him dead. But the mischievous old man was sitting in the rocking chair in fits of silent laughter. He had come to, and comprehending her purpose, he had tied the rope around the leg of the iron kitchen stove, which she had hauled up and which was now swinging clear of the floor. And once the very ancient man who cut the grass in the cemetery paused above our ghost's grave to talk with me and his chief complaint against him was that in life, he had heard, Old Harry had a way on "thrashing" days of rushing to the dining table ahead of everybody and getting a start on the food. Farm wives outdid themselves to feed the "thrashers" well, and it was considered only just and decent for all hands to wait outside the door and go in together, seat themselves at the same time and then fall to without talking for the first fifteen minutes.

The ghost has never molested us, however. Man, woman and children, we have lived peacefully and happily in the house, enlarging it as the babies grew tall and independent. In one such change, we felt it necessary to take the two top panels from the old double door in the south wall of the living room and put in glass. When the panels were removed we found between the inner and outer layers these words written in soft black pencil:

"I, Joseph Housekeeper, made and work this door. August, 1835, I married Magdaleine, my true love."

Thus Joseph Housekeeper, who married his true love, is our tradition, too, although we know no more of him than the hidden words he wrote with his own hand so long ago.

Our ghost brings to my memory two other figures of our countryside, but they are not ghosts for I saw them in the flesh with my own eyes. Yet they were such strangers in a modern age that they might as well have been ghosts.

The first was a little hunchbacked man, a traveling preacher, a small figure always dressed in black and wearing a wide black felt hat, whom I used to meet when I walked in the back roads and lanes. He had a white, thin face and when I spoke to him, he only raised his bony hand in reply and plodded on. He carried a canvas bag slung from his shoulder, and every mile or so he stopped and took from it a hammer and nails and a strip of cardboard whereon was printed in large uneven letters a Bible text, and he nailed it to a tree. This was his way of preaching his gospel, so that wherever people went they would be confronted with the solemn words he could not speak. "Ye must be born again" must have been his favorite, for I came upon it often and in the most unexpected places, even in the deep woods.

The little preacher is dead now and it is ten years since I saw him last and then it was in a thunderstorm. He was walking slowly, against a driving rain, and in a direction opposite to my own. The texts he nailed upon the trees have rotted away. I never knew his name nor ever met anyone who knew it.

The other figure is a woman and I saw her only once. It was on a warm afternoon in late spring and I was going down our long lane to see if the wild strawberries were ripe by the big ash tree. Suddenly I saw her coming up the lane toward me, a woman in a black dress, very full in the skirt and so long that it swept the ground. Her sleeves were long, her collar high, and she wore a close black bonnet. When she came near I saw that she was old and that she looked frightened. Her full round face, white and softly wrinkled, was unsmiling, and her dark eyes were like a child's in terror.

"Can I help you?" I asked.

She shook her head. "I just did want to see the place," she said. "I was born in the house. People say you have made it nice and have planted much shrubbage."

"Please go wherever you like," I said.

We passed, and when I returned with my bowl full of wild strawberries she was gone. I asked my neighbors about her but none knew who she could have been. Our hired man simply insisted that she was a ghost, too.

For myself, I am indifferent to jewels and personal adornment, but I must have roses and a vegetable garden, and some years ago I indulged myself to include camellias, for these flowers, formal and exquisite, are Chinese in origin and were in China one of my favorites. Such roots I put down for myself, for roots are what one must put down, if one is to live. My roots were deep in China, and when they had to be pulled up it was necessary to put them down again as quickly as possible if life were to go on in growth. I have learned that any tree can be transplanted and live, if roots are not left long unsheltered in the drying air. Roots are meant to be in the earth, and quickly, quickly plant them there, pile the common soil around them, stamp it down and water it, and life goes on. But let a tree wait, unplanted too long, and it never roots. It makes a half-hearted attempt, a few leaves are put forth, and inexorably the top begins to die and after it the branches and then one spring there is no green. The laws of life are the same for every kingdom.

My American home, then, has been the root place of my American life, and my first years were absorbed in its building. For the making of a home is a profound educational experience. Thus I grew to know my community as I could never have known it had we not been building together. The workmen, the mason, the plasterer, the plumber, the carpenter, the well digger, the groceryman and garageman, have taught me more than they can imagine. I had the vast human experience of the Chinese behind me, and so trained I could appreciate every likeness and every difference between these citizens of my new world and those of the old. The likenesses were amazing. For some time I could not account for the fact that Americans and Chinese are so much alike. It is not imagination, since the Japanese, for example, are very different from us, and so are the people of Korea. As for the people of India, our temperamental differences are so great that I sometimes fear our permanent misunderstanding.

How are we alike, the Chinese and the Americans? We are continental peoples, for one thing; that is, we are accustomed to think in space and size and plenty. There is nothing niggardly about either of us—there seldom is about continental peoples, possessing long seacoasts and high mountains. We both have the consciousness that we can always go somewhere, we are not hemmed in, we need not be cautious. We are careless, easygoing, loving our jokes and songs. True, the Chinese have existed for so long that they have achieved a naturalism toward which we are still struggling. Ernest Hemingway did much for us in daring to be abruptly naturalistic toward life, and in writing pure naturalism. It was a revolution for the American mind, at first a shock and then an adoration, but to anyone brought up in the Chinese common tradition there is neither shock nor adoration, nothing indeed very new in what is simply a truthfulness, limited only by individual taste. Thus I had since childhood seen as everyday sights and events the life between man and woman, birth and death, starvation and feasting, disease and health, beggary and wealth, superstition, hypocrisy and religion. Superstitions have always interested me, especially, as the unconscious revelations of inner fears and hopes, and it was amusing to discover among the Pennsylvania Dutch farmers of our region many of the same superstitions that I had found among Chinese farm families. I find, too, the same literal and rather casual attitude toward deity. And how it is I do not know, but in the castlelike museum of our county seat, an inspired monstrosity built by one of our local great men—and I say monstrosity because I have never seen another such building, and inspired because there is something beautiful about it and we are proud of it—anyone can see the extraordinary likeness between the tools the early Pennsylvanians used and the tools which the Chinese used and do still use. Our great man saw the likeness and sent his own explorer to China to bring back the evidence, and there it is, and I am not imagining it.

Green Hills Farm

Here are our people at their best. It is two weeks before Christmas of this year, and the weather has turned suddenly cold. I know how cold it is, for when I get up in the morning I always look from my open window into the stone courtyard to see how the rhododendrons are. This morning at six o'clock their leaves were curled tight in little rolls and the hoarfrost upon them was like snow. When I came down to breakfast my good friend in the kitchen told me that during the night a little wooden house on the other side of our hill, which sheltered man, woman and nine children, the youngest seven months and the eldest eighteen years, had burned to the ground and everything with it, including the Christmas gifts. What will they do? Neighbors have taken them in and will keep them until the house can be built again. And when will it be built? Immediately! All the contractors hereabouts and their workmen are beginning at once on the building and they will have a roof on it and equipment enough for living before Christmas. Our whole community, which can be as quarrelsome and divided over certain issues as any in the world, has united instantly in time of need for one of its families. There was never a more generous or spontaneously unselfish people than the Americans, and this same spirit would work, I am sure, if it had the freedom and the knowledge, anywhere in the world. It is said abroad that we Americans are wonderful in an emergency but that we have no sustaining power and never carry through to the end of a problem. This is often true, for we are easily diverted and are swept by many winds of opinion. It is also true that we grow quickly impatient when we detect signs that those whom we help do not also help themselves. I like, nevertheless, on this cold morning with

Christmas on the near horizon, to remember the new house springing from the ashes.

There are many qualities that I like about my neighbors. For example, on the day, now nineteen years ago, when there was something difficult to tell and so we wanted to tell it ourselves. What would our quiet farm community and the little village a mile away over the bridge think of us when they knew that our house was not to be only my house but was to be a family home for a new family, after two divorces were made?

I shrank from the telling and so the man took on the task. He said to our kindly neighbor, who was also the perfect plumber and so continued until his death last year:

"We want you to know, and perhaps you will tell the others, that we have a very difficult experience ahead of us, and we undertake it only out of the deepest conviction that it is right for us. We are getting divorces and plan to be married and live here. We hope you will understand."

The plumber was peering into some recess in the cellar and he came out, dusted his hands together and then held out his right one. "Don't you worry," he said. "It's none of our business. What you are is all we'll care about."

He said this exactly as though he were talking plumbing, with the same slow friendliness and detachment, and when I heard it my roots took a deep plunge down into the earth beneath my feet. This was where I could live.

I packed my bags soon after that and took the long journey westward to a small city named Reno in the beautiful Western state of Nevada, and there settled myself to the strangest six weeks of my existence. I had plenty of time, for I discovered the first day that I could not work at my writing. Everything was too strange, place and situation and people, but mainly the situation, and I had only my decision to stand upon. That was sure and long considered and unchangeable. Yet how persuade the hours to pass, especially as I had by now observed the insatiable need for news in the reporters whose ears were already stretched to windward? I did not blame them, for I had already learned that newspaper reporters are the most tolerant of persons and have less personal curiosity than any other human group. If they are relentless it is because they have their bread to earn, and twenty years ago a divorce was still news. See how we have grown since then! Last week I read in the back pages of a great New York daily a small paragraph stating in dignified terms that a certain well-known man, a high official in the government, had been granted a divorce from his wife. What progress!

We have caught up with the Chinese gentleman who, when Chiang Kai-shek divorced three wives at the moment when he was rising to his first height, still said that it was only "private business."

Twenty years ago we Americans were not so advanced and my dread was not of the six weeks of isolation, for I can always find diversion and I had the companionship of my future mother-in-law, with whom I was entirely congenial and in whose approval I basked. No, larger almost than happiness was the day of abhorrent publicity which I knew that I could not avoid. Reflecting, however, that since I could not escape it, and that there was no need of living it every day before it arrived, I determined to enjoy my enforced stay and learn as much as I could about the Western corner of my country.

After consultation with a lawyer, who made a specialty of such business and performed it with astonishing suavity and ease, I took his advice and settled myself comfortably in the biggest hotel in town, where nobody would expect me to be, and then cast about to find out how I could learn about Nevada. My eyes at that moment fell upon a card under the glass top of the bureau in my bedroom. It announced Madame Kolak, who was prepared to take pounds from any human frame by the most modern methods. Ah, I thought, and why not from my frame? Here was something to show results, even if I could not work at my novel then in progress. I was sixteen pounds above my college weight, and I would take all those pounds from my bones. I called upon the telephone for Madame Kolak and heard a large husky voice reply. Yes, she would come, that day at twelve. Sixteen pounds in six weeks? Yes, if I would help with diet and exercise. I would, and so the bargain was made.

At twelve o'clock I heard a heavy knock upon the door. I opened it and fell back, stupefied. The largest woman I had ever seen stood there in the doorway, not only tall but broad. That is, she was fat, very fat. Her big square face wore no make-up, her hair was drawn straight back and she loomed like a snow-covered mountain in her white uniform.

"Come in," I said faintly.

She came in, very businesslike, and snatched off an untrimmed battered straw hat. "Lay down," she said in the husky telephone voice. "If it hurts, tell me."

I lay down on the bed, and pulling up her sleeves she proceeded to batter the flesh from my resisting skeleton. The method is familiar and doubtless has improved in the years since, for I see many women far slimmer than I was able to stay. What I remember is not the process nor even the hateful dieting, for Madame Kolak put me at once upon

320

a vegetable soup of her own recipe, making me promise to eat nothing whatever except five large cups a day of the watery stew. She told me afterwards that she would not have been so severe except that she supposed of course I would cheat as her ladies "most always did." I never thought of cheating, having been reared to severe honesty when my word was given, and so I starved myself heroically—too thoroughly, alas, as I was afterwards to discover, for during the next year I had to combat a protein deficiency which all but wrecked me for a while, and undid most of our combined efforts, she coming twice a day to pound, and I exercising rigorously between her hours and swallowing the abominable soup.

What I remember clearly now is the incomparable character, Madame Kolak. She was the very embodiment of the American West. She had always lived there, she dabbled in gold mines, she had ridden—in the days when she could still hoist herself on a horse—all through the desert, and she loved it. Sometimes when she was pounding away and both of us were dripping with sweat, she of effort and I of endurance, she would close her eyes and say something like this—

"You know what I saw once? I was ridin' home from a gold mine. It was night but there was a moon, shinin' soft-like. And ahead of me was a little lake, maybe not more than a big pool. An' you know what I see? Nine white horses, drinkin' at the pool, and with 'em a coal-black stallion. Wild horses—"

She smiled, her eyes closed, and we both gazed at those horses drinking from a pool in the moonlight, nine white horses and a coal-black stallion.

"Do you mind," she said one day, while she screwed a pound from my right hip, "if I call my new mine *The Good Earth?* It might bring me luck."

She had not, I surmised, much luck with her mines except for endless excitement and outdoor pleasure. And in those exacerbating days she shared with me, she explained the countryside and the city as well, she described the nature of rattlesnakes, she named the wild flowers, and she told me, bit by bit, the history of the region through the drama of her own life. It was she who whetted me to the point of wandering about the streets of the fabulous derelict, Virginia City, so that, undernourished though I was, I became familiar not only with its present, but with its incredible past.

Twice a day she weighed me, I would not have dared to show less than the prescribed loss. She granted me a reward about halfway through, when I dreaded going on and yet could not bear to give up.

"When you get down to the bottom," she said, "I'm goin' to take you around to the fancy gamblin' places. We'll dress up and I'll bring my husband dressed up and we'll go to all the swell joints."

And so we did on the last memorable night, when, my evening gown hanging on my emaciated frame, I waited for Madame and her husband. They telephoned from the lobby and I went down and there she stood, immense and handsome as the Rock of Gibraltar in a long black satin gown of indeterminate style but massively décolleté and with plenty of shining stones. With her was a trim neat man, rather small, whom I recognized from her descriptions. He was Mr. Kolak. We had a wonderful evening. She urged me to eat all I wanted and was pleased when I wanted very little, my stomach having been properly shrunk. We went to half a dozen places and she, not at all shrunken, ate everywhere and very generously and recommended the wines, and the waiters all knew her and called her "the Duchess." She did, as a matter of fact, look like the Duchess in *Alice in Wonderland,* only a good-natured one and much broader. I went to bed exhausted, although she was fresh as ever, and prepared for the next day, which was the dreadful one when the news would break, and the man would arrive.

And then how maddening it was when he did arrive to have him stare at me with unappreciative eyes, although a very pretty white silk suit had been fitted to my thin figure only the week before, taken in, as Madame said proudly, "inches," and how many I have mercifully forgotten! I had kept the whole process from him to be a delightful surprise, and now he looked peevish. "This is not what I bargained for," he said or something like that, and then stubbornly, "I liked you the way you were."

"I'll be that way again, doubtless," I said gloomily.

Then we laughed. It was a glorious day, the greatest day of our lives, a day, to be sure, which we had both tried to prevent for several years, under the conviction that divorce was horrible, which it had been, and that furthermore nothing was more unfortunate for a publisher than marrying an author and vice versa, thus mixing business with everyday life—and this, thanks be, has been proved not true.

I have heard marriage argued from two contrary points of view, the one that it is wiser for opposites to marry, the other that there should be common interests, hobbies and vacations. My life has proved, for me, at least, the latter point of view. Observing the similar marriages of others, I add this caution—that cooperation and not competition must be the watchword.

Madame Kolak of course had her share in the day, after the court process was over. She and I had escaped reporters through a back exit while they waited on the front steps with poised cameras. We went

322

straight to the back garden of a parsonage where my mother-in-law was waiting for us, and there Madame Kolak and her husband were witnesses to a small quiet wedding. After it was over she handed to the bridegroom a basket which she said was our picnic supper and which later proved delectable in every detail that evening beside Lake Tahoe. But, best of all, when we were in the car and trying to drive away from the parsonage Madame Kolak stood in the middle of the road like a wall and prevented an avalanche of reporters in cars, cameras still poised, from running us down. While she stood placidly outspread, we escaped.

For years after that day Madame Kolak sent to me at Christmastime two large fruitcakes of her own making, one dark, one light, showing her tolerance in the matter of weight and certainly helping to undo all our joint labors. During the war such cakes became impossible and communication ceased between us, for Madame Kolak found letters difficult. Alas, only the other day a woman who had also been to Reno, said, "Did you know Madame Kolak? Oh, my dear, she's dead!" And together we mourned our friend.

The attitude toward divorce has changed somewhat in the many years since I knew Madame Kolak, and slowly our laws and prejudices are coming nearer to the realities of life. This humanizing process would have been more rapid except for the violations of taste and principle on the part of the few who have made of monogamy a progressive polygamy, and, as elsewhere, the outrageous behavior of a few has compelled restrictions upon all. But modern psychology is moving toward the perception that it is impossible to insist that two people remain together physically when communication of mind and heart has proved impossible. Indeed, no law can compel the frantic creature to remain in this prison far more horrible than iron bars and a locked gate. I hope it is not selfish of me now to say, upon long reflection, that I believe one divorce should always be socially and morally accepted as the acknowledgment of a mistake, perhaps merely youthful, but that the second divorce should be made very difficult indeed and that a third should be taken as evidence of lack of seriousness or as proof that the individual should not marry at all, since it becomes obvious that he, or she, is unable to be happy in marriage. There are persons who cannot for temperamental reasons be close to another human being, and to such the marriage relationship is impossible for long.

The condition known generally as incompatibility, or "mental cruelty," has been delicately and devastatingly portrayed by John Galsworthy in *The Forsyte Saga*. There Soames Forsyte, the irreproachable, the successful businessman, whose character as it is revealed has its profoundly moving aspects, but who is simply unlovable for inescapable and yet indescribable reasons, cannot understand why his wife, Irene, does not love him. He has heaped her with gifts, he adores her with terrifying singleness of heart, and though we never hear Irene's side of the story from her own lips, yet we feel the loathing she cannot utter, and we imagine the dreadful midnight scene to which she is compelled again and again, and from which she cannot escape. She spends her days in waiting for her husband to go out, and he knows it, and it is the genius of Galsworthy that we pity Soames and we do not blame him, for he is what he is, and yet we know why Irene cannot love him. We comprehend that love cannot be compelled, for in a woman sensitive and of quick intelligence, and with a dreaming heart, the flesh is not separate from mind and heart. The three are one, and cannot be divided from their whole. When this is understood, and perhaps only the sensitive and the warmhearted and the intelligent can understand it, then there is no cause for condemnation or forgiveness. And it is to be remembered that sometimes it is the man who is the sensitive and intelligent and warmhearted one, and then it is he who must escape or die.

For me a house without children cannot be a home. I do not know why the people who love children are so often prevented by accident from having them, but, God be thanked, there are many who have children and leave them, for one reason or another, and then others can take them for love's sake. My friend, Margaret Sanger, has served humanity well in beginning the great work of birth control, but for honesty I have always made it clear that my devotion is to her as a woman and not to her cause, and this is not that I do not believe her right, for of course she is when it comes to populations. In my case, however, it would be hypocritical to speak for the cause of birth control when other women, without such restraint, have given me wonderful children.

When the house, then, was finished in its first stage, the rose garden planted, a small swimming pool dug under the shade of the big black walnut tree, we approached our one adopted child, then eleven years old, and asked her what she thought of our adopting two little boys as soon as possible, and then a year or so later, a girl and a boy. She reflected for some weeks and then months, and we gave her plenty of time, and when she felt adjusted to her new home, she decided that it would be "nice" to have babies. The three of us then proceeded to an excellent adoptive agency and made ourselves known and began the process necessary to prove ourselves good parents and a "nice" family. It did not take too long in those days, the process was courteous and civilized, and in due course the big third-floor bedroom became a nursery, but without a nurse, for we wanted to take care of the two lively babies ourselves. A year and a half later they were joined by a small but equally lively boy and girl, each a few weeks old.

That was eighteen years ago. The four of them are now in late adolescence and are all but over the last even of that. In the rich years between the day they came home and today I have kept myself abreast of developing adoptive practices as well as a layman can, and have taken an active part as a member on the boards of three adoptive agencies. My interest in this subject is far more than personal. I doubt I am a good mother in the old-fashioned "mom" sense. I love children from the moment they are born until they die of old age on their way to a hundred. The newborn child is to me first a human being and only second a baby. I am not a peasant mother—that is, not an instinctive one. I do not wish to mother the world. I am not infinitely maternal. But I have enjoyed being a mother to my children.

Aside from this, my deep belief is that all human creatures deserve a happy childhood as a right and as a prerequisite to normal adulthood, and that the first essential to happiness is love. I have observed that if a child does not have a wholehearted love from and for someone before he is five years old he is emotionally stunted perhaps for the rest of his life. That is, he is unable to love anyone wholeheartedly and is to that extent deprived of a full life. This loving and beloved person is hopefully father or mother or both, but lacking these, a kindhearted maid or nurse or grandmother will do, but it should be someone who has the physical care of him, so that through the daily washing and dressing and feeding and play he feels the pervading and continuing presence of love. It has to be real love. The professional coddling that a trained nurse or attendant gives a baby in a foundling home or hospital does not fool even the baby. It takes more than a clock-watching employee to make a child feel secure. It is amazing how discerning a baby can be. A child in the care of a good but unloving foster mother soon sinks into impassivity and begins to fade. Love is the sunshine of his growing soul, and when there is no sun, the soul stops and body and mind begin to lag. That is why children in orphanages and boarding homes look dull and are either too silent or too noisy. Babies used to be kept in hordes in orphanages until it was discovered how quickly they died of nothing at all, apparently. Of course they died for lack of true love.

I hardly know where to begin with the many things I want to say about American children. In the first place, I feel that they are the least happy children in the world, outside the war-torn countries, and the unhappiness concentrates in the homeless children, those born outside wedlock and those orphaned and deserted. Next to the segregations and degradation of the Negro in our society I was shocked to discover the way in which our homeless children are cared for, the heartlessness of our methods, the callousness of those to whom the children may be entrusted. I want to say even before this how cruel it is that there are so many homeless children. In the China in which I grew up there were no children born out of wedlock. Perhaps there were a very few but I never saw them or heard of them. If a man wanted a woman and a child was to be born she came into his house as a secondary wife and the child had a family and a surname, and his position was legitimate. At least the child was not punished for the passions of his parents. Children were valued above all else and love was poured out on them however they were born. They were humored and played with and they went everywhere with the family. If parents died, the larger family treasured the child and took the place of the parents, and thus no child was orphaned.

True, there were horrible abuses. Children were sometimes sold into slavery, though, as I have said elsewhere, usually to save their lives in famine time. True, there were individuals who were wicked enough to pander to the white slave trade; true, girl babies were killed at birth sometimes because the head of the family did not want them, or could not care for the extra mouth.

Yet the Chinese are always as shocked as I was, when they find that living newborn children in our country can be abandoned to strangers. Oh, the countless little American children who are left with agencies and in institutions, sometimes for adoption, sometimes just left and visited once or twice a year, or never visited and yet never relinquished! Where are the grandparents, if the parents have disappeared, and where are the aunts and the uncles and the cousins? The child belongs to them, too, and in China they would have kept the child with them. Here, alas, we have no longer the large family feeling that shares responsibility for all its members. It is the child in our society who bears the brunt of the fragmentation of our family life. I was talking the other day with Madame Pandit of India, and I begged her to see to it, as far as she could, that the family system of Asia is not lost as her country modernizes itself. She replied that her people are beginning to recognize the value of their ancient system. And how much it saves the people in taxes! There need be no orphanages, no old people's homes, no institutions for the blind, the insane and the mentally retarded. Yes, my Chinese friends felt it cruel also to put such helpless persons in the care of strangers, and I agree with them. I have visited many institutions and I have seen good employees and bad, but most of them are neither good nor bad. They are unloving, and that is the most cruel of all.

We need therefore to reconsider the whole basis of family life. Since it is obvious that we cannot change our system to one like the Asian, where the generations live together, not usually under one roof, but in small separate houses connected by courtyards, and where each generation is responsible in turn for all the others, we ought nevertheless to make it impossible for the child to be deserted for any reason whatsoever. Certainly the child should not be forced to bear the entire burden of the illegitimate action of the parents. An American man has no responsibility for his child born out of wedlock, unless forced to pay something for its maintenance if paternity is proved. He has none of the blame, he has none of the emotional burden. The mother bears all that. She can retire to a secret place for a while, unknown to her friends, give birth and leave the newborn child to an adoptive agency, and return again to her former position. But the child is the one whose whole life is changed by the fact of his birth. The child is the one who has to find a new place, new parents, a new home among strangers. Sometimes he is carelessly placed by a doctor or a friend or by some relative. The chances are as much against him as for him. Sometimes he grows up in an orphanage where the vested interests of employees, churches and welfare organizations keep him a prisoner without chance of adoption. A well-run orphanage where the children grow up clean and obedient is a wonderful show place. I cannot bear to go into an orphanage. What I see is not the clean faces, the good clothing, no uniforms any more—we have advanced so far—I see only the children's eyes, their wistful looks, the strange still patience, or the belligerence that hides a breaking childish heart.

What about the adoption agencies? Their function is to get children adopted. Alas, they are too often so involved in their professional standards, their lists of questions, their self-interest, that sometimes I fear more children are prevented from finding homes than are ever placed by them. I find a long delay in the boarding homes, far too long. Children ought to go as quickly as possible from birth mother to adoptive parents. Let us say that sometimes this speed would mean a mistake. Even so, I believe, the damage would not amount in total to that which the long delay now causes. There is a fearful lag in the average adoption agency. Workers put in their eight hours a day faithfully enough, I daresay, but far too much of it is spent at paper work and filing and red tape, and this is made necessary to some extent, I know, by the differing and even exclusive laws of the individual states. A child is often limited to one state or one area in chances for adoption, each agency serving only an area without possibility of interchange between areas, and again the child bears the brunt of his sad condition. He continues to wait upon laws and professionalism and bureaucracy. And the prospective adoptive parents wait, eating their hearts out, anxious lest the delay is because they do not measure up to some perfectionist demand of the social worker, that the "matching" in religion or race is not perfect, that the house is not quite big enough, that one bathroom is insufficient, that the father is not a college graduate, or that he is a college graduate, that their marriage is not perfect in its adjustment and security, that they themselves are not perfect but only ordinary human beings.

And the boarding home where the baby waits? There he is probably one of several, all waiting for adoption or else a mixture of the family's own children and the boarding children. Let us bear in mind the significant fact that boarding mothers make money by caring for homeless children. It is true that nearly always they are kind good women, but they are also nearly always ignorant women, not at all suitable for adoptive mothers, and the social worker would not consider them so. Yet the social worker leaves the child there for an indefinite period, seeming to think that because the boarding home is an approved and licensed one, the child is doing well. Meanwhile, during the first months of a child's life, the all-important months, he is without a real mother. For no boarding mother can take the place of the adoptive mother any more than she takes the place of the natural mother. Moreover, I have often found that while an agency may be an excellent one, its supervisor enlightened and well meaning, the social workers all graduates of the best schools, the pediatrician skilled, yet none of this guarantees the child anything. The child has to live in the boarding home alone without any of these officials present. The boarding mother receives from the doctor, for example, a diet list and instructions. More likely than not, being ignorant, and often the mother of many children dead and living, she puts the list in a drawer, saying that she reckons she knows how to take care of a kid, after all she has raised—or lost—so many. And the child is fed noodles and macaroni instead of meat and vegetables and fresh fruits. It is only human nature to save money if possible. And starch fattens a baby and makes a nice show, does it not? And the marvel to me is that many professional social workers know so little about children. They seem not able to see the difference between firm healthy muscular flesh and flabby fat. But too many social workers have never married and have no children of their own to teach them. To my thinking one who works with babies or little children should not be without experience in the daily care of a baby. Even being married is not always enough. There has to be the loving heart.

Yet it seems that the loving heart is the one possession which the social worker is taught to avoid as the disqualifying possession for a professional. Social workers must be "detached." And this is the basic stupidity, for how can one have the right to care for children and place their destinies if one is "detached?" I understand very well what is meant by the term. Emotional clinging to a child is, we are told, the great sin. The social worker must act like God, who pours down rain upon the just and the unjust with equal indifference. A child must therefore simply be a case, "a referral," if you please, and it is very important to have just the right terminology, if you are a social worker, so that other social workers will know that you belong to the gang. The profession is becoming a hiding place for small people, too timid to break petty rules and come out for the great principles of child life. And the greatest of these and the first commandment is love. Everybody who comes near a child or who influences the life of a child in any way, must be capable of love, a love so generous that every child is dear, and every child is a valuable treasure. I have known social workers by the score, and once in a while I do meet one who is right, a warmhearted, generous, loving woman—always a woman, so far—and always one who has known great personal love, given and returned. When I find this one, I sit down and we talk, and she tells me what she thinks and I tell her what I think, and what we think is the same. It is my considered opinion that the whole profession of social workers needs cleaning out, and a new start made. And as I write these words my conscience smites me, for I know a social worker who is sent from heaven in mercy to lost children, and I have the joy of working with her in Welcome House. She is no longer young, and though she has been to schools of social work and knows the rules and laws and jargon, she has forgotten all except the understanding of a little child and what sort of parents he needs, and she has a heart of love and a mind of wisdom, and with these sacred lamps, she searches and finds the parents for the child, and the child for the parents. She is the blessed exception to every rule, and because of her I know there must be many like her, working quietly and doggedly and devotedly in far more places than I know.

I do not say that social workers as a profession are insincere or wilfully cruel or even selfish—not that at all. On the contrary, they are for the most part too conscientious, too careful, too critical—and too self-conscious. They are perfectionists in a far from perfect situation. They complain because doctors and friends and relatives place children for adoption, they give instances, true, I am sure, of misplacements, but they ignore the damage their own failure to solve the problem does to the waiting child, or the "unadoptable" child.

I believe there is no unadoptable child. There are always parents to be found for every child. People need education to help them to accept the so-called "unadoptable" child, but there are always people to be educated, although not all people can be educated, but as it is now, again the child is the one punished for parental unreadiness. Sometimes I have even found in professional social workers a strange hostility toward the adoptive parents. I doubt they know it, but some of them do have it, and the adoptive parents feel it, even when they are approved. It may be the unconscious jealousy of a lonely woman who can never have a child. I have also seen the same strange jealousy in men social workers who are homosexual. Certainly they would deny it, the more hotly if they have it, and will not recognize it.

The social worker has, indeed, a power over human lives which demands a largeness seldom found. She—or he—sits in judgment upon two people, weighing them, examining them, peering into their private lives, and it is this social worker who decides whether or not they shall have a baby. Even God has not such power. Any man and woman who come together, whether they are fit parents or not, may bring a child to life. The child comes according to the law of nature, and if detachment is wanted, here it is. No questions asked, but if healthy people copulate, they have children. But the couple, denied children and wanting a baby more than all else, who submit to the perfectionist's process, are frightened to offend the almighty lest they be refused the joy they long for and to which they are usually entitled.

It will be seen by now that I am angry. I acknowledge it. I have seen too much. I have gone too deep. And I find that it is harder to adopt a child nowadays, thanks to the development of the profession of social work, than it was twenty-eight years ago, when I found my little daughter, or eighteen years ago when our blessed Big Four came home. And I doubt that my husband and I would have passed at all nowadays, as adoptive parents, and certainly we would not have been given more than one child. Yes, the professional gods actually parcel out the children, saying that it is not "fair" for one family to have two children when others have none. What validity the argument might have is destroyed when one visits the orphanages. One such orphanage I know has exactly three hundred children.

"Why exactly three hundred?" I inquired of my guide.

"We are required to have a minimum of three hundred in order to receive our full quota of funds," she replied honestly but without understanding the frightful import of her words.

And I remember the day when a little timid woman, herself a social worker, stole into my office in New York City. She had come from another state to tell me that something had to be done for the children there, because twenty-seven children in an institution or in boarding homes constituted a job and salary for a social worker, and therefore too many of these workers did not want to free the children for adoption, since it meant finding other children to replace the ones adopted.

"I keep seeing their little faces," she said. "Please, can't you do something?"

I could not. The mountain I could not move, for in that state it was imbedded in the corruptions of political life. And so I am glad we began our family before the latter-day social workers had a chance at us, for we have had a glorious life with our children, making plenty of mistakes with them, I am sure, and losing patience on a grand scale occasionally, and they with us, but we have had a glorious time nevertheless, and thank God for every minute of it.

We need social workers, if by that we mean persons devoted to the happiness of children. In a society like ours, where children can be easily lost and ill-treated, there must be organized care for them. But the organization must be watched and criticized continually and rebelled against individually and collectively by those concerned and by the lay public, or else the organization becomes a vested interest. And when children are property, then we have slavery as real as anywhere in the world. The lay mind must always remain in control of the professional, exactly as the civilian mind must remain in control of the military, for once the organization takes over, danger looms. The professional is the specialist, employed to advise and to perform but always under the supervision of the lay mind, for the specialist is too narrow, and made so by his education, to be also the administrator. This is the basic principle upon which alone the citizens of a democracy are safe. For the curse of the professional in any walk of life is his perfectionism. It is all very well to want to be perfect but such heights are achieved only after due process, and the purpose fails if there is such delay that people grow impatient. I read much of the black market in babies, and certainly I do not approve it, but I know the black market in any commodity exists and flourishes only when the proper sources of supply are inadequate for the demand. It is ideal to complete a perfect adoption, taking time to prepare both child and parents, so that one child has a good home and every chance for happiness. But what of all the other children growing too old in the boarding home or orphanage while the one is being perfectly placed, so that many lost children never find adoption?

This is an old war of mine, this war against perfectionism in an imperfect world. I used to fight it in China against the American doctors and the Western-trained Chinese doctors. While millions of people died of preventable disease and millions more went blind from trachoma, the doctors went on with their high professional standards. That is, anyone who practiced medicine must be a graduate physician. But there were few who could be graduates, it was too expensive and there were too few medical schools. To go abroad was prohibitive indeed. I used to argue—why do we need such high training for everybody? Why not train field workers who could give quinine for malaria, treat ulcers and wounds, swab eyelids for trachoma, yet who could realize when a malady was beyond their knowledge? These serious cases could be sent to a medical center and if there too the illness was too grave sent still further to a central hospital. It would mean that the time of highly paid expensive professionals would not be spent upon familiar diseases, easily recognizable, and best of all it would mean people were being cured.

But no, I was told, this was the absurd idea of a layman. I am now enduring considerable secret agony when I hear that the Communists in China are doing exactly what I had hoped could be done by our earlier professionals, and are getting full credit for it. The manner in which a job is done is certainly very important, and the methods should be the best possible. I put only one aim above it—to get the job done, for if one group fails to accomplish it, another group will take over. In the United States the black market in babies flourishes and will flourish, in spite of efforts to control it, until the supply meets the demand. Human nature always prevails.

One personal note I insert here. When I bought the house which became a home for me and mine, my dear elder brother bought the small stone house across the brook. If we stepped out of our front doors together we could wave across the hills. It was our comfortable dream that after being separated all our lives, for he had left our Chinese home for college at fifteen, when I was only four, we could live the rest of our lives side by side. We were still peculiarly congenial, friends as well as relatives. And I think of him here, because I remember how he laughed when we showed him our first two baby boys, then six weeks old! He loved babies and he had a magic with them. I have seen him on a train lift from a mother's arms a fretful crying baby whom he had never seen before and talking gently and half humorously persuade the little thing to quiet contemplation of his kind face, and then to sleep. I could see the adoring uncle in him when he looked at his tiny new nephews and then he decided immediately that since we were spending the winter in New York, only weekending in the country, the babies must have his sun lamp. He was then at the height of his distinguished career in vital statistics and health work, sought in various countries for his wise advice, yet he found time from his busy offices in Wall Street to get the lamp to us that very day.

The next morning he was stricken with a coronary thrombosis as he was about to go to a meeting of his board of directors, and without recovering consciousness he died that day, and with him went our dream.

I have kept his little ancient house all these years, completing its restoration as he had planned and using it to house friends from far countries who needed a home for a while, before moving on.

And while I think of those early years when we still lived in New York and only weekended here at Green Hills, let me remember, too, the kindly men who helped us convey four little children up and down eighteen floors to our apartment. I had been told that children are not welcome in New York apartments but I have not found it true. There was never a complaint when twice a week the doormen and elevator men helped two little boys and two babies into cars and out of them. Once when I spoke my thanks a cheerful elevator man replied, "Shure, ma'am, we'd rather have kiddies than dogs in the house."

And once, I remember, when my husband had left us at his downtown office and had turned over the car full of children and nurse to me, I was stopped at the crossing by the immense policeman at our corner. And oh, dear, I thought, what have I done now? For I was never the best of drivers, being congenitally absent-minded, but the policeman held us there with the flat of his hand against us, while traffic came and went, and the babies began to show signs of hunger. On the second red light, while the cars waited like crouching tigers, he sauntered over to us and leaned amiably into the open window behind me.

"I just wanted to see how the kids are doin'," he explained.

Then he waved us on.

And why do I speak gratefully of elevator men and policemen, and not of the one above all men? For three years of babies my husband, halfway on our way to New York or halfway home, stopped at a way-side diner to heat bottles of milk for those hungry babies of ours. The diner man got to know us well and he took vast interest in the twice-a-week event. But what I remember is my husband's affectionate half-humorous patience as he brought back two bottles of warm milk to insert them gently into the waiting mouths.

When at times I tend to grow impatient with my fellow Americans, and I am only impatient when it comes to large world affairs, at which it seems to me we are still rather stupid, I remember the infinite goodness of my fellow citizens, taken one by one, and the personal kindnesses of daily living, over the years.

During the forty years I lived in China I had kept myself aware of what was going on in the rest of the world, and especially in my own country. I had learned from childhood to recognize the peoples of the earth as members of one family, known or unknown, and had realized the practical meaning of this Chinese view of the globe, first instilled into me by Mr. Kung, as history unrolled before me, enfolding me as it went. So now, living the second half of my life in the United States, I keep close touch with what is going on in China, the country that I have left, and yet which will always be a part of me, in spite of the fact that I am *persona non grata* to the Communists at present in control.

In 1938, therefore, although I was living deeply in my peaceful American farmhouse, I was still close to my other country. Ten years had passed since Chiang Kai-shek set up his government in the old Ming capital of Nanking. They had been difficult years for him and his government, and four severe floods with the inevitable famines following, and one severe drought, had made them no easier. The depression that wrought such havoc with the American people had been, far more than we realized, a world depression, and China in 1933 had all but succumbed to her share of it. Yet the government had pulled through disasters, and in some ways had made progress. The Communists were steadily beaten back into the Northwest, and one province and leader after another gave allegiance to the new Central Government, as it was now called. Anti-Western slogans were dying down, and the influence of the Western-trained officials was growing stronger. Chinese businessmen were eager to increase trade with Western countries, and experts in industry, road making, and scientific research were invited to China to give their advice. An air service was begun and one could fly from the North to the South, from East to West. Many westerners were surprised to see how readily China took to modern modes of travel, but that was because they did not understand the literal and practical nature of the Chinese, who are always ready to improve themselves. It was amusing, even in the days when I was still living in China, to see a stout businessman, his clean extra garments in a small pigskin trunk, mount as confidently into an airplane as he had once climbed into a riksha. Railways, greatly increased, made it possible to travel by train from the coast to as far west as Sian-fu in Shensi. Motor roads were built and buses in various stages of collapse and disrepair bumped along their way into the interior and back again to the ports, although private cars still belonged only to the very rich and to government officials. Perhaps the most notable contributions of the Western-trained Chinese were in the area of roads and railways. The weakness of the young government, however, was still in its remoteness from the peasants who, it must always be remembered, were eighty-five percent of the population. Motor roads and even railroads did not benefit them, and taxes steadily increased. Central control still did not reach far beyond the large cities, and local bullies, in the posts of officialdom, too often exacted levies as they liked. For the peasant there were no courts of appeal. To maintain an enormously increased officialdom he groaned under fresh burdens.

Behind Chiang Kai-shek and his government, however, were the Chinese bankers of the port cities, mainly Shanghai. In spite of the slogans of anti-foreignism upon which the Nationalist government rose to power, the fact is that this government owes more to westerners than it has ever been willing to acknowledge and some of it was because of the treaty ports, where in concessions guarded by Western police and soldiers, the banks and treasuries could be maintained in safety. There, too, the bankers and their families were safe, their children educated in Western schools. The sons of Chinese bankers and other rich men did indeed become the vanguard of a national movement toward Westernism, and through them much of the old Chinese tradition was dying. Young men, growing up in the cosmopolitan cities of Shanghai and Tientsin, wore Western clothes and went to Western dance halls where the hostesses were not only lovely Chinese girls in their slim gowns fashioned on Western lines, but French girls and beautiful White Russians, and even a few English and Americans were available to all alike. A modern theater movement flourished in those cities, and such stars as the Chinese Butterfly Wu, vying with pretty Janet Gaynor of Hollywood, the favorite American star, made motion picture theaters everyday pleasures. Young couples began to want "small family" homes instead of living in the traditional manner with the clan, and much of the literature one read in Chinese magazines and books of the period had to do with the sorrows of young lovers parted from each other by family betrothals. It became acceptable for a man, married by his family, to leave his wife in the ancestral home in the country and to take another wife of his own choosing for his business life in the city. The Chinese is always able to accommodate his principles to the needs of the hour, and for this reason, more than any other, there was never a clean-cut, thoroughgoing revolution in China, let it be said, as there was in Russia. New *mores* developed, but never abruptly. Even the houses changed, and instead of the graceful old dwellings of the past, conforming to landscape, hideous square two-story structures sprang up to mar the ancient Chinese scene. It became fashionable among the modern-minded to be Western in all possible ways, and the effect was often distressing indeed.

Such news and much more reached me here in my pleasant Pennsylvania home, and in the letters of my Chinese friends I read of so many changes—many, it seemed, for the good—that I began to wonder if indeed it had been necessary to leave my childhood land. Not that I regretted the choice—I was entirely happy in my own country, and was already absorbed in the daily discovery of its life, its people, and its manners. But I remembered what my Chinese friends had said when I left. "Go back to your country and discover your ancestors, for this is good," they had told me. "But when you are old, you will come back to us." I had denied this in my heart, for I felt if I left China for the reasons that I had, then I would never return. Yet could I resist? Sometimes I wondered. China was the ideal country for the old, a pleasant place where one achieved honor merely by growing old. How often had I come upon a village, anywhere in China, to find sitting outside the door on a bench at the edge of the threshing floor, a comfortably dressed old man or woman, dozing in the sun, pipe in hand, idle without reproach, loved and cared for and made much of, merely because he or she was old! Old people were treasures and no one was afraid to grow old. When an aged one spoke the others listened, eager for the wisdom of his accumulated years.

It had been a shock to discover how differently the old are treated in my own country, and how pathetically they try to hide the number of their years and pretend themselves still strong and able to do a full day's work. Worse almost than the injustice to homeless children was it to find white-haired parents and grandparents in old people's homes and even in mental institutions, often without mental illness beyond the gentle and harmless decay of age. I suppose that the uncertainty of economic life and the insecurity of the individual alone in his struggle to maintain himself, his wife and children, make thoughtful tenderness too rare between young and old in our country. The aging feel their children's dread and they try to care for themselves and are guilty if they cannot, and so the generations pull apart in a mutual fear which stifles natural love.

I listened not long ago to the conversation of a good elderly man who had for many years been the head of a local bank. He took an interest in an old men's home in a nearby city, and he told me how the superintendent of this old men's home would find upon a doorstep in the early morning an old man left there by son or daughter, abandoned and under injunction not to reveal his family's name. Yes, this happens.

Yet somehow our society must make it right and possible for old people not to fear the young or be deserted by them, for the test of a civilization is in the way that it cares for its helpless members. Thus when Hitler began to destroy the old, I knew that his regime could not last in a civilized world. It was an anachronism, and the laws of human evolution would provide its end—and how quickly did that end come!

To return, however—what might have happened in China had Japan not chosen this hour to enlarge her dream of empire no one can tell. Chiang Kai-shek had not counted upon the speed of Japan's advance and he had continued his policy of internal pacification, encouraged by its seeming success. One by one the provinces had aligned themselves with his government as he drove the Communists to the northwest corner of the country. True, the Communists had set up a rival government there, independent from the rest of China, small but enough to irritate Chiang Kai-shek, determined as he was to unify the country politically. He decided in December, 1936, to make one last march against them, using as his base the city of Sian in Shensi, and as his army local soldiers and the men under Chang Hsüeh-liang, the son of the old Manchurian war lord, Chang Tso-lin. Chang Hsüeh-liang and his men had been exiled ever since Japan seized Manchuria, and now they were discontented exiles, longing to fight Japan but with no heart to fight against the Communists, who were, after all, Chinese. Chiang Kai-shek had heard of their disaffection, and thither he flew by air with his staff on the seventh day of December, 1936, to unite his forces and lead the attack against the entrenched Communists.

What was his surprise, on the twelfth day of the same month as he was resting at a hot springs resort near the city, to find himself taken prisoner by Chang Hsüeh-liang, his ally! The story need not be retold here, so well known is it, for indeed the whole world was shocked by the incident. Yet perhaps the motives behind it may not be so well understood. Briefly, Chang Hsüeh-liang proposed that the Nationalist government make peace with the Communists and join with them immediately in resisting the Japanese, who were daily taking over more northern territory and obviously planning for the whole of China. It may be assumed that the young Marshal, as he was called, saw in the defeat of Japan his only hope of return to Manchuria, and felt there was no sense in a war with the Chinese Communists while foreign Japanese ate up the country. Chiang Kai-shek, a man of well-known and mighty temper, was too angry to listen to such arguments, and insisted upon defeating the Communists first—that is, he insisted upon his own way.

In Nanking not only his family but his government were terrified.

337

It soon became clear that the Nationalist party was splitting upon the issue of the Old Tiger himself. Some members even appeared willing to sacrifice Chiang in order to bring about party unification. Others felt that the whole Nationalist regime would fall if Chiang fell. The family decided to settle the crisis and rescue their hero at all costs, and Madame Chiang then flew to her husband's side.

Meanwhile Chou En-lai, that suave Communist, had talked with the honorable prisoner, and he had put forth a compromise in the best Chinese tradition, albeit one with a big stick behind it. If their terms were accepted, Chou En-lai said, then the Communists would bow to Chiang Kai-shek as their head and the head of the state. The terms? The "rebels" were to be forgiven, an armistice was to be arranged between Nationalists and Communists, and together they were to fight the Japanese. The big stick? That if Chiang did not agree he would be killed at once. Chiang did agree, very reluctantly, and the terms were fulfilled. He was freed again, he was given apparent honor as the accepted head of a united China, and resistance against Japan was planned.

Yet privately everyone knew that the Communists had won a victory and for the first time the young intellectuals, even those in the Nationalist party, began to be interested in the Communist movement. Were there really Chinese who were willing to sacrifice themselves and their own interests to save their country from a foreign enemy? It was something new, and idealism, so sorely weakened under the years of Nationalist rule, stirred again. People began to talk about "agrarian revolutionists," and the Communists themselves took up the term. "We are not like the Russian Communists," they proclaimed. "We are agrarian reformers, and we are Chinese." It was cleverly done, undoubtedly part of a long-laid plan for future conquest, and no one knows whether Chiang Kai-shek understood its full significance. I think he did, for he always denied the validity of the term from the very first. And he was always uneasy in his enforced alliance.

For Americans, too, it must be understood that this was the first victory of the Communists in China, and yet it was a Chinese victory over Chinese. There is little evidence, indeed none, to show that Soviet Russia had any part in it, unless the withdrawal was deliberate, in order to stimulate local or national Communism. The Russians had seemed to repudiate Mao Tse-tung for his separatism, and during the Second World War they were careful at all times to acknowledge Chiang Kai-shek as the head of the Chinese government. Later, when they saw the inevitable fall of the Nationalists, they came forward to ally themselves with the Chinese Communists and thus consolidated their position in Asia by isolating the Chinese from the Americans. Into this plot, if it was a plot, we Americans threw ourselves wholeheartedly, ignorant of what was happening and in our ignorance doing all that we could to help Russia, whom even then we considered a potential enemy.

But I am ahead of my story. Undoubtedly the Chinese Communists wanted a war with Japan, for while they loudly talked of resistance, actually they resisted very little and the brunt fell, certainly at first, upon Chiang Kai-shek—indeed, this was true until Pearl Harbor when the Americans entered the war. It was the hope of the Chinese Communists, of course, that the Japanese would not only destroy the Nationalists but also the old traditional China, that there would be, in short, such destruction and confusion everywhere that the Communists could then step in and offer the only possible organized leadership out of chaos. This was the strong web they wove, and in it Chiang Kai-shek was helpless from the first. Perhaps he knew it, for certainly his resistance to Japan at the beginning was surprisingly strong and successful. His one hope was success in the war against Japan, for if he emerged victor in the struggle, then the people, grown lukewarm and indifferent, would flock again to his side. Thus by victory against Japan he would defeat not only Japan but also the Communists in the Northwest. Both sides were playing against each other, using Japan as the means to victory. The difference was that the Communists counted on the defeat of Chiang by Japan as their means, and for Chiang it was necessary that Japan be defeated. Therefore Chiang would certainly ally himself with the West, for this time the West would be against Japan, and in a Western victory he too would be victorious. This was the situation in which the Chinese found themselves in the year 1938, in the month of November.

In that same year, at the same time, I was in Sweden, where I went to accept the award of the Nobel Prize in Literature.

The preparation for such a journey had been hurried, not only for myself, but also for our family of children, five of them, the eldest twelve and the four babies less than four years old. Though we had a good nurse and a staunch housekeeper, yet I had never before left the children for more than a night or two at a time, and now it was to be for nearly a month. I was determined not to be away at Christmas, and so by careful calculation we planned that we could get home in time for it, although this gave us only four days in Sweden, since it was necessary to have some days in London, and a stopover in Denmark. Though so notable an occasion lay ahead, it was a wrench to leave home for a whole month, and especially to put the sea between children and parents. We went aboard the *Normandie* one grey November day in New York, my husband, my pretty stepdaughter Betty, then just twenty, and I. I have never been happy on the sea, in spite of enjoying it very much from the shore, and I saw with foreboding that although we had not left port, the chairs and tables and heavy furniture were already roped, as though the crew took bad weather for granted. I found, later, that it was only the *Normandie* they took for granted. She was built so slenderly, her breadth too narrow for her length, that she rolled upon the calmest sea. We sailed, and my comfort was the miracle of hearing the children's voices by radio telephone that evening, over the already lengthening miles of water. They sounded cheerful and happy and all was well.

Within a very few days after my arrival in London it was obvious that war in Europe was much nearer than we Americans had thought. Ominous news of course I had heard, and I knew it ominous, even when others seemed indifferent, merely because my life had been spent in the atmosphere of revolution and war, and I could smell strife from afar. In London, however, the portent became certainty, although the comfortable hotel was as luxurious as ever in the staid English way. There was no luxury like traditional English luxury before the last war, and newer hotels, in spite of splendor and dash, cannot equal the subdued richness of the really good London hotel. The bathtubs were vast, the plumbing massive, the water boiling hot, the towels as thick as quilts and as big as sheets. I am one of those, too, who likes the traditional English food, and I ate it that November with a pleasure, a melancholy and a nostalgia, almost foreseeing. Someday, I was sure, there would be no more such thick steaks, such roast beef and Yorkshire pudding, nor even the huge cabbages boiled too long, or the legs of mutton and browned potatoes and rich gravy, the trifles and savories and cups of tea as strong as lye.

For it was already clear that Germany was preparing for war, and the Jews who were wise were leaving that country. Yet everywhere in the London streets there were still the signs left over from the last war, the shelter signs, defense against the bombs. The past was still there, and the future was formidable. Someone much worse than the old Kaiser was now in Germany, someone far more evil. Anxiety was stifling in the air, a sober anxiety that would yield to the last inch of honor, if by so much yielding there could be peace. But the last inch would never be yielded. That, too, was clear.

In Denmark it was different. The people there knew their country was small as Belgium had been small in the First World War. They had no hope of standing against the new German war machine, and it was already decided that Denmark would not resist. She would give but she would not break. She would allow the conquerors to come in but she would never accept them. It was the only way that they could escape total destruction, Danish people told me. And all this went on, this thinking and planning, while the beautiful Danish cities and the rich countryside were calm as ever. When I had last been in Denmark, only a few years earlier on my way back to China, I had visited farms, as I like to do, and I remembered their quiet, their age, their fruitfulness. I had come upon a farmer in his barn one sunny afternoon, and he was busy painting, not woodwork or floors, but upon the whitewashed walls scenes of green trees, fields of grain and still waters. Very convincing scenes they were too, and when I asked why he put them on the walls of his barn instead of upon canvases, he replied:

"It is for my cows, Madame—in the long winter they like to look at these walls and think of the summer. It amuses them."

I could understand why such farmers preferred to yield for the time being rather than to see their homes and barns destroyed.

Nevertheless, the atmosphere oppressed me and I could not enjoy my visit. When an invitation came to me to visit Germany I refused it, and the next day in the Copenhagen newspaper I saw the following report:

"Pearl Buck says, 'I do not wish to visit a country where I am not allowed to think and speak freely.'

" 'Wouldn't you like to visit Germany?' we asked.

" 'Yes,' she replied, 'in one way I should like to see how the Germans live now but I think they would not welcome me there. And I don't want to visit a country where I am not allowed to think and speak freely as I am doing here. I am an individualist and a democrat.'

"Pearl S. Buck has said this in a low and gentle voice, but nevertheless we understand that it has been very important for her to mention it here in Copenhagen."

In Copenhagen I was much depressed, too, by talk with Chinese friends, who, though themselves Nationalists and loyal to Chiang Kai-shek, were nevertheless alarmed at the growing weaknesses of his government. I answered the inevitable questions of newspaper reporters as honestly as I could in the light of my own information. At such a time of crisis in the world, it would be wrong, I felt, to be less honest than I could be. Therefore when asked about China, I said that I did not see peace there for many years to come—yes, perhaps not real peace for as long as fifty years—and what China needed above all just now was a strong central government, able by its acts of concern to win and hold the loyalty of the people. No, I did not believe that Chiang Kai-shek could make such a government—he had lost his opportunity. Was China as poor as ever? Yes, although Chinese diplomats and other

Chinese abroad might try to give another impression of the country, the common people were as poor as ever. I would not say that all officials were corrupt but alas, many were, and at least most of them were not concerned for the welfare of the people.

Such plain speaking might perhaps have been avoided, but I have never believed that truth can be safely ignored, and so I followed my usual habit of speaking as honestly as I knew. The result was that Chinese Nationalist officials in Sweden were offended, and withdrew their presence from the occasion of the award in Stockholm. I was sorry for that, but it was perhaps inevitable. It would have been difficult for me to accept their presence with the grace of ignorance. In politics I have no interest and governments exist, I believe, only to better the life of their peoples. What other good reason have they to exist?

Sinclair Lewis had said to me, "Don't let anyone minimize for you the receiving of the Nobel Prize. It is a tremendous event, the greatest of a writer's life. Enjoy every moment of it, for it will be your finest memory."

I went to Stockholm with this advice, and it was good and true. I have had much happiness in my life and splendid events have come my way, but, aside from the continuing joys of home, the four days in Stockholm in the year 1938 remain my most perfect single recollection. The award came, as I have said before, at a time when I needed it most. I had met that difficult period of a writer's life, when the reaction, which the American public invariably bestows upon anyone whom it has discovered and praised, had set in. Since the praise is always too much and too indiscriminate the opposing criticism and contempt are also too much and too indiscriminate. My head had not been turned by the praise and its excess had only amused and touched me, but the rudeness of unjust criticism, a sort of stone-throwing which became merely imitative once it had begun, did temporarily destroy my confidence. The warmth of the Swedish people, combined with their dignity and their calm, restored my soul. It was good to be received, not with adulation, but with respect and affection. I cherish that memory.

In November Stockholm is almost dark, the sun barely near the horizon at midday, but the city blazed with lights and gaiety. We were met at the train and taken to the Grand Hotel and given the royal suite there, charming and comfortable rooms. Service was perfect and everything had been done to make our stay pleasant. That year there were only two persons to receive Nobel awards, and the other person was a gentle little Italian scientist whose name was Enrico Fermi. I had not heard much of him, but he was pleasant to meet and so were his pretty wife and two dark-eyed children. Later he came to the United

States, and now everyone knows his name for the work that he has done in developing the atomic bomb. But I could not then have imagined that he had anything to do with the deadly weapon. The fission of the atom? At that time it meant nothing to me.

As soon as we were settled in our rooms, we were called upon by a handsome young man, a Swedish attaché, who brought our schedule with him, and who instructed us with exact courtesy in what would be expected of us. He was a little uncertain of me, I could see, not knowing exactly how an American, the citizen of a republic, would behave in a formal setting. For Sweden combines in the most delightful fashion the utmost modernity within the framework of tradition, and I enjoyed both aspects of this most civilized of nations.

"Tell me, please," my young instructor said somewhat anxiously in his perfect but accented English, "is it possible that you will object to moving backward from our King after you have received the award? A Soviet citizen did not do so upon a similar occasion."

I assured him that of course I would not turn my back upon the King. A sigh of relief was my reward for this decision.

He then proceeded to instruct me further, reading aloud from a typed sheet, explaining each detail of the progress planned for the next four days, and I listened with my whole attention, determined to show myself favorably as an American as well as a writer.

The result of such attention is that I remember perhaps in needless detail the procedure of those days. Yet the most memorable hour was of course that of the presentation of the awards, on the evening after the day of our arrival in Stockholm.

When I entered the great Concert Hall the scene was magnificent. Upon the wide platform, decorated with flags and evergreens, the dignified members of the Academy were seated in semicircular arrangement. In the front rows of the crowded hall the royal family, jewelled and splendid, waited in royal calm, while trumpets blared from the galleries.

I sat at the end of the front left row, from whence I could see the whole assembly, and not understanding the preliminary speeches, which were in Swedish, I had time to reflect quietly upon what I saw and to enjoy the occasional music. I shall never forget that scene, yet what I remember most clearly was the instant, half an hour later, when I stood before the dignified and aged King to receive the award, and having made my curtsy, I looked full into his face. In that instant I saw not the King's face, but the face of my old father, long dead, and everything else I forgot. It was incredible that two men could look so much alike. The tall slender figure, the lean face and strong jaw, the frosty

343

blue eyes, the white moustache cut to the shape of the lips, even the hand that held out the big envelope, were like my father's. I was so startled that I could scarcely say, "Thank you, Your Majesty," and I all but forgot my promise not to turn my back. I did not forget, but it was in momentary confusion that I mounted the steps and then backed across the wide stage to my seat. I mention the resemblance here publicly for the first time, but when we were home again I found my father's portrait and showed it to my husband, and he saw the likeness as clearly as I had. It was no more than accidental, of course, or perhaps there was some reason based on geography, for landscape and climate have a way of creating likeness in the human beings who live upon the same bit of earth, and it is true that my own paternal ancestors came two hundred years ago from the same section of Germany from which the King's family had come, for the present royal house of Sweden is not an ancient one. Yet it was strange and certainly meaningful for me to have felt my father come alive for me at the great moment.

I remember next the dinner given that night, by the Crown Prince. It took place in the handsome City Hall, very festive with flowers and fine silver. I enjoyed everything but most of all my conversation with the Crown Prince, who, I found, knew a great deal about China, and had a collection of Chinese art objects. We talked at length about that country, so much that I do not remember at all what I ate, and then we talked of the future, he very guarded, of course. But by this time I had listened to enough people in Stockholm to realize that the gathering resolution in Sweden was of another pattern from that which I had perceived in Denmark. Sweden had all but made up her mind to be neutral when the new war broke. There were some who felt that it would be wise to side with Germany, others that such allegiance was impossible. Decision was trembling in the air, and because I felt it deeply important that as an American I must speak with what strength I could for the cause of human freedom, when it came my turn after dinner to make a brief address, I rose and took my place behind a small lectern and there I made my little speech of acceptance of the Nobel award, a speech of no importance to anyone except myself, I am sure, and yet it had to be made, and here it is, as part of my record.

Your Royal Highnesses:
Ladies and Gentlemen:
It is not possible for me to express all that I feel of appreciation for what has been said and given to me. I accept, for myself, with the conviction of having received far beyond what I have been able to return through my books. I can only hope that the many books which I have

344

yet to write will be in some measure a worthier acknowledgment than I can make tonight. And indeed, I can accept only in the same spirit in which I think this gift was originally given—that it is a prize not so much for what has been done as for the future. Whatever I write in the future must, I think, be always benefited and strengthened when I remember this day.

I accept, too, for my country, the United States of America. We are a people still young and we know that we have not yet come to the fullness of our powers. This award, given to an American, strengthens not only one, but the whole body of American writers, who are encouraged and heartened by such generous recognition. And I should like to say, too, that in my country it is important that this award has been given to a woman. You who have already so recognized your own Selma Lagerlöf, and have long recognized women in other fields, cannot perhaps wholly understand what it means in many countries and even in my own, that it is a woman who stands here at this moment. But I speak not only for writers and for women, but for all Americans, for we all share in this occasion.

I should not be truly myself if I did not, in my own wholly unofficial way, speak also of the people of China, whose life has for so many years been my life also, whose life, indeed, must always be a part of my life. The minds of my own country and of China, my foster country, are alike in many ways, but above all, alike in our common love of freedom. And today, more than ever, this is true, now when China's whole being is engaged in the greatest of all struggles, the struggle for freedom. I have never admired China more than I do now, when I see her uniting her peoples against the enemy who threatens her freedom. With this determination for freedom, which is in so profound a sense the essential quality in her nature, I know that she is unconquerable. Freedom—it is today more than ever the most precious human possession. We—Sweden and the United States—we have it still. My country is young—but it greets you with a peculiar fellowship, you whose earth is ancient and free.

Afterwards, Dr. Fermi's speech following mine, a burst of singing from the huge court below the hall told us that the evening's dance was about to begin and the students were already marching in from the university. My pretty stepdaughter had been invited by the son of the Crown Prince to open the dance with him, and like a little Cinderella in her white gown, her eyes shining, she floated down the broad stairway upon his arm and we stood on the balcony above and looked upon the scene, lovely with gaiety and youth.

The crowded happy days followed fast upon one another, and the chief event of the next day was the dinner at the palace with the King. In the interstices of our full program there were visits and newspaper interviews, as a matter of course, and from each of these I gained further knowledge of Sweden and its remarkable people and was thus provided with a background of understanding for later days. A century and more ago Sweden, worn and consumed by its many wars and conflicts with neighboring peoples, had been compelled to face its own condition and to decide whether it would allow itself to be destroyed by the burdens of war, laid upon the people by military leaders whose career was war, or, on the contrary, deny the leaders and build a life of peace, based upon an unchangeable policy of neutrality in all times of war. They chose peace, and in the decades since that fundamental decision, which every nation must make sooner or later if its people are to survive, Sweden has grown steadily in wisdom and prosperity. Neither wisdom nor permanent prosperity is possible for a nation in the constant turmoil of war.

With such ideas crowding my mind, I proceeded on the evening of that day to the palace and found at its entrance many school children waiting for me. I could not forbear lingering and talking with them until the guards at the gate grew a little impatient with me and urged me on so I mounted the wide curving staircase to the rooms where I was to wait, with Dr. Fermi, for the two who were to escort us to the banquet hall.

My memory of that banquet hall is not very clear, I suppose partly because I had already become accustomed to magnificence. Behind every chair was a steward and across the table from me sat the King between two elderly Princesses, the only ladies of sufficiently high rank to be next him. But the vagueness of my memory is partly, too, because I sat next to the King's brother, Prince William, an explorer and a hunter of big game, a man of wide knowledge and experience, and I became entirely fascinated with his conversation and especially by the account of his visits to the pigmies in Africa. One delicious dish after another was placed before me, the *pièce de résistance* being reindeer steak, I remember, and suddenly, before I knew it, the meal was over. That is, the King rose. The entire extraordinary menu had been served in forty-five minutes! The reason? Court etiquette demands that when the King finishes with a course all plates are removed with his. Some dishes, I fear, I never tasted, for I found my plate gone before I had lifted my fork. The King, a Court lady explained to me afterward, did not usually talk much with the two Princesses, whom he knew very well and had to sit between on many such occasions. Therefore, without

346

conversation, he ate rapidly and hence the fine banquet was soon ended.

In the reception room afterward, we all stood until it pleased the King to seat himself, and I heard a stout Court lady next to me sigh and whisper. "It does seem as though our dear King likes to stand longer every year!"

At last, however, he sent for me as I had been told he would, and seating himself on a couch he bade me sit beside him and then everybody could take seats. I felt at ease for it is the rule that a King must begin a conversation, and this time responsibility was not upon me. Meanwhile his coffee was served in a gold cup, mine in a porcelain one. He stirred in his sugar and kept silence, and I had time to see again how exactly even his profile resembled that of my father. But it would not have been becoming to mention it, and so I did not. After a moment of stirring and sipping, he began to talk, asking me a few questions which I do not remember. What I do remember is that suddenly he leaned forward, his frost-blue eyes mischievous, and glancing affectionately and half ironically about the room, he told me how weary he often was of being a king, and how little freedom a king has, how he must assume not only the heavy responsibilities of state, but also the burden of meticulous personal behavior, so that none of his subjects are hurt in their feelings. But once a year, he told me his blue eyes still sparkling, he had a vacation from being a king. Then, incognito and known only as Mr. G., he went to the Riviera or wherever he liked, and had a holiday, not a king at all, but a gay old man, enjoying his tennis and other games, while his son, the Crown Prince, took over the royal duties. He loved tennis, he told me, and he related with relish a game he had played with the French champion, Suzanne Lenglen. He had missed the line when he served to her, and she had called across the net to him, "You should move a little more to the left, Your Majesty!" To which he had retorted, "Ah, that is what my ministers are always telling me!"

In a little while he rose, we all rose, and the evening was over.

The next day I had somewhat dreaded, for it was the custom for recipients of the Nobel Prize to address the Swedish Academy, a distinguished group of scholars. What did I know to present to them? I had by then lived only long enough in the United States to realize that I knew too little of my own people, that it would take years of living and observation before in our patternless society I could discern the causes behind what we felt and said and did. It would be presumptuous to try to speak so soon. Moreover, I had been reminded often enough of my ignorance. Even when the Pulitzer Prize had been awarded *The Good Earth,* certain critics had objected to so American an award being given to a book about Chinese peasants, written by a woman, and worse than that, a woman who had never lived in her own country.

My address therefore before the Swedish Academy was upon a subject I did know well, and about which very little is known by most westerners. The title of my address was *The Chinese Novel,* and the address itself was later published in a little book under the same title.

From the end of that hour and for the rest of my stay in beautiful Stockholm, the events were pure pleasure, to be enjoyed without responsibility. I must mention, however, that I met at a luncheon given me by Mr. Bonnier, my Swedish publisher, Selma Lagerlöf, a great woman and writer whose books I have loved. She was already very old, but still strong in mind and speech, though simple and modest in manner and looking very pleasant in her grey silk dress and a scarf of violet velvet. She told me that the two biographies of my parents had decided her vote for the Nobel award for me that year, and to hear this of course made me happy. I like to think that the bold and original lives of my father and mother were part of those Stockholm days, as they have been of all my years.

Perhaps this is the place to share a bit of amusement of my own. When the Nobel award had first been announced in the United States, it was mistakenly thought to be for *The Good Earth* alone. This was not true. It was awarded for the whole body of my work, then mainly composed of my Chinese novels and the biographies. My American publishers corrected the mistake, whereupon orders began to come in from bookstore customers for a book, purportedly by me, entitled *The Body of Her Work.*

On the morning of the twelfth of December, the day before we were to leave Stockholm, I rose early, having been gently forewarned, and I wrapped myself in my dressing gown and went back to bed to receive a guest. The door opened at eight o'clock and a pretty girl entered, wearing a crown of lighted candles on her head, and bearing in her hands a silver tray with coffee cups. She walked with slow and graceful steps, singing "Santa Lucia" as she came. In every home in Sweden, I suppose, a similar scene was going on, the Lucia being always the youngest daughter or sister. Thus opened the Santa Lucia Festival, or the Festival of Light, so significant in a winter-darkened country. On that day the sun has reached its lowest point upon the horizon and thereafter the light increases. It is the custom, too, to choose a Lucia for the whole city, and for that year of 1938 Ingrid Lohman, a pretty employee in a furrier's shop, had won the prize. In the evening there was to be a great banquet in the City Hall to celebrate the festival and to crown the queen, and I was invited, too.

I found it a fascinating contrast to the occasions of state which had preceded it. The vast hall was crowded with people sitting closely packed around the simply set tables where we dined. Music and laughter and speeches went on in enjoyable confusion while the pretty queen was crowned, and I saw a different Sweden, a popular one, very free and easy and gay. I liked it and said good-bye reluctantly at the evening's end.

The next morning early we boarded the train that was to take us to the sea again, and it was touching to find at the station a group of Americans. They had come to see us off, and after greetings and handshakings they began to sing as the train moved away, and the sound of their voices in harmony floated after us as they sang:

> *Home—home on the range,*
> *Where the deer and the antelope play.*
> *Where seldom is heard,*
> *A discouragin' word,*
> *And the skies are not cloudy all day.*

We gathered speed under the dark northern skies of Sweden and the haunting melody caught my heart, homeward turned.

The home-coming was the best of all. The sight of the beloved house upon the hill as we drove across the bridge and up the lane, made the heart beat fast. Why did I ever think I had no roots in my own country? I had already put down deeper roots here than anywhere in the world, and never would they be pulled up again for any reason. We were at the end of the lane now, and there were the great red barn and the sturdy stone house. Christmas wreaths were hanging on the doors and at the windows. Four small figures in red coats and leggings came running over the snowy fields to meet us, and here the heart stopped! What embracings and kisses and cries of surprise and how big the four had grown even in a month and how rosy were the cheeks and bright the eyes! Yes, coming home was best of all, the happy end of every journey.

Yet underneath all the joy and peace of home and family at that Christmastime of a memorable year I was acutely mindful, as I shall always be, of what was happening on the other side of my world in Asia. War had begun in deadly earnest, and previous engagements were only skirmishes in contrast. The Japanese armies attacked at Marco Polo Bridge, near Peking. The Nationalist forces, centering their strength around Shanghai and the Japanese aggression there, resisted with more strength than expected, while still the Communists did almost nothing. Alone the Nationalists were to continue resistance through 1939, but failing all along the way to hold their ground. Nanking had been lost in 1937, and the government had retreated up the Yangtse to Hankow, only to lose that city, too, in 1938. The whole coast was indeed too quickly lost, proving what we had sadly feared, that Chiang Kai-shek's hold upon the people was rootless. Thus the richest and most important part of the country fell into enemy control, the industrial areas of the great cities and the fertile plains of the riverland, and Nationalists retreated into the ancient regions of that mountainous West so untouched by modern life. Universities followed the government, which finally settled in Chungking, there to remain for the duration of the war. The Nationalist party was by now divided into two groups, one favoring continued resistance to the Japanese even if only by the guerrilla tactics the Chinese Communists were beginning to use in the North as Japan came close, and the other favoring compromise. It is to Chiang Kai-shek's honor that he refused all compromise with the foreign enemy, as he had with Communism. He continued his waiting position, still hoping that a world war would demand that the United States become deeply involved, this time against Japan, and that in the universal conflict China would emerge on the side of the victorious nations. He did not doubt that the combination of the United States and Britain would be invincible.

How well I remember the day war began in Europe! We had taken a house in Martha's Vineyard that summer, a comfortable place next door to Katharine Cornell's beautiful house on the bay. The water was perfect for our children, shallow, warm and clear, and they tumbled in and out all day, fat and brown and merry. We ourselves spent the day between work and play, my husband devoting himself to the delightful but difficult task of editing Lin Yutang's monumental novel, *Moment in Peking,* and I at work upon my own novel, *Other Gods.* One morning, however, unable to work, and oppressed unreasonably, I hoped, by premonitions of war, I joined the children on the beach earlier than usual. A few minutes later I saw my husband hurrying down the dunes. It was to tell me the fearful news from the radio, that war had been declared in Europe.

It seemed impossible, in spite of certainty. The sun shone upon the calm sea and upon the smooth white sands. Our two babies, hand in hand, were running up and down the beach in the shallow water, while the two little boys dug for sand crabs. Farther up the coast where the sea swept in a great curve, people were swimming in front of Katharine Cornell's house. She had been to visit us, handsome and brown with sun and wind, her dachshunds trailing after her. We had met a few times in New York, without quite becoming well acquainted, each shy, I think, of the other. I have always kept my Chinese trait of reverence for great people—a trait not suited to my American world, where no one is embalmed in reverence. We had talked but not easily, and she said that it was difficult for her to make speeches, I remember, or even to converse easily, because actors use the words of others to express themselves. But she had told me a little of her early life in the city of Buffalo, an incongruous name for the home town of such an elegant and sophisticated woman.

Upon this scene in spite of all its grace and calm, the war broke that day and we knew, my husband and I, that our life would never be the same again, for war would change our country and our people. It would change, indeed, the whole world.

Why, on the other side of that world, did not Chiang Kai-shek do what the Communists did, arm the peasants and bid them fight the invaders? The answer is that he feared the peasants armed. He knew they were not for him, that his government had failed them, and he dared not trust them. He preferred to leave them as they were, defenseless, rather than to give them arms which someday they might use in rebellion against him. He waited, hoping and longing, while Americans remained neutral and unwilling.

And would we remain neutral? Could we? I hoped so. I had seen too much of war to believe in it as a means of permanent victory. And this war would be the worst, I knew, for it would unleash in Asia all the angry forces of the peoples. Each Asian people would use world war to further its own passionate determination for freedom and independence. And after the war, what? Certainly no victory!

I remember a hot day in 1940. My husband and I were driving across the high plains of Kansas. It is one of my favorite states, and I return to it again and again as the heart of our country, its people honest and excellent, intelligent and civilized, while living in simple houses. We were vaguely anxious that day, for President Roosevelt was to make an important speech. At the hour we drew up in the scanty shade of an angular tree so that we might listen with whole attention. We turned on the radio and the rich eloquent voice came rolling over the air. It brought no declaration of war—not yet. But I knew, as I heard it, that war was inevitable, and over the sunny golden landscape the shadows fell.

We continued our journey, sober and silent, we shortened it not at all, turning northward to the Dakotas to visit my sister and her family then living in Pierre, South Dakota—"Peer," as everyone called it. And when we arrived, I remember, I found my small nephews excited with all the other small boys, because on a dry hilltop near the town a huge petrified fish had been found that very day, a creature the size of a whale, and I went with them and there it was, complete in soft stone. It was lifted and taken to the museum, but bits fell off and I brought one home with me and put it beside our pool. It turned quickly to dust, however, as all flesh does, when subject to sun and wind and time.

That was a good journey to make in such a year as 1940 for we wandered through the stupendous Badlands, the Needles and the Black Hills, and again the variety and the beauty of our country were impressed upon me, and not only of landscape, but more than that, of people. In Pierre I wished to find the artist who had made a favorite painting then hanging on our living room wall, a dark red sun setting over the desert and a ruined empty cabin. I found her in a tiny restaurant making potato chips for a living. The reason? People here were too poor to buy paintings, she told us, but she could not leave the magnificent landscapes. She had learned painting in Paris and had thought that she would always live there until she had found South Dakota.

And so we went home again, our memories filled with glorious scenes and good people. We spent another year quietly at home and busy with our usual work, yet always uneasy in the world. In December of 1941 we were enjoying a quiet Sunday afternoon in my stepdaughter's house across the road from our farmhouse. Mutual friends were guests, and we were talking about anything and nothing, while their adolescent son sat outdoors in their car to hear a football game over the radio.

Suddenly he rushed into the room, panting with terror and excitement.

"The Japanese," he gasped, "they've attacked Pearl Harbor!"

My stepdaughter reached for the radio. She turned it on and the news came flooding into the quiet cozy room. It was true. War was certain. We had become part of the whole world. Instantly I thought of China and of Chiang Kai-shek. How happy must he be, far off there in Chungking! Who could blame him? He loved his country, too.

The war years we all know too well for them to be retold again. My task was to keep the children as free from fear as possible, to continue my work, to maintain what is called an even keel. It was a familiar atmosphere, but one I had never expected in my own country. As in China, however, I determined not to allow the war to shadow my existence, nor to prevent me from getting the most possible out of my daily life.

Much of my life in those days centered about the school to which the children were going, a staid Quaker day school conducted in a beautiful old stone schoolhouse, where it had continued for nearly two cen-

352

turies. Next to it was an equally historic meetinghouse. We had always planned to educate the children in Quaker schools, for the philosophy of the Friends was the nearest I had found to the Asian one in which I had grown up. Never shall I forget the first morning I took our little sons to school. They went trustingly and with enthusiasm, believing, alas, that they were about to comprehend immediately the wonders. Thus one, the fair-haired, said joyfully, "I am going to learn how to make an airplane." My heart ached, I confess, when he began to understand how long the road, how weary the hours would be until that day could arrive. But my heart has often ached for such little scholars, their sweet enthusiasm dying in the daily grind. I will not criticize our schools, for I do not know how to make compulsory education pleasant, yet to me learning, learning anything, but especially something I want to know, is the most joyful occupation in life. I do not know when it is that the joy fades out of school for most children, so that they end not only by hating school but even worse, by hating books, and this is grave indeed, for in books alone is the accumulated wisdom of the whole human race, and to read no books is to deprive the self of ready access to wisdom. Even in China such wisdom was relayed generation to generation through centuries until the people were permeated with the sayings of poets and philosophers. But in our mixed ancestry there are no such clear streams, and it is only in books that we can discover what we are, and why we are that, and thus self-knowledge, as well as knowledge of others, is achieved.

It was not only my children who were educated by going to school. Through them as school children, I, too, have been educated, by force if not always by conviction. By background, of course, I am not fitted to have American children. I have nothing to prepare me for the problems they face. My childhood world was spent in an old and sophisticated society, and therefore in one completely natural and simplified as only an ancient society does simplify itself. Take, for example, the matter of tattling. Before the children went to school and we were all at home together every day, I had established as a matter of course the Chinese principle that when something wrong was going on, it was the duty of any child to report to the adult in charge, usually parent or teacher. It was not right to run about telling other people of a person's wrongdoings, but for the sake of order it must be reported to the one who could correct it. This went very well.

Picture my surprise, however, when upon the children's reaching school age and moving out into their larger American environment, they came home to tell me that I was wrong! One of them had duly reported to the teacher misbehavior on the part of a fellow pupil, and she had scolded the little reporter for something called "tattling." I investigated and found that this was true.

"But how," I remonstrated with the teacher, "can you maintain law and order in your school if the law-abiding ones may not report the lawbreakers?"

She evaded this. "It is hateful to tattle," she said.

"Then the children will grow up believing that it is hateful to report a murder to policemen. This would also be tattling," I said.

"I cannot answer that," she replied in a positive voice.

I was to learn that this refusal to face the practical is sometimes characteristic of our people. We act upon emotion—she hated tattling—and upon prejudice—she disliked tattlers—without reference to the very practical question of how a child is to help keep order if he cannot report disorder, and what the confusion is in his own mind if he must remain silent about something he knows is wrong. To what principle is he to be loyal? I am convinced that much of our so-called American lawlessness goes back to this stifling of the child's perfectly right impulse to tell if someone is violating a common rule, accepted by all, and his confusion if he is reproved for obeying the impulse.

Yet when I expressed my conviction the other day to an American friend, he was quite violent in his disagreement with me. I was, he said, "off my base."

"Your argument," he said, "if carried to its logical conclusion, would mean that Soviet children are justified in reporting their parents to the government. Any possible good that might come out of 'tattling' would be more than offset by injury to the child and the community. The informer, at least in Western society, is universally abhorred and even those who use him despise him. There is no way to draw the line and it is better to accept the apparent, immediate evil than to face a much greater one later."

I have reflected much upon his words, and I realize the validity of his point of view in the United States, at least. Yet my own argument holds, too, or so I believe. Perhaps the difference in the two societies, Chinese and American, on this point, lies merely in their organization. Our society is not ordered as the Chinese was. A child reported only to the adult in charge of his little world and when he was grown his primary loyalty was by tradition still to his family and not to the state. Perhaps it is basically a question of primary loyalty, and on this matter of loyalty we Americans are indeed confused. It does seem contradictory to me that we elect representatives to make laws and enforce them and yet absolve ourselves of responsibility when we see those laws broken. There is something wrong in the logic, and in the result, too, since we are the most lawless of all nations, and our rate of individual crime incredibly high. It is, as the King of Siam said, "a puzzlement."

Green Hills Farm

"Please," my youngest daughter said to me this morning, "come with me."

Should I or should I not? In trying to be a good American mother how often I have asked myself the question. Where exactly is the point for a parent to stand back so that the child may be independent? In China the parent was always welcome, the parent always went. She is sixteen, this child, and she is near the end of high school. She wants to be a kindergarten teacher and she had decided, quite by herself, that she would go into our public school system, and therefore the State Teachers' College is the place for her next year, after high school. The formalities had been finished, many papers signed and questions answered, and today was the day for the interview.

"Please," she said again.

"Sure you want me?" I asked.

"You could sit outside," she said.

So I have come and here I am outside. That is, I am sitting in a large pleasant room, the reception hall of the college, in a comfortable chair, alone, while my daughter is being interviewed somewhere in the bowels of the building. She went off bravely with a group of young women, looking serious and independent, though she is a small girl, very blue eyes under dark brown hair. I watch the people who come and go while I wait, a pastime which I always enjoy. Meanwhile I meditate upon the passage of life. This daughter of mine, whom I remember clearly as she was when I first saw her, a minute creature, perfect in detail, the same great blue eyes, already black-fringed, but so small that she fitted comfortably into the crook of my arm, is now a young woman with a mind of her own. She has rejected a fair amount of the education offered her, as most American children seem to do, and until she reached high school I did not know whether to be exasperated with her or with her teachers. Why, oh, why can learning not be made more exciting, more rewarding? I was exasperated with her teachers when she came trudging home from school, weary and pale with too many hours out of the sunshine, and yet with a pile of books under her arm. What wickedness, I cried in my heart, to keep a child sitting on a hard bench all day and then crowd the night hours, too, with homework! The children of

355

Europe sit through long hours, too, but they have more to show for it than our children have. They achieve a prodigious amount of book learning, they can speak several languages, they understand mathematics and the abstractions of philosophy, but our poor children end their school days with pitifully little in the way of sound knowledge. I rebel against the waste of time, remembering my own free childhood, the lessons quickly learned and then the hours of sunshine and play and pleasant freedom. Not until I reached college did I study at night, except for the one year at Miss Jewell's School in Shanghai where what I learned was not in books.

And I cannot remember at all when I learned to read. I know I read quite comfortably at four, because on my fifth birthday I received a small book as a gift, entitled *Little Susie's Seven Birthdays* and I envied Susie for having seven instead of five. Yet my American children learned reading with strange difficulty, and I am shocked at the number of our people, men and women, but especially men, who read slowly, word by word, and are never comfortable in reading and do not enjoy it, although the purpose of education should be to make reading as simple and easy as listening to a voice, for only when a person can really read will he surely continue his own education. And examining into the cause for this slow and painful reading I am convinced that it is chiefly because we have wasted the value of the alphabet. Today's children—or perhaps it is yesterday's, since my own, except for the one whom we call our little Postscript, are past the early grades—are taught reading as though each word were a separate entity, exactly as Chinese children are taught their ideographs, or characters, of which five thousand must be separately learned before one can read, and for this reason the Chinese need two more years than we do with our alphabet language in order to complete the same work. The Koreans have an alphabet even more compact than ours and profited thereby until the Japanese conquerors made Japanese the language of the schools, and Japanese is no better than Chinese for learning to read. But English is a matchless language, and the alphabet, each letter with its own sounds, is the key, yet in this generation the teachers have thrown the key away. I rebel, I say, though very little good does the rebellion of the lay mind do against the professional, and this dominance of the professional is a weakness in our civilization, for the professional gets no over-all view of the people and the culture, and we are only torn hither and thither by one professional opinion and another.

When our Postcript came along, a little German war child, I taught her secretly at home how to read, but I knew better than to mention it abroad. Her teacher, an excellent one incidentally, told me the other day that our child, though only in second grade, is reading fifth grade books and needs no help whatever. I smiled and kept my counsel. Of course she knows how to read, and knowing she enjoys it. She learned as I learned, easily and unconsciously, for I gave her the key to reading, as my mother gave it to me, by teaching her how to use the alphabet.

But upon education one can write many books. Examinations, tests, grades, competition, these are all obstacles to true learning. Were I young again—how many things I would do if I were young again and in my own country! I would create a school where children could drink in learning as they drink in fresh milk. They drink because they are thirsty, and children are always thirsty for learning, but they do not know it. And in schools sources of learning are fouled with tensions, anxieties, competitive sports and the shame and fear of low marks, and it is no wonder that we are not a book-loving people. We have been made to hate books and therefore to scorn, with private regret mixed in, the educated man because he is an intellectual. Compulsory education? I doubt the wisdom of it, and certainly the use of the word compulsion is not wise. Education, yes, but not this sausage mill, this hopper, into which our children are all tossed at the age of six, and from which they emerge, too many of them, in dazed confusion, somewhere along the way, as rejects or as mass products.

Education? It is now a Saturday morning, after breakfast, the hour sacred to homework—work before play, and so on. But Rusty, the frivolous cocker spaniel widow, has foolishly neglected to get to the kennel in time to have her current batch of mongrel pups, and waiting greedily at the kitchen door for her morning meal she was overtaken by nature. Instead of retiring in prudence, she continued to wait but the puppies did not, and my second son, a six-foot adolescent, opened the door on her. Seeing her plight, he immediately rushed to her aid. Fresh straw in the kennel, a bowl of warm milk, a blanket-lined basket for the puppies shivering in the raw January air, and then Rusty herself, transported tenderly in his arms into the dry comfortable kennel—all this has, I am sure, taken most of the study hour. He will have to make it up, of course, but meanwhile, absorbed in life, he is learning. I daresay he will do more reading for the next few days than he has done in a month. He will want to know. And probably as a result he will fail his chemistry test on Monday. And his teacher will complain. And the irony is that I can sympathize with her, too. It is hard to teach a boy who has not done his homework, especially a charming boy of whom one is fond, and especially if one is a teacher with a conscience.

Part of the home education of the children has certainly been in the many visitors from abroad who have come to our house and they are too many to mention by name, and many of them have come again and again until our house seems linked to the other countries of the world by the memories of known and unknown friends, their faces, their voices, their letters. At this moment I recall an incident during the war, actually before Pearl Harbor. I had written some articles, quite strong ones, against Japanese militarism and I knew of course that they had reached Japan. But Japan was on the other side of the world, cut off from me, I imagined, by what had happened. Yet here is the story.

One cold winter's night we sat by the living room fire in our home. The snow lay on the ground, deep and unploughed. No one could come in, none go out. It had been a wonderful day, the snow falling, the wind blowing, the children playing outside until they were half frozen, and in the evening after their supper we had popcorn before they went to bed. They were bathed and read to and tucked into their snug covers, and the father and I had settled ourselves to our books before the fire when suddenly the telephone rang. I answered unwillingly, wondering what neighbor could be calling, and acknowledging my name to the operator. Then I heard her say excitedly, "Hold on, please—Tokyo calling!"

Tokyo? But how did Tokyo have my unlisted private number?

"Wait," I said, and I called my husband. "Will you take it for me?" I said.

I felt a strange unaccustomed fear. Could Tokyo reach across the sea like this and pluck me out of my house on a faraway hillside, in my own country, and in the darkness, too, of a winter's night? And for what reason?

He took the receiver from my hand and listened. Then he laughed. "It's only a newspaper—*The Mainichi*," he said. "They want to wish you a happy New Year and ask you a few questions."

I need not be afraid, then? But still I was, a little. Nevertheless, I took the receiver from him, and almost instantly heard my name called and a very Japanese voice wishing me a happy New Year, quite as though Japan had not attacked China, and then the questions. They were the usual ones. What do you think of Japanese literature? What is your next book? Have you some message for us, please? Ah, *sodeska!* Thank you very much. Good-bye. Exactly as though there were no war going on! I put up the receiver, feeling dazed, and went back to my chair by the fireside. No, I paused on the way and looked out of the window. The snow was still falling. I could see it by the glare of the snowplow just now turning into our lane from the road, and throwing great clouds of frothing white into the darkness. Around us were miles of white countryside, miles of plains and valleys and mountains and beyond them miles of ocean between this house and Japan and yet Tokyo had reached across them all and found me! And the voice was friendly, though nations were at war! There was a moral somewhere, but I let it lie. For me the fact simply was that I could not escape any of my several worlds.

And so the visitors have continued through the years to come and to go and to come again, faces, voices, letters. James Yen, the great simpleminded Chinese, once stayed long enough for us to write a little book together, entitled *Tell the People,* and it is made from his own words spoken to me while I listened, and it tells of his work in mass education in his own country. Many years he carried it on, and now he is exiled but his methods are being used by the Communists in their effort to make the people quickly literate. And that little book, he tells me, has gone far and wide over Asia, where other peoples want to learn to read because reading is the key to learning, and they have never had the key. And Nehru's nieces came to us in the summers that Madame Pandit was in India and they were here at school, and we learned to love the beautiful warmhearted girls. They are married now and all but the youngest have children. I remember that youngest one because sometimes when I rested in the evening on the couch she stroked my feet with such gentle skilful movements of her palms that the weariness went out of me, and I felt rested even in my spirit. It is an Indian gift, natural in a country where the people go barefoot and walk many miles because they must. Uday Shankar, the Indian dancer, and his wife and Ananda, their little boy, have been our guests, and they, too, were so beautifully gentle and graceful that we all watched them in fascination.

Madame Pandit has come many times, and the memory of her statuesque beauty recalls itself, and I remember especially the evening of the day when her brother, Jawaharlal Nehru, left the United States after his visit here. We had talked with him alone, had dined with him, had met as best we could his long weary brooding silences and the sudden outpourings when a remark stirred some interest of his own. The deep affection between brother and sister was touching. Two lonely people, obviously, they shared their memories and each was better for the other's presence. When he had gone, she was alone again and in our house I saw that it was a loneliness that could not be healed. Life has set them both apart, as great men and women are always set apart, and therefore lonely perhaps because they know too much, have felt too much, and can never do enough of what they see needs doing to satisfy themselves or even others.

Josuè de Castro of Brazil came here after writing his brilliant book,

The Geography of Hunger, and what power there was in his strong and flashing mind! Shizuè Masugi, the woman novelist of Japan, was another guest, and Sumie Mishima, and Lin Yutang and his family many times through the years, and Wang Yung and her husband, Hsieh, and Toro Matsumoto, now master in a famous school in Japan, and with him, too, his family. I must not forget Mbono Ojike, now an official in Nigeria. Ojike, a tall, merry fellow, told us many tales and made us laugh very often. His father was an African chieftain who had ten wives, and the old man, deciding to become a Christian, went to church one Sunday, with all his wives behind him in procession. At the door he was met by the Christian missionary who in consternation cried, "But you cannot come to church with ten wives!"

"Why not?" Ojike's father asked. "They are all good women!"

"It is not Christian to have ten wives," the missionary objected. "You must choose one and send the others away."

The chieftain retired to the shade of a tree to consider the matter, his ten wives waiting in a circle about him. How could he dismiss nine good women? He could not be so cruel. Beckoning to them to follow him he went home again and gave up church and Christianity.

Ojike, by the way, went travelling for The East and West Association, creating mirth and joy wherever he went, a proud gay creature, tall and black. In some Midwestern city where he was scheduled to speak, he arrived by train and seeing a large hotel whose sign was "The Chieftain," he decided it was appropriate for his stay, and so he strode into the lobby—with that graceful jungle panther stride of his—and asked for a room.

The clerk looked at him sidewise. "We don't have a room for you," he said at last.

"Why not, sir?" Ojike demanded.

"We don't take colored people," the clerk said.

Ojike's great eyes flashed. He drew himself up to his most tall, haughty as the prince he was. "Sir," he said majestically, "I am not colored. I am black!"

"Colored," in his country was an insult. "Colored" were people mixed with white blood, and he had no white blood in him. He would not budge and demanded that the leading citizen who had arranged his visit with our office be called for. Much telephone conversation followed and at last the clerk, dazed and stammering, found a room and Ojike went upstairs in majesty, his bags carried by a bellboy. Next morning so he told us, when he came out of his room to go to the dining room for breakfast, a Negro maid in the corridor fell on her knees at the sight of him.

"Oh Jesus," she babbled, "Lord Jesus Christ done come!"

"Get up, woman," Ojike said with dignity. "I am not Jesus. I am Ojike."

"Jesus," she insisted, "you must be Jesus! They wouldn't let no black man sleep in this hotel unless he was Jesus come again."

Pages I need to write down the names of the men and women and the children who have come to bless our house and bring the world to us here, so that our children, wherever they go, will see no face which seems strange to them, for such faces are their lively childhood memories and among the happiest they have. This also has been their education.

And if I have shared my friends from other worlds with family and neighbors, others have drawn me deep into my American world. My first friend was Gertrude Lane, then editor of *The Woman's Home Companion,* and she was the first American woman that I knew well. Gertrude Battle Lane—I write her full name because it suited her. She had come as a girl from a little New England town, and with a single ambition, she told me, which was to work for that magazine. Her first job was errand girl, office girl, the lowest possible, she said, and at the beck and call of everyone. And from that place she rose by sheer ability to be the editor and the highest paid woman in the United States. She loved to tell the story of it, not only because it was her story but because it was an American story, for where could it have happened except in our country? She was not young when I first knew her, her hair was grey, her face and figure no longer youthful, but her spirit was dauntless. She loved good talk and good food and she had a shrewd wisdom, not intellectual but practical and sound. We met often for luncheon and it was characteristic that she chose quiet expensive places and pondered over the menu. And I had pleasant visits in her country house and with her friends.

I came to know Dorothy Canfield Fisher, and visited her, too, and through her another American life revealed itself to me, and in as American a home as was ever built, founded nearly two centuries ago, and still maintained in the same Vermont town. In a strange sorrowful way my worlds met again through Dorothy Canfield, for she lost her son in the Philippines during the war, a brave young doctor who gave his life for his fellow Americans when he went to rescue American troops. For a monument to him, his parents brought to this country the young Filipino doctor and his wife, also a doctor, who had been the son's best friends while he was with them, and the parents gave these two the opportunity for postgraduate study which enabled them to return to their homeland and set up their own hospital.

Thus my worlds meet again and again, until the several are fused in one. Oscar Hammerstein and his wife Dorothy, world citizens, our friends and neighbors, have stood beside me in the work for Welcome House, and not only they, but others as steadfast here in our own community. James Michener, friend and neighbor, too, world citizen again in spirit and in act, and others who have never left this American world and yet have had hearts as wide as the globe, and minds as free, these who have stood with me in the work for Welcome House are my friends.

And now, I suppose, it is time to tell of Welcome House, for the children of Welcome House do indeed unite my worlds in one.

It all began one Christmastime and I have already told that story under the title "No Room at the Inn," and here I shall compress the years into a few pages.

I have never, I believe, willingly undertaken a job outside of my home and my work, which is writing novels. I have inherited no crusading blood and I dislike publicity with a fervor which may as well be called hatred, for that is what it is. When I have undertaken a task which has nothing to do with home or my writing, it has always been with reluctance and only after a period of desperate search for someone else, anyone else, to do it. Certainly I had no thought of opening a child adoption agency in the United States and this after I was fifty years old. Yet that is exactly what I did.

I had long since ceased to think of adoption agencies. My own children were all but grown up, and my interests were in their age group. Then suddenly one cold December day, when our house was all in ferment with approaching Christmas and long-legged boys and girls with their skis and their dances and glorious hodgepodge of Christmas presents and holly wreaths, the postman brought me a special-delivery letter from a distant child adoption agency, asking if I could help them place for adoption a little baby, the son of an American white mother and an East Indian father, but rejected by both families on both sides of the globe. Do not ask why a child is rejected, for I cannot understand it, whatever the reason. The agency workers had exhausted every possibility in the whole of the United States, they told me, and they had even tried to place him in India, but no one wanted him. They enclosed his picture. I looked into the sad little face of a lonely child, and the happy world in which I lived dropped away. What I saw was hundreds of little faces like his in India, hundreds and thousands of young men and women, born of the white man and the Indian woman, not wanted by either and therefore lost, for the unwanted child is always the lost child. But this little boy was American, born here in my own country, and for me it was unendurable that he should be lost here as he would

362

have been lost in India. I hastened to the telephone and called every friend I had who was Indian, or partly Indian, everyone, too, whom I knew who had been to India and might know other Indians, and over and over again I told the baby's story. Still nobody wanted him. The agency letter said, "If we cannot place him by the first of January, then regretfully we shall have to put him permanently in a Negro orphanage where he does not belong because of course he is Caucasian on both sides. We have no prejudice against the Negro but we are reluctant to put upon any child's shoulders the burden of prejudice which they bear and which he might be spared."

Yes, I understood that. Hastily I gathered my family around me and told them the story. What should we do? There was not one dissenting voice, from the father to the youngest daughter. All of them said, "Bring him here. If we can't find a better place for him, we will keep him."

Thus authorized, I telephoned the agency. Soon after Christmas in the darkness of a winter's night, a small dark boy was deposited in my arms, his enormous brown eyes quietly terrified and he utterly silent because his thumb was buried permanently in his mouth. The people who brought him went away again, and I took him upstairs to the crib we had prepared and I put him to bed. He did not sleep much that night and neither did I. He did not cry aloud but now and then he cried in a small voice subdued by fear, and then I held him until he slept.

Astounding as this advent was, yet another came and in the same month. A friend wrote me that a little half-Chinese child was to be born in a certain city hospital. The child had nowhere to go, for the Chinese father, already married, could not acknowledge him and had returned to China, and the American mother had no way to keep him. Could the child be sheltered with me until I could find some family for him? The local adoption agency could not accept him. By now I felt that I was under some guidance I did not understand. My family said, "We may as well have another," and so, on a cold January day, we brought home from the big city hospital a little baby boy, nine days old, literally naked, for we took clothes with us to put upon him. And he, too, began to live with us.

We all took care of our babies together, except at night when they were my responsibility, and we all shared the joy of seeing them grow strong and happy. The little American-Chinese never knew anything but love and he thrived from the first, but the little American–East Indian had to be won into believing that we loved him. Yet that did not take long. The months passed and our family did a great deal of thinking. If there were these two children there must be many others. I began to inquire among child adoption agencies and found indeed that the American child of Asian or part-Asian ancestry was their greatest problem, greater even than the Negro child. Many agencies would not accept them at all, feeling their adoption was impossible. What became of them then? Nobody knew. A child can be lost here in the United States more easily than in countries where the big family system still prevails.

I reported back to my family. Behind our two babies were perhaps hundreds of others. Were we to do nothing about them? I had now a special concern. No one perhaps can love his country so logically and deeply as the person who has lived away from it for many years and returns with ardent patriotism. I could not bear to see in my country the same evils that I had seen in others. That is, I could not bear to believe that these beautiful children could find no adoptive homes because of their mixed origins. I would not believe it. The job was simply to find parents for them.

Yet suppose I could not? Hundreds of agencies had tried and failed. I could not take all the children, that was obvious. Also, as I reminded our grown children, their father and I were too old to start another family of babies. These little American-Asians needed special love and care right through the years and we were no longer young. We must plan for a sound future. Then I asked myself—why not then find younger parents in our own community for our two American-Asian babies, and let theirs be the home center while we helped as grandparents? And why not plan for all such children until other agencies were convinced that they are "adoptable"? Our community has many generous and kind people in it, and perhaps they would help. I invited our leading men and women one evening to talk over the plan. "If you will stand behind it with us," I said, "I believe we can do something really useful not only for this, after all, rather small group of American children, but for our nation. Communist propaganda in Asia says that we Americans despise people with Asian blood. But we will show them that we care for these exactly as we care for all."

The man who keeps our general store spoke for everybody. He was a big Pennsylvania Dutchman, our oldest citizen and our most respected and influential. He said, "We won'dt only be willin', we will be proudt to have the childtern."

Thus began Welcome House, Incorporated. It has grown through the years to gather many children. A few live permanently in our community, established in two families before the adoptions began, but the others, the babies, now go to adoptive parents. For there are many parents who want the American children of Asian blood. Some of these parents are white Americans, some Asian, some part-Asian. All of them are people who have unusual background, advantages in understanding and education and experience. We are particular about our parents. They must want our babies for what they are, they must value the Asian heritage and be able to teach the child to value it. Once a prospective mother, looking at a lovely little girl whose Japanese mother had given her Asian eyes, asked me, "Will her eyes slant more as she grows older?" My heart hardened. That woman would not be given one of our children. She had to think the tilted eyes were beautiful, and if she did not, then she was not the right one. Plenty of people do think such eyes beautiful. We have at last a list of waiting parents who want our babies. And when they are approved, our babies go with them into their communities and make their way, without fail. For the blood of Asia adds a gentle charm to the American child and there is no gainsaying this fact.

The job has not been easy. Has it been worth doing? Yes, and for many reasons. For me it has been deeply satisfying to find Americans who are generous and widehearted, who help to find the children, help to support them, and help to place them with good adoptive parents and thus insure good lives. It has been worth while, too, to discover the Americans of different caliber, the small-minded narrow-hearted prejudiced ones, the men and women unworthy of the great name they carry, the un-American Americans. I find it as useful to know these as the others. Not all the people even in our community are the right kind of Americans—the kind that I can be proud of before the whole world.

And I hope I am not too selfish in finding comfort in the children for myself. At night in the solitary hours before dawn, when, wakeful, I find my wilful mind dwelling upon the problems of the world and particularly upon our American problems, which seem increasingly severe, I find myself thinking of all our Welcome House children, each one of them belonging now to an American family, loving and loved, and I remind myself that thousands of people, maybe millions of people, in Asia know about them, too. As I write these very words, I was stopped by the ringing of the telephone and when I answered it, I heard the voice of a man from Indo-China, a Vietnamese, who broadcasts regularly to his own country against Communism and for democracy, and he put a familiar question to me. "May I come and visit Welcome House? I want to know all about the children, how they get adopted into American families, so that I can tell my countrymen about it. This is what they ought to know about the United States."

"Come," I said as I always say. "We are glad to tell you everything."

Yes, and Welcome House is worth while, too, not only for what it does now, but for what it proves to other adoption agencies—that no child is "unadoptable" if they find the parents who want that particular child. There are parents for every child born in the United States of America.

Green Hills Farm

We have many exiles with us nowadays, here in our country. I used to see exiles in my Chinese world often enough but they were the white men who could never go home. Sometimes it was their own fault. They had married Chinese women, or had children by them, and the little creatures they had made, inadvertently perhaps, had laid such hold upon them that they stayed until it was too late to leave them. More often they were exiles merely because they could not enjoy living in the small American towns and on the farms where they had been born. The magic of Asia had caught them, the inexplicable richness of ancient life, the ease and freedom of belonging nowhere, and they could not return to the tight circle of family and friends who could never understand the magic.

Today I see other exiles, the Chinese here in the United States, who dare not return to their own land because they have committed themselves against the Communists and now fear for their lives if they go home. It interests me to see how the state of exile affects these people I have known for so many years, the famous as well as the unknown, the rich as well as the poor. Some of the Chinese exiles are very rich. They have prepared against this day by storing away in American banks wealth enough to last their lifetime through. They live here much as they did in China, in comfortable houses or apartments, but waited upon by American servants and deferred to by Americans who sympathize with them. The ladies play mahjong in New York as they did in Shanghai, all afternoon and most of the night, sleeping in the early hours to wake up and play again. They invite each other as guests, travelling in sleek automobiles with Negro chauffeurs. They are not seen often in public and their circle is themselves and the Americans who defer to them.

Others are well-known scholars and writers, exiled because they are Confucianists in an age which rejects the order of Confucius. They live in cities in small apartments, their wives doing the housework and finding it hard. "In China I had three servants," such a Chinese lady said to me the other day. "Here I cannot afford one. I pity the American women, slaves to housework! Life is too difficult here in America."

Yes, it is hard for a Chinese exile. In his own country the scholar and the intellectual had honor. Here there is not as much honor for the scholar as for the successful prize fighter or football player or crooner or movie star. And the exile who is a scholar often has his principles. He will accept as his friends only those Americans who believe as he does. Traditionally the Chinese scholar was the administrator of Imperial government and today he reasons, though wrongly, that he who is not for Chiang Kai-shek is certainly for Mao Tse-tung. Tell him that it is possible to reject both equally and he cannot believe you—or he will not. In his narrowed world, for he does not accept the American, either, this exile grows bitter and ill-tempered. "He can be very mean," the great Chinese novelist, Lau Shaw, once said, and I did not know then what he meant.

But nowadays Lau Shaw himself is an exile of a sort, I suppose, living in Peking, and speaking what he is told to speak, and writing what he is told to write. I see quotations sometimes from his articles and stories. I hear echoes and I marvel at his obedience. But I know he has compensations. He is in Peking, he is in China, and his heart is free. He was not happy here in the United States as a visitor, for nothing could lift the shadow of exile from him. Once when he came to spend a weekend with us, it happened that we had invited a crowd of wounded veterans from the Valley Forge Hospital to a party in our big barn. They were tragic young men, soldiers who had been half blown to pieces in the war by booby traps and hand grenades. Their faces were all but obliterated, and the plastic surgeon was trying to rebuild them bit by bit. Our party was the first time they had been away from the hospital and the officer in charge had warned us not to be shocked. I had tried to explain to the children, but the explanation had been almost impossible. Luckily our cocker spaniel had a litter of puppies at their best and most lovable age, six weeks, their eyes open and mischief beginning to invade. I was a few minutes late for the party and from the house I could see the Red Cross station wagons arriving with the men. The children were already in the barn. I braced myself, dreading the next hours, and then I went over to be hostess.

I need not have feared. With infallible instinct the children had taken the basket of puppies to the barn with them and Rusty, the mother, and Silver, the father, then alive, had gone with them. When I entered the barn what I heard was laughter, the loud self-forgetting laughter of young men and children at play, and what they were playing with was the puppies, and the puppies were performing at their best and funniest. The men had forgotten their faces, forgotten for the moment the war. They had gone back to being boys at home, and the children, proud of the puppies, had forgotten that the boys had no faces. They were all laughing, laughing at the puppies. The evening was off to a roaring success.

What I really wanted to tell about this story, however, was that Lau Shaw was already there, too. I had asked him to speak to the men and I introduced him after the solid refreshments, explaining that he was China's greatest novelist. I had no idea what he would say. Lau Shaw is really a very old-fashioned Chinese. If he had his way, I am sure that he would like to have lived in China five hundred years ago. He is a sensitive man, oversophisticated perhaps, instinctively avoiding anything painful, even in conversation. What then would he say to the pitiful young men?

He got up, diffident as ever, he stood before them a moment, and I could see that his eyes were closed. Then he began to speak in his deep gentle voice. What did he talk about? About shadowboxing in old Peking, if you please, surely as alien a subject as could be imagined! I doubt whether one of those young Americans had ever heard of shadowboxing. Of course Lau Shaw knew that, and so he proceeded to explain the art, its meaning, its story, its historical significance, all in the simplest and most charming fashion, and then without the slightest self-consciousness he illustrated his talk himself by making the movements of shadowboxing into a sort of formal dance, a set of stylized motions. I knew the subject well, I had often watched shadowboxers in Chinese theaters, but I was entranced. And looking about me I saw that the men were entranced, too, comprehending without knowing, perhaps, just what it was they comprehended, but fascinated and carried away into another world they had never seen. When Lau Shaw stopped, there was silence, a great sigh, and then wild applause. And this is what I mean by human understanding.

Once again I heard Lau Shaw wield the same magic, this time in New York, before a sophisticated city audience. It was at an East and West Association meeting and he had been very reluctant to speak. He was averse to any publicity, hating to be known, wary of politics and political questions and discussion. He made the same hesitation before he spoke and then he delivered a delightful discourse, exactly as he might have done in Peking. The subject? "Crickets, Kites and Pekinese Dogs and Their Significance in Chinese Life," and the audience was enthralled.

So gentle a creature as Lau Shaw was of course cheated again and again by the cruel-hearted in the United States, as well as elsewhere. He made friends once in his lonely existence in New York with a man who professed to admire him, and after a month or so of acquaintance, the man, seeming intelligent and well informed, and therefore trusted by Lau Shaw, asked for a twenty-four hour loan of a hundred dollars. It was Lau Shaw's allowance for the month, but in the Chinese tradition which does not deny a friend he handed the sum to the American who never appeared again. Several such experiences, I am ashamed to say, this Chinese great man suffered. We Americans do not know how often crimes are thus committed against guests in our country. If we knew we would not prate so much of how we are cheated when we go abroad.

Undoubtedly the revolution in China has had a disastrous effect upon Chinese scholars and intellectuals and not one of them has fulfilled his early promise. Even Hu Shih's great books, so brilliantly begun, have never been finished. Yet the cause, if not the blame, for this rests partly upon us, too, who belong to the West. Hu Shih and Ch'en Tu-hsiu, the two leaders of the literary revolution in China—and it is necessary to remember that in revolutions scholars and intellectuals were always the leaders—had early committed themselves to the West, as I have said. Ch'en Tu-hsiu, indeed, even attacked Confucianism as a denial of human rights and Hu Shih maintained in those days that the culture of the West was not to be considered materialistic merely because it made life easier. Both declared themselves for an outright adoption of Western ways.

Yet the literary revolution, so brilliantly begun by these two young men, failed in its purpose of reaching the people, for the First World War revealed deep faults in Western civilization. War was shocking to them as Asians, to whom civilization meant a universal humanism whose inevitable fruit was peace. After the war, the vitality, even the ferocity, of the Russian revolution attracted the fiery nature of Ch'en Tu-hsiu, for, he reasoned, if violence be the secret of power in the world today, then choose the most violent means to the designed end. He became the founder and leader of the Chinese Communist party. Hu Shih, a man of different character, left his work permanently unfinished and retired into the life of a scholar and cosmopolite.

One is not inclined to blame. The writer suffers in profound ways from the injustices and the griefs of the times. It is inevitable, too, that in the loneliness of exile—for many Chinese will never see their homeland again, I fear, they are too old, and they know it—they feel keenly the indifference of their American neighbors and sometimes even of their American friends, and they cannot love America. We ought therefore to remember them and show them full respect, for we are honored by their presence.

In these years while my personal life was absorbed in home and growing family, I had at the same time been learning about my own people.

Life in China and with the Chinese had taught me much about human beings, for in ancient countries humanity and human relationships are the primary concern. To know how a person feels was to my Chinese friends more important than anything else about him, for until one knows how another feels no friendship can be established nor even business carried on with mutual benefit. I applied this education and its skills to those who surrounded me in my new life, to neighbors and to acquaintances and to the casual contacts of everyday. That I might learn more widely, I travelled to various parts of the country, so that I could see the contrasts beneath North and South, East and West, contrasts far more striking than their geographical counterparts in China or indeed in any other country that I had ever seen.

I began to know my fellow Americans for what they are, a generous, impulsive, emotional people, unstable, not only from nature, but also from environment. This environment is historical as well as present. We have changed so quickly from a pioneer and rural culture to industrialism and its consequent urbanism that we are still divided between the two major types of civilization. Our political system, too, abetted and even partly caused the instability of our life. The complete overturn every four years in our central government, or at least the effort to make the overturn, the intervening upset of local politics, the shortness of the term of office, not only for major officials, but for the lesser ones as well, make impossible the development of enduring policies and principles. A sense of haste and hurry pervades our daily life, bred of the necessity for action before the change again, and this permeates our thinking. The safety valves of English democratic procedures, whereby a government remains until the people overthrow it, are not ours. Good or bad, certain men can count upon remaining in office for a certain number of years, to do good or evil or nothing at all. Yet however beneficial the good, it may be impermanent, for in four years or eight, seldom more, the whole regime is upset or can be upset. To this, more than to any other single cause, I began to ascribe the superficiality of American life and thought. We live from day to day, unable to plan for long years ahead, lest a new government bring about far-reaching changes. I cannot sufficiently stress the disastrous effect upon the life of our people of continual political uncertainty, especially when in addition to it we have the heavy task of amalgamating a population which has come from so many varying parts of the world, and so quickly that there has not been time to create the real union to be found not in political organization so much as in the deep human roots of tradition and custom developing through a long common life together.

Thus reflecting, I began to be alarmed in the year 1941, for the future of Americans. I knew very well that at the end of the war we would be the ones on the victorious side, and undoubtedly, too, the strongest among the victors, and therefore the peoples of Asia would be expecting a leadership from us which we would be unable to give, mainly because of our own instability but also because of our ignorance of Asian peoples, their history and their importance in the postwar world. When I say importance I mean not only in potentiality but also in the ferment and trouble and struggle in which we would inevitably be involved in the whole world, but centering this time in Asia because of the coincidence of the Second World War with Asian determination for independent modern life. Try as we might we could not again escape as we did after the First World War, by withdrawal. Asia this time must be reckoned with. Yet how could our people meet such a future with these peoples when we knew nothing about their past? I grew wretched with continual pondering upon such matters, aware as I was of the deep hostilities of Asia against the white man. Could Americans escape those whirlwinds of history? The only hope, I came to see, lay in the possibility that we could establish ourselves as a separate people, a new people, not to be allied even in thought with old empires and colonialisms. We must deal with the Asians as Americans not involved with the past, and we were fortunate in the possibility, since we had indeed waged no active wars for colonial purposes nor established any real colonies, and since our regime in the Philippines had been relatively enlightened, and it was clear that we had no wish even to stay there. We were lucky enough, that is, to have already a great fund of good will in Asia, and especially in China, upon which to draw for the future. Only new and reckless action could forfeit it. This was always possible in a war, when many young men are shipped willy-nilly and without real preparation into a foreign country. We had experienced that in Europe in the First World War.

I have never been an evangelical missionary, and indeed abhor the general notion, and yet I know very well that my missionary beginnings have shaped me to the extent of feeling responsible at least for what I can personally do about a given situation which needs mending. What then could I do, I asked myself, to help my countrymen, even a few of them and even on a small scale, to know something of the lives and thoughts of the peoples with whom they must inevitably deal, either as friends or enemies, in the future and that very near? The one gift I had brought with me to my own country was the knowledge of Asia and especially of China and Japan, gained not only through years of living there but through years of concentrated study, travel and observation. True, I wrote books. But books, even best sellers, reach only a small number of the total population of our country. Do they not reach the leading minds? Yes, but in a democracy such as ours the leading minds seldom achieve a place of permanent influence. And the men who sit in Congress or even in the White House are usually not our leading minds. They are not the thinkers. Still less have they time for reflection, or even for thoughtful travel. In a democracy, I reasoned, it is the people who must be informed.

But how?

For a number of years my husband had been editor of *Asia Magazine*, a monthly started in 1917 by Willard Straight, then American Consul in Peking. Impressed by the fabulously interesting scene in which he worked, Willard Straight put a portion of his wealth into a magazine designed to inform and amuse and interest the American public by describing in authentic prose and pictures the colorful and powerful Asian peoples. I had a sentimental interest in the magazine because some of my own first writing had been published there, and I had continued to write for it occasionally. Yet it had never been able to find the number of readers it deserved. Americans could not be interested in Asia, it seemed. The magazine, maintaining high standards of excellence, had through the years lost much money annually and only a wealthy family could have continued it, as Mrs. Straight did continue it after Mr. Straight's death, and after her marriage to Leonard Elmhirst. My husband had steadfastly reduced the loss over the years of his editorship, maintaining authenticity above all, but the number of readers did not greatly increase. There were, it seemed, only about fifteen thousand or at most twenty thousand Americans who were interested in Asian peoples, in spite of the inevitable future looming ahead.

Could this be true? It seemed impossible to me, and in 1941 when Mrs. Elmhirst decided to close the magazine, my husband and I wished to continue it for a while to see whether this small interest could be increased. There was no other magazine in the United States which carried full and authentic information about Asian life. At that moment it seemed folly to end the last means of informing our people and providing the knowledge essential to their own safety and welfare. It was as near a missionary impulse as I ever had, and my husband shared it. We were given the magazine and all its assets in the hope, encouraged by Mrs. Elmhirst, that it could be saved. Suffice it to say that we did keep it going for another five years, until events after the end of the war made it impossible. There was, as a matter of fact, an increase in American interest in Asia during the war years, and had there been enough paper available, the magazine might have become self-supporting.

In those ten years, too, I founded The East and West Association and from it learned enough for many books. Even a magazine, I could see, did not educate our people. They learned better from hearing than reading, and best of all from seeing. Why not then, I thought, bring to them men and women of Asia who could speak for themselves, show what they were, explain their own history and civilization? Why not devise a sort of Asian adult education for American communities? In this way our people could get firsthand, from Asian citizens, the story of Asia, without bias and without persuasion. The idea was very simple. In the United States were many pleasant and learned visitors from various countries. I was interested especially in Asians, but if there were such visitors also from Europe why not include them, as well? The world of peoples, I had early learned from Mr. Kung, was indeed one family under heaven. If average Americans could see themselves as part of the human race, they might be stimulated to curiosity and thus to interest and thus to understanding. It was the usual technique of learning.

We set up a small organization, secured tax exemption and a good list of sponsors, and began our work with an opening dinner in Washington, followed by a large meeting in New York, to explain the purpose of the Association. Wendell Willkie made the main opening speech in New York, and it was there that I first heard him speak of his one world. Hu Shih, then Chinese Ambassador to Washington, spoke, too, and various dignitaries from other Asian embassies. The job was begun. It was not to be carried on by such meetings, of course, but by men and women travelling far and wide over the country, sometimes alone, sometimes in couples, or in groups if they were entertainers, and their task was never to be political but always cultural, and even culturally it was first of all to be simple and friendly and vivid. They were to speak of everyday life in their own countries, of their ways and thoughts and hopes, illustrating what they said with costumes, pictures, instruments of music or drama. We chose good people, not necessarily famous or even highly skilled, and indeed I preferred not to have the very famous. I wanted our average Americans to see men and women of Asia who were like themselves, teachers and students and technical men here to learn American methods. One of the best men we ever had was a quiet little Indian professor, here on his sabbatical year, who visited many communities and spoke to all kinds of groups and stayed in American homes and answered questions over the dinner table and around the evening fire. Expenses for such visitors were paid by the local groups, and I was touched and amazed to find that I had been wrong in thinking that Americans cared nothing about the people of Asia. Asia, it is true, roused no interest as such, but a man or woman from Asia, in the flesh and in their own town, speaking in the high school auditorium, or from the pulpit on a Sunday, staying over the night and cooking an Asian dish for supper, and helping to wash the dishes, making himself human and friendly, Americans were very much interested in him. Nor was the interest one-sided. The visitors themselves came back with shining eyes to our little East and West Association office in New York. Not only had they told the Americans about their countries and their peoples—and how they appreciated the opportunity to do this—but they learned about Americans as they had never had a chance to do before. It was so different, they said, from living in a hotel, from walking the streets of a strange city, even very different from living in a university dormitory and sitting in a classroom. They had stayed in American homes, they had played with the children, they had helped with the chores, they had met real people in the school auditorium and had answered thousands of questions. They had showed American women how to wear a sari, how Korean women put on full skirts and jackets, how to cook Chinese food; they had talked with businessmen and teachers and preachers and workingmen. Now they could go back to their own countries and tell their own people how friendly and good the Americans really are—different indeed from politicians and officials.

One year we even rented a bus and sent out a troupe of young Chinese actors and actresses to give plays of their people, old and new. Their opening performance was given for Mrs. Roosevelt and some friends at the White House, and there Wang Yung first gave her remarkable roles of Chinese peasant life. This young actress was a star of modern motion pictures in Shanghai, before the war, and when the Japanese attacked she had joined her fellow artists in organizing a travelling theater whose purpose was to educate the peasant into resistance against the Japanese. The group had divided into several units in order to cover the Chinese countryside as well as they could, singing and acting in impromptu plays for propaganda, as well as performing historical plays. Wang Yung and her troupe walked over many provinces of China. In Hong Kong at last she escaped capture by the Japanese, disguising herself as a beggarwoman, and though she was young and pretty, she prepared herself down to the very dirt on her skin that an old beggar would naturally accumulate and so saved her own life. Safely out of China the troupe played again in Malaya and Burma, and when it finally disbanded Wang Yung was allowed a visit to the United States as a reward. Here she came to see me and then to give her talents to The East and West Association. She was an unusual young modern in that, belonging to a good old family, she was also thoroughly rooted in Chinese tradition and grace.

I do not know whether even Mrs. Roosevelt knew how accurately and richly Wang Yung portrayed the Chinese peasant woman that night in the stately East Room of the White House, but I felt a deep happiness as I watched. Here at last, in the very heart of my own nation, a Chinese woman revealed her people. And I had the same happiness months later in New Orleans, where I went to meet the troupe on its journey. In that wonderful and beautiful city, where the old life of Europe mingles with the modern world we Americans have made, again I saw our young Chinese appear before a great audience to give a play of just such intermingling of old and new in China.

The American audiences could not of course appreciate the delicate nuances of the Chinese play and I did not expect it. But they caught, perhaps, the reality of life and love in conflict between old and new, and this human struggle is the same everywhere. I wish that we could have continued with our travelling troupe, for their work was vivid and true, but expenses are always high for such a venture and even generous gifts from Chinese in America, whose sympathies were with the Nationalists, could not maintain the troupe and so its work came at last to an end.

By such simple means good people from Asia went into many American communities, and though I had thought primarily of my own people, it gave me satisfaction that the visitors took back to Asia new understanding of Americans, too, and a very favorable one. Our "East and West" visitors were not always Asians, but sometimes white men and women who had special knowledge of Asia and occasionally of other parts of the world. But Asia was my primary concern, naturally, because it was the field of the most profound American ignorance.

Why did that most interesting and, I hope, valuable work ever end? For after ten years I did suspend its activities, although it had been an education for me, too, for it had brought me to many communities, myself, and into contact with large numbers of Americans whom I might otherwise never have met. There were two reasons, one financial, for though local communities paid their own expenses, the growing demand for the Asian visitors, as speakers and entertainers and friends, made necessary an increased office staff, and for this I was never able to get any help. Foundations give for research or charity, and The East and West Association was neither. It was an educational experiment, designed for friendship and mutual understanding between the peoples, especially of Asia and the United States. There was nothing very daring or even very new in the idea, but the practical application of an ideal, however old, may be alarming to persons who have not thought of such a possibility before. There was another reason. It was too late, and so I had feared even as early as 1946, when our chief American representative announced at the San Francisco conference in the presence of many distinguished Asians, that American policy for the future would not concern itself with the independence of colonial peoples in Asia.

What a death blow were such words to those Asian peoples who knew our history far better than we did theirs, who had glorified George Washington because he fought for the freedom of his country from an imperial power, who had revered Abraham Lincoln because he had freed dark-skinned slaves! Their hopes, their own ideals, they had found expressed in our American Constitution and Bill of Rights. And now, they heard, these were not principles for all peoples, as they had supposed, but only for Americans. I knew instantly the words were spoken that nothing anyone could do now could prevent the inevitable future. China at least would be lost to our leadership, and perhaps the whole of Asia. It was incredible to me that the words could have been uttered, that any man could be so incredibly naïve and ignorant of the world, both historically and in the present, as to utter them at such a moment in such a place. I went into mourning for many months, literally. If I did not wear black garments on my body, my mind was clothed in shadows and my heart was desolate. We closed *Asia Magazine* in 1946, and four years later, convinced that there was no way to bring about human understanding in our dangerous age, I closed The East and West Association. The organization remains, if ever the time comes to revive it again, but it is inactive. Yet here and there groups of people still gather by their own efforts, under its name, determined to learn understanding by knowing men and women from Asia. But they are independent.

Had I been able to foresee the strange atmosphere that has pervaded my country since 1946, where good men and true scholars have lost their jobs and their reputations because of their knowledge and their understanding of the areas which, without American leadership, have gone over to Communism, I should have been confirmed in my decision. For though The East and West Association never sent a Communist or political figure to any American community, yet today it is dangerous even to declare belief in the brotherhood of peoples, in the equality of the races, in the necessity for human understanding, in the common sense of peace—all those principles in which I have been reared, in which I do believe and must believe fearlessly until I die. No, but I would have closed The East and West Association also because I would not have been willing to subject my friends from Asia to the lies and suspicions and false accusations so rife in our times. Yet I am grateful for those ten years in which we were able to meet each other face to face, good citizens from Asia and good citizens in the United States, and now and then the seed sown still bears its fruit.

Much of my life, my thought, my time, my money for ten years went into this work. Through it I, too, learned a lesson. A nation, like a child, cannot comprehend beyond the capacity of its mental age. To teach calculus to a child of six is absurd. One has to begin at the beginning, one has to wait for maturity and it cannot be hastened.

It was increasingly difficult as the war years went on to gain even for myself a true picture of what was happening in China. There was much pleasant propaganda about our Chinese allies, but the sad truth, as I discovered from honest Chinese friends who in rueful talk admitted what I had feared, was that in the positional war which Chiang Kai-shek was waging by remaining in Chungking without much active resistance, the armies under his control were gradually deteriorating. Poor food, irregular pay, a stagnant life were combining to take the heart out of the men. They were growing impatient and bitter as well as idle, while they waited for the World War to decide their fate. Inevitably, too, corruption set in and secret and unlawful trade with the enemy began to flourish. The West would win, they were told, and since they were the allies of the West, it remained only for them to wait until Japan was defeated. The Communists meanwhile carried on a brisk war, and not entirely unselfishly either, for they were consolidating the peasants behind them in the rural areas, penetrating even into Nationalist-held territory. The two parties had no communication with each other, except in a formal fashion in Chungking between Communist representatives and those of the Nationalist government, and they made no mutual military plans. Since neither told the other what it was doing resistance was divided. Their very hopes were divided. Chiang wanted a quick end to the war while his position was still strong enough to claim the leadership in peace, whereas the Communists hoped for a long war, because in the interval they could consolidate more and more territory under their control in the guise of resistance to the aggressive enemy. Civil war was actually being waged, though undeclared, and thus it continued until 1945 when Germany surrendered.

Japan did not surrender at the same time and Chinese of both parties thought that the war would still go on perhaps for many years, the Nationalists fearing, the Communists hoping for such a situation. I remember that my Chinese friends in New York argued with me that the United States must certainly send forces to land upon the Chinese coast and face Japanese troops in hand-to-hand battle. If this were done, they promised, the Nationalist troops would be at their side. The Communists, I reasoned, for I had no means of knowing, would do their best against such an outcome, for by it the whole southeast area which they had begun to penetrate through their guerrillas would automatically be restored to the Nationalists.

My Chinese friends were wrong, as any American might have guessed they would be. We did not, and doubtless never had planned to land American troops on the Chinese coast to meet the Japanese face to face. Instead, as everybody now knows, the Japanese forces were much nearer collapse than had been supposed, and when suddenly and without warning to anyone the atomic bombs were dropped, the end came. Chiang Kai-shek acted with speed. With the power of his office as Commander in the China Zone, he demanded that his troops be taken by American airplanes to the occupied areas and that the Japanese not be allowed to surrender to the Chinese Communists, but only to his own representatives. Upon this the Civil War flared into the open.

We Americans were in an embarrassing position. We were obliged to fulfill Chiang Kai-shek's demands, and yet by so doing we put ourselves on the side of the Nationalists as against the Communists, and this made impossible the atmosphere of neutrality essential to the position we assumed later as arbitrators. That is, the compromise so heroically worked for by General Marshall was always hopeless in view of what had already taken place. The situation was only the first of others that were to follow, the most notable and dangerous one being our support of France as a colonial power in Indo-China. I am convinced that such a position is abhorrent to all good Americans, for in spite of confusions and betrayals we are committed by conviction and by choice to the independence of peoples, and yet, because we stand against Communism, we feel ourselves compelled to accept as allies those with whom we are most deeply incompatible. It has always been and is now, however, a mistake to assume that we are actually compelled to such compromise. An enlightened leadership by men informed of the actualities of life in Asia would have found an alternative that could have given to American democracy its true expression. I say American, and yet the power and the attraction of our way of life, based upon the deep principles of the human heart, lie in the fact that what we believe in is what all mankind craves, the freedom of the individual within the limits of universal law. Had we been able to fulfill ourselves, we might have found world friendship and peace far easier to achieve. Instead we have slipped unwillingly into the place of the burden-bearers of Asia, responsible for old sins that we never committed.

General Marshall went to China in 1946, therefore, with a vain hope.

He faced two lawless parties, each equally lawless, for neither was the elected of the people. Chiang Kai-shek had never made a real—that is, a constitutional—government, and the members of his Cabinet were merely his lackeys, without security of tenure except as they were loyal to his person. Long ago the hope of any organized government had been taken from them. Chiang Kai-shek remained a military leader and no more.

But the Communists had nothing better, either. They also were not elected by the people. They, no more than the Nationalists, had set up an organized legality, within which the people could express their choice. The framework of the nation was gone, the old patterns were destroyed. Had there been no revolution, no Sun Yat-sen, at least there might have been the throne to seize, the Imperial Seal to possess. Even the Old Empress had been careful, however often she fled, to take with her the sacred seal, which alone could prove her right to rule.

Our brave old American general faced two groups of warring men, neither of them with the right to rule a great people, for the people had not spoken and could not speak. Even though a compromise were reached, a government had still to be made. It was indeed a hopeless task, and thinking of it in these days I wonder if he knew it. And why, I wonder, did not our own government know it? A few educated Chinese clung to a vague shred of remaining hope that if a short working compromise could be made they themselves could plunge into the effort of creating a government. They were older and wiser than they had been in the first years of the Nationalists, and though now they no longer believed in Chiang's government, they were not yet won to the Communists, either, and in their no man's land they kept their resolution and tried to form a new group, the Democratic League. The only result of this was to be called pro-Communist by the Nationalists and pro-Nationalist by the Communists, and the little effort soon faded, although it was courageously begun.

Between these two equally selfish forces, the people were all but lost. War-torn and weary, their homes destroyed, the remnants of their families gathering again, they wanted only peace—peace from foreigners, peace to save what they could of their old life. The Communists made quick propaganda for that end. The Americans, they proclaimed, were backing Chiang for their own purposes. A new imperialism was growing in the West. The old European and English empires were ended, but the United States was a rising young power, white men again hungry to possess the world. As loyal Chinese, the Communists declared, they would fight if the United States handed China back to Chiang Kai-shek. Even if this meant years of civil war, they would never yield.

The weary people counted their cards. They cared nothing for Communism and knew very little about it anyway. But they did not want civil war. If Chiang took over the government, civil war would drag on year after year, for the Old Tiger was stubborn and would not acknowledge defeat so long as he lived. Had he not carried on such a war for years before the Japanese attacked? But the Communists promised peace.

The people chose peace, even though it was only a promise, against the certainty of war. And when the people of any country choose peace at all costs, not even generals can make war. The people chose peace, not Communism. It is what Americans must remember, now more than ever, for in this one fact lies the hope for our future friendship in Asia.

When it became clear to me that we had lost, as day after day the Nationalist armies surrendered without battle, handing over their American-supplied arms to the Communists, I spent much thought upon what could next be done. I had no blame in my heart for those yielding soldiers. Soldiers? They were not soldiers. Chiang's real army had been kept intact and would retreat with him to Formosa as had been planned long before. No, the soldiers who faced the Communists were for the most part just country boys, sent in from the provinces upon order. They had been seized, impressed into army service as in the American Civil War our own men were impressed, taken by force if no consent were given, tied with ropes and chained and compelled to march perhaps hundreds of miles, to the battle scene. There guns were thrust into their hands and they were told to fight. But why should they fight? What had the Nationalist cause ever done for them or for their families? They were the sons of average Chinese parents, home-loving and hating war. Of course they surrendered easily and why should they not? Perhaps they did not even know how to fire the American weapons they held.

No, there was no use by now in blaming anyone. The question remained, how could American democracy prevent Chinese Communism from following the harsh Soviet pattern? Much was in our favor. Mao Tse-tung, the acknowledged Communist leader of China, had never been really *persona grata* with Soviet Russia, or so one heard. At one time it was even rumored that he had been expelled from the International party for insubordination to Communist principle and discipline. Certainly he had followed a pattern of his own. Moreover, I could not believe that the good record of Americans in China for a hundred years had been forgotten. American boys living in China during the war had, it is true, left behind them mixed impressions. The intelligent and civilized ones were liked and became good ambassadors for their people. But many of them were not civilized and intelligent and being mere children in years, for what man is mature before twenty-five at least, they had acted like naughty boys, drinking too much and insulting women and sometimes behaving like criminals. I had grieved about this for a while, hearing directly as I did in those years from Chinese friends, and then I reflected that perhaps the time had come for the Chinese and the Americans to know each other exactly as we were, good and bad. On the whole, the record, I say, is good.

I felt, then, that we should capitalize upon the good and should immediately strengthen every tie with the Chinese people by trade and benefit and interchange of goods and citizens, hoping that the American influence would be stabilized before the Russians could step in. As a matter of fact, all during the war there was very little direct Russian influence in China and this remained so for a considerable period after the war during which time we might indeed have consolidated our position as friends of the Chinese, so that the new government would come to depend upon us for trade and technical help, instead of upon Soviet Russia. Our policy, however, developed in quite the opposite direction when Chiang Kai-shek was defeated. We cut ourselves off from the Chinese people, withdrew our citizens, and retired from the Chinese scene. Once again the new Chinese rulers turned to Soviet Russia, as Sun Yat-sen had done in his time, so many years before, for the necessities of their existence.

In the intervening years of increasing tension and the outbreak of the Korean war, I pondered much upon the history of China in my lifetime. I have come to the conclusion at last that it is dangerous, perhaps the supreme danger, for persons or parties to destroy the framework of government which a people has built for itself, not consciously or by sudden choice, but by the slow and profound processes of life and time. The framework is the structure upon which people hang their habits and their customs, their religions and their philosophy. An old house can be changed and strengthened and remodeled and lived in for centuries if the essential framework holds. But once the whole structure is pulled down into dust it may never be rebuilt, and the people who lived in it are lost and wandering.

A revolution, therefore, inevitable in the history of any people when living conditions become intolerable, should always stop short of total destruction of the framework. Thus Sun Yat-sen, when in desperation he overthrew the Manchu dynasty, should not, I have come to believe, also have overthrown the form of government. The Throne should have been upheld, the system maintained, and within that framework reforms carried out. The Chinese people, like the British, were accustomed to a ruling figure. They had developed their own resistances to tyranny, and with increasing knowledge of Western democracy and its benefits they would have assumed modern manners of their own. The English system might have provided better guidance for them than ours. We are not an ancient people. The Chinese background is very different from ours.

This will seem a heretical conclusion, doubtless, not only for many westerners but also for a considerable number of Western-educated Chinese. Nevertheless I maintain it. Sun Yat-sen was an honorable and selfless man, whose integrity is beyond doubt. He deserves the homage of his people. He is not to be blamed that in his burning desire to serve them he destroyed the very basis of their life, which was order.

It is dangerous to try to save people—very dangerous indeed! I have never heard of a human being who was strong enough for it. Heaven is an inspiring goal, but what if on the way the soul is lost in hell?

When I reflect upon the years that I have spent in this American world of mine, I discover that against the quiet steady background of home and work, they divide into what I have done over and beyond my daily life. For example, our farm—

Twenty-one years ago—it is as long as that—when I first saw my house, postage stamp size on a real-estate folder, I scarcely realized its environment. I saw the sturdy thickset old stone building on the hillside, flanked by the tall black walnut tree on one end and the maple on the other, and across a grassy road the big red barn. Forty-eight acres of woodland and meadow went with the house, edged by the brook. They seemed then as wide as an empire. In China the average farm is less than five acres. At first I contended with what seemed rank wilderness. The land had not been tilled for seventeen years, and weeds and briars covered it like a blanket. I attempted the unattainable. I tried to make those woolly acres look like a Chinese farm, neat and green and fruitful. I coaxed the old apple trees, but they remained unresponsive, I tried to confine the brook, and it remained rebellious. An old neighbor looked doubtfully on, and said, "It's a vild critter, that there run." For a while I thought he meant "vile," but then I discovered that it was Pennsylvania Dutch accent. Wild our brook was and wild it still is, as mild as milk in summer, but when the spring snows melt, or after a thunderstorm, it imitates the raging Yangtse. No retaining wall is strong enough. We built a dam fit to hold back a monster, and that alone compels it into a small lake where the children can boat and fish and skate in winter.

Eventually, of course, I realized that American land is rebellious, and, besides, our own land had been ill-treated. Generations of farmers had neglected to fertilize, and had further robbed the earth by planting nothing but corn, until the shale and clay pan that underlie our shallow topsoil emerged like skeletons from old graves.

I had been taught in my Chinese world that earth is a sacred possession and I was horrified at what I saw I had. How could I replace what had been lost before I came? I longed to buy cattle and treasure the manure for the land. But those were the days when no one was encouraged to farm, the incredible days when people were actually making a living by not farming the land upon which they lived. Government subsidy was for nonproduction, and my neighbors, all farmers, divided themselves into the good and the evil, the good men refusing to let their fields lie idle even when times were awry, and the evil, who had more cash than ever before, because they were only too ready not to work. It was no time to begin a farm, at any rate. Therefore I planted trees, thousands of them, upon our hillsides. After my brother died, I planted trees upon the land which he had left, and then, that our right flank might be protected against small bungalows, I bought still another farm as derelict as either of the others, and planted trees there, too.

This went on until the war came, and then I felt that the time had come really to farm, as I had been secretly longing to do. For another reason, the children were drinking quarts of milk every day, and I was not satisfied with the milk supply. To live in the country and drink pasteurized milk as one must in the city, seemed absurd. The precious vitamins of raw milk, so essential to children, are too often destroyed or all but, by pasteurization, especially if it is well done. If it is carelessly done as it may be, then such milk is more dangerous than raw milk, for the process gives the excuse for all sorts of milk to be poured into the vats, certainly not all of it clean. And I am prejudiced against dirt, dead or alive, in food. I wish that my countrymen were all clean, but the truth is we Americans are not a very clean people, not nearly so clean as the Japanese, for example, or the Swedish, or several others. Our farmers are content too often with dirty barns and dirty cows hastily swabbed around the udders before milking time. I did not at all like what I saw on farms, and this, too, moved me to have my own. Rejoicing when war directives urged the raising of food, I hastened to obey. It meant the buying of three more run-down farms adjoining our land. The average farm in our region is fifty acres. Each of the farms had on it a good stone house, though without modern conveniences, and a good-to-middling barn. One good stone barn remodeled would do for the herd, the other barns were left for storage.

I plunged into the job, deciding that I must learn myself before I could know what should be done, for this was the United States and not China. For two years I listened, read, observed and worked. My neighbors said, "Be you goin' to do real farmin' or book farmin'?" This, I discovered, meant was I going to try to have a Bangs-free herd? Our state requires herds to be free of tuberculosis but not yet of Bangs. Therefore if I wanted to have a clean herd I would have to work alone. None of my neighbors approved the effort. In kindliest spirit they warned me that one could lose a whole herd if he got the idea of not having any Bangs. Best thing, they said, was just to pay no heed to Bangs. There was no law against it. I listened and smiled and said nothing, determined for the children's sake to have a clean herd, and so we began by being clean, and have so continued, tested constantly, unceasingly watchful, but successful. I look at my hearty brood of children now, much taller than I am, and reflect that all these years they have been drinking the best milk that can be produced, raw milk as fresh as the morning, all the vitamins intact, and rich with yellow cream. Through the war I made our own butter and we did not take our share of the nation's supply. Last spring when there was a glut of milk on the market for a month or two and we could not sell all we had I made butter again, in quantities to last for months, and we raised extra pigs on the skim milk, and gave it to the chicks and they came through in prime shape. The price of our grade of milk is high enough so that usually it pays to sell it whole. Yet I am sufficiently irritated in true democratic fashion when I see the difference between what we get for our clean excellent milk wholesale and what the consumer has to pay for it bottled after the middlemen are through with it. The boys urge me to go into the retail milk business, and run a milk route, but that I refuse. My concern is for the children, and the land is showing a satisfactory return to what good land should be. The marginal acres we still keep in trees, and will always do so, replanting as we cut each year. The cows have done well enough. They take prizes at shows and so on, and I have more than my share of ribbons and silverware. But I am not much interested in such goings on. I feel that unless a cow can produce milk and manure, her good looks are useless. Pretty is as pretty does, my mother used to say. Unless the help wants very much to show a cow or bull we have bred and of which they are proud, my eyes remain upon the milk and crop records.

Farms with hired help are not, of course, for making money. Yet, all in all, I feel we have done well with our farm, better than we feared, and I refuse to count the money alone. Besides milk, the farm has given the children an endless source of interest and pocket money. There is always work to be done, free or for pay, and the boys have grown up

384

farmwise. They know how to milk, they know the care and feeding of the herd, they understand the soil, they can use farm machinery and care for it as a capital possession. They know the urgency of harvesting and of work that has to be done long after hours because hay and grain will not wait upon a storm. The farm has given us family roots, not only in the community, but in the very earth itself. It has even sifted human beings for us. We have learned to know a rascal from an honest man, whether he be farm manager or hired hand. We have had both kinds, at all levels, and it has taught the children lessons they cannot learn in school. They have learned, too, that kindness to animals pays, as well as to human beings, not only spiritually but materially. It is true that a contented cow gives better milk and more milk than an unhappy one, and she is only contented when she is kindly treated. We have fired men because they pushed the cows around.

There are the lesser creatures, too, on a farm like ours, the turkeys that we raise for ourselves and our farm people and our relatives at Christmas. Turkeys are temperamental birds, and they cannot have their feet on the ground, for they die of reality. They must be maintained in cages above the earth, and carefully fed. And American chickens are delicate, not at all the robust brown creatures that scratch in the dung and the dust of the Chinese threshing floors and country roads and take care of themselves. Even the pigs here are inclined to pettishness unless they are carefully tended. Pigs I did not know very well in China, for there I saw them merely as farm scavengers, prized because they would eat anything and then could be butchered to provide food in turn for the farm family. It was only when we began to keep a few pigs here on our American farm for our own ham and bacon and sausage that I took time to watch them and reflect upon their personalities. They are interesting creatures, not at all simple, as I had supposed.

Yet I doubt if I could have understood fully how complex and intelligent pigs are had it not been for Tiny, a runt in one of the litters, who amused us by his insistence upon life, midget though he was born, so that when I saw him doomed merely by size as he fought with his mates for his dinner at the trough, I felt nature had been unjust and, yielding to the children's pleas, I let them bring him to the house. Such was Tiny's intelligence that it was a matter only of hours before he realized that he was, so to speak, in clover, and began to impose himself upon us in the most astounding manner. I used to wonder why it was that Chinese farm families allowed their pigs to roam in their houses, and my mother told me that in Ireland, too, the pigs were in the farmhouses. I thought it a deplorable habit until I discovered that pigs anywhere are so determined that they do whatever they wish. In two days

Tiny was clamoring at every door to get into our house, and only the screen doors kept him out. I say clamoring, but the proper word is screeching, or screaming, or loud bawling in a high key. The microscopic creature, standing only three inches or so above ground and no larger than a kitten, had a voice of such volume and discord that it was distracting beyond any I had ever heard. I used sometimes on Chinese roads to speak reproachfully to a sweating Chinese farmer transporting two fat pigs to market, tied by ropes on either side of the central wheel of his barrow. Their noise was so appalling that I am sure they were in severe pain, and I begged him to loosen the ropes somewhat to relieve them. No farmer ever did more than grin at me and go on his way. Once a farmer did stop to wipe his sweating brow with his blue cotton girdle cloth, "Foreigner," he said, while he paused, "it is the noise pigs make."

I discovered that he was right. Tiny made the same noise, not because he was tied or confined, for he ran about the lawns like a puppy, but because he was not continuously waited upon or petted or noticed or fed, or because he was lonely and wanted to sleep in someone's lap. Once every hour, regularly, he trotted to the screen door of my own study where I was busy writing a book and stood there squalling until I came out and poured his dish full of milk. Sometimes he came back to squall again merely because he wanted to be with me. There were times when I let him sleep on my lap to stop his raucous cries while I worked. If we took a walk he would scamper after us and then squall because we went too fast for his three-inch legs. He grew fat but not much bigger, and within a month had become such a tyrant that even the children agreed he had to go. We missed him in a queer relieved half-regretful fashion. He was so full of personality that we still laugh when we remember him, but too much personality is not good, at least in a pig. In fact, it was impossible to live with him and in this reflection there is a moral, I suppose, but let it be.

Cats and kittens of course belong to a farm and we had as many as thirteen at the house one spring, not to mention the barn cats necessary for keeping down the rats and mice. We have always had dogs and puppies, both wanted and unwanted. Our pair of cocker spaniels, a little husband and wife, produced beautiful purebred puppies for some years in an ideal monogamy. The little female never looked at a male except her mate. One day, always self-confident, he stepped across the road to speak to a neighbor dog and was run over by a car and the female was left a widow. Her degeneration has been almost human. She mourned for a while and seemed inconsolable. Suddenly she threw sorrow to the winds, grew plump and pretty and left off her homekeeping ways.

386

Within a few weeks she was on the lowest terms of good fellowship with every canine Tom, Dick and Harry in the township and mongrels are now the order of her day, and ours.

Our farm abounds in pleasant wild life, new to me. The hills about my Chinese home were populated by wild boar and wolves and slim mountain panthers, and there were pheasants and wild geese and ducks and cranes. Now I live among squirrels and muskrats and ground hogs. The pheasants are the same, however, the beautiful Chinese ring-necked pheasants, and since I could not tolerate the trespassing ways of city hunters who cannot remember that all land belongs to someone and certainly not to them, we have a state game preserve on our land. And the pheasants abound and also the deer. A few months ago as we sat at luncheon in the dining room, we saw under the locust trees three deer, the buck statuesque and on guard, while the does nibbled the azaleas. Though I am angry for a moment sometimes in the garden to see lettuce beds destroyed or our best early strawberries consumed, I remember that life has to be shared with somebody and that I have chosen the hunted and not the hunters. Rabbits dash over the lawns, their white tails flying, and the boys trap them alive and sell them to the state to transplant to other places. And here, as in my Chinese home, the herons come and stand beside the pool in the shade of the weeping willow trees, and when I see them, I feel my roots reach around the world.

New York City

A cold grey day in this city, where I make a transient home when business demands it. Today's business is the Academy of Arts and Letters of which I am now a member. Each honor that has been given me has come with the shock of surprise and pleasure, for each has been unexpected, and none more so than the invitation to join the Academy. I accepted for my own enjoyment, and though I feel stricken with a familiar shyness when I enter the great doors, I am pleased, nevertheless. I am ashamed of this shyness, and perhaps it is not really shyness, for surely I am accustomed by now to being anywhere and with anyone. Perhaps it is only the slight sense of strangeness with which I still enter any group of my own countrymen. In this case the gender is correct, for I am the only woman who attends the meetings, thus far. There is one other such member, I am told, but she never comes. I am pleased, too, that the chair assigned me was occupied before me by Sinclair Lewis. His name is the last on the plaque, and when I take my seat I reflect that after his name will one day come my own.

The hall where we meet is a place of dignity and beauty. While the simple ceremonies are performed, I gaze from the great window on the opposite side of the room, upon a city hillside, inhabited not by living human beings, but by the dead. It is a graveyard, well kept and permanent, the resting place, I suppose, of comfortable persons who in their lifetimes were also well kept and permanent until death carried them on. A great tree spreads its aged branches across the window, and in the winter, on such a day as this, the graves stand severely plain. When spring comes the tree puts out small green leaves, not hiding the dead but interposing a delicate quivering screen. In summer the graves are all but hidden.

Most of us are old who sit in the seats whereon are the names of the dead. I am, I believe, next to the youngest member, and I am not young. I put my vote the other day for several younger than I, so that new life may come in and early enough to enjoy the company of the learned. For there is no doubt that the Academy is the company of the learned. I keep a respectful silence most of the time, for the learning of these learned men is not profoundly my own. They are the musicians, the painters, the writers, the architects of the United States. I am still studying the subjects which they have made theirs long since and in which they are eminent, while I can never be but an amateur. I comfort myself with the thought that there are also many things I know which they do not.

For example, although they discuss so beautifully the symbolism of Mallarmé, do they know the symbolism of the famous essayists, or the hidden novelists, of China? These are never discussed. And for another example, among The Hundred Books, those classics which Western scholars have chosen to represent the sources of human civilization, there was not one Asian book, although in Asia great civilizations flourished long before our day and still exist in revitalized strength. "Why," I asked an American scholar, "are there no books from Asia in The Great One Hundred?"

"Because," he said quite honestly but without the least sign of guilt, "nobody knows anything about them!"

Nobody? Only millions of people! Ah, well—

Meanwhile I like very much to be in this company of the learned, deservedly or not. They are truly learned men and therefore without conceit and bombast. They are simple in manner, kind and mildly humorous, and they are careful not to wound one another. This is because they are civilized as learning alone can civilize the human being. I like to hear them speak even of unfamiliar subjects, for their voices are pleasant and their language often quite beautiful. Whatever their appearance, they have the gentle look of scholars, not dead but living in a pure and vital atmosphere. They jest now and then about the graves outside the window, for they are aware of their destination, but none is afraid. They are part of a stream, a river, that, broadening, carries mankind toward a vast eternal sea. Each knows his worth and yet his humble place. In this atmosphere I feel at home, for it is the atmosphere of scholars in every country and, I daresay, in every age.

Today it is winter, the tree will be bare against the grey sky and the tombstones will stand stark. But the next time we meet it will be spring.

When I look back over the twenty years that I have now lived in my own country, I realize that I still do not see my people plain. The years are rich with living, but life does not flow here in a river as it did in China. I see it as a series of incidents and events and experiences, each separate, sometimes complete, but always separate. The parts do not yet make a whole. And I am quite aware of the historical fact that our national life broke in two pieces in 1914, when the First World War began, so that what we were before we never can be again. There is no normalcy for us, no point of return. We can only go on, whatever the risks of the future.

Take the subject of women, for example. American women always absorb my interest, I watch them everywhere I go, I ponder upon them, I observe the way they talk and think and behave. Years ago I wrote a little book called *Of Men and Women*. So changeful is the American scene that while the book remains true in principle—that is, as it pertains to the relationship between men and women in the United States—yet women have changed very much since I wrote it. The present generation of young women, the daughters of the mothers about whom I wrote, are not "gunpowder women" as I called their mothers then. They are almost Victorian in their desire to marry, to be supported by their husbands, to have children, to do nothing outside the home. In spite of the fact that these young women are compelled to do a great deal outside the home, they seldom enjoy it, and they want now above all else, it seems, to be given an excuse, a moral reason, why they should give up outside interests. They want big families to provide the reason, they proclaim boldly that they take jobs only because they must. In this generation a girl is not ashamed to say that she wants to marry, and she appraises every man she meets, married or not, as a possible husband for herself.

Perhaps men do not accept marriage as necessary to a man's estate as once they did. Military life, it is said, does a damage to normal life for a man. It not only increases the number of homosexuals, but it persuades men to consider life without marriage as good enough. In military life men find their companionship with men, and sex becomes a physical rather than an emotional experience. Once in so often a man needs a woman physically, and when that time comes he can go out and find her easily enough and often without paying money for it. Why, then, the emotionally dwarfed man inquires, should he burden himself with the responsibilities of wife and children? The number of men who find civilian life unsatisfactory and return to the shelter of the armed forces has never been made public but it is worth study, and women ought to be the students. If they crave home and family as they now seem to do, they had better find out how to fulfill their longings.

The pursuit of men by women is not healthy. It is a portent of totalitarianism. In prewar Germany homosexuality was rife as it usually is in militaristic societies, and women, knowing or not knowing, felt that they were not desirable in the old ways and they became abject and fawning before men. I do not like to see American girls in this generation give up their own individualities in order to attract men, for if men can be attracted by such behavior, then it is alarming. And it is alarming that girls stake so much on marriage so that if they do not marry they consider themselves failures, even though marriage should be the proper goal of men and women alike, an inevitable and desirable state, if society is in balance.

There will come a time, I daresay, when a sensible means will be developed for men and women to marry and as a matter of course, so that any one who wishes to marry will have a dignified and sane opportunity to meet persons suitable for marriage, and when, if individuals need help for the final arrangements of betrothal and wedding, it can be provided. In China this was done by the parents of both boy and girl. Who, the Chinese used to say to me, can know son or daughter better than his own parents, and who therefore is more suited to find a proper mate? Americans, unless family life becomes much broader and more stabilized than it is at present, will scarcely accept the parental control of marital fate, but it may be that our increasing trust in scientists will lead us to put our faith in those who may specialize in matching mates. Adoption agencies make great ado about matching adoptable children to the color, creed, environment, temperaments, the race, and the likes and dislikes of adoptive parents, thereby incidentally forcing many good people to remain childless because their individual peculiarities are not reproduced in children available for adoption, any more than they would probably be if they gave birth to a child. I have known parents with red hair and freckled complexions who gave birth to a black-haired, black-eyed child, and no one took the child away from them.

Indeed I once knew a Canadian storekeeper in China who was brunette, and so was his wife, and in honorable matrimony they had six children, two black-haired and black-eyed, two red-haired and green-eyed and two yellow-haired and blue-eyed, with complexions to match the three varieties. Yet they were allowed to keep all these children, the ones that matched them and the ones that did not. But social workers are trained to be careful of their colors and their creeds, and I daresay that as time goes on we shall develop social work still further and then we shall find ourselves in the hands of matchmakers in marriage as well as in adoption. Men and women being born in about the same assortment, however, some shuffling will doubtless result in everybody finding the right person, scientifically at least, to marry.

Meanwhile I feel sorry for the women today who want to marry and cannot. Their mothers were the gunpowder women of yesterday, bursting out of their kitchens, and here are their daughters trying to get in again. I sat one evening in our living room and listened to a fine young woman, a little too tall and a little too old for the average marriage market—the girls grow up so quickly nowadays that a child of twelve or thirteen is already beginning to be competition to the woman of eighteen and twenty, and she in turn to the chances of the woman of thirty and this one was thirty-five. She talked and I listened, and she told me of the plan upon which she and two of her friends were working. They had made a list of the marriageable men they knew, and had divided the men between them in terms, first of preference, and then of possibility. A certain number they gave up as impossible. One was too attached to his mother, another was a confirmed bachelor, the result of being more handsome than needful for a man, another was stingy, another had tantrums, and so on. A year later I received a wedding announcement from her. She had married number four, the last of her list of preferences. I could have wept for her. But I hope, oh, I do hope, that she has lovely children!

Green Hills Farm

Yes, I remember the American years in scenes, unconnected. For example, when the war stopped, we were at New Bedford, in a hotel with all our children for the night, and expecting to get to the island of Martha's Vineyard in the morning. And that very night the news came that the war was over and everybody in the town went crazy and took a holiday, and even the steamer's crew was drunk next day. But we had to leave the hotel because our rooms were engaged by other people and so we were quite without a shelter over our heads, while men and women went mad and got drunk and fell into fights, all because of joy. At last we were able to persuade a fisherman in Woods Hole to take us across the Sound in his motorboat and so we arrived, starved and tired and dazed with all we had seen and heard.

And I remember the day I spent with the children on a set in Hollywood. It was my only visit there, and I went because my novel *Dragon Seed* was being made into a picture with Katharine Hepburn in the leading role and I was secretly distressed because she wore a man's Chinese jacket instead of a woman's, and when I inquired of someone in command why this was allowed, I was told that she liked the lines of the man's jacket better than the woman's. Just as she would not cut off her bangs, although anyone who knew China would know that a farmer's wife would not wear bangs. They are plucked out the night before her wedding, as a sign that she is no longer to be a virgin. And the bridge they had on the set was all wrong. It was the sort of bridge they used in South China but not in Nanking. And, worst of all, the terraces should never have been on the mountains. The rounded hills outside Los Angeles are very much like the hills outside Nanking, but for *Dragon Seed* they were terraced with bulldozers, whereas there is no terracing on the Nanking hills, and what confounded me most was that some of the terraces ran perpendicularly like great ditches up and down, impossible to imagine except in Hollywood, for terracing prevents erosion and the ditch provides it. When I inquired why the ditches, I was told that they made a contrast to the terraces running horizontally, and this only confounded me further.

Yet why dwell upon such matters now? Pictures improve, I daresay, and later in that same day the people on the set had their chance to laugh at me, too, when they produced the water buffalo which had been an important character in the filming of *The Good Earth* and now had become a sort of pet. I suppose they thought I would fall affectionately upon the beast's neck but I did not. I remembered that water buffaloes in China have a deep prejudice against white persons and will always attack if they can. It was as much as I could do to put my hand on this one's horn for a photograph. We eyed each other with mutual distrust, I because he was a water buffalo, and he eyed me because he smelled my fear, and was stirred by ancestral antagonisms. Meanwhile the Americans watching us laughed heartily and I let them laugh.

And this brief and single visit to Hollywood brings to my memory the strange story of the filming of *The Good Earth*. I have always disliked mystery stories in which the villain is an Oriental of unknown and sinister character, just as in my childhood I used to dislike the crude Chinese plays where the villain was always a Western man with blue eyes, a big nose and red hair, yet—well, here is the story, and in time it properly begins in that last winter which I spent in the old city of Nanking.

When the stage version of *The Good Earth*, prepared in 1932 by Owen Davis, was sold by the Theater Guild to Metro-Goldwyn-Mayer, I wished very much that the chief characters in the motion picture could be played by Chinese actors, for the stage play had convinced me that it was impossible for Americans to portray the parts of Chinese with any reality. Nazimova, who took the part of O-lan, was a brilliant exception, but she had some background in Eastern Europe which gave her an almost Asian grace of movement and pose. I was told, however, that our American audiences demand American stars and so I yielded the point, as indeed I had to, for I had no control over the matter.

As soon as I reached Shanghai, the representative there of Metro-Goldwyn-Mayer came to see me in a state of despair. He had been sent to take preliminary photographs of scenes and people and he had found himself frustrated at every attempt. Finally his studio was burned down by unknown persons and he was giving up and returning to the United States. There are "forces," he said, who did not want the picture made at all.

"Forces?" I inquired, unbelieving.

He nodded and went away without explaining. Later, I heard that he had committed suicide before reaching the United States, although not, I believe, from artistic frustration but from some private and domestic tragedy of his own.

I discovered, as the months passed, that the "forces" were familiar enough, for they were simply the prickly inverted patriotism of some members in the new government who did not want an authentic film made of Chinese villages and peasants lest it might provide unflattering views of China to foreign audiences abroad. I had a certain amount of sympathy with this, and so I declined at once any association with the making of the film, for friendly relations were more important to me than its succeess. Nevertheless, during the winter I heard a great deal about the making of that film, and I read of it, too, in Chinese newspapers. For a company was sent from Metro-Goldwyn-Mayer complete with cameras and technical equipment, and the story of their travail was relayed to me regularly by my friend the American Consul, who was compelled in the course of duty to be the mediator between the American motion picture group and the Chinese authorities, who objected at every step, and even after mediation, unwillingly acceded to, insisted upon dressing up the villages before pictures were allowed. Every woman, I heard, had to appear in clean clothes, and wear a flower in her hair, the rugged streets had to be cleaned and the houses decorated. The authorities even tried to substitute a modern American tractor, a machine that few Chinese had ever seen, for the redoubtable water buffalo who was an essential character in my story. If I heard the American side of the troubles from the Consul, I had the other side from editorials in the Chinese papers, which ran something like this:

"We fear that in spite of our government's every precaution, there will be some child in this film with an unwashed face or some farmer's wife with a dirty apron."

My sympathies were with both sides by now, and I kept a prudent silence and followed my usual pursuits. It was only after the motion picture was finished and shown and I was living in the United States that I heard of the incredible ill luck that dogged its making. One misfortune followed another until the tale became a legend. It was told to me by a member of the company, and proceeded from minor accidents too numerous to mention to the major disaster of discovering, when the company left China to come home, that most of the film material brought back from China in tin containers had somewhere along the way been destroyed by acid, so that of the entire length of a long film, as it was eventually shown, only about twelve minutes was composed of the original photography taken in China. Even the famous locust scene was made in one of the Western American states, where an opportune locust scourge supplied the necessary local color. The final tragedy was of course the death by sudden illness of the brilliant director, Irving Thalberg, leaving the picture uncompleted.

His successor confessed to his own secret fears one evening when the picture was finished, or so I was told, and at the moment he happened to be standing by a chimney piece in his house, or in some other, and as he spoke an immense and heavy-framed portrait fell from above the mantelpiece, narrowly missing his head.

My own memories of the film are not so sinister. I did not go to the opening although I was in New York at the time, for I dreaded the fanfare and publicity. I waited for a few days and then my husband and I went quietly to the theater and took seats in the gallery. It is an amazing experience to see the characters one has created come alive on the screen, and I was much moved by the effort that had been made, especially by the incredibly perfect performance of Luise Rainer as O-lan. She not only looked like a Chinese woman but she moved like one and every detail of action, even to the washing of a rice bowl, was correct. When I asked her how she had accomplished this, she told me that she had chosen from among the many Chinese employed on the set for the crowd scenes a young woman whom she thought most like O-lan. She had then followed this woman everywhere, watching her until she felt identified with her. When later the film was shown in China, as well as in other Asian countries, where incidentally it was a great success, Chinese friends wrote to me of their surprise and appreciation of Luise Rainer, marvelling, as I had, at the miracle of her understanding.

As for the evening at the New York theater, when I got up to leave my seat after the picture was over, I heard a gusty sigh from behind me and a hearty male voice said:

"Well, it's a good show, but I'd ruther see Mae West."

I knew what he meant. I had seen Mae West, but in a small crowded theater in Java, and hearty males had enjoyed her there, too!

Now and again during these years I have taken the children to see the house where I was born in West Virginia. It stands back from the road in the shelter of the mountains looming behind it, and it belongs to another family, a friendly one, to whom my first cousin went in sad distress, decades ago now, when speculations forced him to sell the homestead he had inherited from my eldest uncle who had it from my grandfather, in old-fashioned primogeniture. I am glad that friends live there but nevertheless the house is sorely changed. It needs paint and carpentering and the great old trees are gone, although the wisteria vine still hangs from the pillared portico. Inside, the house is entirely changed, only the shape of the rooms remaining. The formal old life that I can remember is no more.

But much is gone that is no more and it would be ungrateful of me to be sorry. And I remember instead that the young son of the family who lives in the house now came back a captain from the Second World War, as his father did from the First World War, and as his grandfather did from the Civil War, but this young captain has lost half his body. We were shocked—nay, our children at first were terrified—when he came rolling out of his car that day of our first visit, a stump of a man with no legs. For some impatience in him had made him to decide to live as he is, without artificial legs if he cannot have the ones he was born with, and thus he goes about his business, making his living and managing with the help of friends even to go fishing, a pastime that he loves. He has a good young wife and he has fathered two children, and he told me on a later visit that the only time he cannot bear his loss is when one of his children asks him to do something which he cannot and then he must explain that he has no legs. He has plenty of courage, nevertheless, and I am glad that my sons know him. It takes courage indeed to live as he does, and to wonder sometimes, as I am sure all young men must, whether there is not common sense enough somewhere in the world so that the folly of such loss can never be again.

What else do I remember? One winter I was charmed by radio, and I planned a novel written for that fine medium, so new to me then, and I went quietly to a class at Columbia taught by an excellent radio writer, and there, unknown among young men and women green to the craft, too, I learned and wrote my assignments until the professor's sharp eye picked me out, and then he told me I had learned enough and there was no more he could teach me. I never wrote the novel, but I wrote a few radio plays during the war, one of which was included in the anthology of that year. Now television has come, and sometimes I ponder how a novelist can use that magic medium, too. It remains to be discovered. Meanwhile, I learned not only from the professor but from those young men and women who were my fellow students.

The young American entices me to ask many questions. I observe him everywhere, in my own house and on the streets of the village and the city, everywhere I go. There is a basic lack in his life, I feel, although I cannot define it. Our young are strangely insecure. I ascribe this, primarily, after much thought and observation, to the general lovelessness of their life as children. In old countries, France, for example, in Europe, and anywhere in Asia, the child is so well loved that he can survive any disaster of his life in childhood, except death itself, because he is always with his family, and in later life because he has had his foundations laid in love. Only in Germany did I see harshness to the young, and I wonder how much that early harshness had to do with their life-unhappiness, the restlessness, the discontent which have forced them into war again and yet again, and compelling them, perhaps, to find a kindly father in any leader who promises them good things.

Our Americans are not harsh to their children so much as indifferent and withdrawn, or anxious and critical. The parent world is too far separated from the childhood world, there are too many absolutes conflicting one against the other, so that our children grow up uncertain of their own worth as human beings. I am amazed when sometimes an unperceptive foreigner tells me that Americans are proud. Bombastic sometimes, yes, and boastful, but this is because we are not proud, but secretly self-distrustful and doubtful of what we do and say and think. A man who knows his own worth does not boast, is not self-seeking, will not domineer or force his own opinion upon others, respects his fellow man because he respects first himself. When we Americans fail in these virtues it is because somewhere we have lost our faith in ourselves, and this happens, I believe, in early childhood. How I wince when I see a mother, or a father, but more often a mother, because

American men do not usually take their proper share of responsibility for their children, jerk a child's arm upon the street, slap the little creature, shout at him, walk too fast for small legs! I long to have the courage to speak, to tell the mother to be careful what she does, because it is by such cruelty that she will lose her child's heart. I have never dared to speak because I discover that to the American parent his child is a private possession, to deal with as he likes, and this is not as it was in China, where the child belonged to all the generations, and was always defended from parental injustice.

Our children, I say, are not treated with sufficient respect as human beings, and yet from the moment they are born they have this right to respect. We keep them children far too long, their world separate from the real world of life. In towns and cities, for example, the young are not allowed to take responsibility. Is this not also a form of disrespect? The opinion of children is a valuable point of view and should be put to use. They are part of the community and they have their thoughts and feelings. The energy, too, of children is an asset which should be expressed for the benefit of the community. I see dirty streets, filthy areas, evidences of careless if not of bad government in most communities, yet the children do not consider it their business. But if I were the mayor of a town, I would want the children to have a voice in putting me in that place, and I would hold the young, at this level, as responsible as the elders at theirs, for the conduct of community life. Americans are citizens from the moment they are born, and not when they become twenty-one years of age. By then, if they have not performed the acts of a citizen in a democracy, it is too late. They remain irresponsible and therefore immature. From the first grade on, the child should be taught his duties as a citizen, and given his voice in municipal matters and then in state and nation. But here I begin to ride a hobby and I dismount.

In the years during which I have lived in my own country the greatest advance, perhaps, has been made in race relations. I say this in the full knowledge that the advance, measured in terms of the goal, is still very small, but it has begun in the minds of the white people, and in the determination of the Negroes. We do learn, we Americans, though the process is slow and we are not always willing to admit that we are changing. Perhaps the outspoken criticism of Asians whose skins are not white, and of South Africans, black and colored, has made us think. I believe that prejudice in the American, as a matter of fact, is very shallow, and could easily be cast away altogether.

I am the more inclined to this belief when I see the generous praise and respect given to Negroes who prove themselves great artists and great human beings. When Negroes ask me, "What would you do if you were a Negro?" I always reply, "I would devote myself to the discovery of the most gifted and most intelligent children among my race and I would collect money somehow to educate them to their fullest development, and with responsibility for others."

The intelligent men and women of India and Pakistan have in recent years, too, had much to do with our realization that people with brown skins can be wise and cultivated, in the ways of the West as well as of the East. I hope that such voices will not allow themselves to be silenced, for Americans are human beings first of all, and we can be won by humanity wherever it is shown. The extraordinary patience and grace with which the leaders of India, in particular, have borne our rash speeches and newspaper articles have increased their influence over us, in spite of loud and raucous cries from certain public figures here. Dignity is a wonderful weapon when it is consistently used, and if never lost, it always wins.

Many friends have helped me know my country. Dorothy Canfield, for example, means Vermont to me, and knowing her inspired me to build our small house, our sons learning by helping to build it, Forest Haunt in the Green Mountains. There we face the Wilderness. Much as I love people and find my life among them, I like sometimes to sit in our forest-circled cabin and know that for thirty-five miles to the north of us, there is no man or woman living, but only woods and brooks and silence. Each state in this great union lives for me not only in landscape and experience, but in the people who belong there and have taken me with them to their homes, if not in body, then in letters.

Of my American family, next to husband and children, I remember my dear mother-in-law, now dead. Reared in China, I could not but respect her position in my life. It was essential to me that she like me and approve me, but what if she had not? She did, however, and from the first the relationship was what it should be, honor from me and love, and from her an affection, kind and easy. I do not know why at this moment I see her on a certain morning here at our farmhouse, where she often visited us, but would never live, somewhat to my hurt at first, for I would have liked to have her live with us and give our children the benefit of a grandmother in the house, the grandfather being dead and so beyond the reach of our daily life. But no, she would only come for visits, and on one such morning, as we lingered over the breakfast table after the children had finished and gone away, we talked of England and the royal family in whom, as one born in England, she took much personal interest. She was a handsome white-haired lady, substantially built and always well dressed and cheerful, afraid of nothing except mice. She sat with her back to the big window at the end of the table, my husband on one side of her and I on the other, and behind her the sunlight fell upon the polished red brick floor.

Suddenly, as she talked, a kangaroo mouse darted out from the logs piled in the fireplace which was not lit, and without an instant's hesitation, the fragile lively mite rose upon its hind legs, its front paws waving like little hands, and began to dance in the sunshine. The sight was so exquisite, the dance so minutely dainty and graceful, that my husband and I caught each other's glance, longing to speak. Yet did we speak, the mouse would be revealed to our mother, and then the dance be broken. In silent ecstasy we watched while our elder talked, until the mouse had finished its dance and fluttered back into the fireplace. I see the scene yet, like a painting on a wall, except that no painting could convey the fairy movement of the little wild thing behind our mother's chair.

And still another memorable picture in my intermingling worlds is of a cold November day in New Jersey, the twenty-third, to be exact, and at Freewood Acres. The occasion was the consecration of a Lama Buddhist Temple. Actually it was a garage made into a temple, and there is something strange and fascinating about the very idea of such a transformation, the first in the history of our country, I am sure. But it was a true temple, for all that, and made by a devout people now becoming American citizens. They were the anti-Communist Kalmuks, more than a hundred of them, men, women and children, and they had worked on the building themselves, the woodwork, the masonry, the plastering. The asphalt shingles they had painted a bright yellow, the sacred color of Buddhism, but over the door was a huge American flag as well as the red and yellow flag of their religion.

The Kalmuks are the descendants of the Mongolian warrior-followers of Genghis Khan, who conquered much of Asia and Europe in the thirteenth century. They settled on the steppes between the Don and the Volga rivers, and after the revolution in Russia they were formed into the Kalmuk Socialist Soviet Autonomous Republic. In spite of this fine name they never were friendly with the Kremlin and during the Second World War many of them were taken, or allowed themselves to be taken, by the German armies, and thus they found their way into DP camps, whence they were brought to the United States, mainly through the efforts of Protestant Christians. In New Jersey now they work in carpet factories, on farms and on construction jobs.

We arrived early that day, the air very frosty and cold, and were met by friendly representatives who led us into a crowded small room in somebody's house, made festive as a guest room, and there we were offered cakes and tea. Though it was so early, the entire population, even the children, looked clean and rosy, the babies amazingly fat and round-faced and wrapped like little papooses against the cold. After two hours or so the services began. We were invited into the tiny temple and given places of honor behind ropes at the right side of the altar.

How strange the familiar Buddhist gods looked to me that day! I had never seen them before in an American setting, or even in so simple a building, but here they were, sitting in a row behind the altar, and before them were heaped the offerings of the people, food of every sort including boxes of crackers and breakfast cereals, and I daresay the gods had never been given such gifts before, either. Of course, actually, they were gifts to the lamas. But it was all very solemn and to me inspiring as well as touching. My old friend, the Dilowa Hutukhtu, who is the eighteenth recorded incarnation of the Indian saint Tolopa and is therefore the primate of all the Mongol Buddhists in our country, officiated in the brief half-hour ceremony. To his right and slightly lower sat nine lamas, who had come, I think, with the Kalmuks. The Dilowa himself is a tall man, now growing old, and his wide Mongolian face is as peaceful here as though he were not an exile. On that day in the little garage temple he was quietly radiant, though once he had been the head of nine hundred lamas in three great lamaseries, one in Outer and two in Inner Mongolia. But that was in the days before the Communists drove him out and before Owen Lattimore saved his life.

Now in the new little temple he put on his yellow silken hat, which signified his rank, comparable, perhaps, to the red hat of a cardinal in the Catholic Church, the Dalai Lama in Tibet being comparable to the Pope. He sat cross-legged on a high seat when we came in, then he rose and walked slowly to the altar, his robes flowing about him. He sounded a delicate small bell, and the other lamas gathered beside him and in chorus they began the sacred chants. When this part of the service was ended the Dilowa made a short sermon, and these, translated, are among the words he spoke:

"This day, by the saving grace of Buddha, is a day of great rejoicing for the completion of a deed of blessed merit.

"All ye Kalmuk Mongols of pure faith did succeed in escaping from the dreadful circumstances of Red Russia, where false beliefs prevail, and did come to this great America where peace and happiness are broadly based and you have built a new temple in the pure sincerity of your devotion, to affirm your faith in the Buddha, which you held from of yore, and now invoke its consecration. That you have founded a congregation of the faith, that verily this day you have completed a palace of the Lord Buddha to be his dwelling, to uphold and accomplish that which is in the heart of Buddha, a place of prayer and sacrifice, a place for the sowing of the harvest of blessedness, is your reward because in previous incarnations you were valiant in the faith. . . .

"Upon all of you, the Kalmuk Mongols, who, in raising this temple, have perpetuated in it the name of Arashi Gimpling, your temple in your ancient homeland, I invoke this blessing: That, having fulfilled all that you sought and all that you hoped for, in the fulness of the Law and to your heart's desire, your happiness may be overflowing, your words of merit ever increasing, your very rebirth bring you together with the religion of the Buddha, and that speedily and in peace and without toil you may be united with the pure saints on high."

When the services were over we all went out into the cold and brilliant sunshine, and there on the tiny porch of the temple I saw a pleasant sight. Five-year-old Sally, the small but extremely beautiful daughter of my friend, the Mongol prince, had paused to give voice to the exuberance of her soul. She was dressed in gorgeous red and green satin robes from her throat to her feet, as were all her family, and thus attired she stood beneath the American and the Buddhist flags, and overcome with religious feeling, she burst into spontaneous song. The hymn? It was "Jesus Loves Me." I retired behind the building and enjoyed private and soul-shaking laughter, but the Kalmuks seemed to find nothing either amusing or strange in the incident.

"How nicely Sally sings," they said, admiring this little Sunday-school princess.

The next event was a mighty dinner, given by the White Russian colony at Rova Farms to the Kalmuks and their friends. We sat down, three hundred of us, to a feast such as only Russians know how to provide, and while excellent food and drink progressed from course to course, speeches began and went on. Russians rose and spoke with great vitality and vigor, and I listened, unable to understand except as a neighbor translated hastily. What was most moving, however, was the final speech which the leading Kalmuk gave, a sturdy moonfaced man in a grey business suit. He held a paper before him and after he had expressed his thanks for the dinner and also for the great kindness otherwise shown the new colony by the White Russians, he went on to give thanks to the gods that his people had been brought safely to the United States, where, he said, they were doing well. Not only, he told us, had they built the temple consecrated this day, but thirty families owned their own houses, more than twenty had cars, and, he was glad to say, more than fifty had television sets!

Tremendous applause followed these figures of achievement, and after the speeches people really fell upon the food.

It was a wonderful, heart-warming, soul-inspiring day. My many worlds came together for the space of it, at least, and I think something like this happened to us all. The Countess Alexandra Tolstoi was there, and we clasped hands, and looking into her honest and good face, I saw reflected my own feelings.

And I remember, like another painting, an evening when Asia was in my house again, this time in the shape of beautiful young women who had come to contribute their presence in a fashion show that my friend and neighbor Dorothy Hammerstein was giving for the benefit of Welcome House. They had spent the afternoon at her house, had modeled their stunning costumes on the platform by the swimming pool, and having visited the Welcome House children had come to spend the night with us. Japan had given me Haru Matsui and the famous young actress, Shirley Yamaguchi, on her way to Hollywood to make a film. Both were lovely to see, but Shirley Yamaguchi had a French grandmother, and the foreign blood had made her eyes larger and more lustrous than any I have ever seen, her skin pure cream, and her features clear as carved marble, but still all Japanese. A pretty girl from Pakistan, a big handsome Chinese girl, the daughter of a famous war lord, a graceful Indonesian, a tall young beauty from India—they grouped themselves on the couches in the living room after dinner, and no men being present they prepared themselves for female chatter and good talk, eagerly turning to one another to ask how life was in their separate countries. The Chinese girl was the least cultivated, I suppose, not because Chinese girls are so, but being the daughter of a war lord, she had not had the advantages of scholars and artists in her lineage. She came of the plains people of the North and her big body, her handsome heavy features, her broken English, for English was their only common tongue and all the others spoke it with silvery perfection, set her somewhat apart. I noticed that she was restless, and I asked her if she were not feeling well. She replied that she had eaten too much. The night before, in New York, friends in exile had made a feast for her because her father was a high general in Formosa, and tonight she had enjoyed the fried chicken and rice at my dinner table, and now her girdle was too tight.

"Go upstairs and take it off," I suggested. "We are only women here."

Upstairs she went, and came back looking much relieved, but only for a few minutes. Then she rubbed her midriff ruefully. "I am still too full," she said frankly, in Chinese. I translated and the other young women were all mirthful sympathy.

"A little bicarbonate of soda in hot water?" I suggested.

She was willing to try anything, and so I mixed the brew and she drank it, relieving herself thereafter at regular intervals by loud unblushing belches, which startled and shocked the others, but not at all the war lord's daughter.

"How did you come to America?" I asked at last, to change the situation, for shock had given way to laughter scarcely controlled behind the pretty ringed hands of India and Pakistan, Japan and Indonesia.

The war lord's daughter answered with hearty honesty. "When the Communists came," she said, "it was time for my father to go to Formosa. But he has a very large family, several wives and more than thirty children. Which should he take? The sons, he said, could watch over their own wives. His youngest and prettiest concubines and daughters he took with him to Formosa. The ugly ones he left behind because, he said, they would be safe even from the Communists."

"But how is it you are here?" I inquired.

She was quite literal and quite without rancor toward the old war lord who was her father. "I am not pretty, also not ugly," she replied, "and so my father sent me to America to school."

Flooding my living room with irrepressible music came gales of laughter from Asia.

Postscript to this story: The beautiful woman from Indonesia arrived that afternoon in a state of such polished calm that I was sure something had gone wrong. Upon questioning, she confessed that it had. She had decided to model at Dorothy Hammerstein's garden party a formal costume of her country, to which jewels were an essential decoration, and so she had brought her jewelry bag with her—and had left it in the taxicab in New York! With magnificent fortitude she had come on without the jewels, had told no one, since she did not want to disturb her hostess, had modeled her gown without the jewels, trusting that the American audience would not know the lack.

Now, however, she fervently asked for help. The jewels were priceless—rubies, pearls, diamonds and emeralds in ancient and heavy gold settings. We telephoned at once to the taxicab office in New York and found that the bag had been turned in a few minutes before by the driver. He had opened the bag and had decided the contents were worthless.

"Some show girl's stuff," he had reported, "Costoom jew'lry—"

The very rugs I walk upon in this American house of mine remind me of Asia. They are good Peking rugs, bought in the year before I left China never to return. I left them where they were when I shut the door in 1934, for the last time, lest I might change my mind, or unchanging, that my last sight would be what I had always known. Six years later, knowing that the Japanese were probably in occupation of all such houses in Nanking, I wrote to a friend asking if it were possible to have the rugs sent me. I doubted it, but the impossible is sometimes possible. So it proved to be again. In an incredibly short time bales of rugs arrived safely. Chinese friends had sent them to me across two hundred miles of Japanese-occupied territory. The Customs officers in New York asked that the goods be checked before release, because there were oil stains on some of the bales. They were checked, and not one rug was stained or missing, and I asked that they be sent on by express to our farmhouse.

When they arrived here five bales were gone. I reported the matter to the Railway Express Agency office in New York and was told in a courteous letter to write to the Philadelphia office, stating the money value of the rugs, and the sum would be sent me. My temper, usually calm, rose up in a truly American fashion. I wanted the rugs. I wrote a letter saying that the rugs had been sent across miles of enemy-occupied China, across the Pacific and to New York. Why, then, should they be lost in the eighty miles between the New York Customs and our farmhouse in Pennsylvania? The reply to this was another courteous letter saying that if I would state a sum, etc. Whereupon I wrote to the president of the company on the theory that the best man is always at the top. He was, at least in this case. I got back not only a courteous letter but a sensible one, telling me that the rugs would be found and asking me to wait. I waited for months. Now and then a telephone call would come, asking me to wait a little longer, that the search was going on. At last after half a year or so, the missing bales arrived. Where they had been I shall never know.

When I had laid the Chinese rugs upon my American floors, still the century-old floors of wide old oaken boards, I was astonished to see how new they looked, as though they had scarcely been used. Yet for six years the Nanking house had been lived in, first as a bachelor quarters for American professors at the university, and later by strangers. The mystery was explained some years afterward when I met one of those professors.

"How," I inquired, "did you keep my rugs so new?"

He laughed. "Don't think we were allowed to use them! Your too faithful servants rolled them up as soon as you were gone and put them in the attic, packed in camphor. Once a year we saw them, when the servants brought them down and sunned them. Then they were rolled up and put away again, for you."

I tell this story here in gratitude to a fidelity beyond the call of duty, for those faithful servants I have neven seen again, nor can we ever meet, but God go with them always.

Other feet beat a path to my door, too, not because I have made excellent mousetraps or anything else that surpasses the products of others. No, it is because of something that my invalid daughter has done for me. I open the door and there stand two parents, mother and father, and with them a child, a little boy or girl, and I look at the child and I know why they are here. The child is retarded.

"Come in," I say.

They come in and I open the big old French *armoire* in the living room that serves as a toy closet for the Welcome House children when they come to spend the day, or for grandchildren and neighbor children, and the little child amuses himself while the parents tell the story I know too well. It is part of my own life, repeated again and again, and when it is told, we consider together what the child's future shall be, where and how. So much, so tragically much, depends upon money. If the parents are poor and if they cannot keep the child at home, then the only place will be a crowded state institution, and I brace myself for their instinctive cry against it. They have been to see it and they cannot bear to think of their child left in so lonely a place, lonely because who will love him, who indeed will have time to love him there, where there are too many children and too few people to care for them?

Most of the parents are too poor to afford the fees of a private school, and even if they can afford them, can they also afford to arrange for the terrifying future when perhaps they are dead and the child lives on? We talk for hours, the child growing hungry, and I fetch cookies and milk and we talk again. There is no solution and I know it, but still we talk.

For the most neglected children in our entire nation are these little ones whose minds have been injured by some accident before, during, or after birth, the ones who cannot grow. Public schools too seldom carry the classes which would teach them what they could learn, for all of them can learn something and be the better and happier for it, and with what relief to their sorrowing families can scarcely be expressed. But the Boards of Education are oblivious or hard pressed, budgets are strained, and so nothing, or very little, is done for these American citizens. Children with polio, children with heart disease, children with cerebral palsy, children with cancer, children with every possible handicap have their foundations, their hospitals, their shelters, but not yet the little ones who will always be children and innocent. And when their parents leave them they are left to shift with unwilling relatives and hostile communities, and they live and die in a daze of misery.

I have seen with my own eyes what it means in a society like ours, where the family is only father and mother, sisters and brothers, when a child who is physically handicapped in the brain instead of in some other part of his body, is left alone. Lost children these, often used by clever ones to do the evil deeds that we call juvenile delinquency, and so it will be until the parents together rise up to defend their own. I appeal again to the family, for family must be the individual's stronghold, his safety and his shelter, and there is no welfare agency or state institution or public organization which will do so well for the needy child, or adult for that matter, as the concerned family. Somehow the American family must be taught responsibility for its own again.

Yes, when I survey the memories of the twenty years that I have lived in my country I see very much and yet I realize that still I see no finished story, nor even consecutive pages of the years. I see my America in scenes and episodes, experiences so varied that I scarcely know how to put them together. The daily life goes on, rich and deep and good, and I am rooted in it, but I know that it is only as much of America as one family can live upon one farm in one community, from which it is true, paths lead around the world. When a visitor from Asia presses me to tell him what Americans really are, that he may have the key to our hearts, the clue to our minds, I shake my head.

"I have to take my compatriots one by one," I tell him. "I have no key, I do not know the clue—not yet."

I say that I see no unifying thread which ties together these rich and varied American scenes of my present life, and yet I feel a unifying spirit abroad in our land. In spite of our incredible differences in thinking, our seemingly irreconcilable conflicts in action, we have a unity of spirit, the American spirit. It is difficult to define, and yet I feel it steadfast, the deepening and strengthening expression of a people still in growth, still in the process of welding a new nation out of human material, from everywhere in the world. Whatever were the motives of our ancestors in leaving old countries to come to this continent, and the reasons were as various as themselves, good and bad, we who are their descendants are creating something unique in our own selves, a nature native to our soil, a character peculiarly American.

Our contribution to the solutions of the world's problems will come only from the working of the American spirit. Our approach will be practical, though sometimes impatient; optimistic, though humorously rueful; energetic, though occasionally reluctant. In short, if I am sometimes critical of my own people, it is in excess of love, for I perceive so clearly the needs of humanity and our own amazing ability to aid in fulfilling them, that I grow restless with the delays preventing the realization of ourselves and of what we can do, at home and abroad, to create a sensible and pleasant world.

Yet the advance in our national thinking since the end of the Second World War should pacify and encourage even the most exacting and loving of critics. In spite of embarrassing mistakes and alarming missteps in the process of learning our world lessons, I see the American spirit reaching new levels of common sense and enlightenment. We are already beginning to give up our destructive prejudices in color, creed and nationality, and we are no longer so boastfully sure that we can lead the world. Indeed the idea of world leadership is becoming distasteful to us, and we are considering cooperation instead of leadership. Americans learn quickly and well from experience, if not from preaching or even from books. Our own men, coming home from abroad as soldiers and diplomats, are proving to us that we can like other peoples—not all of them, but enough of every people so that we do not dislike all of any one kind. Given half a human chance, we like rather than dislike, but we are not sentimental about it.

We are not empire builders. How important this fact is no American who has not lived in Asia can appreciate. For a while even I was not sure of it but now I know. We do not want an empire, for we do not enjoy the task of ruling. It goes against our conscience, which is a very tender part of the American spirit. Therefore we are learning how to hold our allies, not by force of arms and government, but by mutual benefit and friendship. So much is already clear. If we have not yet discovered the whole means we search for to persuade others of our common need and benefit, we have persuaded them, or almost, that we do not want their territory or their subjection. By this great negative their fear can be allayed, and when fear is cast out, hope soon takes its place.

I am therefore hopeful. In spite of dismaying contradictions in individuals in our national scene, I feel the controlling spirit of our people, generous, decent and sane.

In this mood of faith and hope my work goes on. A ream of fresh paper lies on my desk waiting for the next book, I am a writer and I take up my pen to write—